Edited by Philip S. Foner

The Factory Girls

A collection of writings on life and struggles
in the New England factories of the 1840s by
the Factory Girls themselves, and the story,
in their own words, of the first trade unions
of women workers in the United States

UNIVERSITY OF ILLINOIS PRESS
Urbana   Chicago   London

© 1977 by the Board of Trustees of the University of Illinois
Manufactured in the United States of America

Library of Congress Cataloging in Publication Data

Main entry under title:

The Factory girls.

  Includes bibliographical references and index.
  1. Women—Employment—New England—History—Sources.
2. Factory system—New England—History—Sources.
3. Women in trade-unions—United States—History—
Sources.   I. Foner, Philip Sheldon, 1910–
HD6096.N36F3   331.4'0974   77-22410
ISBN 0-252-00422-1

The operatives in our factories are intelligent; exceedingly so. We have the testimony of a bookseller in Troy, that the operatives in Ida Mills are the largest class of readers he has, according to their numbers. We have often wondered at their amount of knowledge, considering the hours which they have to devote to labor. This testimony is flattering to them; and the literary works of the girls at the Lowell Factories speak volumes for them also, not because of their condition, but because they rise above it.

—*Mechanics' Mirror* (Albany, N.Y.), reprinted in
Voice of Industry, November 27, 1846

The factory operatives of New England, now hold a prominent position in the ranks of respectability and tone. Time once was when they were hooted at by every dandy jackanape in creation; but they united against oppression, have risen above all opposition, and will ere long receive ample justice from those who now endeavor to oppress them.

—*Factory Girls' Album* (Exeter, N.H.), March 14, 1846

We are a band of sisters—we must have sympathy with each other's woes.

—An Operative in *Voice of Industry*,
January 8, 1847

We war with oppression in every form. . . .

—Sarah G. Bagley in *Voice of Industry*,
May 15, 1846

Preface

More has been written of the female factory operatives of New England, especially those of Lowell, Massachusetts, than of any other pre–Civil War labor group. These were the operatives who worked in the mills established by the great Boston textile merchants. They were young women from seventeen to twenty-two years old who came from the farms and villages of New England to work in the cotton mills. Many of them wrote verse or fiction and their literary magazine, the *Lowell Offering*, gained international fame. Two of them, Harriet H. Robinson and Lucy Larcom, went on to write distinguished memoirs of life in the mills.

In a 1930 article entitled "Early Factory Magazines in New England" (*Journal of Economic and Business History,* II, 685–705), Bertha M. Stearns called attention to the fact that these were also the female operatives who repudiated the *Lowell Offering* as a company organ, publishing their own militant magazines and periodicals to voice their discontent over conditions in the mills and to mobilize for improvements. Unfortunately, although Harriet H. Robinson's *Loom and Spindle,* Lucy Larcom's *New England Girlhood,* and the *Lowell Offering* (as well as its successor, the *New England Offering*) have recently been reprinted, the writings of the female operatives to which Bertha Stearns called attention a quarter-century ago have remained buried in the weeklies and monthlies in which they originally appeared. Even recent collections of writings of American women, which have fortunately increased in number since the rise of the contemporary women's liberation movement, have included selections from Harriet H. Robinson, Lucy Larcom, and the *Lowell Offering,* but have not reprinted even a single page of the writings of the militant female factory operatives. (See Aileen S. Kraditor, ed., *Up from the Pedestal: Selected Writings in the History of American Feminism* [Chicago, 1968]; Miriam Schneer, ed., *Feminism: The Essential Historical Writings* [New York, 1969], and Nancy F. Cott, ed., *Roots of Bitterness: Documents of Social History of American Women* [New York, 1972].) It is curious, moreover, that in the anthology *America's Working Women,* comp. and ed. Rosalyn Baxandall, Linda Gordon, and Susan Reverby (New York, 1976), all but one of these documents of the 1840's are from secondary sources, and only one, "Factory Life As It Is, by an Operative," is by a factory girl herself. The present volume seeks to fill this vacuum. It includes selections from the magazines of the genteel factory girls—the *Lowell Offering,* the *New England Offering,* and their contemporaries—but the bulk of the volume is devoted to the hitherto neglected literary output of the militant female factory operatives.

There will be some objection to the use of the term "girls" for the young women who worked at the looms in the New England mills. But, as the reader will quickly discover, this is precisely what they called themselves, the militant as well as the genteel. (There were also factory boys, and a novel published in 1839 was entitled *The Factory Boy.*) Nor did the term cease with the Civil War. In 1903 Mrs. John Van Vorst and Marie Van Vorst published *The Woman Who Toils: Being the Experience of Two Ladies as Factory Girls.* On September 5, 1913, the *Socialist and Labor Star* of Huntington, West Virginia, carried a poem entitled "The Factory Girls"; on March 3, 1917, the *Norfolk Journal and Guide,* a black weekly, published on its front page the headline, "Factory Girls Resent Abuse," and on June 24, 1933, the *Chicago Defender,* another black weekly, published, also on its front page, the headline: "1,500 Factory Girls Walk Out. Demand More Money." In England, the *Woman's Dreadnought,* edited by Sylvia Pankhurst and published by the East London Federation of Suffragettes, carried in its issue of December 26, 1914, an article entitled, "Factory Road! As a Factory Girl Saw It."

Writing to George Henry Evans, editor of the New York *Working Man's Advocate,* in the issue of September 12, 1835, a female champion of the ten-hour day noted: "Whilst I was writing the above I was half asleep, for the long time system deprives me of time to write or think, unless I take it out of the time my boss allows me to sleep, so you will please to make any corrections you think wanted." To this Evans replied: "We saw no corrections of consequence in the above letter to make, and therefore have made none. We wish that many of our *legislators* had as much good feeling and good sense in their whole career as this single letter evinces." It is in this spirit that the present volume has been edited. All documents have been reproduced without substantive change, but misspellings and grammatical errors have been corrected if they appeared in printed sources and clearly were typographical mistakes. Original headings have been retained, but where there were none, they have been furnished by the editor. All introductions and notes are the editor's.

A work of this nature would have been impossible to produce without the kind cooperation of many libraries and historical societies. I owe a deep debt of gratitude to the staffs of the public libraries of Lowell, Fall River, and Chicopee, Massachusetts; Manchester, Dover, and Nashua, New Hampshire; the Boston Public Library; the New Hampshire Historical Society; American Antiquarian Society; New York State Library; New York Pubic Library; Tamiment Institute Library of New York University; Lincoln University Library; Wisconsin State Historical Society; and the Library of Congress.

—Philip S. Foner

Lincoln University, Pennsylvania
May, 1977

Contents

Introduction

The War for Independence burst the shackles imposed upon American industry by the British mercantilist system, but political independence did not bring immediate industrial development. In 1800 the vast majority of Americans were still isolated farmers. Transportation and communication facilities were so limited that a considerable market for industrial products could hardly exist. For the most part, the rural household was self-sufficient. Alexander Hamilton estimated in 1791 that in many districts "two-thirds, three-fourths and even four-fifths of all the clothing of the inhabitants are made by themselves."[1]

Other obstacles impeded the rise of industry. Capitalists were not interested in investing in manufactures. Merchant princes like Elias Hasket Derby of Salem and Stephen Girard of Philadelphia were reaping huge fortunes in foreign commerce. By 1805 profits from the carrying trade ranged from $50,000,000 to $70,000,000 annually. The total failure of many of the industrial enterprises convinced most merchants that surplus funds should be invested in real estate. Robert Lee, a budding industrialist, in a letter to the Newark (New Jersey) *Centinel of Freedom* of August 14, 1810, complained of "the scarcity of capital for manufacturing purposes or the diversion of capital into other channels of employment, where there is a greater prospect of gain, or where it can be employed with greater facility and ease to the proprietor."

Another obstacle was the tendency to view the rise of industry with disfavor because of the belief that it would bring in its wake vice, profligacy, and demoralization of the population. In his *Notes on Virginia,* published in 1782, Thomas Jefferson expressed the hope that America would never see its citizens occupied at a workbench, and that it would be best for the nation if "for the general operations of manufacture . . . our workshops remain in Europe." The controversy over industry got under way with this publication, and for the next three decades the "establishment of manufactures" was a focus of debate. Alexander Hamilton urged that the national government should nurture the development of industry, while Jefferson argued that to follow this advice would guarantee that the United States would go through the same demoralizing experience as England, where factory workers were sinking into pauperism, forced by the workings of human nature and economic law to "the maximum of labor which the construction of the human body can endure, & to the minimum of food . . . which will preserve it in life."[2]

In time Jefferson changed his view, and many Jeffersonians became ardent advocates of industrial development. But for a quarter-century after the adoption of the Constitution, most Americans agreed that industry ought to stay in Europe. The news that came from Manchester, Birmingham, Leeds, and other British manufacturing centers concerning the horrors of child and female labor, the miserable living conditions of the working class, and the transformation of the worker into an appendage of the machine, convinced them of the correctness of their stand.

The need to avoid a repetition of the English industrial experience was thus widely recognized in the United States at the opening of the nineteenth century. Rather than avoid industrialism altogether, a school arose in the United States that argued that it was possible to develop manufacturing without the accompanying human degradation characteristic of the factory system in England. A leading figure in this school of thought was Francis Cabot Lowell, the creator of the "Waltham system," that remarkable innovation in the cotton textile industry which set out to introduce large-scale manufacturing into the United States without reproducing the horrors of the English factory system, and, in the process, brought the first factory girls into being.

The "Waltham experiment" was not the beginning of the factory system in the United States. This system was inaugurated by Samuel Slater, who, in 1790 in Pawtucket, Rhode Island, had begun spinning mills based on English inventions. The British jealously guarded against the export of those machines or plans for them, but Slater stored away the details of the new devices in his memory and came to the United States in the hope of finding sponsors to start a cotton spinning mill. In Rhode Island the wealthy Quaker merchants William Almy and Moses Brown supplied the capital. Slater drew up the plans of the Arkwright spinning machine from memory and turned them over to David Wilkinson, a Pawtucket blacksmith, who in 1790 built the first Arkwright machinery to be successfully operated in the United States. A year later several machines were producing satisfactory yarn.[3]

Not only were the Pawtucket spinning mills based on English invention; they also copied the English system of labor. Here, as in England, whole families were employed to tend the carding and spinning machinery, with children working long hours doffing and slubbing. The yarns were sent out to be woven into cloth, but manufacturing villages were created as families with large numbers of children were induced to settle in the factory neighborhood near the spinning mill. The more children a family had, the more eagerly they were sought by the factory, for they provided a constant supply of cheap labor. Often only the children were regularly employed, and the whole family lived on their small wages, usually paid in store orders, plus what the parents could earn by weaving or farming. When Josiah Quincy, the New England educator, statesman, and reformer, visited a textile mill in Pawtucket in 1801, the owner pointed with pride to the number of children at work. By keeping out of mischief and not wasting time playing games, he said, these children were serving God as well as aiding their families. Quincy, however, was not impressed by this eloquent defense of child labor: "But an eloquence was exerted on the other side of the question more eloquent than his, which called us to pity these little creatures, plying in a contracted room, among flyers and coggs, at an age when nature requires for them air, space, and sports. There was a dull dejection in the countenances of all of them."[4]

While religious imprecations against idleness reinforced child labor in New England, there opposition to its spread was beginning to emerge. The "Waltham System" was introduced partly to avoid the creation of conditions characteristic to the Rhode Island factory system. Actually, the Pawtucket factory was by no means a full-fledged factory. Machinery was used only for turning raw cotton into yarn; weaving was still done by local farmers in their cottages. Hence the "Waltham System" introduced both the first modern factory in America and a new labor system different from the English factory system.

Francis Cabot Lowell toured the British Isles during 1810–12. During the latter part of his stay he investigated the textile industry in England, Scotland, and Ireland. He did not fail to notice two developments. One was the fresh invention of the power-loom which enabled spinning and weaving machines to be placed under one roof. The other was the ill effects that the factory produced on its operatives and its environment. Lowell saw what life was like in the English mill towns: the poor were packed in slums, with families living and sleeping in one room; such overcrowding meant a high death rate. He was quick to realize that the combination of spinning and weaving in one place would increase the profits from textiles, but he was also intelligent enough to realize that duplication of the horrors of Lancashire would intensify opposition to industrial growth.

When he returned to Boston, Lowell engaged a talented mechanic, and together they reconstructed a workable power-loom. Lowell's brother-in-law, Patrick Tracy Jackson, rounded up the necessary capital. Twelve Boston merchants put up $100,000 at first and later $400,000 to turn Lowell's loom into a profitable industry. The Boston Manufacturing Company was incorporated in 1813 to produce cotton, woolen, and linen cloth, although only cotton was ever fabricated. Two years later the first power-loom in the United States was patented by Lowell and Jackson. By this time the factory was operating in Waltham, Massachusetts, on the Charles River, manufacturing cotton textiles in a fully integrated mill in which, for the first time, all the machinery was power driven. Production workers were not, as in the case of the Rhode Island system, whole families and especially children, but adult females.

The decision of the Boston Associates (as the founders came to be known) to employ adult females in preference to whole families was partly due to the fact that the equipment at Waltham was too complicated to be operated by children. (In Lancashire, too, technological problems barred children from employment at the power looms.) If the labor of children could not be used, the cheap-labor advantage of the family system was lost.[5] But another significant reason was the necessity to overcome the argument that the factory system would bring in its wake an impoverished, vice-ridden, ignorant laboring class as it had in the Old World, and that this would be a threat to a democratic republic. In any event, having elected to employ hundreds of farm girls in their mill, the Boston Associates had to decide how such a work force was to be accommodated. Clearly Yankee farmers would not send their daughters into the factories if they became known as breeding places for sin and corruption. Nor would the community permit the invasion of a large number of youthful maidens to become a regular work force without assurance that they would not be tempted into vice.

The answer was the famous system introduced by the Boston Associates: boardinghouses under the direction of a matron, usually a widow, who represented the company and its interests in strict adherence to regulations of behavior and mandatory church attendance. The girls were required to reside in the boardinghouses, where the doors were locked at ten o'clock each night. They were also required to be constant in attendance at religious worship.

In addition to the provision of company housing, house mothers, and the establishment of proscriptive rules and regulations so as to insure a labor force for its large-scale operation, the Boston Associates found it necessary to introduce payment of wages in money rather than in scrip and to avoid company stores. Here, too, necessity rather than moral values forced the decision. The girls employed at Waltham, provided with room and board by the company, did not spend most of their earnings within the community. Instead, they sent a large portion home to help their families. They had, therefore, to be paid in currency which was good anywhere and not merely at a company store.[6]

This unique system, first introduced at Waltham, came to full flower at Lowell. Further expansion of the factories at Waltham was limited by the water-power capacity of the slow-flowing Charles River, and so after completing the third mill on that site in 1820 the Boston Associates sought other sites on swifter streams. The farming community of East Chelmsford at the junction of the Concord and Merrimack rivers, some twenty-five miles from Boston, was chosen. With the Pawtucket Falls providing motive power and Boston close by and connected by water by the Middlesex Canal, the area held out great promise. The land was purchased from unsuspecting farmers in 1821, and construction of the first mills began in 1823. The Merrimack Manufacturing Company, created for the venture but made up predominantly of the original Waltham group, planned not merely a single mill this time but an entire community. The community of East Chelmsford was renamed Lowell after Francis Cabot Lowell, who had died prematurely in 1817.

The town of Lowell grew rapidly. The Merrimack factory was up in December, 1823; two new mills went up in 1828, another in 1830, three more in 1831, and yet another in 1835. Between 1822 and 1839 nine cotton textile companies were formed. The population of Lowell also mushroomed, leaping from 200 in 1820 to 17,633 in 1836 and over 30,000 in 1845. In 1835 the Boston and Lowell Railroad was opened.

The success of the Lowell mills—dividends rarely fell below 10 percent—led to their expansion, along with their boardinghouses, throughout New England. The mills in Manchester, Dover, and Nashua, New Hampshire, Chicopee, Holyoke, and Lawrence, Massachusetts, all followed the Lowell pattern. Outside New England there were only a few integrated companies. At Whitestown, New York, on the Unadilla River, and at Pittsburgh, Pennsylvania, on the tributaries of the Ohio River, companies started in the 1820s which also combined the processes in the production of cotton textiles under one room and employed factory girls who lived in company boardinghouses.

In most cases these new textile enterprises were financed by the profits first gained at Lowell and Waltham, and in fact many were established by the same individuals who were connected with the Boston Associates—the Jacksons, Abbots, Appletons, Lawrences, Bootts, Lowells—a well-knit group, holding tightly to patents and controlling blocks of corporate stock. Absentee owners, these capitalists rarely visited the factory towns they had created. The mills were operated for them by an agent or manager who lived at the site of the factories and was in actual charge of production. These agents, the Boston capitalists acknowledged, were "gentlemen selected for their offices, not on account of any mechanical knowledge or experience in manufacturing, their training before their appointments having been wholly mercantile or professional, but for their executive ability, their knowledge of human nature, their ability to control large numbers of operatives, and their social standing."[8]

Who were the female operatives at Lowell, the Harriets, Sarahs, Ellas, Clementines, Marys, and the others whom Harriet H. Robinson recalled as having "queer names"—"Samantha, Triphena, Plumy, Kezia, Aseneth, Elgardy, Leafy, Ruhamah, Almaretta, Sarpeta, and Florilla . . . among them."[9] They were, in the main, farmers' daughters who came from all parts of the rural districts of New England by stage or baggage wagon, usually recruited by agents of the corporations. They came to the city of spindles for a variety of reasons—to earn some money with which to buy finery and save for the future, to help their fathers eke out an existence, or to assist a brother in furthering his education. Many also came because they were smitten by what was known as "Lowell fever," attracted by the educational opportunities provided by the Lowell library (begun in 1825 with a contribution of $500 by the corporation), the Lyceum (built at company expense, which offered twenty-five lectures per season for the price of fifty cents), and night-school courses. (These educational facilities were also supported by community taxes.) "We had all been fairly educated at public or private schools," Lucy Larcom, herself a mill operative, recalled, "and many of us were resolutely bent upon obtaining a better education."[10] Although circulating libraries were encouraged, reading was strictly forbidden in the mills themselves. But the Lowell operatives "pasted their spinning frames with verses to train their memories," and "pinned up mathematical problems in the 'dressing room.' "[11]

Under the Waltham system, and as it was enlarged upon at Lowell, young women were employed to tend the roving and spinning frames and to mind the looms. Men were engaged primarily as overseers, machinists, teamsters, and in other heavy occupations, or those requiring a definite skill, such as calico printing. Children were used only as bobbin boys and girls. When the Irish came into the mills in large numbers in the 1850s, their children were employed directly in all phases of the production process.

The wages of men under the Waltham system were arrived at through individual bargaining and were usually established at the prevailing New England rate for each trade or skill group. In the case of females, however, there was no well-developed going rate. Wages were set at a level which would be high enough to induce young women to leave the farms and stay away from competing employment, such as household manufactures and domestic service, but low enough to offer an advantage for employing females rather than males, and to compete with unskilled wages of the British textile industry.[12]

In the late 1830s the Lowell female factory operative earned about $1.75 a week clear of board. The board itself came to about $1.45 a week. The boardinghouses were crowded with fifty or sixty young women who slept ten or twelve in a room, two in a bed, and ate in a large communal dining room. They were controlled by the corporations, supervised by a woman appointed by the corporation, and in order to enter such a boardinghouse the factory girl had to agree to the observance of certain regulations. She was to be answerable for any "improper conduct." If she was habitually absent from public worship on the Sabbath, she could not be employed by the company. In addition, the doors of the corporation establishment were locked at ten o'clock at night, as noted earlier. As the Reverend Henry Miles, a Lowell clergyman and an enthusiastic propagandist for the corporations, pointed out: "The sagacity of self-interest as well as more disinterested considerations, has led to the adoption of a strict system of moral police." Without "sober, orderly, and moral" workers, profits would be "absorbed by cases of irregularity, carelessness, and neglect."[13]

The factory operative was awakened at 4:30 A.M. by the bells that called the workers to the mills. She worked in a badly ventilated, tall, narrow building. The light was so poor that she was forced to depend upon a "petticoat lamp" fastened to her loom and filled with whale oil. She needed the light, for she worked at least twelve or thirteen hours a day, starting before seven on a winter morning, before five in the summer, and continuing until seven at night, with a half-hour off for breakfast and another half-hour free for midday dinner.

Contemporaries and many later writers, ignoring the long hours and low wages, placed great emphasis on the evenings at Lowell, the pianos in some boardinghouses, the Lowell lyceum for lectures, the literary meetings with ministers in the Improvement Circles (which led eventually to the publication of the world-famous magazine, the *Lowell Offering*). Foreign visitors were especially impressed with the literary mill operatives. Charles Dickens (who visited Lowell in 1841) was amazed that the young women who worked such a long day could be interested in anything more taxing than climbing wearily into bed in the evening. That they were relentlessly bent on improving themselves, attending lectures and school, flabbergasted him, as did the report that the "factory ladies" had joined together to buy a piano for their boardinghouse parlor.[14] William Scoresby, vicar of Bradford, Yorkshire, who visited Lowell in 1844, recorded his impressions and presented them in a series of lectures on America which were enlarged upon and published in 1845 as *American Factories and Their Female Operatives*. His book is almost completely a glowing account of the operation of the Waltham system at Lowell, and he particularly emphasized the "general superior tone of moral principle and propriety of behaviour prevalent among the young women of the operative classes of New England." Gratifying to Scoresby were "the watchful consideration and moral care for the young women taken by their employers and others." His final chapter is devoted to suggestions, based on his Lowell experience, for the improvement of the condition of English factory operatives—"especially that of females."[15]

Although most foreign observers found Lowell a "philanthropic manufacturing college" (a term used by Anthony Trollope)[16] and supported the rigid moral formula by which the women's lives were ordered, the language of some reveals a strong undercurrent of doubt and uncertainty. For the French traveler Michael Chevalier, the characteristic sound of Lowell was the noise of hammers and spindles and of bells calling the hands back to their machines: "It is the peaceful hum of an industrious population, whose movements are regulated like clockwork." And he termed the hundreds of young women tending the machines "the nuns of Lowell," who, "instead of working *sacred hearts,* spin and weave cotton"—certainly a very revealing remark, implying that the excessive prudery and code of virtue imposed on her prevented the factory operative from realizing her feminine potential. Indeed, he observed that the workers had taken their vows to their machines, "ere they had unfolded themselves."[17]

Alfred Pairpoint, another visitor, while admiring the clean, neat factory and the operatives' efficiency, noted "a certain pallor and anxious sadness in their countenances" as they worked at "the most beautiful specimens of machinery."[18] Frederika Bremer, who also visited Lowell, noticed that "some of the 'young ladies' were about fifty," and was struck by the fact that the factory operatives seemed more like the victims than the beneficiaries of their industrious labor.[19]

The spread of industrialism affected women throughout society. For some it meant working long hours in the factory; for others it meant increasing isolation in the home. And all of them were subjected to the spread of a consciously articulated ideology which preached new definitions for men and women in accordance with the developing class structure and separation of work life and home life. "The Lady" had always been the ideal for upper-class women. What was new was the possibility for middle-class women to "aspire to the status formerly reserved for upper class women." A lifestyle of genteel leisure became a status symbol and was held up as an ideal for all women, whether they could afford it or not. Idleness, formerly considered a sin for women in an early colonial and labor-scarce economy, became a virtue. Women of the growing wage work force would thus be looked down upon for having to work and were easily set apart by their dress, speech, and manners.[19]

Quite a few of the female operatives, especially those associated with the *Lowell Offering,* were convinced that the fame of Lowell gave standing and respectability to the women who worked for wages in the factories, and this kept not a few from protesting about the conditions in the mills. But many of the level-headed Yankee girls quickly saw that the corporations were capitalizing on the favorable image of the factory girl created by the operatives' own efforts. It did not take long for them to realize that a favorable image was no compensation for exploitation.

The genteel operatives continued to center their social life in the churches, learning foreign languages, writing verse or fiction, learning how to play the piano, or taking instruction in the fine arts. But they also began to seethe with revolt and react with "independent and solid character" to the existing working conditions. They were tired of endless labor, of tending as many as three looms, of long hours of daily indoor work, broken only for two hastily gulped meals, with only Sundays and four holidays off during a year: Fast Day, the Fourth of July, Thanksgiving, and Christmas. Even Saturday evenings were denied them—the boardinghouses would not allow lamps to be lighted so the girls would retire early in preparation for church on Sunday.

Ironically, as Hannah Josephson notes in *The Golden Threads: New England's Mill Girls and Magnates* (published in 1949 and still the best general study of the female factory operatives), by 1845 the oft-maligned English system had four to six fewer hours in the working week and two more holidays per year, and most British operatives were required to tend but two looms. In 1847, the ten-hour day became law in England; it was not until 1874 that the same applied for women and children in Massachusetts.[20]

Increasingly, as stockholders multiplied and greater profits were demanded, the wages of the Lowell operatives were reduced and a speed-up of work and a longer day became the rule. "Since 1841," declared the *Lowell Advertiser* of October 28, 1845, "the operatives' wages have been cut down twice directly, besides being cut down indirectly by requiring them to do at least 25 per ct. extra work." Lowell, moreover, set the pattern for all mills using the Waltham system, and agreements existed among employers to follow the wage rates and production speed of the machines adopted at Lowell.[21]

Convinced that they had made possible a life of beauty and culture in the factories, the capitalists felt themselves betrayed when the factory operatives rebelled.[22] They struck back viciously. In an early year, a single Lowell mill discharged twenty-eight women for such reasons as "misconduct," "captiousness," "disobedience," "impudence," "levity," and even "mutiny."[23] Later, young women working for mills operating under the Waltham system were required to "agree . . . to the Regulations which are now, or may

hereafter be adopted, for the good government of this Institution."
Included were provisions which bound the signers to work for such
wages as the company saw fit to pay, not to leave the company's
service without first giving two weeks' notice of intention, and, in
any event, to be subject to loss of two weeks' pay. Finally, signers
had to agree "not to be engaged in any combination, whereby the
work may be impeded, or the Company's interest in any work injured; if we do, we agree to forfeit to the use of the Company the
amount of wages that may be due to us at the time. We also agree
that in case we are discharged from the service of the Company for
any fault, we will not consider ourselves entitled to be settled with
in less than two weeks from the time of such discharge."

Any operative who refused to sign such regulations would have
her name sent abroad to other companies as a "troublemaker" and
would find herself effectively blacklisted throughout the mills.[24]

In 1834 and again in 1836, the female factory operatives took to
the streets and paraded and rallied in response to wage cuts and
accumulated grievances. These were indeed acts of great courage in
light of the social conventions of the day, which frowned on such
"unladylike" activities. But rarely did these demonstrations last for
more than a few days, and never did they result in the formation of
a trade union. Most of the young women either went back to work
on the old terms or returned to their farm homes, cursing the factory
owners who were trying to reduce them to the status of slaves,
denouncing the "mushroom aristocracy of New England who so
arrogantly aspire to lord it over God's heritage," and warning others
to stay away from the "factory prisons."[25]

A few of the unmarried factory operatives and penurious widows
worked for the rest of their lives in the mills. But the majority were
not proletarianized. They came from the nearby farms, and their
earnings in the factories were their sole means of support. They
could leave whenever they desired. Under these circumstances, their
demonstrations were bound to be short-lived, more spontaneous
outbursts of protest than trade union activity. But in the 1840s the
situation was drastically altered; gradually a more or less permanent
working class began to emerge in the factories. During the economic
crisis of 1837–40, a good many farmers in New England had lost
their farms. "As the New England farms disappeared," writes Norman F. Ware, "the freedom of the mill operatives contracted. They
could no longer escape. . . . a permanent factory population became
a reality."[26] Or as a contemporary labor journal emphasized in the
summer of 1845, the workers in the mills were composed "of a large

share of poverty's daughters whose fathers do not possess one foot of land, but work day by day for the bread that feeds their families. Many are foreigners free to work . . . according to the mandates of heartless power, or go to the poor house, beg or do worse."[27]

Once the female factory operatives became the primary wage earners in the family, they became fully committed to improving their conditions on a more systematic basis than through brief turn-outs. The factory operatives of Lowell, Manchester, Dover, Nashua, Fall River, and Waltham, already famous for their cultural and literary activities, were now to earn a new reputation. They were the ones who, in the mid-1840s, formed the first trade unions of industrial women in the United States—the Female Labor Reform Associations—and furnished the first women trade unionists of note in this country, Sarah G. Bagley, Huldah J. Stone, and Mehitabel Eastman.[28] By their ability, militancy, and hard work, they won the respect of the men leading the New England labor movement. They served as delegates to labor conventions and became officers of regional labor organizations along with men. They moved about the towns and villages of New England soliciting subscriptions for the labor press, and they took a leading part in the great struggle for a ten-hour-day law, initiated by the male operatives of Fall River. They gave impetus to a number of important reforms including antislavery, anti–capital punishment, and temperance. Moreover, these militant mill workers were among the real pioneers in the movement for women's rights. They were pressing for full citizenship for women, through voice and pen, precisely at the same time that Elizabeth Cady Stanton, the Grimké sisters, and Susan B. Anthony were active, and they used many of the same arguments. Nor had these militants ceased to be the literary factory girls. They wrote as frequently as ever, but now they wrote in their own magazines and papers and set forth their own points of view on the issues confronting them, rather than reflecting what the corporations would like to hear.

In 1839, following a visit to Lowell, Michael Chevalier asked: "Will this become like Lancashire? Does this brilliant glare hide the misery and suffering of the working girls?"[29] Most historians of the Lowell mills have concluded that the glare of the model factory town, the showcase of the Waltham system, did indeed hide the existence of exploitive wages and working conditions, and that this became even more pronounced from the 1840s onward.[30] A few scholars, however, have recently challenged this thesis; they have argued that the more favorable contemporary accounts of the conditions of life and work in the factories should be taken seriously, and that the conditions in the textile mills must be compared with conditions in the rural communities from which the young women had moved and in other occupations where they fared even worse.[31] One is reminded of what Mrs. Cooke Taylor, a London aristocrat, wrote after a visit to the industrial areas of Lancashire in 1843: "Now that I have seen the factory people at work. . . . I am totally at a loss to account for the outcry. . . . They are better clothed, better fed, and better conducted than many other . . . working people or than they were before they found factory jobs."[32] Perhaps the best way to end the controversy over the well-being of the female operatives is to read what they themselves had to say of life in the mills and the boardinghouses. These young women were not the least bit reluctant to tell their side of the story once they found a medium through which they could communicate. Some of their writings contain a strong strain of morality, a concern with respectability, and perhaps a naive faith in Progress of Man and Woman, and the inevitability of justice for the laboring or producing classes. But the militant factory girls made it clear that justice was due them because they produced the wealth that enabled the corporation owners and their agents to live in luxury, while the mill women endured unceasing toil, inadequate wages, and stunted lives. They also made it quite clear that justice would come only through organization and struggle.

What follows is their message.

NOTES

1. Victor S. Clark, *History of Manufactures in the United States* (New York, 1929), I, 379–80.

2. Samuel Rezneck, "The Rise and Early Development of Industrial Consciousness in the United States, 1760–1830," *Journal of Economic and Business History*, IV (December, 1932), 784–98; Philip S. Foner, ed., *Thomas Jefferson: Selections from His Writings* (New York, 1943), p. 30.

3. W. R. Bagnall, *Samuel Slater and the Early Development of the Cotton Manufacture in the United States* (Middletown, Conn., 1890), p. 44; Caroline F. Ware, *The Early New England Cotton Manufacture* (Boston, 1931), p. 64.

4. "Account of a Journey of Josiah Quincy in 1801," *Proceedings, Massachusetts Historical Society*, ser. II, vol. IV (1888), 124.

5. Samuel Batchelder, *Introduction and Early Progress of the Cotton Manufacture in the United States* (Boston, 1863), pp. 72–74; Jonathan Taylor Lincoln, "The Beginning of the Machine Age in New England: Documents Relating to the Introduction of the Power Loom," *Bulletin: Business History Society*, VII (June, 1933), 6–20.

6. Howard M. Gitelman, "The Waltham System and the Coming of the Irish," *Labor History*, VIII (Fall, 1967), 228–32; Kenneth F. Mailloux, "The Boston

Manufacturing Company of Waltham, Massachusetts, 1813–1848: The First Modern Factory in America" (Ph.D. thesis, Boston University, 1957), pp. 60–65.

7. Vera Shlakman, "Economic History of a Factory Town: A Study of Chicopee, Massachusetts," *Smith College Studies in History*, XX (Northampton, Mass., 1935), 31, 37, 48.

8. Hannah Josephson, *The Golden Threads: New England's Mill Girls and Magnates* (New York, 1949), p. 103.

9. Harriet H. Robinson, *Loom and Spindle: Or Life Among the Early Mill Girls* (New York, 1898), pp. 62–63. For a biographical sketch of Harriet H. Robinson, see below, p. 1. In the manuscript, "Names of Females Hired by Me in Weaving Room No. 1 Manchester Mills in the Year 1846," a report of the agent which is in the New Hampshire Historical Society, there are the following among the first names listed: Harriet, Lydia, Fanny, Mary, Rosanna, Jane, Louisa, Nancy, Sophancie, Adelina, Mehitabel, Lydia, Rebecca, Paulina, Sarah, Cynthia, Phebe, Elisabeth, Ellena, Clarissa, Abigail, Amenta, Jerusha, Abby, Lucretia, Teressa, Hanna, and Diantha. The girls were listed as coming from such communities as Dexter, Portland, Augusta, and Wales, Maine; Thetford, Sharon, Strattford, and Montpelier, Vermont; Lowell, Boston, Haverhill, and Gloucester, Massachusetts; and from at least twenty small communities in New Hampshire.

10. Lucy Larcom, *A New England Girlhood* (Boston, 1890), p. 142. For a biographical sketch of Lucy Larcom, see below, p. 20.

11. Edith Abbott, *Women in Industry* (New York, 1910), p. 122.

12. Malloux, "The Boston Manufacturing Company," pp. 66–69; Gitelman, "The Waltham System," pp. 232–33, 44–45.

13. Henry Miles, *Lowell as It Is and Was* (Lowell, 1845), pp. 128–30. The agent of Manchester Mill No. 1 informed the absentee capitalist owners that it was essential to make certain that the factory girls attended church regularly, and that "without reference to any feelings of philanthropy, self-interest, in the preservation of our property would dictate a watchfulness on our part" (manuscript, New Hampshire Historical Society).

14. Charles Dickens, *American Notes* (New York, 1842), pp. 76–80.

15. William Scoresby, *American Factories and Their Female Operatives* (London, 1845; reprinted, New York, 1968), pp. 81–88, 123–35. There does not appear to have been an equivalent to the literary output of the New England mill girls among their counterparts in old England. None is mentioned in Edward P. Thompson, The Making of the English Working Class (London, 1963), which pays special attention to the literary forms of working-class cultural expression, or in Kathleen Eleanor McCrone, "The Advancement of Women during the Age of Reform, 1832–1870" (Ph.D. dissertation, New York University, 1971), which deals with the female factory workers of England and with literary expressions of English women.

16. Anthony Trollope, quoted in Herbert G. Gutman, "Work, Culture, and Society in Industrializing America, 1815–1919," *American Historical Review*, LXXVIII (June, 1973), 551.

17. Michael Chevalier, *Society, Manners and Politics in the United States* (Boston, 1839), pp. 129, 143.

18. Alfred Pairpoint, *Uncle Sam and His Country* (London, 1857), pp. 163–65; Frederika Bremer, *The Homes of the New World*, trans. Mary Howitt (New York, 1854), I, 210.

19. Gerda Lerner, "The Lady and the Mill Girl: Changes in the Status of Women in the Age of Jackson," *American Studies Journal*, X (Spring, 1969), 2–10. See also Barbara Ehrenreich and Deirdre English, *Witches, Midwives, and Nurses —A History of Women Healers* (Oyster Bay, N.Y., 1972), pp. 4–8.

20. Josephson, *The Golden Threads*, p. 281.

21. Robert G. Layer, "Wages, Earnings, and Output in Four Cotton Textile Companies in New England, 1825–1860" (Ph.D. thesis, Harvard University, 1952), p. 176. A published summary of Layer's thesis is available as *Earnings of Cotton Mill Operatives, 1825–1914* (Cambridge, Mass., 1955).

22. *Ibid.*, pp. 496–503.

23. Robinson, *Loom and Spindle*, p. 38.

24. *The Man*, New York, March 26, 1834. *The Man* was a labor weekly published in New York City and edited by George Henry Evans.

25. Philip S. Foner, *History of the Labor Movement in the United States* (New York, 1947), I, 108–10. See also below, pp. 9–14.

26. Norman F. Ware, *The Industrial Worker, 1840–1860* (Boston and New York, 1924), p. 74.

27. *Voice of Industry*, July 3, 1845.

28. There are no biographical sketches of Huldah J. Stone and Mehitabel Eastman, not even in the recently published three-volume *Notable American Women* (Cambridge, Mass., 1971). There is a sketch of Sarah G. Bagley in volume I, but a more complete one may be found in Madeline B. Stern, *We the Women: Career Firsts of Nineteenth-Century America* (New York, 1963), pp. 84–94. Strangely, Stern lists Sarah Bagley as "America's First Woman Telegrapher" (which she was) and not as what she also was, "America's First Woman Labor Leader." For biographical notes on Huldah J. Stone, Mehitabel Eastman, and Sarah G. Bagley, see below, Part IV.

29. Chevalier, *Society, Manners and Politics*, p. 144.

30. See Caroline F. Ware, *Early New England Cotton Manufacture*, pp. 113, 268; Norman F. Ware, *The Industrial Worker*, pp. 120–24; Abbott, *Women in Industry*, pp. 125–30; Shlakman, "Economic History of a Factory Town,", p. 63; Josephson, *The Golden Threads*, pp. 294–96; Layer, "Wages, Earnings, and Output," pp. 130–35; Malloux, "The Boston Manufacturing Company," p. 213.

31. The leading dissenter is Ray Ginger in "Labor in a Massachusetts Cotton Mill, 1853–1860," *Business History Review*, XXVIII (March, 1954), 67–91. See also Stephen Thernstrom, *Poverty and Progress* (Cambridge, Mass., 1964), pp. 126–31. Recent studies of conditions in the New England mills include Thomas Louis Dublin, "Women at Work: The Transformation of Work and Community in Lowell, Massachusetts, 1826–1860" (Ph.D. dissertation, Columbia University, 1975); Dublin, "Women, Work and Protest in the Early Lowell Mills: 'The Oppressing Hand of Avarice Would Enslave Us,' " *Labor History*, XVI (Winter, 1975), 99–116; Dublin, "Women, Work and the Family: Female Operatives in the Lowell Mills, 1830–1860," *Feminist Studies*, III (Fall, 1975), 30–39; Bettina Eileen Berch, "Industrialization and Working Women in the Nineteenth Century: England, France, and the United States" (Ph.D. dissertation, University of Wisconsin-Madison, 1976); Carl Gersuny, " 'A Devil in Petticoats' and Just Cause: Patterns of Punishment in Two New England Textile Factories," *Business History Review*, L (Summer, 1976), 131–52; Allis Rosenberg Wolfe, "Letters of a Lowell Mill Girl and Friends," *Labor History*, XVII (Winter, 1976), 96–102; Lise Vogel, "Their Own Work: Two Documents from the Nineteenth-Century Labor Movement," *Signs*, I (Summer, 1976), 787–802; Thomas Bender, *Toward an Urban Vision: Ideas and Institutions in Nineteenth Century America* (Lexington, Ky., 1975); John Kasson, *Civilizing the Machine: Technology and Republican Values in America, 1776–1900* (New York, 1976); and Lise Vogel, *Women of Spirit, Women of Action: Mill Workers of Nineteenth-Century New England* (Somersworth, Mass., 1977).

32. Quoted in *Capitalism and the Historians: Essays by T. S. Ashton, Louis Hacker, F. A. Hayek, W. H. Hutt, and Bertrand de Jouvenal* (New York, 1974), p. 35.

Prologue

The First Factory Girls

The First Factory Girls

Although Harriet H. Robinson gives the impression that the women who labored in the New England textile mills during the 1830s were not discontented, poems and songs by the factory operatives themselves presented a different picture. Moreover, even Harriet Robinson later recalled strikes when industrial depression sent wages downward. Two of the earliest strikes in Lowell and Dover are described here in contemporary accounts. The section closes with Harriet Robinson's account of the 1836 strike and with several extracts from the diary of a factory operative in Lowell.

Harriet Hanson Robinson (1825–1911), one of the famous Lowell mill operatives and later a woman suffrage leader, was born in Boston. Her father's death in 1831 forced the poverty-stricken family to move to the mill town of Lowell, where her mother boarded workers for the Tremont Corporation while all four children found employment. Harriet entered the mill at age ten as a bobbin doffer, attended school when she could until age fifteen, and took private lessons in drawing, dancing, and language. In 1848 she married William S. Robinson, the young free-soil editor of the *Lowell Courier,* and became active herself in the antislavery cause. After the Civil War she took up the cause of woman suffrage, organized, with her daughter, the National Woman Suffrage Association of Massachusetts, and became widely known as a lecturer and club-woman. Among her numerous writings are *Early Factory Labor in New England* (1889) and *Loom and Spindle* (1898), recollections of her years in the Lowell mills. ☐

Factory Population of Lowell in 1832

In 1832 the factory population of Lowell was divided into four classes. The agents of the corporations were the aristocrats, not because of their wealth, but on account of the office they held, which was one of great responsibility, requiring, as it did, not only some knowledge of business, but also a certain tact in managing, or utilizing the great number of operatives so as to secure the best return for their labor. The agent was also something of an autocrat, and there was no appeal from his decision in matters affecting the industrial interests of those who were employed on his corporation.

The agents usually lived in large houses, not too near the boarding-houses, surrounded by beautiful gardens which seemed like Paradise to some of the home-sick girls, who, as they came from their work in the noisy mill, could look with longing eyes into the sometimes open gate in the high fence, and be reminded afresh of their pleasant country homes. And a glimpse of one handsome woman, the wife of an agent, reading by an astral lamp in the early evening, has always been remembered by one young girl, who looked forward to the time when she, too, might have a parlor of her own, lighted by an astral lamp!

The second class were the overseers, a sort of gentry, ambitious mill-hands who had worked up from the lowest grade of factory labor; and they usually lived in the end-tenements of the blocks, the short connected rows of houses in which the operatives were boarded. However, on one corporation, at least, there was a block devoted exclusively to the overseers, and one of the wives, who had been a factory girl, put on so many airs that the wittiest of her former work-mates fastened the name of "Pukersville" to the whole block where the overseers lived. It was related of one of these quondam factory girls, that, with some friends, she once re-visited the room in which she used to work, and, to show her genteel friends her ignorance of her old surroundings, she turned to the overseer, who was with the party, and pointing to some wheels and pulleys over her head, she said, "What's them things up there?"

The third class were the operatives, and were all spoken of as "girls" or "men;" and the "girls," either as a whole, or in part, are the subject of this volume.

The fourth class, lords of the spade and the shovel, by whose constant labor the building of the great factories was made possible, and whose children soon became valuable operatives, lived at first on what was called the "Acre," a locality near the present site of the North Grammar schoolhouse. Here, clustered around a small stone Catholic Church, were hundreds of little shanties, in which they dwelt with their wives and numerous children. Among them were sometimes found disorder and riot, for they had brought with them from the *ould counthrey* their feuds and quarrels, and the "Bloody Fardowners" and the "Corkonians" were torn by intestinal strife. The boys of both these factions agreed in fighting the "damned Yankee boys," who represented to them both sides of the feud on occasion; and I have seen many a pitched battle fought, all the way from the Tremont Corporation (then an open field) to the North Grammar schoolhouse, before we girls could be allowed to pursue our way in peace.

I had been to school constantly until I was about ten years of age, when my mother, feeling obliged to have help in her work besides what I could give, and also needing the money which I could earn, allowed me, at my urgent request (for I wanted to earn *money* like the other little girls), to go to work in the mill. I worked first in the spinning-room as a "doffer." The doffers were the very youngest girls, whose work was to doff, or take off, the full bobbins, and replace them with the empty ones.

I can see myself now, racing down the alley, between the spinning frames, carrying in front of me a bobbin-box bigger than I was. These mites had to be very swift in their movements, so as not to keep the spinning-frames stopped long, and they worked only about fifteen minutes in every hour. The rest of the time was their own, and when the overseer was kind they were allowed to read, knit, or even to go outside the mill-yard to play.

Some of us learned to embroider in crewels, and I still have a lamb worked on cloth, a relic of those early days, when I was first taught to improve my time in the good old New England fashion. When not doffing, we were often allowed to go home, for a time, and thus we were able to help our mothers in their housework. We were paid two dollars a week; and how proud I was when my turn came to stand up on the bobbin-box, and write my name in the pay-master's book, and how indignant I was when he asked me if I could "write." "Of course I can," said I, and he smiled as he looked down on me.

The working-hours of all the girls extended from five o'clock in the morning until seven in the evening, with one-half hour for breakfast and for dinner. Even the doffers were forced to be on duty nearly fourteen hours a day, and this was the greatest hardship in the lives of these children. For it was not until 1842 that the hours of labor for children under twelve years of age were limited to ten per day; but the "ten-hour law" itself was not passed until long after some of these little doffers were old enough to appear before the legislative committee on the subject, and plead, by their presence, for a reduction of the hours of labor.[1]

I do not recall any particular hardship connected with this life, except getting up so early in the morning, and to this habit, I never was, and never shall be, reconciled, for it has taken nearly a lifetime for me to make up the sleep lost at that early age. But in every other respect it was a pleasant life. We were not hurried any more than was for our good, and no more work was required of us than we were able easily to do.

Harriet H. Robinson, *Loom and Spindle: Or Life Among the Early Mill Girls* (New York, 1898), pp. 13–19

The Little Factory Girl to a More Fortunate Playmate

I often think how once we used in summer fields to play,
And run about and breathe the air that made us glad and gay;
We used to gather buttercups, and chase the butterfly—
I loved to feel the light breeze lift my hair as it went by!

Do you still play in those bright fields? and are the flowers still there?
There are no fields where I live now—no flowers any where!
But day by day I go and turn a dull and tedious wheel,
You cannot think how sad, and tired, and faint I often feel.

I hurry home to snatch the meal my mother can supply,
Then back to hasten to the task—that not to hate I try,
At night my mother kisses me, when she has combed my hair,
And laid me in my little bed, but—I'm not happy there—

I dream about the factory, the fines that on us wait—
I start and ask my father if—I have not lain too late?
And once I heard him sob and say—"Oh better were a grave,
Than such a life as this for thee, thou little sinless slave!"

I wonder if I ever shall obtain a holiday?
Oh if I do, I'll go to you, and spend it all in play.
And then I'll bring some flowers, if you will give me some;
And at my work I'll think of them and holidays to come!

The Man, May 13, 1834

The following lines from Frazer's Magazine, although intended for English readers, apply with full force to many cases in this country.—They abound with thrilling incident and matter of fact circumstances, and are well calculated to fill the hearts of tyrannical factory agents here, with a deep rooted conviction of the abominable wrong they are continually doing the poor girls in their employ. Therefore, we commend them to their especial attention, and hope they will have a tendency to soften their flinty hearts.

The Little Factory Girl
Founded on Fact

Twas on one winter's morning,
  The weather wet and wild,
Three hours before the dawning,
  The father roused his child;
Her daily morsel bringing,
  The darksome room he paced,
And cried 'the bell is ringing,
  My hapless darling, haste!'

'Father, I'm up, but weary,
  I scarce can reach the door,
And long the way and dreary,—
  O, carry me once more;
To help us we've no mother,
  And you have no employ;
They killed my little brother,—
  Like him, I'll work and die!'

Her wasted form seemed nothing,
  The load was at his heart;
The sufferer he kept soothing,
  Till at the mill they part;
The overlooker met her,
  As to her frame she crept,
And with his thong he beat her,
  And cursed her as she wept.

Alas! What hours of horror
  Made up her latest day,
In toil, and pain, and sorrow,
  They slowly passed away;
It seemed, as she grew weaker,
  The threads they oftener broke.
The rapid wheels ran quicker,
  And heavier felt the stroke.

The sun had long descended,
But night brought no repose;
Her days began and ended
As cruel tyrants chose.
At length a little neighbor
Her halfpenny she paid,
To take her last hour's labor,
While by her frame she laid.

At last, the engine ceasing,
The captives homeward rushed;
She thought her strength increasing—
'T was hope her spirits flushed.
She left, but oft she tarried;
She fell and rose no more;
Till, by her comrades carried,
She reached her father's door.

All night, with tortured feeling,
He watched his speechless child,
While close beside her kneeling,
She knew him not nor smiled.
Again the factory's ringing,
Her last perceptions tried,
When, from her straw bed springing,
' 'T is time!' she shrieked, and died.[2]

Mechanics' Offering (Concord, N.H.), May 13, 1834

The Lowell Factory Girl[3]

When I set out for Lowell,
Some factory for to find,
I left my native country,
And all my friends behind.

Refrain.
Then sing hit-re-i-re-a-re-o
Then sing hit-re-i-re-a-re-o

But now I am in Lowell,
And summon'd by the bell,
I think less of the factory
Than of my native dell.

Refrain.

The factory bell begins to ring,
And we must all obey,
And to our old employment go,
Or else be turned away.

    Refrain.

Come all ye weary factory girls,
I'll have you understand,
I'm going to leave the factory
And return to my native land.

    Refrain.

No more I'll put my bonnet on
And hasten to the mill,
While all the girls are working hard,
Here I'll be lying still.

    Refrain.

No more I'll lay my bobbins up.
No more I'll take them down;
No more I'll clean my dirty work,
For I'm going out of town.

    Refrain.

No more I'll take my piece of soap,
No more I'll go to wash,
No more my overseer shall say,
"Your frames are stopped to doff."

    Refrain.

Come all you little doffers
That work in the Spinning room;
Go wash your face and comb your hair,
Prepare to leave the room.

    Refrain.

No more I'll oil my picker rods,
No more I'll brush my loom,
No more I'll scour my dirty floor
All in the Weaving room.

    Refrain.

No more I'll draw these threads
All through the harness eye;

No more I'll say to my overseer,
Oh! dear me, I shall die.

   Refrain.

No more I'll get my overseer
To come and fix my loom,
No more I'll say to my overseer
Can't I stay out 'till noon?

   Refrain.

Then since they've cut my wages down
To nine shillings per week,[4]
If I cannot better wages make,
Some other piece I'll seek.

   Refrain.

No more he'll find my reading
No more he'll see me sew,
No more he'll come to me and say
"Such works I can't allow."

   Refrain.

I do not like my overseer,
I do not mean to stay,
I mean to hire a Depot-boy
To carry me away.

   Refrain.

The Dress-room girls, they needn't think
Because they higher go,
That they are better than the girls
That work in the rooms below.

   Refrain.

The overseers they need not think,
Because they higher stand;
That they are better than the girls
That work at their command.

   Refrain.

'Tis wonder how the men
Can such machinery make,
A thousand wheels together roll
Without the least mistake.

   Refrain.

Now soon you'll see me married
To a handsome little man,
'Tis then I'll say to you factory girls,
Come and see me when you can.

Broadside, Harris Collection, Brown University

The Turn Out at Lowell

We learn, by the latest accounts, that the Yankee girls at Lowell are doing themselves much credit by their determined resistance of the attempt of their taskmasters to visit punishment upon them for the sins of Bankism.[5] The run upon the Lowell Banks still continued, and the Banks had been obliged to send to Boston for specie. The following is some account of the proceedings of the factory ladies.

THE TURN OUT AT LOWELL.—We are informed by a gentleman from Lowell, that our account of the "Turn out" amongst the female operatives was far from being exaggerated. The disturbance continued through Saturday. Many of the operatives had left Lowell for their homes, and others had returned to their mills. The following proclamation, declaration, manifesto, or whatever the reader pleases to call it, was circulated at Lowell on Saturday:

Issued by the Ladies who were lately employed in the Factories at Lowell to their associates, they having left their former employment in consequence of the proposed reduction in their wages of from 12 to 25 per cent, to take effect on the first of March.

UNION IS POWER

Our present object is to have union and exertion, and we remain in possession of our own unquestionable rights. We circulate this paper, wishing to obtain the names of all who imbibe the spirit of our patriotic ancestors, who preferred privation to bondage, and parted with all that renders life desirable—and even life itself—to procure independence for their children. Their oppressing hand of avarice would enslave us; and to gain their object, they very gravely tell us of the pressure of the times; this we are already sensible of, and deplore it. If any are in want of assistance, the Ladies will be compassionate, and assist them; but we prefer to have the disposing of our charities in our own hands; and as we are free, we would remain in possession of what kind Providence has bestowed upon us, and remain daughters of freeman still.

All who patronize this effort, we wish to have discontinue their labors until terms of reconciliation are made.

Resolved, That we will not go back into the mills to work unless our wages are continued to us as they have been.

Resolved, That none of us will go back unless they receive us all as one.

Resolved, That if any have not money enough to carry them home, that they shall be supplied.

> Let oppression shrug her shoulders,
> And a haughty tyrant frown,
> And little upstart Ignorance
> In mockery look down.
> Yet I value not the feeble threats
> Of Tories in disguise,
> While the flag of Independence
> O'er our noble nation flies.
> —*Boston Transcript.*

The Man, New York, February 22, 1834

Factory Girls' Meeting

In consequence of the notice, given by the Agent to the Females, employed in the Manufacturing establishments in this town, that from and after the 15th instant, their wages would be reduced, to enable their employers to meet the *"unusual pressure of the times,"* the girls, to the number of between 600 and 700, assembled in the Court-House on Saturday afternoon, to devise ways and means to enable themselves to meet the *"pressure of the times"* anticipated from this threatened reduction.

The meeting was organized and a committee of three appointed to prepare resolutions and a report of the proceedings. The notice of the Agent, informing them, that when the mills were again started, it would be upon the *"new prices,"* was then read and the following Resolutions unanimously passed:

1st. *Resolved,* That we will never consent to work for the Co-chaco Manufacturing Company at their reduced *"Tariff of Wages."*

2d. *Resolved,* That we believe the *"unusual pressure of the times,"* which is so much complained of, to have been caused by artful and designing men to subserve party purposes,[6] or more wickedly still, to promote their own private ends.

3d. *Resolved,* That we view with feelings of indignation the attempt made to throw upon us, who are least able to bear it, the effect of this *"pressure,"* by reducing our wages, while those of our overseers and Agent are continued to them at their former high rate. That we think our wages are already low enough when the peculiar circumstances of our situation are considered; that we are, many of us, far from our homes, parents and friends, and that it is only by strict economy and untiring industry that any of us have been able to lay up any thing. That we view, with feelings of scorn, the attempt made by those, who would be glad to see us bond slaves for life, to magnify the small amount of our earnings into fortunes, that their oppressive measures may wear the appearance of justice.

4th. *Resolved,* That we view this attempt to reduce our wages as part of a general plan of the proprietors of the different manufacturing establishments to reduce the Females in their employ to that state of dependence on them, in which they may openly, as they do now secretly, abuse and insult them, by calling them their *"slaves."* That while we feel our independence, we will neither be cajoled by flattery nor intimidated by threats, from using all the means in our power to prevent the accomplishment of a purpose so much to be deprecated.

5th *Resolved,* That we view both the ungenerous accusation of our effecting *"riotous combination"* and the poor compliment of our being *"otherwise respectable"* with like feelings of contempt: and consider them both as the last degree insulting to the daughters of freemen.

6th *Resolved,* That however freely the epithet of "Factory Slaves" may be bestowed upon us, we will never deserve it, by a base and cringing submission to proud wealth or *haughty insolence.*

7th *Resolved,* That it be considered base in any one to depart from the determination expressed by our first resolution.

After the adoption of the above resolutions a communication from one of the members was read, exhorting them to persist in the endeavors to obtain the old prices for labor and not to work for the new, and to correspond with those of their own sex similarly situated in other places, to encourage them to adopt a like course.

The communication was well received and after it had been read the following Votes were passed.

Voted, That a committee of twelve be chosen to communicate the proceedings of this meeting to the girls employed in the Factories at Great Falls, Newmarket, and Lowell.

Voted, That a fund be raised and appropriated to defray the expenses of those, in returning to their homes who may not have the means at their command.

Voted, That the proceedings of this meeting be published in the Dover Gazette and N. H. Globe, and in all other papers printed in this State whose editors are opposed to the system of slavery attempted to be established in our manufacturing establishments.[7]

Dover (N.H.) *Gazette,* reprinted in *The Man,* New York, March 8, 1834

The 1836 Strike in Lowell

One of the first strikes of cotton-factory operatives that ever took place in this country was that in Lowell, in October, 1836.[8] When it was announced that the wages were to be cut down, great indignation was felt, and it was decided to strike, *en masse.* This was done. The mills were shut down, and the girls went in procession from their several corporations to the "grove" on Chapel Hill, and listened to "incendiary" speeches from early labor reformers.

One of the girls stood on a pump, and gave vent to the feelings of her companions in a neat speech, declaring that it was their duty to resist all attempts at cutting down the wages. This was the first time a woman had spoken in public in Lowell, and the event caused surprise and consternation among her audience.[9]

Cutting down the wages was not their only grievance, nor the only cause of this strike. Hitherto the corporations had paid twenty-five cents a week towards the board of each operative, and now it was their purpose to have the girls pay this sum; and this, in addition to the cut in the wages, would make a difference of at least one dollar a week. It was estimated that as many as twelve or fifteen hundred girls turned out, and walked in procession through the streets. They had neither flags nor music, but sang songs, a favorite (but rather inappropriate) one being a parody on "I won't be a nun."

> "Oh! isn't it a pity, such a pretty girl as I—
> Should be sent to the factory to pine away and die?
>   "Oh! I cannot be a slave,
>   I will not be a slave,
>   For I'm so fond of liberty
>   That I cannot be a slave."

My own recollection of this first strike (or "turn out" as it was called) is very vivid. I worked in a lower room, where I had heard the proposed strike fully, if not vehemently, discussed; I had been an ardent listener to what was said against this attempt at "oppression" on the part of the corporation, and naturally I took sides with the strikers. When the day came on which the girls were to turn out, those in the upper rooms started first, and so many of them left that our mill was at once shut down. Then, when the girls in my room stood irresolute, uncertain what to do, asking each other, "Would you?" or "Shall we turn out?" and not one of them having the courage to lead off, I, who began to think they would not go out, after all their talk, became impatient, and started on ahead, saying, with childish bravado, "I don't care what you do, *I* am going to turn out, whether any one else does or not;" and I marched out, and was followed by the others.

As I looked back at the long line that followed me, I was more proud than I have ever been since at any success I may have achieved, and more proud than I shall ever be again until my own beloved State gives to its women citizens the right of suffrage.

The agent of the corporation where I then worked took some small revenges on the supposed ringleaders; on the principle of sending the weaker to the wall, my mother was turned away from her boarding-house, that functionary saying, "Mrs. Hanson, you could not prevent the older girls from turning out, but your daughter is a child, and *her* you could control."

It is hardly necessary to say that so far as results were concerned this strike did no good. The dissatisfaction of the operatives subsided, or burned itself out, and though the authorities did not accede to their demands, the majority returned to their work, and the corporation went on cutting down the wages.

And after a time, as the wages became more and more reduced, the best portion of the girls left and went to their homes, or to the other employments that were fast opening to women, until there were very few of the old guard left; and thus the *status* of the factory population of New England gradually became what we know it to be to-day.

Harriet H. Robinson, *Loom and Spindle: Or Life Among the Early Mill Girls* (New York, 1898), pp. 86–88

Diary of Mary Hall

Feb. 1, 1834   Today some excitement amongst the girls in the factories respecting the wages and many of the girls have left their work.

15.   The excitement increases and many more have left.

Dec. 30, 1835   Been to the Lyceum Lecture Mr. Elliott from Boston. Subject Ancient Rome.

Jan. 20, 1836   Been to the Lyceum Lecture. Professor Mussey from Hanover, N.H. Subject, Reasons and Objections to Galls and Sperzheims System of Phrenology.

May 14   Today left the factory again. Health so poor not able to work.

Dec. 28   This is my birth day. Twenty-five years of my life on earth are numbered and spent. And is it not possible that all the years of my probationary state are numbered. How solemn the thought when I reflect I have thus suffered in so trifeling a manner. God grant that this holy spirit may descend and direct my thoughts aright so that if my years on earth should be protracted they may in future be spent more in conformity to the great end for which I should live.

Extracts from Diary of Mary Hall, weaver in the factory of the Merrimack Corporation, Lowell, Mass. Manuscript in New Hampshire Historical Society

NOTES

1. It was not until 1874 that Massachusetts passed a ten-hour law for women and minors.

2. The poem also appeared in *The Man* of May 13, 1834, without any acknowledgment of its English origin, under the title "The Factory Girl," and with an additional concluding verse which read:

> That night a chariot passed her,
>   While on the ground she lay;
> The daughters of her master
>   An evening visit pay—
> Their tender hearts were sighing,
>   As negroes' wrongs were told;
> While the white slave was dying,
>   Who gained their father's gold!

Some held the view that factory owners who supported the abolitionists were hypocrites, since they were responsible for white slavery in their factories; hence the poem, with its final stanza as above, was reprinted in the labor press of the 1840s. See, for example, *The Mechanic* (Fall River) of May 25, 1844, where it is called "The Factory Child."

3. John Greenway dates the song from around the 1830s, and the internal evidence supports this conclusion. See his *American Folksongs of Protest* (Philadelphia), p. 2.

4. About $2.25 per week.

5. The reference is to the charge, widely believed in labor circles, that Nicholas Biddle, head of the Bank of the United States, retaliated against President Andrew Jackson's removal of government funds from the bank by creating a panic by calling in balances from state banks, raising exchange rates, and using

other financial tricks. A wave of failures swept Philadelphia, New York, and Washington early in 1834.

6. This was a reference to another charge, also widely believed in labor circles, that pro-Bank employers reduced wages to turn workers against Jackson's anti-Bank policy.

7. In a later circular the Dover girls appealed: "We beseech the farmers of our country not to permit their daughters to go into the Mill *at all*, in any place, under the present regulations, if they value the life and health of their children" (*The Man*, New York, March 26, 1834).

8. This is an error. The first strike occurred early in 1834. This is the second strike.

9. This also is not accurate. During the 1834 strike in Lowell, one of the leaders of the strike was reported to have made a "flaming Mary Wollstonecraft speech on the rights of women and the iniquities of the monied aristocracy" (*The Man*, February 22, 1834).

In 1790 Mary Godwin Wollstonecraft (1759–97) published her *Vindication of the Rights of Women*. The modern women's rights movement is dated from that publication.

Part 1

The Genteel Factory Girls

The "Beauty of Factory Life"

During the 1840s newspapers and magazines were filled with glowing pictures of life in the Lowell mills. Unlike the dark, gloomy, wretched life led by workers in the manufacturing plants of Europe, the workers in the Lowell mills were depicted as living in a workers' paradise. In her reminiscences Harriet H. Robinson presented a typical picture of the benevolent factory system in Lowell and the happy life of the factory operatives. However, she conceded at the end: "Undoubtedly there might have been another side to this picture, but I gave the side I knew best,—the bright side!" She may have meant that factory work had a "bright side" compared with work on the farms or competing female employments, such as household manufactures and domestic service.

The female factory operatives received considerable attention because of their interest in culture. The picture of the average operative was that of a person reading a book. Without doubt the young women who came into the mills from rural districts were interested in reading. Many of them were attracted to Lowell by the fame of the circulating libraries, where for 6¼ cents a week they could get books and periodicals unobtainable in their homes. The more ardent carried their volumes of stories and poems into the factories with them, and when books were forbidden during working hours they devised ingenious methods of going on with their reading. Lucy Larcom, herself an operative, recalled one such method.

The picture of the benevolent factory system and of the factory operative whose sole concern was (after helping her family in need) to develop her mind, was presented in novels of the period. This section includes the preface to one such novel, *Lights and Shadows of Factory Life in New England, by a Factory Girl,* published in 1843. Even poets wrote verses in praise of the factory system. This section closes with a typical poem, "Song of the Factory Girls."

Lucy Larcom (1824–93), the most famous of all the Lowell mill operatives, was the daughter of a sea captain who died when she was a small child, leaving his widow and children without adequate provision. Her mother moved the family from Beverly, Massachusetts, to Lowell and became supervisor of one of the mill company dormitories for the female factory operatives. Lucy cut short her grade school training to enter the mill at the age of eleven. She worked, while pursuing independent study on the side, until 1846, when she quit Lowell to live with her sister in Alton, Illinois. Before leaving Lowell she had made the acquaintance of John Greenleaf Whittier, the libertarian poet and antislavery editor. In 1852 she graduated from the Monticello Female Seminary at Alton and returned to Massachusetts to teach. After several years as a teacher at Wheaton Seminary in Norton, she left to become editor of *Our Young Folks,* a popular magazine published in Boston. Her reminiscences of life as a Lowell mill operative are set forth in "Among Lowell Mill-Girls: A Reminiscence," *Atlantic Monthly* (November, 1881), and *A New England Girlhood* (1890). Miss Larcom never expressed sympathy for those seeking to improve working conditions in the mills, and, unlike Harriet H. Robinson, she took no interest in woman suffrage. □

The Pleasant Life in the Factory

Except in rare instances, the rights of the early mill-girls were secure. They were subject to no extortion, if they did extra work they were always paid in full, and their own account of labor done by the piece was always accepted. They kept the figures, and were paid accordingly. This was notably the case with the weavers and drawing-in girls. Though the hours of labor were long, they were not over-worked; they were obliged to tend no more looms and frames than they could easily take care of, and they had plenty of time to sit and rest. I have known a girl to sit idle twenty or thirty minutes at a time. They were not driven, and their work-a-day life was made easy. They were treated with consideration by their employers, and there was a feeling of respectful equality between them. The most favored of the girls were sometimes invited to the houses of the dignitaries of the mills, showing that the line of social division was not rigidly maintained.

Their life in the factory was made pleasant to them. In those days there was no need of advocating the doctrine of the proper relation between employer and employed. *Help was too valuable to be ill-treated.* If these early agents, or overseers, had been disposed to exercise undue authority, or to establish unjust or arbitrary laws, the high character of the operatives, and the fact that women employees were scarce would have prevented it. A certain agent of one of the first corporations in Lowell (an old sea-captain) said to one of his boarding-house keepers, "I should like to rule my help as I used to rule my sailors, but so many of them are women I do not dare to do it."

The knowledge of the antecedents of these operatives was the safeguard of their liberties. The majority of them were as well born as their "overlookers," if not better; and they were also far better educated.

The agents and overseers were usually married men, with families of growing sons and daughters. They were members, and sometimes deacons, of the church, and teachers in the same Sunday-school with the girls employed under them. They were generally of good morals and temperate habits, and often exercised a good influence over their help. The feeling that the agents and overseers were interested in their welfare caused the girls, in turn, to feel an interest in the work for which their employers were responsible. The conscientious among them took as much pride in spinning a smooth thread, drawing a perfect web, or in making good cloth, as they would have done if the material had been for their own wearing. And thus was practised, long before it was preached, the principle of true political economy,—the just relation, the mutual interest, that ought to exist between employers and employed.

Those of the mill-girls who had homes generally worked from eight to ten months in the year; the rest of the time was spent with parents or friends. A few taught school during the summer months.

When we left the mill, or changed our place of work from one corporation to another, we were given an "honorable discharge." Mine, of which I am still quite proud, is dated the year of my marriage, and is as follows:—

"HARRIET J. HANSON has been employed in the Boott Cotton Mills, in a dressing-room, twenty-five months, and is honorably discharged."

(Signed) J. F. TROTT

Lowell, July 25, 1848.

The chief characteristics of the early mill-girls may be briefly mentioned, as showing the material of which this new community of working-women was composed. Concerning their personal appearance, I am able to quote from a magazine article written by the poet John G. Whittier, then a resident of Lowell. He thus describes,—

THE FACTORY GIRLS OF LOWELL

"Acres of girlhood, beauty reckoned by the square rod,—or miles by long measure! the young, the graceful, the gay,—the flowers gathered from a thousand hillsides and green valleys of New England, fair unveiled Nuns of Industry, Sisters of Thrift, and are ye not also Sisters of Charity dispensing comfort and hope and happiness around many a hearthstone of your native hills, making sad faces cheerful, and hallowing age and poverty with the sunshine of your youth and love! Who shall sneer at your calling? Who shall count your vocation otherwise than noble and ennobling?"[1]

They [the mill-girls] went forth from their *Alma Mater*, the Lowell Factory, carrying with them the independence, the self-reliance taught in that hard school, and they have done their little part towards performing the useful labor of life. Into whatever vocation they entered they made practical use of the habits of industry and perseverance learned during those early years.

Skilled labor teaches something not to be found in books or in colleges. Their early experience developed their characters . . . and helped them to fight well the battle of life.

Such is the brief story of the life of every-day working-girls; such as it was then, so it might be to-day. Undoubtedly there might have been another side to this picture, but I give the side I knew best,— the bright side!

Fourteenth Annual Report of the Massachusetts Bureau of Statistics of Labor (Boston, 1883), pp. 132–35; Harriet H. Robinson, *Loom and Spindle: Or Life Among the Early Mill Girls* (New York, 1898), pp. 13–16

How to Read in the Mills

Work in the "dressing-room" was liked for its cleanly quietness; and here, also, one might have wider spaces of leisure. A near relative of mine, who had a taste for rather abstruse studies, used to keep a mathematical problem or two pinned up on a post of her dressing frame, which she and her companions solved as they paced up and down, mending the broken threads of the warp. It has already been said that books were prohibited in the mills, but no objection was made to bits of printed paper; and this same young girl, not wishing to break a rule, took to pieces her half-worn copy of Locke on the Understanding, and carried the leaves about with her at her work, until she had fixed the contents of the whole connectedly in her mind. She also, in the same way, made herself mistress of the argument of one of Saint Paul's difficult Epistles. It was a common thing for a girl to have a page or two of the Bible beside her thus, committing its verses to memory while her hands went on with their mechanical occupation. Sometimes it was the fragment of a dilapidated hymn-book, from which she learned a hymn to sing to herself, unheard within the deep solitude of unceasing sound.

Lucy Larcom, "Among Lowell Mill-Girls: A Reminiscence," *Atlantic Monthly* (November, 1881), pp. 603–4

Preface of "Lights and Shadows of Factory Life in New England, by a Factory Girl"

In a review of Mrs. Trollope's "Michael Armstrong," a work written as an exposé of the factory system in England, one of the editors of the "Ladies' Companion," says:

"The tale is very affecting, but we do not think it well managed. The rescued factory children are elevated, in the end, to too high a station. It is ill-judged, and it may be said, absurd, to make as good as 'lords and ladies' of them."

Yes, in aristocratic, proud, old England, where the factory operatives are so degraded, and the barriers in the way of their onward progress so numerous. But those acquainted with Factory Life in New England, will bear me witness, that in making "so good as lords and ladies" of some of the characters in this little book, there has been no sacrifice of truth.

I saw a gentleman from Washington, who fills a "high place" under the government, and in polite circles there, and elsewhere. . He said, when speaking of the factory girls: "Please inform me on one point—are they intelligent, well educated, graceful, and amiable, as a class?"

One might as well ask, are members of Congress a polite, dignified, and learned class of men? Are the cadets at West Point talented, honorable, and pleasing, as a class? Are the ladies of Troy Seminary graceful, intelligent, and amiable? For the factory girl of to-day, was the school girl, the village belle, or the country maiden, the daughter of affluence, or the destitute orphan, yesterday. A few weeks, months, years, pass away, and she is—perhaps the factory girl still; toiling patiently on, for the subsistence of worthy and beloved, but unfortunate parents; perhaps she is again the school girl; perhaps she is the faithful and efficient helpmeet of the farmer; perhaps the elegant wife of the merchant, mechanic, minister, physician, or lawyer, the accomplished mother of accomplished daughters and honorable sons, who "rise up and call her *blessed.*"

In '40, and '41, there were at school in ———, five beside myself, who had been factory girls. One of them had studied French and Italian, and was then studying Greek and Latin. She is now in the Mill working for funds to complete her education. Another was attending to Greek and Latin. She is prosecuting her studies now with her husband, who is, or is about to be a clergyman. Two others commenced the study of Latin. One of these left school, and became the wife of a physician in the neighborhood. The other is now in the factory, with the object of attending school again. Another studied the Latin, Greek, and French, *un peu, tres peu.* The other was the daughter of one of the first men in the village. Her scholarship was above mediocrity. She is now successfully engaged in teaching.

I do not suppose a knowledge of these languages so common as might be inferred from this fact; but were we all to return to the Mills, we should, by no means, be "literary curiosities" there.

I do not say this in the spirit of vain-boasting. I have not written to show to the world what a factory girl can do; or to prove that the operatives are "intelligent, well-educated, graceful, and amiable as a class." But I love them, and would do them good. I have attempted to clothe rules of duty in an attractive garb, that they may thereby have access to those, who would pass them by, if they appeared in a series of didactic essays. I do not know—I never can know—how far I have been successful. But if the prayers I have breathed over these pages are answered, their mission will be one of benefit and peace.

The New World (New York, February, 1843), pp. 1–2. Copy in Columbia University Library, Rare Book Division

Song of the Factory Girls

Oh, sing me the song of the Factory Girl!
So merry and glad and free!
The bloom in her cheeks, of health how it speaks,
Oh! a happy creature is she!
She tends the loom, she watches the spindle,
And cheerfully toileth away,
Amid the din of wheels, how her bright eyes kindle,
And her bosom is ever gay.

Oh, sing me the song of the Factory Girl!
Who no titled lord doth own,
Who with treasures more rare, is more free from care
Than a queen upon her throne!
She tends the loom, she watches the spindle ,
And she parts her glossy hair,
I know by her smile, as her bright eyes kindle,
That a cheerful spirit is there.

Oh, sing me the song of the Factory Girl!
Link not her name with the Slave's;
She is brave and free, as the old elm tree
Which over her homestead waves.
She tends the loom, she watches the spindle,
And scorns the laugh and the sneer,
I know by her lip, and her bright eyes kindle,
That a free born spirit is there.

Oh, sing me the song of the Factory Girl!
Whose fabric doth clothe the world,
From the king and his peers to the jolly tars
With our flag o'er all seas unfurled.
From the California's seas, to the tainted breeze
Which sweeps the smokened rooms,
Where "God save the Queen" to cry are seen
The slaves of the British looms.

Chicopee (Mass.) *Telegraph,* March 6, 1850

The *Lowell Offering;* the *Operative's Magazine and Young Ladies' Album;* and the *Olive Leaf, and Factory Girl's Repository*

The young women in the Lowell mills formed "improvement circles"—little clubs in which they produced sketches, essays, and short tales modeled on those they found in the popular periodicals of the day. The circles were fostered and encouraged by the clergymen of Lowell and by the mill owners, who looked with favor upon their employees devoting themselves to culture rather than to complaining about their conditions in the mills and acting together to remedy them.

Out of one of these little clubs emerged the *Lowell Offering.* Under the supervision of the Reverend Charles Thomas, pastor of the Second Universalist Church, four small quartos of sixteen pages each, containing the literary efforts of factory operatives, made their appearance at irregular intervals between October, 1840, and March, 1841. The major emphasis in these issues was to dispel the notion that factory work was degrading and that the mill operatives were exploited.

Occasionally the *Lowell Offering* carried a piece of fiction or poetry which revealed dissatisfaction with the conditions of work, but they ended in the same escapism that characterized the main bulk of the contributions. Susan, explaining her first day in the mill to Ann, said the operatives awoke early and sang, "Morning bells, I hate to hear./Ringing dolefully, loud and clear." Susan went on to describe how she was set to work "threading the shuttles, and tying weaver's knots and such things and now I have improved so that I can take care of one loom. I could take care of two if I only had eyes in the back of my head." When she went out at night, the sound of the mill was in her ears, "as of crickets, frogs, and Jew-harps, all mingled together in a strange discord. After it seemed as though cotton-wool was in my ears." But just as it appeared that Susan would suggest to Ann that the factory operatives unite to change such conditions, she wrote: "But now I do not mind it at all. You know that people learn to sleep with the thunder of Niagara in their ears, and the cotton mill is no worse."

Soon the *Lowell Offering* attracted national and international attention, the attitude summed up by the statement of the Reverend William Scoresby, a visitor from England, who called it "the ninth wonder of the world, considering the source from which it comes." Another improvement circle in Lowell, guided by the Reverend Thomas Thayer, pastor of the First Universal Church, envied the success of the *Lowell Offering*. Not to be outdone by the other factory girls, the young women of this group began in April, 1841, a rival publication, called the *Operatives' Magazine,* edited by Lydia S. Hall and Abba A. Goodard. Unlike the *Offering*, it did not advertise itself as exclusively feminine, but "solicited communications from the operatives of both sexes." Printed by William Schouler for the "association of females" which published it, the *Operatives' Magazine,* like the *Offering,* had no intention of criticizing factory conditions or urging the factory operatives to unite to change them. With the July, 1841, number the publication appeared as the *Operatives' Magazine and Lowell Album,* "written, edited, and published by females alone." It continued its course of dealing only with moral questions until August, 1842, when Schouler became the proprietor of the *Lowell Offering* and united the *Operatives' Magazine* with that more famous publication.

Still another magazine which espoused the escapist outlook of the genteel factory operative was the *Olive Leaf, and Factory Girl's Repository,* published in the mill town of Cabotville, Massachusetts.

The most famous of the magazines of the genteel factory operatives was, of course, the *Lowell Offering.* Harriet Farley and Harriot F. Curtis, both former mill operatives and contributors to the *Offering,* were co-editors, though Miss Farley soon became sole editor and Miss Curtis took charge of the subscription department.

Harriet Farley (1813?–1907) was the daughter of the Reverend Stephen Farley, a Congregational minister in New Hampshire. One of ten children, she had to seek work to help support the family at the age of fourteen. After work at straw-plaiting, binding shoes, tailoring, and other trades, she entered the Lowell mills. She had studied at Atkinson Academy, of which her father was principal; once in Lowell, she joined an improvement circle. She first won notice in December, 1840, when the *Lowell Offering,* then edited by Abel C. Thomas, printed her reply, signed "A Factory Girl," to transcendentalist Orestes A. Brownson's attack (in his magazine *Boston Quarterly Review)* upon textile mill owners and the exploitation of factory labor. Brownson observed that few of the factory girls "ever return to their native places with reputations unimpaired. *'She has worked in a factory.'* is sufficient to damn to infamy the most worthy and virtuous girl." Miss Farley defended the mill owners, attacked Brownson as a "slanderer," and called work in the textile mills "one of the most lucrative female employments." Her defense of the corporations came to the attention of Amos Lawrence, Lowell textile magnate, and when in the fall of 1842 the Lowell *Courier* purchased the *Offering,* he assisted her financially so that she could leave the mill and devote herself to the editorship. A year later, Harriot F. Curtis joined her as co-editor. Miss Farley wrote editorials, including autobiographical sketches in the *Lowell Offering* of July and August, 1845.

Harriot F. Curtis, a descendant of Miles Standish, was born in Vermont; before she entered the Lowell mills she had published *Kate in Search of a Husband,* a popular novel. After working as a highly skilled harness-knitter in the mills, a relatively highly paid position, she quit to become co-editor of the *Offering.* Among her contributions to the *Offering* was a novel called *The Smugglers,* which was published serially beginning with the issue of November, 1843.

In this section will be found a list of the writers for the *Lowell Offering,* a few selections from the famous magazine, and selections from the *Operatives' Magazine* and the *Olive Leaf.* The selections from the *Lowell Offering* include Miss Farley's reply to Orestes Brownson, which reflects her sensitivity to the charge that the *Offering* was concerned not with the real problems facing the factory operatives but mainly with demonstrating the workers' culture and respectability. It also includes "Pleasures of Factory Life," by Sarah G. Bagley (S.G.B.), who, as we shall see in the next sections, was to become Miss Farley's most vigorous opponent, the outstanding critic of the *Lowell Offering,* and the leading voice of the militant factory operatives. One of the selections is the only piece on women's rights ever published by the *Offering;* in keeping with the tone of the magazine, it is very moderate in its approach. □

Editor's Preface to the *Lowell Offering*

In the early part of 1840, an "Improvement Circle," as it was denominated, was formed in this city. The meetings were holden one evening each fortnight. The entertainments consisted solely of reading communications. Shortly afterwards, a second Circle was formed. In October, 1840, the first number of the "Lowell Offering" was published—the articles, selected from the budgets of those Circles, being exclusively the productions of Females employed in the Mills. Nos. 2, 3, 4, followed at intervals of a month or six weeks. In April, 1841, a new series of the work was commenced. The first Volume, completed, is now presented to the public.

The two most important questions which may be suggested, shall receive due attention.

1st. Are all the articles, in good faith and exclusively, the productions of Females employed in the Mills? We reply, unhesitatingly and without reserve, that THEY ARE, the verses set to music excepted. We speak from personal acquaintance with all the writers, excepting four; and in relation to the latter, (whose articles do not occupy eight pages in the aggregate) we had satisfactory proof that they were employed in the Mills.

2d. Have not the articles been materially amended by the exercise of the editorial prerogative? We answer, THEY HAVE NOT. We have taken *less liberty* with the articles than editors usually take with the production of other than the most experienced writers. Our corrections and additions have been so slight as to be unworthy of special note.

These statements rest on our veracity. Those who wish to inquire concerning our standing and reputation, are respectfully referred to His Honor, Elisha Huntington, Mayor; Samuel Lawrence,[2] Esq.; Jacob Robbins, Esq., Post Master; or any of the Superintendents of the Corporations in Lowell.

In estimating the talent of the writers for the Offering, the fact should be remembered, that they are actively employed in the Mills for more than twelve hours out of every twenty-four. The evening, after 8 o'clock, affords their only opportunity for composition; and whoever will consider the sympathy between mind and body, must be sensible that a day of constant manual employment, even though the labor not be excessive, must in some measure unfit the individual for the full development of mental power.

Yet the articles in this volume ask no unusual indulgence from the critics—for, in the language of the North American Review, "many of the articles are such as satisfy the reader at once, that he has only taken up the Offering as a phenomenon, and not as what may bear criticism and reward perusal, he has but to own his error, and dismiss his condescension, as soon as may be."

Lowell Offering, n.s. I, 1841

Writers for the *Lowell Offering*

The names of The Lowell Offering writers, so far as I have been able to gather them, are as follows: Sarah G. Bagley, Josephine L. Baker, Lucy Ann Baker, Caroline Bean, Adeline Bradley, Fidelia O. Brown, M. Bryant, Alice Ann Carter, Joanna Carroll, Eliza J. Cate, Betsey Chamberlain, L. A. Choate, Kate Clapp, Louisa Currier, Maria Currier, Lura Currier, Harriot F. Curtis, Catherine Dodge, M. A. Dodge, Harriet Farley, Margaret F. Foley, A. M. Fosdick, Abby A. Goddard, M. R. Green, Lydia S. Hall, Jane B. Hamilton, Harriet Jane Hanson, Eliza Rice Holbrook, Eliza W. Jennings, Hannah Johnson, E. Kidder, Miss Lane, Emmeline Larcom, Lucy Larcom, L. E. Leavitt, Harriet Lees, Mary A. Leonard, Sarah E. Martin, Mary J. McAffee, E. D. Perver, E. S. Pope, Nancy R. Rainey, Sarah Shedd, Ellen L. Smith, Ellen M. Smith, Laura Spaulding, Mary Ann Spaulding, Emmeline Sprague, S. W. Stewart, Laura Tay, Rebecca C. Thompson, Abby D. Turner, Elizabeth E. Turner, Jane S. Welch, Caroline H. Whitney, A. E. Wilson, Adeline H. Winship, and Sabra Wright, fifty-seven in all. Most of the writers signed fictitious names such as Ella, Adelaide, Dorens, Aramantha, Stella, Kate, Oriana, Ruth Rover, Ione, Dolly Dindle, Grace Gayfeather, and many others.

Harriet H. Robinson, *Loom and Spindle: Or Life Among the Early Mill Girls* (New York, 1898), pp. 118–19

Defence of Factory Girls

"SHE HAS WORKED IN A FACTORY, *is sufficient to damn to infamy the most worthy and virtuous girl."*

So says Mr. Orestes A. Brownson;[3] and either this horrible assertion is true, or Mr. Brownson is a slanderer. I assert that it is *not* true, and Mr. B. may consider himself called up to prove his words, if he can.

This gentleman has read of an Israelitish boy who, with nothing but a stone and sling, once entered into a contest with a Philistine giant, arrayed in brass, whose spear was like a weaver's beam; and he may now see what will probably appear to him quite as marvellous; and that is, that a *factory girl* is not afraid to oppose herself to the *Editor of the Boston Quarterly Review.* True, he has upon his side fame, learning, and great talent; but I have what is better than either of these, or all combined, and that is *truth.* Mr. Brownson has not said that this thing should be so; or that he is glad it is so; or that he deeply regrets such a state of affairs; but he has said it *is* so; and *I* affirm that it is *not.*

And whom has Mr. Brownson slandered? A class of girls who in this city alone are numbered by thousands, and who collect in many of our smaller towns by hundreds; girls who generally come from quiet country homes, where their minds and manners have been formed under the eyes of the worthy sons of the Pilgrims, and their virtuous partners, and who return again to become the wives of the free intelligent yeomanry of New England, and the mothers of quite a proportion of our future republicans. Think, for a moment, how many of the next generation are to spring from mothers doomed to infamy! "Ah," it may be replied, "Mr. Brownson acknowledges that you may still be worthy and virtuous." Then we must be a set of worthy and virtuous idiots, for no virtuous girl of common sense would choose for an occupation one that would consign her to infamy.

Mr. Brownson has also slandered the community; and far over the Atlantic the story will be told, that in New England, the land to which the Puritans fled for refuge from social as well as religious oppression—the land where the first blood was shed in defence of the opinion that all are born free and equal—the land which has adopted the theory that morals and intellect are alone to be the criterions of superiority—that *there,* worthy and virtuous girls are consigned to infamy, if they work in a factory!

That there has been prejudice against us, we know; but it is wearing away,[4] and has never been so deep nor universal as Mr. B's statement will lead many to believe. Even now it may be that "the mushroom aristocracy," and "would-be-fashionables" of Boston, turn up their eyes in horror at the sound of those vulgar words, *factory girls;* but *they* form but a small part of the community, and theirs are not the opinions which Mr. Brownson intended to represent.

Whence has arisen the degree of prejudice which has existed against factory girls, I cannot tell; but we often hear the condition of the factory population of England, and the station which the operatives hold in society there, referred to as descriptive of *our* condition. As well might it be said, as say the *nobility* of England, that *labor itself* is disgraceful, and that all who work should be consigned to contempt, if not to infamy. And again: it has been asserted that to put ourselves under the influence and restraints of corporate bodies, is contrary to the spirit of our institutions, and to that love of independence which we ought to cherish. There is a spirit of independence which is averse to social life itself; and I would advise all who wish to cherish it, to go far beyond the Rocky Mountains, and hold communion with none but the untamed Indian, and the wild beast of the forest. We are under restraints, but they are voluntarily assumed; and we are at liberty to withdraw from them, whenever they become galling or irksome. Neither have I ever discovered that any restraints were imposed upon us, but those which were necessary for the peace and comfort of the whole, and for the promotion of the design for which we are collected, namely, to get money, as much of it and as fast as we can; and it is because our toil is so unremitting, that the wages of factory girls are higher than those of females engaged in most other occupations. It is these wages which, in spite of toil, restraint, discomfort, and prejudice, have drawn so many worthy, virtuous, intelligent, and well-educated girls to Lowell, and other factories; and it is the wages which are in a great degree to decide the characters of the factory girls as a class. It was observed (I have been told) by one of the Lowell overseers to his superintendent, that he could get girls enough who would work for one dollar per week. I very much doubt whether it would be possible; but supposing it true, they would not be such girls as will come and work for two, three and four dollars per week. Mr. Brownson may rail as much as he pleases against the real injustice of capitalists against operatives, and we will bid him *God speed,* if he will but keep truth and common sense upon his side. Still, the avails of factory labor are now greater than those of many domestics, seamstresses, and school-teachers; and strange would it be, if in money-loving New England, one of the most lucrative female employments should be rejected because it is toilsome, or because some people are prejudiced against it. Yankee girls have too much *independence* for *that*.

But it may be remarked, "You certainly cannot mean to intimate, that all factory girls are virtuous, intelligent," &c. No, I do not; and Lowell would be a stranger place than it has ever been represented, if among eight thousand girls there were none of the ignorant and depraved. Calumniators have asserted, that *all* were vile, because they knew *some* to be so; and the sins of *a few* have been visited upon *the many*. While the mass of the worthy and virtuous have been unnoticed, in the even tenor of their way, the evil deeds of a few individuals have been trumpeted abroad, and they have been regarded as specimens of factory girls. It has been said, that factory girls are not thought as much of any where else as they are in Lowell. If this be true, I am very glad of it; it is quite to our credit to be most respected where we are best known. Still, I presume, there are girls here who are a disgrace to the city, to their sex, and to humanity. But *they* do not fix the tone of public sentiment, and their morals are not the standard. There is an old adage, that "Birds of a feather flock together;" and a Captain Marryatt could probably find many females here who do not appear like "woman as she should be"—but men of a better sort have found females here of whom they have made companions, not for an evening or a day, but for life. The erroneous idea, wherever it exists, must be done away, that there is in factories but one sort of girls, and *that* the baser and degraded sort. There are among us *all sorts* of girls. I believe that there are few occupations which can exhibit so many gradations of piety and intelligence; but the majority may at least lay claim to as much of the former as females in other stations of life. The more intelligent among them would scorn to sit night after night to view the gestures of a Fanny Elssler.[5] The Improvement Circles, the Lyceum and Institute, the social religious meetings, the Circulating and other libraries, can bear testimony that the little time they have is spent in a better manner. Our well filled churches and lecture halls, and the high character of our clergymen and lecturers, will testify that the state of morals and intelligence is not low.

Mr. Brownson, I suppose, would not judge of our moral characters by our church-going tendencies; but as many do, a word on this subject may not be amiss. That there are many in Lowell who do not regularly attend any meeting; is as true as the correspondent of the Boston Times once represented it; but for this there are various reasons.There are many who come here for but a short time, and who are willing for a while to forego every usual privilege, that they may carry back to their homes the greatest possible sum they can save. There are widows earning money for the maintenance and education of their children; there are daughters providing for their aged and destitute parents; and there are widows, single women, and girls, endeavoring to obtain the wherewithal to furnish some other home than a factory boarding-house. Pew rent, and the dress which custom has wrongly rendered essential, are expenses which they cannot afford, and they spend their Sabbaths in rest, reading, and meditation. There may also be many other motives to prevent a regular attendance at church, besides a disinclination to gratify and cultivate the moral sentiments.

There have also been nice calculations made, as to the small proportion which the amount of money deposited in the Savings Bank bears to that earned in the city; but this is not all that is saved. Some is deposited in Banks at other places, and some is put into the hands of personal friends. Still, much that is earned is immediately, though not foolishly, spent. Much that none but the parties concerned will ever know of, goes to procure comforts and necessaries for some lowly home, and a great deal is spent for public benevolent purposes. The fifteen hundred dollars which were collected in one day for Missionary purposes by a single denomination in our city, though it may speak of what Mrs. Gilman calls the "too great tendency to overflow in female benevolence," certainly does not tell of hearts sullied by vice, or souls steeped in infamy. And it is pleasing to view the interest which so many of the factory girls take in the social and religious institutions of this place, who do not call Lowell aught but a temporary home. Many of them stay here longer than they otherwise would, because these institutions have become so dear to them, and the letters which they send here after they do leave, show that the interest was too strong to be easily eradicated. I have known those who left homes of comfort and competence, that they might here enjoy religious privileges which country towns would not afford them. And the Lowell Offering may prove to all who will read it, that there are girls here whose education and intellect place them above the necessity of pursuing an avocation which will inevitably connect them with the ignorant and vicious.

And now, if Mr. Brownson is a *man,* he will endeavor to retrieve the injury he has done; he will resolve that "the dark shall be light, and the wrong made right," and the assertion he has publicly made will be as publicly retracted. If he still doubts upon the subject, let him come among us: let him make himself as well acquainted with us as our pastors and superintendents are; and though he will find error, ignorance, and folly among us, (and where would he find them not?) yet he would not see worthy and virtuous girls consigned to infamy, because they work in a factory.

A FACTORY GIRL

A social meeting, denominated Improvement Circle, was established in this city about a twelve-month since. At the sessions of this Circle, which have been holden one evening in a fortnight, communications (previously revised by the gentleman in charge) have been read, the names of the writers not being announced. The largest range of subject has been allowed, and the greatest variety of style indulged: Fiction and fact; poetry and prose; science and letters; religion and morals:—and in composition, the style has been humorous or otherwise, according to the various taste or talent of the writers. The reading of these articles has constituted the sole entertainment of the meetings of the Circle. The interest thus excited has given a remarkable impulse to the intellectual energies of our population.—At a social meeting for divine worship connected with one of our societies, communications, chiefly of a religious character, have been read, during several years past. The alternate weekly session of this conference was appropriated mainly to communications, and denominated Improvement Circle, soon after the institution of the one above mentioned; and the interest has thereby been greatly increased. A selection from the budgets of articles furnished to these circles, together with a few communications derived from other sources, constitutes THE LOWELL OFFERING, whereof the two gentlemen in charge of the meetings aforesaid are the Editors.

We have been thus particular, partly to gratify the curiosity of our readers, and partly to call attention to the advantage of such social institutions for improvement in knowledge and in the art of composition. The meetings being free to all who are disposed to attend, they may be likened to so many intellectual banquets; the writers furnishing "the feast of reason," while all present participate in "the flow of soul."

EDITORS

Lowell Offering, December, 1840

Pleasures of Factory Life

Pleasures, did you say? What! pleasures in *factory* life? From many scenes with which I have become acquainted, I should judge that the pleasures of factory life were like "Angels visits, few and far between"—said a lady whom fortune had placed above labor. [Indolence, or idleness, is not *above* labor, but *below* it.—EDS.] I could not endure such a constant clatter of machinery, that I could neither speak to be heard, nor think to be understood, even by myself. And then you have so little leisure—I could not bear such a life of fatigue. Call it by any other name rather than pleasure.

But stop, friend, we have some few things to offer here, and we are quite sure our views of the matter are just,—having been engaged as an operative the last four years. Pleasures there are, even in factory life; and we have many, known only to those of like employment. To be sure it is not so convenient to converse in the mills with those unaccustomed to them; yet we suffer no inconvenience among ourselves. But, aside from the talking, where can you find a more pleasant place for contemplation? There all the powers of the mind are made active by our animating exercise; and having but one kind of labor to perform, we need not give all our thoughts to that, but leave them measurably free for reflection on other matters.

The subjects for pleasurable contemplation, while attending to our work, are numerous and various. Many of them are immediately around us. For example: In the mill we see displays of the wonderful power of the mind. Who can closely examine all the movements of the complicated, curious machinery, and not be led to the reflection, that the mind is boundless, and is destined to rise higher and still higher; and that it can accomplish almost any thing on which it fixes its attention!

In the mills, we are not so far from God and nature, as many persons might suppose. We cultivate, and enjoy much pleasure in cultivating flowers and plants. A large and beautiful variety of plants is placed around the walls of the rooms, giving them more the appearance of a flower garden than a workshop. It is there we inhale the sweet perfume of the rose, the lily, and geranium; and, with them, send the sweet incense of sincere gratitude to the bountiful Giver of these rich blessings. And who can live with such a rich and pleasant source of instruction opened to him, and not be wiser and better, and consequently more happy.

Another great source of pleasure is, that by becoming operatives, we are often enabled to assist aged parents who have become too infirm to provide for themselves; or perhaps to educate some orphan brother or sister, and fit them for future usefulness. And is there no pleasure in all this? No pleasure in relieving the distressed and removing their heavy burdens? And is there no pleasure in rendering ourselves by such acts worthy of the confidence and respect of those with whom we are associated?

Another source is found in the fact of our being acquainted with some person or persons that reside in almost every part of the country. And through these we become familiar with some incidents that interest and amuse us wherever we journey; and cause us to feel a greater interest in the scenery, inasmuch as there are gathered pleasant associations about every town, and almost every house and tree that may meet our view.

Let no one suppose that the 'factory girls' are without guardian. We are placed in the care of overseers who feel under moral obligations to look after our interests; and, if we are sick, to acquaint themselves with our situation and wants; and, if need, be, to remove us to the Hospital, where we are sure to have the best attendance, provided by the benevolence of our Agents and Superintendents.

In Lowell, we enjoy abundant means of information, especially in the way of public lectures. The time of lecturing is appointed to suit the convenience of the operatives; and sad indeed would be the picture of our Lyceums, Institutes, and scientific Lecture rooms, if all the operatives should absent themselves.

And last, though not least, is the pleasure of being associated with the institutions of religion, and thereby availing ourselves of the Library, Bible Class, Sabbath School, and all other means of religious instruction. Most of us, when at home, live in the country, and therefore cannot enjoy these privileges to the same extent; and many of us not at all. And surely we ought to regard these as sources of pleasure.

S.G.B.

We have taken the liberty to change several sentences in the preceding article, and to transpose two of the paragraphs. The hints of the writer might be amplified in a series of illustrations. Who will undertake it? Eds.

Lowell Offering, December, 1840

Lowell—A Parody on Hohenlinden

When Lowell once desired to show
What factory girls had power to do,
Her heaps of cloth as white as snow,
   She largely piled, and rapidly.

But Lowell saw another sight,
When intellect proclaimed her right,
And operatives by her clear light,
   To Science brought their OFFERING.

By pen and pencil fast arrayed,
And scheme, by thought's deep doings laid
On reason's rock, in fancy's shade,
   They wrought their spirit's imagery.

Then felt the land the impulse given,
Then rushed each pen impetuous driven,
And bright as meteor of heaven,
   Far flashed the mind's artillery.

And brighter yet these minds shall glow,
'Mid Lowell's drifts of mimic snow:
And swifter yet shall be the flow
   Of genius, rolling rapidly.

'Tis morn; but scarce can Truth's bright sun
Undo what slander's night has done;
Yet time shall write the victory won,
   Upon a truth-lit canopy.

The world is gazing. Oh, and save
Your name from ignominy's grave.
Wave, Science, thy bright banner wave
   Above each Lowell factory.

Here poetry and prose shall meet
Upon the Offering's flying sheet,
This blushing calumny retreat—
   Then lock her in her sepulchre.

L.S.H.

Lowell Offering, December, 1840

Woman

Woman's Mission, Woman's Sphere, Woman's Rights, Woman as she should be—and many similar phrases, are titles of books which have within a few years issued from the press. I have read none of them; for I am one of those who have more time for reflection, than for the perusal of books; but the feeling which has prompted so many of our own, and of the other sex, to write and speak of woman's duty and influence, cannot but be shared by all of us who have heads to think, and hearts to feel. My opinions, then, may claim the merit of originality; and if they possess no other, I may plead in excuse that a more extensive knowledge of the thoughts and opinions of nobler minds, might have corrected my errors, and reformed my sentiments.

It cannot be thought strange, that in this country, where the rights of man are so vehemently asserted, those of woman should also receive some attention; and that the questions should arise whether her mission is duly performed—her sphere the only one for which she is fitted—her rights appreciated—and whether she is indeed "as she should be." Man is every where lord of creation: here, he is lord also of himself; and while he now takes a higher stand than he has ever claimed before, woman has not arisen in a corresponding degree. Here, every man may share in the government of his country; but woman is here, as elsewhere, the governed; and if her natural rights and duties are the same as his, she is also the oppressed. She has here no privilege which she might not enjoy under the enlightened monarchs of Europe, and no distinction but that of being the mothers and daughters, the wives and sisters, of *freemen.* Several kingdoms are now governed by females; and probably as well governed as they would be by those of the other sex; and thus it is evident, that woman is capable of being trained to reason, and to rule; but it is an important query, whether this is her most appropriate and congenial sphere?

Mrs. Sigourney[7] has most beautifully expressed an opinon, which I believe to be true. I repeat not her words—but her sentiment is this:—that while the sexes might exchange occupations—while man might be taught to steal around the chamber of the sick, and perform the quiet duties of domestic life, woman might also be taught to sway the senate, and lead her country's armies to battle; but violence would be done to the nature of each. Yes, man might be taught to bend his energies to the still duties of house-hold life; but his spirit would pant for a wider sphere, and his mind would writhe and chafe beneath its shackles; and woman might engage in noise and strife, but the overtasked heart would yearn for a humbler lot, and prematurely exhaust itself in the violence of self-contest.

The Bible, and every ancient tradition, has awarded to man the honor of being first created; but a companion and help-meet was needed; and as he had been gifted with an immortal mind, so none but a being destined to share with him a glorious immortality, could call out his affections, and share his sympathies. In those feelings and moral sentiments, the exercise of which is to constitute his future happiness, she is fully his equal—apparently his superior; for in her they exist uncontrolled by those selfish and intellectual qualities which fit *him* to go forward in this earthly existence. But if there be no difference of mind, there is a difference of body which must compel her to yield to him the palm of superiority. He is made more strong, that he may protect and defend; she more lovely, that he may be willing to shield and guard her; and that physical difference which in one state of society, makes woman the slave of man, in another makes him her worshiper.

Woman has always been obliged to take that station in life which man has been pleased to allot her. Among savage nations, where those faculties of mind in which she equals him have little exercise in either sex, she is but little more than a beast of burden; but in those stages of society where refinement, and the love of the beautiful, were predominant, she has been the object of chivalrous adoration. She has been knelt to, and worshiped, with all the enthusiasm of gallantry; but the same hand which raised her to the throne, had power to overturn it; and while she sat upon it, it was at his caprice.

It has been truly said, that Christianity alone has truly elevated woman. And how has it done it? Not by infusing any new power into his mind; but by awakening in man the love of the true, the good, and the just; by making him sensible of the superiority of right over might; by arousing those holier sympathies and desires in which he feels that woman is not indeed his inferior; and should the time come when earth is to bear some resemblance of heaven, woman's influence will be found to mingle equally with man's, in hastening on the era of happiness and love.

But though in many respects his equal, she will never be like him. Her duties and pleasures must always be different. Were the sexes willing to exchange places, they could not do it; and each has been so formed, as to enjoy most in a separate sphere. *She* can never obtain his strength and vigor, and some of her duties he could not perform, if he wished. Woman must be the mother, and that fount of "deep, strong, dealthless love," has been implanted in her breast, which can turn a mother's cares to pleasures. In that station where woman is most herself, where her predominating qualities have the fullest scope, there she is most influential, and most truly worthy of respect. But when she steps from her alotted path into that of the other sex, she betrays her inferiority, and in a struggle would inevitably be subdued.

It is now asserted, by some, that woman should here share in the toils, duties and honors of government; that it is her right; and that it is contrary to the first principles of our constitution to deprive her of this privilege.

That woman, if not now capable of doing this, might be rendered so by education, cannot be doubted; and should our sex rise *en masse,* and claim the right, I see not how it could be denied. But this will never be. To be happy, and to contribute to the happiness of others, is her aim; and neither of these objects would be attained by engaging in party politics. The general principles of government, and the welfare of her country, should always be subjects of interest to her. They may occupy part of her thoughts and conversation; but to become a voter, would be contrary to the feelings which she ought principally to cherish, and the duties she should never neglect—those of home.

Man, says Lady M. W. Montagu,[8] by engrossing to himself the honors of government "has saved us from many cares, from many dangers, and perhaps from many crimes." Let woman, with her warm sympathies, engage in the political wrangle, and the strife will not be less bitter. If she go at all upon the battlefield, it should be "as (to use an expression of William Penn's) the physician goes among the sick—not to catch the disease, but to cure it." But to do this she must go, not as a partisan, but as a mediator. She should endeavor to speak words which would allay the wrath of the combatants, and to say to all who will listen, "Sirs, ye are brethren." She must stand on neutral ground, with the white flag in her hand; for if she show herself upon either side, she may become the victim of her own violent feelings, if not the slave of the perfidious and designing of the other sex.

Women once madly and unrestrainedly engaged in political strife; and while some, with the most ardent patriotism, preserved their purity and tenderness, others became the "Furies of the Guillotine." Even then, though nominally as free as the other sex, the stronger spirit ruled. They were urged on for a time, and when that time was over they were obliged to yield a power which they could not maintain, and which the other sex wished to resume.

But though woman may not personally approach the ballot box, or mingle in the caucus, yet she can there be represented. Men consider their interests as identified with those of their families. They do not vote for themselves alone, but for their mothers, wives, and daughters. Females who think at all upon politics, usually think as the males of their families do; their sympathies lead them to adopt the opinions of those they love best, and the result of elections would probably be the same if they were voters. But if they are not always represented—if their opinions do sometimes differ from those of their male relatives, it is well that this difference cannot create more trouble. It is well that the bickerings and contentions of the club-room and tavern-house, are not to be brought into the family circle. It is well that the sounds of "home, sweet home," are not to be displaced by bitter words and party disputations. Differences of religious opinion create enough of discord and misery in family circles; but religion, though mingled with superstition, and darkened by bigotry, is religion still. It is the exercise of the heart's best affections, and no persons can embitter the fire-side with religious quarrels, and conceive themselves following in sincerity the example of Him whose mission was peace and love. Political feuds would not have as a counteracting influence this glaring inconsistency of principles and practice; and may we never take a more active part in them.

Let woman keep in her own sphere, and she can do much for herself, and much for society; but her influence is weakened in proportion as she deviates from the true path. Her domestic duties should claim her first thoughts; and then society should receive her unwearied efforts to elevate, to gladden, and to beautify. If social evils are to be remedied by reforming public opinion, woman's influence, when properly excited, may do much; and thus they *will* be remedied, if she is true to the nature God has given her, and the station he has assigned her. She may do this by her influence over the rising generation, especially that portion of it who will one day be voters, and perhaps rulers of their country. Her exertions should be to throw around her the sun-shine of gentleness and affection, and her aim should be

"To solace, to soften, to cheer, and to bless,
With the streams of her gushing tenderness."

But many who think that woman should never interfere in political affairs, assert that in religious and benevolent enterprises she should act publicly and unrestrained. If woman had been intended to grace the pulpit or the lecturer's desk, I think she would have been gifted with a voice more suitable for them, and been endowed with less of that delicacy which she must now struggle to overcome. Women have harangued public audiences, who are to be respected for their faithfulness to the dictates of conscience; but while my ideas of female duty differ so widely from theirs, I cannot admire them, and would not imitate them, if I could.

If a woman is sensible that she has talents which might be of service to her country, let her exercise them; but in a quiet way. Madame Roland[9] says, that in the seclusion of her own chamber were written documents which entered into all the cabinets of Europe; and far more influence had those opinions, while passing under the sanction of her husband's name, and far more noble does Madame Roland appear, than if she had entered the National Assembly, and expressed them vocally.

There are exceptions to all rules, and there may be times when woman will do what man could not perform. She may depart from her appropriate sphere, and the very novelty of her position will create enthusiasm in her behalf; and the fervency of her feelings will excite her on, to deeds requiring the utmost moral energy. Yet happy is she, if the thunderbolts she launches around, return not upon her own head. Witness, for example, Joan of Arc.

Many who think woman inferior in every other mental capacity, maintain that in literary talent she is man's equal. She may be, in some respects, and in others his inferior; but in those departments of literature which have usually been considered highest, she appears to be his inferior. We cannot well judge from what woman has done, what she is capable of doing. Under happier auspices, much might have been performed of which she has been deemed incapable; still I do not think that if the literary arena had been always as open as it now is, that woman would ever have written an Iliad, or a Paradise Lost. When an anonymous work appeared, called "Sartor Resartus," which evinced much originality and talent, there were many conjectures concerning the authorship; but it was never suspected to be the production of a woman; and had the sweet "Songs of the affections" come forth into the world unsanctioned by the name of Hemans, they would never have been attributed to a man.

Women who now write upon subjects which have heretofore been the exclusive subjects of man's talents, do it usually in a more familiar, and sometimes in a more beautiful manner. As, for instance, Miss Martineau upon Political Economy; and Sir Walter Scott declares, that it was Miss Edgeworth who taught him to write novels.

But how great the difference between the sexes, with regard to literary talent, can be better decided at some future time. It cannot at all events, be said of woman, that in this respect "she hath done what she could."

Those females who have been blessed with beauty of form and face, need not fear that their graces will be lessened by mental cultivation. The natural desire in our sex to please the other, has often led them to adorn their persons at the expense of their minds; and if they have succeeded, they must have pleased men who were not worth pleasing.

Much of the prejudice which even now exists against educated females, has probably been caused by the fact, that too many literary women have been pedantic, assuming, and arrogant. They have laid aside the graces of their own sex, without attaining the vigor of the other; but they cannot become men—let them therefore not cease to be women. They should cherish those feelings, and virtues, which alone can render them pleasing, and cultivate those faculties which will command respect.

Yes, woman can climb the Hill of Science, and let her go; let her bind the laurel and the myrtle with the roses which already bloom around her brow, and the wreath will be more beautiful; but she should guard well the flowers, lest the evergreens crush, or overshadow them, and they wither away, and die.

ELLA

Lowell Offering, January, 1841, pp. 129–35

Editorial Remarks

We offer this number of the OPERATIVES' MAGAZINE as a specimen of what our operatives can do upon subjects of utility and importance. We shall wear no disguises, but shall endeavor to encourage the cultivation of the intellectual and moral energies of our operatives, by offering them a medium of communicating their thoughts upon moral, religious and literary subjects, but not for the publication of nonsense.

The Magazine will contain original articles on religious and literary subjects. Those upon literary must be moral in their tendency and manly [sic] in their style. Those upon religious subjects must be written with candor. Articles of a sectarian character entirely, will be excluded.—Those which inculcate the doctrines of the Bible as understood by evangelical christians, without their peculiarities, will be admitted.

Here the muse may sing, provided she does not make discord with truth. Here the poet and wit may bring their "thoughts that breathe and words that burn," provided the breathing be not poison, or the burning "strange fire."

We expect success in this undertaking, because our object is a good one, and our whole motive for action are before the public. Judge ye of the merits of the work and then decide, but never let it be said that our operatives are degraded or incapable of maintaining their proper rank and standing in the moral and intellectual world.

We solicit communications from operatives of both sexes, which may be left with the publishers, requiring only, 1st, that all articles shall be entirely original; 2nd, that, (whatever may be the signature,) the real issue of the writer shall accompany each communication.

We have no apology to make for any lack of variety, and also for the arrangement of the articles in this number, hoping to make up such deficiencies in future. The publication being in a great measure unknown necessarily rendered the communications few. We have however a number of very interesting articles on hand which will appear in our next.

Operatives' Magazine, April, 1841

Lowell and Its Manufactories

So much has already been said under this caption, that it seems hardly possible for a new idea to be broached, or another paragraph cogitated. Enough that the object of the present article is, simply to advert to a few *facts* among the many *probabilities* which have been heretofore recorded. It has been customary with a certain class of *readers,* as well as *hearers,* to set down all the *ill* which can be said of manufacturing villages as true, while its opposite can scarce obtain credence. A few of the many facts, which have been, or may be, gathered from the annals of Lowell morality, are here presented, so that a candid mind will acknowledge at a glance, that *good* may and does exist in an almost chaotic mass of *seeming* evil.

A witness of mechanical operations is not surprised at an occasional friction, as the rough edges of unfinished workmanship come in contact; neither does a resident of a city like our own, suppose there will be no confliction of thought or feeling: on the contrary, we expect in the crooks and turns of *business life,* to meet often with much which we would rather had never been seen.

It has been customary, from the first, to cry down manufacturing communities simply because incorporated bodies exercise the control, as if the fact of capitalists associating for the profitable investment of money tended to deteriorate from the character of persons in their employ.

Premises like these are false, and so, of course, are all such conclusions. In pointing directly to the actual standing of our female population, I would specify one of our large, and one small establishment (that is, comparatively speaking). The Appleton corporation, by an investigation, presents the number of 189 members of different churches. These, it must be recollected, are some of the many "factory girls" of Lowell. Again, the Merrimack company employ 1,098. Of this number, 442 are members in *good* standing of some evangelical church—more than one-third of the whole number employed. Of the remaining two-thirds, a large majority rank high in the scale of nominal christianity. This surely does not look much like what has been sometimes said: "that the population of Lowell is made up of 'scraps' and 'refugees'—the cast off 'non-essentials' of refined society."

Taking these as a true criterion, may we not fairly judge our population to be all that has been claimed in self-defence. Show me a community where one-third are not only nominally, but (so far as man may judge) truly the followers of the Redeemer, and I will allow them to possess an undoubted right to the name of "refinement and respectability." We have, it is true, many among us who are a "shame, a grief, and a vexation," but what is this more than what is common to other places? An agent of one of our establishments related the following incident, in proof of his statement respecting the difficulty with which a person of doubtful reputation obtains employment. Two young females called at his counting room for "regulation papers," as they had engaged a place in one of the rooms. They were given, and the girls went to the overseers for further orders. Before they had taken off their bonnets, they were recognized by those already at work; the overseer was informed, and the ladies had the pleasure of calling somewhere else for employment.—"This," he added, "is only one of the many I could relate; and it shows the impossibility of retaining a situation at the expense of character." And such is the fact. There is not a class of persons more tenacious of reputation, or more discriminating in its code of morality. But it is needless to waste words. If minds are so weak as to decide upon a point where both sides are examined, I can only say, I pity their weakness, and despise their narrowness.

In connection with this subject, I would speak of the literary abilities of operatives generally, It is true, but a small proportion accustom themselves to writing their thoughts, but this does not prove them incapable of the faculty. In illustration, I would point to the articles which appear from time to time, ostensibly from their pens. That they are actually written by them, I *know;* and many more dwell in the midst of us, who, if they do not possess the talents of a "Signorey," may boast an "Adelaide."

In conclusion, I would advise those who know *nothing* of Lowell as it *is,* to defer their decisions till they have given the subject a fair examination.

Ella

Operatives' Magazine, December, 1841

A Word about Us

In presenting the last No. of the present Vol., we appear in the garb we intend to wear for the ensuing year. Our pages will be increased to twenty-four. We shall accompany our work with engravings—and those will be suited to our ability. If our circulation warrants the expense, we shall add music. Our work has been thus far, an experiment. We know of no publication, beside our own, conducted exclusively by females. There may be such, but we do not at this moment remember one. The Magazine from July, '41, has been written, edited, and published by females alone.[10] 'Tis true we don't all work in the mill—for were we confined within the limits of the factory thirteen out of the twenty-four hours, it would be impossible for us to issue our work ourselves. The majority of our correspondents are now employed in the mills. We have others who are not, but have been.

We have heard it said that we were not honest in our pretensions —this we deny. We said in July last, that our pages were free to those who had been, as well as those who are operatives; and this we did, presuming that those who had spent four or five years of life in the mills did not lose their identity by coming out of this employment, and laboring in a sphere more congenial to their tastes. Our pages are still open to such, and we hope to add many more to our list of regular correspondents. Meanwhile we should give the elbows of many of our friends still within the sound of the shuttle, a kindly jog.

Don't you know, friend, that you can write better than any of our present contributors, and won't you exercise a little benevolence in our behalf? We have catered to the taste of our readers to the best of our ability—and we have the vanity to think that the general scope of our work has done credit to the class it is intended to represent. We do not pretend to claim superior talents; we only assert that the fact that we are or have been employed in a manufactory, does not detract aught from our intellectual capacities.

We have foreborne to notice the encomiums the press at large have so liberally heaped upon us. That we have been gratified, we confess with pleasure, and yet our only determination has been to stand or fall by our intrinsic merits. If our work is morally good, then we claim for it the support of a generous public: if not, let it be numbered with things that were. Since we commenced our efforts, we have lost but *"one subscriber."* We hope our present subscribers will continue their patronage. We need a larger list. Our income for the present year, has not defrayed our actual expenses. This we think should not be, for if we are what we profess to be, an enlightened community will not, we think, forget our claim for a liberal support.

To the conductors of the press, at large, we tender our thanks for the kind words they have spoken of, and for us. If the thanks of females are worth anything, we beg you accept them, and with them our kindest recollections. Our work as editors, has been new —entirely so. We have been better accustomed to the dignities of the cotton mill, than those of the chair editorial. We hope, however, to "get accustomed" to the last, and bear them with credit to ourselves, and the class whom we are proud to represent. Will this portion of our friends still cheer us by their kind notice and kinder regards. We will try and deserve all the good which may be said of us.

To our subscribers we would say, we hope you will pardon our deficiencies, and continue your patronage, and not this only, but induce your neighbors and friends to follow your example. We do not beg anybody's good will or support; we ask it on the ground of returning to each of our subscribers their money's worth, and will guaranty to all, a satisfactory return of all obligations they may confer.

Reader, we offer you our hand, and with this, we bid adieu to the present volume, though we hope to give you many a hearty shake for the year to come.

EDS.

Operatives' Magazine, March, 1842

Editorial

Our friends may be somewhat surprised at our announcement of "a change" in the spirit of our dreams, but we fancy they will be pleased withal; for we are confident, changes for the better are always acceptable. We have disposed of the "responsibilities" of editors, while we hold the same interest in its prosperity.

In vacating the chair editorial, we surrender our charge to abler hands—though we doubt whether hearts are more willing. We have felt our incompetency, and this consciousness induces us to make the present transfer.

The Magazine will be united with the "Offering," both having been purchased by William Schouler,[11] Esq., a gentleman well known as the able conductor of a spirited political paper. The new publication will assume the name of "The Offering and Operatives' Magazine,"—and its articles will be so blended that the most fastidious can scarce fail of being satisfied. We are confident the publication will maintain its distinctive character,—its pages ever open to the communications of those who hail under the euphonious name of "Factory Girl." The articles will be written, as heretofore, by an association of females—its only difference, being its outward embellishments, of better paper, and more expensive engravings—its internal improvement will of course depend upon the ability of its writers.

Our present subscribers will be supplied during the year, on the same terms as heretofore. The office of publication will be duly announced. Those who prefer, can have their papers left at Mr. Upton's. Our agents are informed that all business relative to the "Magazine," will be promptly attended to by Mr. Schouler.

In vacating the sanctum, we do not intend to lose our identity. We are happy in the consciousness that we have sought to do right. We have never aimed at parade of learning, for this we have not: we have labored to improve, and this we have accomplished.

Those who have aided us by their counsels and words of encouragement, must take our thanks as their reward, for we have nought else to give. And we further express the hope, that what has been done, is but as the dew, when compared to a refreshing shower. We make our adieu, confident that "no body" will be sorry, while many "bodies" will be gainers in the end.

LYDIA S. HALL
ABBA A. GODDARD, *Editors*
In behalf of the Association.

Operatives' Magazine and Young Ladies' Album, August, 1842

Prospectus

The Olive Leaf is a semi-monthly paper, devoted to the interests of the operatives at Cabotville and Chicopee Falls, and throughout the New England States.

The matter will be chiefly original, containing articles—Religious, Literary, and Historical.

The paper will ever be free from a party spirit, and nothing will be admitted to its columns with a view to establishing any particular opinion.

Virtue and Morality will be its leading characteristics, while the chief aim of the Editor shall be to benefit that class, to whose welfare it is devoted and at the same time endeavor to make it interesting to all.

Olive Leaf, and Factory Girl's Repository, April 25, 1843

To the Ladies of Cabotville

This paper if we understand its object, is to be devoted to the interest, or more especially, the mutual improvement of that class, whose name in part it bears. Now if others are so much interested in our intellectual welfare, ought not we be prompt in showing that we appreciate that interest; not only by giving our subscription for the support of the paper, but by devoting some of our leisure moments in supplying its pages.

The time allowed us for mental improvement, it is true, is extremely limited; but if we are zealous to redeem each moment as it flies, there are but few, we trust, but will have something to offer on the side of virtue and morality.

Here is a field of enterprise open before us; and shall we not improve it? By communicating our ideas to each other through the medium of the Olive Leaf, we may be successful in aiding its Editor, in his noble work of advancing good morals within our village, and scattering precepts that shall fall in healing beams upon the mind. Then let us give him our hearty co-operation.

If acceptable, he shall have the humble efforts of A FACTORY GIRL.

Olive Leaf, and Factory Girl's Repository, April 25, 1843

Communications

The following is from a self educated girl in one of the mills in this village, as will appear. We hope that many will follow her example and endeavor to secure to themselves that which is worth more to them than all the show of fashionable life,—an education. We also hope the writer will remember us often, and induce many of her companions to join her in advancing the good of those with whom they associate. Ed.

For the Olive Leaf.

Mr. Editor:—

It so happened that I was born in New Hampshire, where my mother still resides, with a large family of young children, dependent on her for support, and hard does she have to struggle to gain a living for herself and offspring; and but for the charity of several friends and kind hearted neighbors, she would have to put them out before they knew the first rudiments taught in our common schools. Sensible that she had a weight upon her heavy to be borne, to lighten the load, I left home and came into one of the factories in Cabotville. When I came here I could not read, except by spelling out the words like a child of very few years. I had not commenced learning to write, and all the learning I now have has been gained without instruction, having obtained it alone, and that too, after I had labored in the mill twelve hours a day on the average through the year.

I have often murmured and repined at my lot, thought my case a solitary and hard one, to be thus constantly confined in the factory, and after all could hardly gain a subsistence, while so many were enjoying high life, and "faring sumptuously every day," without labor. But the views I had embraced in this respect, are now entirely changed; and I have begun to think that idleness is the parent of nearly all the sins that have been committed since the morn of creation.

Not long since I visited New York for the first time; and there spent a fortnight with a friend, who is the daughter of a wealthy merchant in that city; and while I was with her, I became like herself, a 'lady at large,' quite above work, and made amusement my occupation. I visited the Park Theatre, Niblo's Garden, Peel's Museum; attended a soiree, went half a day to the Cathedral, a Roman Catholic Church on the corner of Mott and Prince Streets. Spent two evenings down at the Battery viewing the display of fire works; passed up and down half a dozen times a day, the great promenade and thoroughfare, Broadway; called in at the fancy stores to see the new goods, bent down prices, and learn the fashions, &c. &c. Dropped in at most of the ice cream, candy and soda shops; bought liberally, and made an off-hand market for my bright sixpences; went down to Staten Island and over to the Jersey shore; visited Hoboken, Elysian Fields, Weehawken, the Pavilion; took a ride in the grove upon the circular railroad, the cars upon which are propelled by cranks, turned by men. Visited the Navy Yard at Brooklyn; went to Williamsburgh, the Wallaboat and East New York, of recent origin; went up the far famed horse racing ground, &c. &c.

Having spent the time allotted to myself, and visited most of the places of resort in New York and its environs, I left the city with some thing out of pocket, tired of being in the bustle and vain show of the modern Babylon. I came home, worn down with fatigue, and went cheerfully to my accustomed employment in the factory, better contented and more happy than when I left, resolving never again to 'despise the day of small things;' and not again envy those who wear better and finer clothes than I can afford; and live at their ease, and move in the circles of the rich, gay and fashionable. Believe me, I would not exchange situations with my New York friend on any account, and be obliged to keep up the routine of fashionable life. My humble origin and limited means forbid that I should be extravagant in dress, or purchase an article that I do not stand in need of. I seldom make a visit to New Hampshire to see my mother, but I do not forget her, nor the debt of gratitude that I owe her. I often send her two new dresses with other things; also ten dollars in money.

During my residence in this village, the perusal of valuable books, reflection and conversation have been indeed of great benefit to me; and suffer me, my young friends and associates, to recommend this practice to you. Believe me, we shall then be able to furnish matter for the Olive Leaf, without murdering the 'King's English,' and our compositions will be such, that if a Dickens should again visit this country, and go into the New England factories, and we girls should happen to be the focus for his eyes, when he returns to his native land, he can speak of us and the Olive Leaf in high terms of commendation, as the author of 'Notes on America' has done of the Lowell Offering and the operatives there.[12] It may be that some distinguished writer may visit Cabotville; if so, may he not find a single moping, slatternly girl in the mills, wearing 'clogs and pattens,' but see them, one and all, dressed as neat, clean and looking more tidy than Queen Victoria in all her attire of royalty, together with a cluster of fine trinkets, and a thousand dazzling ornaments.

MARY JANE

Olive Leaf, and Factory Girl's Repository, September 16, 1843

NOTES

1. It is interesting to note that Harriet H. Robinson does not mention Whittier's reaction when he arrived in Lowell to edit the *Middlesex Standard*. In his column "The Stranger in Lowell" (August 15, 1844), he wrote: "Not as a matter of taste and self-gratification have many of them [the factory girls] exchanged the free breezes . . . of the country for the close, hot city, and the harshness and whirl of these crowded and noisy mills. Nor am I one of those who count steady, daily toil, consuming the golden hours of the day, and leaving only the night for recreation, study and rest, as in itself a pleasurable matter. There have been a good many foolish essays written upon the beauty and divinity of labor by those who have never known what it really is to earn one's livelihood by the sweat of the brow. . . . Let such be silent."

2. Agent of the Merrimack and Middlesex textile companies in Lowell and one of the leading figures among corporate executives.

3. Orestes A. Brownson (1803–76), clergyman and writer, who worked for a short time with the Workingman's party, became a Universalist and Congregationalist minister and founded a new Church of the Future. His *Boston Quarterly Review* was one of the most influential magazines of the time, and his essays on "The Laboring Classes" in the *Review* of July and October, 1840, in which he discussed the Lowell textile mills and the factory girls, were widely discussed. In 1844 Brownson converted to Roman Catholicism.

4. Miss Farley may have been referring to the series of articles published in the *Lowell Courier*, July 20, 23, 25, 27, 30, 1839, by Dr. Elisha Bartlett, later reprinted as a pamphlet, *A Vindication of the Character and Condition of the Females Employed in the Lowell Mills, Against the Charges Contained in the Boston Times, and the Boston Quarterly Review, by Elisha Bartlett, M.D.* (Lowell, 1841). In the preface to the pamphlet, Dr. Bartlett praised Harriet Farley for her reply to Orestes Brownson.

5. Fanny Elssler (1810–84) was an Austrian dancer, famous for performance of the Spanish Cachucha.

6. Sarah G. Bagley also wrote a similar piece, in the form of a short story ("Tales of Factory Life, No. 1"), published in the *Lowell Offering* of February, 1842 (pp. 65–68), which described the experiences of a penniless farm girl, a runaway, who found work in the Lowell mills. It closed: "Sarah has studied and faithfully learned the lessons of usefulness and practical benevolence. In

my last interview with her, she expressed a sort of pride in saying, that although she had been a runaway beggar, she had been more fortunate than many within the circle of her acquaintance; and though there may be difficulties, yet a little perseverance will overcome them. I went, by her invitation, to the Savings Bank, and learned that she had deposited four hundred dollars, since the commencement of 1838."

7. Lydia Howard Sigourney (1791–1865), American author.

8. Lady Mary Wortley Montagu (1689–1762), famous English writer, acclaimed especially for her letters.

9. Madame Jeanne Phlipon Roland (1754–93), French Republican politician during the Revolution.

10. At first the magazine had been edited by "an association of Gentlemen of Different . . . Denominations," but soon Lydia S. Hall and Abba A. Goodard, who had graduated from mill work to become teachers in the public schools, took over the editorship of the *Operatives' Magazine*.

11. William Schouler (1814–72), owner and editor of the *Lowell Courier*, champion of corporation interests, served those interests not only through his newspaper but also as a representative from Lowell in the Massachusetts legislature. In 1845 Schouler became chairman of the Committee of Manufacturing in charge of investigating working hours in the mills; he wrote the report adverse to any ten-hour legislation. Defeated for re-election, he was returned to the legislature in 1847 and in that year became editor of the influential *Boston Daily Atlas*. He retained that position at the Whig paper until he was forced to resign because he criticized Daniel Webster's March 7 speech, defending the Compromise of 1850.

12. In his *American Notes*, Charles Dickens wrote: "Of the merits of the Lowell Offering as a literary production, I will only observe, putting entirely out of sight the fact of the articles having been written by these girls after the arduous labors of the day, that it will compare advantageously with a great many English Annuals."

Part 2

The Militant Factory Girls

The Debate over the *Lowell Offering:*
Sarah G. Bagley versus Harriet Farley

Writing of Harriet Farley's editorship of the *Lowell Offering,* Norman F. Ware points out in his book, *The Industrial Worker, 1840–1860,* that she "began by defending the operatives against attacks that were levelled at the corporations, and finished by defending the corporations at the expense of the operatives." This was recognized by contemporary labor reformers, who criticized the editor of the *Offering* for being deferential to employers and indifferent to the real needs of the factory operatives. On July 3, 1845, the *Voice of Industry,* a labor paper then published in Fitchburg, Massachusetts, criticized the *Lowell Offering* for helping strengthen the myth surrounding the so-called beauties of factory life. "One would suppose that the Lowell mills were filled with farmers' daughters who could live without labor and who go there merely as a resort for health and recreation, instead of a large portion of poverty's daughters whose fathers do not possess one foot of land, but work day by day for the bread that feeds their families. Indeed, many of the operatives are foreigners free to work there according to the mandates of heartless power, or to go to the poor house, beg or do worse." When, it asked, would the *Offering* reflect the real problems of these workers?

The factory operatives themselves, however, remained silent, influenced no doubt by the prevailing view that it was unfitting for mere female employees to question a magazine supported by the men who owned the mills. It was Sarah G. Bagley who broke this silence. She initiated a public debate which made it widely known that the world-famous magazine did not meet with the approval of the female operatives it was supposed to represent.

Miss Bagley, the first woman labor leader in American history, was apparently born in Meredith, New Hampshire, and received a common school education before moving to Lowell in 1836 to work in the Hamilton Manufacturing Company, where she was employed for six and one-half years, and then at the Middlesex Factory. She joined the Lowell Improvement Circle, became active in temperance work, and contributed articles on the "Pleasures of Factory Life" for the *Lowell Offering*. Becoming increasingly discontented over conditions in the mills as wages declined and working conditions deteriorated, especially with the rapid increase of machine operations, she began to contribute articles to the *Offering* that were critical of the corporations. Denied access to the timid and genteel magazine, Miss Bagley voiced her anger at an Independence Day rally in 1845 attended by 2,000 workingmen at Woburn, Massachusetts. When one of the speakers praised the *Offering*, Miss Bagley took the platform and, according to the reporter for the *Lowell Advertiser*, "made some statements . . . which will do much to correct the impression abroad that it is the organ of the 'Factory Operatives'—stating that she had written articles in relation to the condition of the operatives, and their insertion had been invariably *refused!*"

Miss Bagley's attack on the *Offering* was widely reported and Miss Farley promptly responded through the editor of the *Lowell Courier*, William Schouler, denying that any article by Miss Bagley had ever been rejected by her. If any had been refused, it must have been when Mr. Thomas was in charge of the *Offering*. This started a debate between Miss Bagley and Miss Farley in the columns of the *Lowell Express* in which the mill operative challenged the editor of the *Offering* to cite one article that she had published which was critical of corporation policies and conduct. When Miss Farley refused, Miss Bagley called her a "mouthpiece of the corporations" in the *Express* of August 7, 1845. On this note the debate ended, but undoubtedly Miss Bagley's attacks won support among the factory operatives, for the popularity of the *Offering* declined markedly. Late in 1845, despite assistance from the corporations and their agents, it died for lack of support.

Miss Bagley was not content merely with criticizing the famous magazine and its editor. She insisted that the factory operatives organize and protest to improve their conditions. She helped form and became first president of the Lowell Female Labor Reform Association, and when the *Voice of Industry* moved to Lowell in October, 1845, she served on its publication committee; for a time in 1846, after its purchase by the Lowell Female Labor Reform Association, she was its chief editor. Active in the ten-hour movement, Miss Bagley helped the Association round up over 2,000 signatures to a petition to the Massachusetts legislature calling for a law limiting the length of the working day. When the legislative committee set up to consider the problem of working hours in the mills opened its hearings in February, 1845, Miss Bagley was among those who testified. Shortly afterward she left her position in the mill, perhaps as a result of displeasure caused by her militant activities.

Miss Bagley now plunged into full-time labor activity, helping to build the Lowell Female Labor Reform Association's membership to several hundred, organizing branches in other mill towns, and serving as an organizer and speaker for the New England Workingmen's Association. In Lowell she helped found an Industrial Reform Lyceum to discuss controversial subjects ignored by the regular town lyceum.

On February 13, 1846, the *Voice of Industry* carried the following announcement: "The Magnetic Telegraph is now completed from this city to Boston, and will be in successful operation in a few days. This enterprise has been prosecuted under the direction of Mr. Paul R. George, whose democracy in selecting a superintendent in Lowell is truly commendable; having appointed to that office Miss Sarah G. Bagley, one of our publishing committee. This is what we call '*the people's*' democracy. Miss Bagley having served ten years in the factories, is now entitled to the situation she has received, and for which she is eminently qualified." When Miss Bagley began operating the telegraph machine at the Lowell Telegraph Depot on February 21, 1846, she became the first woman in the United States to do so.

In the summer of 1846 Miss Bagley was elected vice-president of the Lowell Union of Associationists. This organization was part of a reform movement based upon the utopian socialist principles of Charles Fourier, whose ideas were also incorporated in the colonies at Brook Farm and Hopedale in Massachusetts and in Fourierite societies in New York, New Jersey, Pennsylvania, Ohio, Illinois, Indiana, Wisconsin, and Michigan. In 1847 Miss Bagley became the Lowell agent for *The Covenant,* a monthly magazine published in Baltimore by Mrs. Catherine Nielson, devoted to "Odd Fellow-ship and General Literature." Little is known of her life after this.

Miss Bagley was a prolific writer on conditions in the mills and the need for militant struggles to improve them; these writings will be found in several of the sections that follow. In this section are the letters of Miss Bagley and Miss Farley relating to the *Lowell Offering,* as well as an account of the speech by Miss Bagley which started the controversy. Also included is an interesting piece by Amelia Sargent, a mill operative, describing what followed as a result of the controversy in the *Lowell Advertiser.*   □

Report of Speech by Sarah G. Bagley

A convention of the workingmen and women of New England was holden on the 4th inst at Woburn in a beautiful grove. Dele-gates from the vicinity continued to arrive until about 11 o'clock, principally from Lowell, Boston, and Lynn, numbering in the ag-gregate about 2,000. The delegates from Boston and Lowell were escorted by a band of music from the cars to the grove, which was tastefully arranged for the occasion. . . . Miss S. G. Bagley, of Lowell, a lady of superior talents and accomplishments, whose re-fined and delicate feelings, gave a thrilling power to her language and spell-bound this large auditory, so that the rustling of the leaves might be heard softly playing with the wind between the intervals of speech; she spoke of the Lowell Offering,—that it was not the voice of the operatives—it gave a false representation to the truth—it was controlled by the manufacturing interest to give a gloss to their inhumanity, and anything calling in question the factory sys-tem, or a vindication of operative's rights, was neglected—she had written several pieces of this character, which were rejected,—she said she had served an apprenticeship of 10 years in the mills, and by her experience claimed to know something about it,—and that many of the operatives were doomed to eternal slavery in conse-quence of their ignorance—not knowing how to do the most com-mon domestic work, many could not do the most common sewing, and notwithstanding the present lengthened time of labor, which deprived them of the most human comfort, the proprietors or agents of these mills were striving to add 2 hours more to their time of labor, thus cutting off all hope of bettering their condition; but said she, the girls have united against this measure, and formed a society to repel this movement, she took her seat amidst the loud and unanimous huzzas of the deep moved throng, and was followed by some closing remarks from Mr. Albert Brisbane[1] of New York, after which adjournment was called for and adopted.

Voice of Industry, July 10, 1845

Sarah G. Bagley Defends Her Speech

The following from the pen of Miss S. G. Bagley, and published in the Lowell Advertiser,[2] was called forth in reply to a statement of Miss Farleys,' editress of the Lowell Offering, which appeared in the Courier, reflecting somewhat upon Miss Bagley's remarks at Woburn on the fourth. We had the pleasure of listening to Miss Bagley's remarks at Woburn, and can testify that she spoke in kind and courteous terms of the present editress—brought no charge whatever against the Offering, farther than it was controlled by corporation influences—stated that she had written articles for the Offering, which were rejected because they spoke of *Factory girls wrongs*—but by whom rejected she did not inform us—nor was it the least consequence whether by Miss Farley or some of her predecessors, as it was the general character of the Offering that she wished to illustrate.

We hold the literary merits of the Offering in high esteem—it reflects much honor upon its talented conductors—but still we were pleased to hear this exposition in relation to its true character and standing. It is, and always has been under the fostering care of the Lowell Corporations, as a literary repository for the mental gems of those operatives who have ability, time and inclination to write— and the tendency of it ever has been to varnish over the evils, wrongs, and privations of a factory life. This is *undeniable,* and we wish to have the Offering stand upon its own bottom, instead of going out as the united voice of the Lowell Operatives, while it wears the Corporation lock and their apologizers hold the keys.

In looking over the Courier of Wednesday last, we found our name in connection with the Lowell Offering saying that we had never presented an article that had been refused since Miss Farley had been its Editress. Well, as we did not say that we had we do not see any chance for controversy. But we did say (and we hold ourself responsible) that we have written articles for the Offering that have been rejected because they would make the Offering "controversial" and would change its "original design," which was that there is "mind among the spindles."

If any one will take the trouble to look at No. 2, specimen copy, that was published previous to the commencement of Vol. 1, they will find that controversy has not always been studiously avoided, and that the defence made was against O. A. Brownson and not corporation rules, which would change the *propriety* of "controversy" very materially. We preferred no charge against Miss Farley, but spoke respectfully of her, and should not have spoken of her or the Offering, had not Mr. Mellen, of Boston, made an attack upon the operatives of our city, and as an argument in favor of our *excellent* rules, stated that we had the Offering under our control, and had never made one word of complaint through its columns.

We were called upon to state the *original* design of the Offering; and gave it in nearly the same language in which it was expressed in a note by the editor in the No. referred to.

We stated that it had never been an organ through which the abuses of oppressive rules or unreasonable hours might be complained of; but that both exist cannot be denied by the editress— and stranger still it has been admitted by the editor of the Courier. We stated that the number of subscribers to the Offering among the operatives, was very limited; we were authorized to make such an assertion in conversation with Miss Farley a few months ago; and we would not charge her with telling an untruth either directly or *indirectly,* lest we should be deemed *unlady-like.*

We asked the question what kind of an organ of defence would the operatives find with Mr. Schouler for a proprietor and publisher?[3] We repeat that question, and if any one should look for an article in the publisher's columns, they would find something like the following:

"Lowell is the Garden of Eden (except the serpent) the gates thereof are fine gold. The tree of knowledge of *good* is there, but the evil is avoided through the *judicious* management of the superintendents. Females may work nineteen years without fear of injuring their health, or impairing their intellectual and moral powers. They may accumulate large fortunes, marry and educate children, build houses, and buy farms, and all the while be operatives." Thus would the Offering under such a control, and those who are as stupid as Mr. Mellen made himself, *would believe it.*— We have not written this article to evince that there is "mind among the spindles," but to show that the minds here are not *all spindles.*

SARAH G. BAGLEY

Voice of Industry, July 17, 1845

Harriet Farley Responds to Sarah G. Bagley

Friday Eve.

MR. EDITOR:—I see by the Patriot[4] of to-day that you have again devoted quite a generous portion of your columns to the LOWELL OFFERING. A short time since, I stated to you my disapprobation of any thing tending to bring the Offering into a political controversy. And this I dislike because I know, and can know but very little about party politics, and could not do myself or my cause justice in a discussion of this kind. Party politics and party politicians, as such, have ever been my aversion—but I see not now how I can well avoid coming forward, unless I would be recreant to my cause, and a deserter of my poor Offering in its last days. You and I have, I think, conversed upon this subject so sufficiently as to understand each other. We do not agree in all things; but I thank you for your assertion that you believe me unwilling to become the medium and producer of false impressions—you do me no more than justice.

You say though, that you do not suppose I am conscious that the Offering is used by the corporations to produce erroneous impressions;[5] I do not think I am so unconscious of the impression it produces as you suppose me. The corporations do not take that lively interest in it that they have been represented to do; any thing like an effort to foist it upon the community, cannot be attributed to them, and I do not believe they wish it to be looked upon as aught but what it simply professes to be—a collection of articles written by *Factory Girls*—creditable to the writers, so far as they indicate talent and education, as well as kind feelings and discriminating judgment; and creditable to the corporations so far as they represent them as the home of New England females, who, in spite of weariness, toil, and long confinement, retain or improve the characters which they brought from their country homes.

You may possibly know of some who would wish it to be taken as a proof of more than this, but it is not the general feeling. There is not a livelier interest taken in the Offering any where than is evinced in our southern and south-western States. Indeed Boston and Lowell do very little for the Offering in comparison with New York and Baltimore, Augusta and Savannah; though these latter can only be considered as doing more in proportion to the efforts made in them; and everywhere *out of New England,* the interest manifested in our magazine is entirely irrespective of political feelings. They profess to look upon it as a national affair, (don't laugh!) and are proud of their toiling countrywomen. A gentleman to whom it was sent while in France, and that when he had convinced a member of the Chamber of Deputies that it was indeed written by Lowell female operatives, his ejaculation was—"Sirs, yours will be the greatest country in the world."

It is impossible for the Offering to benefit the corporations only as it elevates the character of the operatives, and removes the unjust prejudice against them. If the Offering has produced erroneous impressions, and of late I have feared this might be the case, it has been by representing the mass of operatives in too favorable a light—that is, the light emanating from some, seemed, to distant observers, as reflected from all.—As there are yet four numbers to be issued we shall have an opportunity to retrieve this wrong.

But we challenge any one to find a misrepresentation or false assertion in the pages of the Offering, or articles written by others than those with whom they profess to originate.

As I have alluded here and elsewhere to the proposed discontinuance of the Offering, you can inform those who are rejoicing over the fact—and inform them upon the authority of your friend Os-GOOD, who mails them for us—that it is not on account of a meagre or decreasing subscription list.

That the Lowell girls do not support it we have ever thought more a discredit to themselves than to us. Once for all, I repeat that from the bottom of my heart, I believe the wrong impressions that *may* in some minds be created by the Offering, are but a tittle in comparison with those which it removes.

But I have almost filled my sheet and not alluded to Miss Bagley; I beg her pardon, but will write now as much as I dare hope you will publish.

She has cleared herself, at one bound, from all difficulty, by asserting that she did not say I had refused her articles an insertion; but she intimates that some one has, and you know *I* should be the sufferer from such an intimation. She was understood as speaking of the Offering as it exists now, and she must have been aware of it. Indeed the paragraph has commenced the rounds of the papers, as we can both see, as something of recent or constant occurrence, and many will read that item who will never be informed of this refutation. The world INVARIABLY, so emphatically printed, would necessarily convey the "erroneous impression," that at least, each of the only two editors had refused these long suffering essays.

Miss B. says "there is no chance for controversy," as though I had thrown down the gauntlet to her.—There was a brief and positive denial of a brief and positive assertion: And I am ready for aught of controversy which is necessary to maintain it, though I had ever before considered Miss B. and myself upon one side of that great question—what are the rights and capacities of the laborer?

Not that I can do all the things that she can, for I cannot make a speech or talk politics, or speak of the factory system as she represents it, for it never seemed to me a "durance vile," or Inquisition torture, or slave driven task work. I never felt disposed to croak or whine about my factory life, and have endeavored to impose a cheerful spirit into the little magazine I edit; yet I suppose all my efforts to be upon the same side of the great question as Miss Bagley's. I know that my aim was like hers, to raise the operative. Vapid and inane might my exertions appear, compared to theirs, but they were on the same side. The Labor Question is the great Reform taper of the day. William Ellery Channing, Lydia Maria Child,[6] and many others, work upon the same side with Geo. Ripley,[7] Michael Walsh,[8] and Sarah Bagley. In each of these I find something in which I can and must sympathize, though they are widely different.

I honor the laborer in this capacity, though as a man I may love, fear, or despise him. By my time, my strength, and whatever I may possess of ability, is enlisted in *his* or *her* cause.

Miss B. speaks of things which *cannot* be denied by me. The hours of labor have been explicitly stated in the Offering, and frequent allusions to them may be found, and to all the abuses *I have known*.

Miss Bagley speaks of the limited circulation of the Offering among the operatives as something ascertained from me, though not generally known, of course; apparently placing herself in the unenviable position of a reporter of a confidential conversation.

Yet I can bear very well to be misunderstood and misrepresented by the operatives, when I think they are, those, whose manner of advocating their cause must be more congenial to the promiscuous mass, who are treated little better, indeed whose veracity is impeached, whose kind sympathy is doubted, and whose most earnest endeavors in their behalf are attributed to an unwomanly love of notoriety. But we must all keep silence if we cannot run the risk of being misrepresented.

Miss B. it appears, spoke respectfully of me while endeavoring to undo the wrong which the Offering has so innocently done. It seems to me that I must have been represented as a very respectable dunce, and herself as a lady of endowments far superior to those of the person of ordinary abilities, whose wise steps she was excusing and rectifying.

There are more allusions in Miss B.'s article entirely beyond my comprehension. But one is to an article reprobating the assertion that *"To work in the factory is sufficient to damn to infamy the most worthy and virtuous girl."* As though the Offering was not now open to any refutation of such assertions—indeed it is of itself a refutation, and Miss Bagley, and myself, with every other factory girl in Lowell, have cause to bless the originator of The Lowell Offering.

Excuse this long trespass upon your patience and columns.

Yours respectfully,
HARRIET FARLEY

Lowell Advertiser, July 15, 1845

Sarah G. Bagley Answers Harriet Farley

MR. EDITOR; I notice by the Advertiser of last week that I have been *favored* with a specimen of *refined* literature, from the pen of one of the *geniuses* of the age, and feel myself highly honored with a passing notice from such a *high* source, although it comes in the form of personal abuse. Miss Farley, in her comments on her "poor Offering," says that you do her no more than justice when you say that she would be "unwilling to become a medium or producer of false impressions,"—a *justice* she could not accept at *her own hands;* for in another paragraph she says "she is not so *unconscious* as you suppose her to be of the *erroneous impressions* made by the Offering; and of *late* that it might be the case that at a distance the light emanating from some, might seem to be reflected from *all.*"

Now, to my *weak* judgment such a conclusion is very extravagant; for if such a glorious illumination as the Lowell Offering could emanate from fifty or an hundred female operatives, if seven thousand should lend their radiant beams the brightness would not only illuminate our own planet, but would be viewed by those surrounding ours, with wonder and admiration.

Miss Farley says that she "has ever thought it more discredit to the girls that they do not support the Offering than to the publishers." Now, in my judgment the Offering has no more claim upon the operatives of this city than any other paper, nor so much as some; for there have been some papers, (one in particular,[9]) that have always called for reform in factory labor and rules.

In commencing her comments upon me she begs pardon for neglecting *me* so long. Now, I always feel *obliged* to pardon one where there is *such strong manifestations* of penitence as are evinced in the remainder of her communication. She prefers a very serious charge against me for the typographical arrangement of a word that was written by a special reporter for the Advertiser, an article I never read *before* nor *since* it was published, with the exception of an extract in another paper. If Miss Farley expects by the *generous* course she has pursued to drive me to an acknowledgement of making a misstatement, she mistakes me altogether; for I have not made *one* statement that I cannot abundantly *prove,* to the satisfaction of my candid mind. I have not the least objection to a controversy with Miss Farley on the Offering, although *she* has literary talents to which *I* lay no claim; but I have *facts,* and that is better.

She speaks of the labor question as the "reform topic of the day," and in her classification assigns me a place I could not hope to have attained, with all my "unwomanly love of notoriety."

Miss Farley has been a defender of the rights of operatives, it would seem, for she has not only defended them, but exposed *"all the abuses she has known"* to exist. It is somewhat strange that the operatives have not better appreciated her labors in that department.

She has complained of "all the abuses she has known."—Three sisters came from New Hampshire to work in the mill. They were placed by the mother in the care of her sister, who, by the way, lives across the street from the Corporation. A short time after an investigation was made by the agent, to find those who did not board in the Company's buildings. The sisters' boarding place was discovered to be off the Corporation, and they were notified to go to one of the Corporation boarding-houses or leave their employ forthwith. The eldest sister went to the agent—told him the circumstance—and was told that it was a *universal* rule from which he *would not depart.* She told him she would like to leave his employ, for which she received the *consolatory* assurance that he would report her at every Corporation in the city, and prevent her from getting work if she left his employ!

Has the Offering ever rebuked such exercise of power? Has its columns ever contended against oppression or abuse in any form? If so, I would like to read the number containing such an article; not because I *want* such facts to exist, but because they *do* exist and should not go unrebuked. The Offering, edited by an operative, (or, one that *has* been, and still retains the name,) should be the appropriate communication to the community of any abuses that exist.

Miss Farley says those that she knows are exposed. What says the pages of the Offering? Those that read can understand.

So far as she has made herself *agreeable* by personalities, I have nothing to say, only that I am accountable to public opinion for my saying and doings, and in that case Miss Farley can only be an *offended* witness.

In conclusion Miss Farley calls on me, with every other sister operative, "to bless the originator of the Offering." Now, as Miss Farley says of me, so I say of her, I cannot do all that she can. She can be thankful for "erroneous impressions" and their circulation; but owing to some constitutional *inability* I never could thank God nor Miss Farley for falsehood, nor "erroneous impressions," in any form whatever.

I am, yours, in behalf of justice.

SARAH G. BAGLEY

Lowell, July 23, 1845

Lowell Advertiser, July 26, 1845

Report of an Adjourned Meeting of the Improvement Circle Held in Lowell, Mass., Sept. 16th, 1845

MR. EDITOR:—Having received from Miss Farley, editress of the Lowell Offering, and mistress of ceremonies at the above named, and in our humble estimation, misnamed Improvement Circle, an invitation to be present on this important occasion, and understanding also, that the discussion recently laid before the public, relative to the Offering; its origin, commencement past and present character, was to form part of the evening's entertainment; and that Miss Bagley her opponent therein, was to be present with such of her friends as she chose to accompany her, we felt no small curiosity to know "what manner of things these were," or in other words, what would be the result of a private comparison of these principles which had been so thoroughly proved in public, viz: Truth and Falsehood, and accordingly, an early hour found us at the appointed place, prepared to become an attentive listener to the exercises of the evening. The first in order, was an article from Col. Schouler, editor of the Courier, showing the manner in which the Offering passed from his hands to those of Miss F., which for low scurrilous abuse and party prejudices we have seldom seen equalled.—This Miss F. requested a gentleman present to read, which he did, stating however, at the close, that he did not wish to be considered as endorsing all the sentiments therein contained, far from it, on the contrary, he deemed many of them unjust and reprehensible in the extreme. Then followed the remarks of the same editor (on an extract from the Advertiser, concerning Miss B.'s statement at Woburn, respecting the Offering, viz: "that it was not, and never had been a medium, through which the Operatives could complain of unreasonable hours, or abusive treatment from the Corporation's, that she herself had written articles of this kind, and that they had been invariably rejected,") out of which the discussion grew, stating that Miss F. requested a contradiction of the above statement, which she positively denied stating to the meeting, that she did not request such contradiction, but merely authorized him to make such if he pleased. Here then is falsehood somewhere, where shall it rest? with Miss F., or Col. Schouler; they must settle this matter to their own satisfaction, it is immaterial to us, but one query we should really like to have answered, which is; if Miss F. had never received any such articles, why did she apply to J. G. Whittier, Esq., for advice respecting them, for that she most certainly did, as we have it on the authority of one of her most intimate friends, who moreover told us that he advised her to refuse all such, and on no account whatever, to meddle with such matters at all, but keep her publication, what it always had been, purely literary and I also, added the friend in question, gave my advice to the same amount, and Miss F. resolved to act in unison with the same, yet after all this, Miss. F. has the effrontery to come before the public, and makes it appear, that she never received any such articles; but to return to our subject. Miss F. also stated, that no article of Miss B.'s had been rejected since she published the work in question, and moreover, that she had received information from very respectable sources, that Mr. Thomas, while editor of that work, had never rejected one single article of hers on such grounds, but on the contrary, quite a number, because very badly written, &c. Now had not the gag law been so ridgedly enforced, Miss B. might have presented to the meeting at least one article rejected by Mr. Thomas on the ground, that it would render the Offering controversial, and change its original design, which was to show that there is mind among the spindles, and also a note written about the same time (which by the way, we have at this moment before us) requesting a continuance of her other articles for the Offering. But no, that would never do, they would have seen why one article was rejected and the other accepted, accordingly when at the close of the article, Miss B. would have offered some explanation of the matter, and defended herself against the charge of falsehood so pitifully made, but the *honorable, refined, lady-like* Miss F. turning toward her peremptorily commanded her to be silent, and speak not one word in her defence. Was not this the very quintessence of justice, and generosity, if it was not, we know not what is. But jesting aside, was not this mean, contemptible course, all sufficient proof of the falsehood of her assertion, did it not savor strongly of the declaration, "We love darkness rather than light, because our deeds are evil." Next followed the principal article of the discussion in regular succession, commencing with one from Miss Bagley, proving the statements made at Woburn, to be true, with the various comments on the original character and design of the Offering, and finally asking the question: "What kind of an organ of defence would the operative find, with Mr. Schouler for proprietor and publisher, saying that were any one to look for an article in the publisher's columns," they would find something like the following. "Lowell is the garden of Eden, (except the serpent,) the gates thereof may be of fine gold, the tree of knowledge of good is there, but the evil is avoided through the judicious management of the superintendents. Females may work nineteen years without fear of injuring their health or impairing their intellects or moral powers. They may accumulate large fortunes, marry and educate children, build houses and buy farms, and all the while be operatives." This, Miss F. stated she had used her best endeavors to discover the meaning of, but as yet, had been unable to do so. Now taking into consideration the fact that it is almost an extract verbatim from an editorial which appeared in the gentleman's columns not many months ago, and has since been the rounds of nearly every paper in the union; we can only account for the lady's ignorance of its meaning, by allowing her an unusual share of stupidity in such matters. Much more might be said on this article, but we pass to Miss F.'s rejoinder, if such it may be called, as more than half of the same is addressed to the editor of the Advertiser, instead of her opponent. She commenced by stating her "disapprobation of any thing tending to bring the Offering into a political discussion," for which she has, doubtless abundant reason, knowing as she does, that its political character is such, as utterly to sink it in the estimation of every honorable mind, if once fairly displayed before them; she then goes on to thank him for his assertion, that he believed her unwilling to become the medium, and producer of false impressions stating that he did her no more than justice, and quoting his remarks, that he believed her unconscious, that it was used by the Corporations to produce those impressions. She declares herself not so unconscious of the impressions it produces, as he supposed her to be; thereby verbally admitting that she does know it is used by the Corporations for that purpose, and is willing to become their agent in the matter. She then goes on to state that the Corporations have not that lively interest in it, which they have been represented to do, as proof of the falsity of this assertion, we need only give her own evidence, which she presented to the meeting as follows: "Many of the agents subscribe for two, five and even ten copies, and did all they could for it," liberal efforts truly for those altogether uninterested. The next thing worthy of notice, is the declaration "that the Lowell girls do not support it, we have ever thought more discredit to them than to us." Here she added by way of comment for the especial edification of the company present, that had she lowered or degraded the character of the Offering so as to have made it the medium of low scurrilous abuse, and complaint against the corporations, she would undoubtedly have received as much greater support from the operatives, than she had done, though not so much from the class to which it now owed its existence, and we ask, are the class which it is principally indebted for support; who but the wealthy aristocratic slaveholder of the South, the no less guilty capitalists of New York and Boston, and the miserable drivelling agents of fraud and oppression in Lowell. It is from these and such as these it has ever found a welcome, and not from those who know full well, that it is but a specious link in the chain of oppression weaving around them. After putting a few worthless remarks, she continues "I never felt disposed to croak or whine about my factory life," in connection with this, she read to the meeting a short extract from some paper, which gave so good an idea of her position, that we insert it, here it is as follows:

"Miss Farley's remarks that she never felt disposed to croak or whine about her factory life, reminds us of the answer of a petted and pampered negro slave, who perchance had lived in luxury and ease, being his master's favorite, when interrogated about becoming free, 'they say slavery is an evil, but me no feel it.'" She remarked that she had never been a pet or a favorite in any sense of the term —had never asked or received any favors whatever; she was capable of doing without them. How happens it then, that the Company employed another person to take charge of her looms one half of the time, while she remained absent arranging matter for the same

Offering; was it as a favor to her, if not, then it must have been, as many already said, because they saw in that work a medium, through which to defend and strengthen their darling system of slavery and oppression.—Miss F. next goes on to state, that she "has exposed all the abuses she has known," which according to her own admission, are just none at all, for she says (perchance by way of explanation,) that she wished to be distinctly understood, that in her estimation, there were no abuses connected with the factory system, that there might be evils, she would not deny, but none that could be avoided. She quotes Miss B.'s remark, that she spoke respectfully of her, remarking that she ought not to have done so, (and we are of her opinion) but the last paragraph in this precious article is something of a curiosity, it reads thus: "There are more allusions in Miss B.'s article, entirely beyond my comprehension. But one is an article respecting the assertion, that 'to work in a factory is sufficient to doom to infamy the most worthy and virtuous girl.' As though the Offering was not now open to any refutation of such assertions—indeed, it is of itself a refutation, and Miss Bagley and myself with every other factory girl in Lowell, have cause to bless the originator of the Lowell Offering." So Miss B.'s allusion to said article, is entirely beyond her comprehension is it; well, we sincerely pity the poor soul's want of understanding, and will endeavor to enlighten her concerning it; and first, let us prove the allusion itself. "If any one will take the trouble to look at No. 2, specimen copy that was published previous to the commencement of Vol. 1, they will find that controversy has not always been studiously avoided, and that the defence made against O. A. Bronson [*sic*], and not Corporation rules which would change the *propriety* of controversy very materially." Now does not every one comprehend at a glance, that this allusion was made, to show that when the character of the operative was attacked from abroad, it might be defended through the Offering, it was considered a fit subject for its columns, controversial though it might be; but when their rights were trampled upon, themselves insulted and abused by their employers, then it was a different affair altogether, then the Offering was no longer controversial; and as to our blessing the originator of the Offering, it is the opinion of a majority of the operatives, that we have much more reason to bless the day of its death, which is now close at hand. We would gladly comment upon the remaining articles, but must pass them by, lest we transcend the limits of this communication, but one circumstance we cannot forbear mentioning. Miss Farley stated at the close of the meeting, that the editor of the Advertiser, utterly refused to publish a reply to Miss B.'s last article, whereas we have it on good authority, that by the advice of her friends, Miss Farley herself requested said editor to stop the discussion. Now to quote the words of another, we will not say that she has told a lie, but this much, we will say, she has "walked all round the truth, and that at a very respectful distance too;" but the length of this article admonishes us that it is high time we draw to a close, and asking your pardon for this long trespass on your columns, we are,

Yours Respectfully,
AMELIA SARGENT

—Since writing the above, we have received positive information, that one agent in this city, is at this very moment a subscriber for 25 copies of the Offering, another for 20, some for 10, 12 &c., while the whole number of female operatives, who support it, are but 52, 12 of whom only reside in the city.

Voice of Industry, September 25, 1845

The Factory Girls Expose the "Beauty of Factory Life"

Even before the *Lowell Offering* surrendered in December, 1845, to the attacks made upon it by the factory operatives, the women had acted to set up their own magazines and periodicals, and these grew when the *Offering* expired. In 1842 a fortnightly periodical, *The Factory Girl,* saw the light of day in New Market, New Hampshire. It was edited by men, but they were assisted "by several operatives of undoubted ability," and the bulk of the material published was by the young factory women. In 1842 the *Wampanoag, and Operatives' Journal* came into existence in Fall River, Massachusetts. It was edited by Frances Harriet Whipple (1805–78), a native of Rhode Island who became active in the movement led by Thomas Dorr for a more democratic suffrage in that state, and who was also a leading figure in the Rhode Island antislavery movement, writing poetry for the cause. Miss Whipple's interest in labor is indicated by the fact that in addition to editing the *Wampanoag, and Operatives' Journal* during its year of existence (1842–43), she also was the author of a pro-labor novel, *The Mechanic* (1841).

In 1844 the *Factory Girl's Garland,* published by a man but edited by female factory operatives, appeared in Exeter, New Hampshire. Exeter was also the site for the publication of the *Factory Girl's Album and Operatives' Advocate,* which began its career in 1846. Although published by a man, it was edited entirely by "an association of females who are operatives in the factories, and consequently well qualified to judge the wants of those whose cause they will advocate."

On November 7, 1845, the *Voice of Industry,* originally published by William F. Young in Fitchburg, but now issued in Lowell, carried the notice: "We cordially invite the Factory Girls of Lowell, and the operatives and working people generally, whether they agree with us or not, to make the *Voice* a medium of communication; for it is your paper, through which you should be heard and command attention. The Press has been too long monopolized by the capitalist non-producers, party demagogues and speculators, to the exclusion of the people, whose rights are as dear and valid." So many factory operatives made the *Voice* "a medium of communication" that it soon came to be known as "the factory girl's *Voice.*" In May, 1846, the paper was taken over entirely by the young women in the factories.

These new periodicals carried their share of genteel poetry, stories, and advice on general conduct. But they also spoke out vigorously in defense of the factory operatives and supported all of their efforts to organize to improve their conditions. Moreover, through their columns the young women began at once to demolish the myth concerning the so-called Beauty of Factory Life. They did this in letters, articles, and even poetry describing the actual conditions in the mills. Liberal papers like the *Manchester Democrat* also opened their columns to letters and articles from factory operatives that described the real conditions they faced in the mills.

In addition to demolishing the myths surrounding factory life, the factory operatives used these publications to point out that it was impossible to take a neutral position "while manufacturers and operatives were diametrically opposed in their pecuniary interests." This note of class consciousness was sounded in many forms, including poetry and definitions. ☐

An Appeal to Consistency

The pay of the operatives in the Lowell factories has been considerably reduced, for the reason, as declared, that the depression of trade is so great and the sale of goods consequently so limited, *they are running them at a loss!* If this be a fact, (though nobody believes it,) why do they not cut down the fat salaries of their Agents, who roll about this city in their carriages, living at ease in fine houses, with servants of both sexes to do their bidding? But this is never done. The poor *laborers* must bear all the *burthens.* If there are any losses to be sustained, or any diminution of profits likely to affect the *dividends,* the difference must always be made up by the hard working female operatives, who are occasionally very *pathetically* told that the factories are only kept running at all from motives of *pure charity towards them.* Let us see a little more equality—a little more sincerity in this matter, and then perhaps we may have a little more charity.

A Lowell Factory Girl

*Wampanoag, and Operatives' Journal,*10 Fall River, July 9, 1842

What Are We Coming To?

MR. EDITOR:—The bustle and heartburning created by my former correspondence having nearly subsided in New Market, I shall venture to address you a short note respecting our condition in the mill.—What are we coming to? I can hardly clear my way, having saved from four weeks steady work, but three hundred and ninety-one cents! And yet the time I give to the corporation, amounts to about fourteen or fifteen hours. We are obliged to rise at six, and it is about eight before we get our tea, making fourteen hours. What a glorious privilege we enjoy in this boasted republican land, don't we? Here am I, a healthy New England Girl, quite well-behaved bestowing just half of all my hours including Sundays, upon a company, for less than two cents an hour, and out of the other half of my time, I am obliged to wash, mend, read, reflect, go to church!!! &c. I repeat it, what are we coming to? What is to make the manufacturing interest any better? Our overseer says America will never be able to sell any more cottons than she does now; then how are we to have any better times? I have been studying some new writers on Manufacturers, and shall ask this question often.

OCTAVIA

The Factory Girl, New Market, N.H., March 1, 1843

New Definitions

Overseer.—A servile tool in the hands of an Agent; who will resort to the lowest, meanest and most grovelling measures, to please his Master, and to fill the coffers of a soulless Corporation.

Operative.—A person who is employed in a Factory, and who generally earns three times as much as he or she receives.

Contemptible.—For an overseer to ask a girl what her religious sentiments are, when she applies to him for employment.

Dastardly—The conduct of an Agent when he (instead of going himself) sends one of his minions to notify a watchman, that he is to be turned out of employ.

Oppressive.—To make two men do the work of three, without making any addition to their wages.

The Factory Girl, New Market, N.H., January 15, 1845

The Factory Bell

Loud the morning bell is ringing,
　Up, up sleepers, haste away;
Yonder sits the redbreast singing,
　But to list we must not stay.

Not for us is morning breaking,
　Though we with Aurora rise;
Nor for us is Nature waking,
　All her smiles through earth and skies.

Sisters, haste, the bell is tolling,
　Soon will close the dreadful gate;
Then, alas! we must go strolling,
　Through the counting-room, too late.

Now the sun is upward climbing,
　And the breakfast hour has come;
Ding, dong, ding, the bell is chiming,
　Hasten, sisters, hasten home.

Quickly now we take our ration,
　For the bell will babble soon;
Each must hurry to her station,
　There to toil till weary noon.

Mid-day sun in heaven is shining,
　Merrily now the clear bell rings,
And the grateful hour of dining,
　To us weary sisters brings.

Now we give a welcome greeting,
　To these viands cooked so well;
Horrors! oh! not half done eating—
　Rattle, rattle goes the bell!

Sol behind the hills descended,
　Upward throws his ruby light;
Ding dong ding,—our toil is ended,
　Joyous bell, good night, good night.

Factory Girl's Garland, Exeter, N.H., May 25, 1844

A Beautiful System

We are informed by a gentleman that at a small manufacturing village in Massachusetts, the manner of employing hands is as follows:—The owner induces poor people who have large families to move there—they live in his houses, and their children are taken into the mills at 12 or 13 years of age—they are generally paid in goods from the store of the employer, and settle at the end of every year; and if, as it sometimes happens, they cannot get along without a dollar or two in money, they are charged interest until the end of the year. A beautiful system, truly.

Factory Girl's Garland, Exeter, N.H., May 25, 1844

Aristocracy

There is far too much of an aristocratic feeling existing among our people. Many causes have contributed to produce this state of things. To inquire into them at this time would be unnecessary. We will therefore only allude to the aristocracy which is so prevalent in manufactoring villages, and the groundless prejudice existing against the factory girl. Her industry is to be commended—she toils from morning until night at the loom, or on some portion of the work which goes to make up the Whole. But does she receive an adequate reward for her services? Not so. Her pay is too little in comparison to the profits derived from the work, it must be acknowledged that the employer receives too much, the operative too little.

But aside from this, there is another feature abounding in grievous wrong, that is the difference in caste which the employers create between their sons and daughters and the sons and daughters whom they employ to increase their wealth. We are opposed, to this distinction. It is wrong; it is unjust to give the latter a supremacy in society over the former. We have something more to say on this subject in a future number.

Sarah

Factory Girls' Album, Exeter, N.H., February 14, 1846

Advice to Mill Owners

Don't be so hard with your girls. If they wish to go away an hour or two, or a day even, let them go and be happy. They will work all the better for you. You don't realize how unpleasant it is for females to be confined in a factory month after month, with no time to enjoy the sunshine and flowers—the blue sky and the green grass. And when a sweetheart invites them on a little excursion, you must know it would be a great disappointment for them to be denied the gratification. Remember you were once young, and once gallanted the young women about. Can't you enter into their feelings and be kind and pleasant? The man who is unkind to his female help, cannot be a christian, if he is a church member, a deacon, or even the carrier round of the contribution box.

A Factory Girl

Factory Girls' Album, Exeter, N.H., February 14, 1846

The Operatives' Life[11]

The numerous class of females who are operatives in mills, are required to devote *fifteen twenty-fourths* of every working day to the laborious task incumbent upon them, being thirteen hours of incessant toil, and two hours devoted to meals &c. Is not this fact a painful one? Is it not degrading to the age in which we live? It indicates that barbarism still exists among us, and it would be well for some people to take moral and humane lessons from savage life even. It is not a matter of marvel, that the Lowell girls should rebel against such treatment and petition the legislature of Massachusetts to establish a ten hour system; neither is it surprising that the federal *wise-acres,* who constituted that body, considered it inexpedient to legislate upon the subject—*they* do not legislate for the protection of the *poor,* but for the protection of the *rich;* the *gold* that lies within their grasp benumbs their sensibilities; and prevents the administration of that *justice* which humanity demands. We begin to doubt the utility or justice of any legislation for the protection of capital; indeed, if *barbarism* is to be the result of *protection,* we trust that the enlightened and philanthropic inhabitants of this country will cheerfully dispense with such *aid,* and, (as experience teaches it,) consider that legislation for the benefit of the *few,* is inimical to the best interests of the *whole.*

Think of girls being obliged to labor *thirteen* hours each working day, for a net compensation of *two cents per hour,* which is above the average net wages, being $1.56 per week. Two cents per hour for severe labor! Is not such a lesson enough to make an American curse the hour, when in an evil mood our lawmakers first granted a charter to enable the *few* to wield the wealth and power of *hundreds?* Is it not necessary to the maintenance of our rights, that some change be speedily effected in those laws by which our corporations are governed. We trust the friends of *equal rights,* will petition our legislature to make such a revision of these laws, as will cause the more general distribution of those benefits which were designed for all. If such a course is taken, let the tyrants tremble.

Factory Girls' Album, Exeter, N.H., June 20, 1846

Independence

Dialogue of a Lowell girl with the overseer of a factory:—"Well, Mr. Buck, I am informed that you wish to cut down my wages?" "Yes, such is my determination." "Do you suppose that I would go into that room to work again, at lower price than I received before?" "Why, it's no more than fair and reasonable, considering the hard times." "Well, all I have to say is, that before I'll do it, I'll see you in Tophet, pumping thunder at three cents a clap!" It is needless to say that she was invited to resume her duties.

Factory Girls' Album, Exeter, N.H., September 19, 1846

A Curiosity for the Exeter Museum

The soul of a factory agent (not visible to the naked eye) a sight of which, alone is worth a ticket.

Factory Girls' Album, Exeter, N.H., October 31, 1846

Beauties of Factory Life

Hundreds of operatives who work in our mills, are scarcely paid sufficient to board themselves, and are obliged to dress poorly, or, run in debt for their clothing. The consequence is, they become discouraged—lose confidence in themselves, and then, regardless of consequences, abandon their virtue to obtain favors. A goodly proportion of those in large cities, who inhabit "dens of shame," are first initiated into this awful vice in manufacturing places. Soon after, most of them commence the downward road to destruction—

they become known, and are compelled to leave their work in the mills and emigrate to large cities. We repeat what we have often done—girls leave not your homes in the country. It will be better for you to stay at home on your fathers farms than to run the risk of being ruined in a manufacturing village.—Man. Pal.

How painfully true is the above. Many young, amiable and virtuous girls are yearly initiated into a life of vice and shame, through the baneful influences of the present corrupt factory system in New England. And when we hear of the depraved condition of those whom we had formerly known as the fairest of their sex, but who have since gone astray through dire necessity, or been duped by the arts of the wily men who frequent manufacturing villages, we are led to exclaim in the language of Cowper,[12]

> My ear is pained,
> My soul is sick with every day's report
> Of wrong and outrage with which earth is filled.
> There is no flesh for man; the natural bond
> of brotherhood is severed as the flax,
> That falls asunder at the touch of fire.

Factory Girls' Album, Exeter, N.H., October 31, 1846

A Dream

"I had a dream which was not *all* a dream."

One night, when worn and weary I sunk to slumber, after thirteen hours of toil in the suffocating heat of a cotton mill, I fell into a feverish fitful sleep, and a vision of the day of Judgment passed before me. I was surprised to see that the children of men were often times arraigned in groups like criminals, whenever it appeared that their sins were of the same deep dye. A crowd of various mingled tongues and nations passed by to receive their sentences, and at last came the Amoskeag Manufacturing Company.[13] I noticed that the agents stood in front of the owners and seemed still to act as their agents and chief spokesmen. As they stood trembling before the supreme Judge of the world, methought that the following dialogue occurred:

JUDGE.—What were you doing on Sunday, the—day of—1844?

AGENT.—Attending church.

JUDGE.—But I am informed that you were blasting rocks.

AGENT.—Oh, ah, ye-yes-I, that is, we employed some common people to do that for us, *I* attended church *myself*.

JUDGE.—You must go below.

AGENT.—What apartment shall I take?

JUDGE.—About the centre of the pit.

After this case was disposed of, I was curious to see who would come next; and lo and behold it was a factory girl, whom I at once recognized as my old room-mate in the Stark mills.[14]

JUDGE.—What were you doing on Sunday the—day of—1844?

GIRL.—I attended church in the morning and in the afternoon rambled off into the woods.

JUDGE.—How came you to ramble in the woods on Sunday?

GIRL.—I had no time on week days.

JUDGE.—How many hours did you work each day in the Stark mills?

GIRL.—Thirteen.

JUDGE.—How much time had you for meals?

GIRL.—One hour and a quarter—sometimes less.

JUDGE.—This makes fourteen and a quarter which deducted from twenty-four, leaves nine and three quarters. How much time had you for relaxation, religious and moral instruction, reading, social visiting, and intercourse with your family?

GIRL.—Only what I stole from my sleep; and I was so tired at night that I had to retire immediately to rest.

JUDGE.—You may go to Heaven.

GIRL.—What seat shall I take?

JUDGE.—Any of the upper seats that you like.

THAT OTHER FACTORY GIRL

Manchester (N.H.) Democrat, September 5, 1845

Letter from a Local Factory Girl

I write to let the public know the cruel story of a sister operative of mine in Lowell. She is a young woman who had been employed in one of the factories of that city and left it, for the purpose of removing to another of the mills in which she thought she could labor with much better satisfaction to herself. But on application for work at that mill, she was denied employment, because the overseer (*driver* in the Southern term) of the mill she had left, had denounced her to the overseers (or drivers) of every mill in the place, as a girl not worthy to be employed. She applied to each mill in the city for employment, but was repulsed at all in succession for the same reason that employment was refused her at the first one. She sued the driver in a civil suit for slander, but was defeated in her suit for damages because the mill owners had established amongst themselves a rule, which custom had made law, making the ill-report of the overseer of one mill imperative cause of rejection by all the mills of the place;—for which ill-report as reason is asked of the overseer, and it stands by itself unexplained, final and imperative.

The issue of this case proves the existence of a rule and combination among the Lowell corporation that prevents any person upon leaving a corporation from obtaining work in any other corporation, if, *in the opinion of the overseer* of the corporation where the person formerly worked, he or she is not a suitable person to be employed. And it is of no consequence what induces that opinion—bad temper, immoral conduct, or nothing, on the part of the girl, or private pique, the gratification of an envious favorite, revenge for disappointed lechery, or any other cause, no matter how trivial or how wicked, on the part of the overseer—it may and does result in hunting and driving a girl out of the city if the overseer chooses to exercise his power over her destiny and her reputation.

Now I defy the most vehement ranters against Southern slavery to produce a section of the "black code" of any State,[15] which makes more of a slave in the Southern plantation driver the female negro who has a master and an owner to protect her, than under the rule above established by the mill owners of Lowell, and as "priviledged communications" *made supreme over the common law of the State,* are the thousands of unprotected white females of Lowell slaves to the overseers of a dozen or two of cotton mills, who hold not only the bread, but the characters of those girls, in the palms of their hands, and can do with them as any passion may dictate or any caprice suggest, with perfect impunity of the law, and safety from all consequences to themselves.

When chartered and specially protected monopolies obtain such power and exercise such outrageous tyranny over the *women* of the U. States, making their laws of *custom* and *"privilege"* paramount to the common law of the land, placing thousands of virtuous and noble females under worse than Turkish subjection to the male tyrants of the cotton mills, whose associated millions pension United States Senators and buy up legislators "like cattle in the market," it is indeed high time for the men of the United States, if there are any left this side of the Rio Grande, to seriously inquire whether these things are tending, and whether there is no remedy for such a slavish condition of *American white women?*

A Factory Girl in the Nashua Corporation

Nashua (N.H.) Gazette, October 1, 1846

Are the Operatives Well Off?

MR. EDITOR:

We are told by gentlemen both in this country and abroad that the Lowell factory operatives are exceedingly well off. Good wages, sure pay, not very hard work, comfortable food and lodgings, and such unparalleled opportunities for intellectual cultivation, (why, they even publish a Magazine there!!) what more can one desire? Really gentlemen! would you not reckon your wives and sisters fortunate if they could by any possibility be elevated into the situation of operatives? When in the tender transports of first love, you paint for the fairest and fondest of mortal maidens a whole life of uninterrupted joy, do you hope for her as the supremest felicity, the lot of a factory girl? The operatives are well enough off!—Indeed! Do you receive them in your parlors, are they admitted to visit your families, do you raise your hats to them in the street, in a word, are they your *equals?*

OLIVA

Lowell, Sept. 16, 1845

Voice of Industry, September 18, 1845

The Voice of the Sufferers

It is a subject of comment and general complaint, among the operatives, that while they tend three or four looms, where they used to tend but two, making nearly twice the number of yards of cloth, the pay is not increased to them, while the increase, to the owners is very great. Is this just? Twenty-five cents per week for each week, additional pay, would not increase the cost of the cloth, one mill a yard; no, not the half of a mill.

Now while I am penning this paragraph, a young lady enters my room with "Oh dear! Jane, I am sick and what shall I do? I have worked for three years, and never gave out, before. I stuck to my work, until I fainted at my loom. The Doctor says I must quit work and run about and amuse myself; but I have nowhere to go, and do not know what to do with myself." I have given the language, as it struck my ear; the conversation going on behind me. It is but the feelings of a thousand homeless, suffering females, this moment chanting "the Voice of Industry in this wilderness of sin."

One of the Vast Army of Sufferers

Voice of Industry, March 13, 1846

The "Beauties of Factory Life"

MR. EDITOR:

Those who write so effusively about the "Beauties of Factory Life,"[16] tell us that we are indeed happy creatures, and how truly grateful and humbly submissive we should be. Can it be that any of us are so stupified as not to realize the exalted station and truly delightful influences which we enjoy? If so, let them take a glance at pages 195 and 196 of Rev. H. Miles' book,[16] and they will surely awake to gratitude and be content. Pianos, teachers of music, evening schools, lectures, libraries and all these sorts of advantages are, says he, enjoyed by the operatives. (Query—when do they find time for all or any of these? When exhausted nature demands repose?) Very pretty picture that to write about; but we who work in the factory know the sober reality to be quite another thing altogether.

After all, it is easier to write a book than it is to *do* right. It is easier to smooth over and plaster up a deep festering rotten system, which is sapping the life-blood of our nation, widening and deepening the yawning gulf which will ere long swallow up the laboring classes in dependent servitude and serfdom, like that of Europe, than it is to probe to the very bottom of this death-spreading monster.

JULIANA

Voice of Industry, June 12, 1846

Corporation Tyranny

DEAR VOICE:—I was about to head this article Corporation Sharing, but when I come to reflect that females are not accustomed to that troublesome operation, and that it was their wrongs which I was about to set forth, I at once discovered its inapplicability, and have headed it as above. It is an old maxim that if the cents are looked after the dollars will take care of themselves; this I believe is universally admitted to be true, so much so, that the son who has not been taught this lesson by his father, would be considered ill fitted to set up for himself, amid the ups and downs of life. Now sir, I see not why the same principle may not with propriety be applied to Hours and Minutes, in connexion with "our labor" in our mills.

You are laboring hard to show the injustice of compelling the operatives to labor the unreasonable number of hours which they now do. I rejoice to see it, and bid you God speed; but the thought struck me, that there are Minutes also to be looked after. I know sir, it will be said we are dabbling in "small matters," but when I reflect that many littles make a great whole, and that these littles are daily being wrenched from the operative, particle by particle, I am constrained to speak out, that this ever grasping, tyrannizing spirit may be rebuked and receive the contempt which it so richly deserves. Perhaps those who are accustomed to reflect and mourn over the fact that thousands of hard working females are allowed but thirty minutes to lave themselves, go down three flights of stairs, travel one fourth of a mile to their boarding house, eat their meal and return the same distance to their work; I say perhaps those who are acquainted with these facts are not aware that it is even worse; *it is so.* On some of the Corporations in this city, two of which I will name, the Boot[17] [*sic*] and Massachusetts,[18] it is, and has been since 1841, an established rule to hoist the gate twenty-eight minutes from the time it shuts down for meals, and on commencing in the morning it is to be hoisted eight minutes from the time that the Merrimack[19] bell strikes, which is two minutes earlier at each time of hoisting, than is practiced on that Corporation. Thus you see by tightening the screws in this way, the operatives lose from four to six minutes per day, under the pretence of allowing them thirty minutes for meals. A little calculation will show how it would stand at the end of five years; and it will be recollected that many of the operatives have worked in the same mill more than five years. Four to six minutes per day, say average five minutes—thirty minutes per week, two hours per month, two days of thirteen hours each per year, and ten days for five years. This is the practical effect of this irresponsible, over-working, oppressive system.

Now Mr. Editor is it right? ought these things so to be? I do hope that the former agent of the Boot, and the present agent of the Massachusetts Corporation, will examine this matter candidly and use their official influence to undo the wrong which themselves have (unauthorized) inflicted on hundreds and thousands of the laboring poor of this city, and restore to them that which is just and honest in the sight of God.

LOWELL OPERATIVE

Voice of Industry, January 8, 1847

The Condition of the Operatives

MR. CASE:—DEAR SIR:—In the last No. of the Voice, I notice a letter from you, in it, you desire information in relation to the condition of the operatives, in our factories.—Since I was between seven and eight years old, I have been employed almost without intermission in a factory, which is almost 18 years. During this time I have not attended school more than one year. Probably not that. So whatever you may think of my composition, you must acknowledge I ought to be a judge of factory life. I should like to give you my whole experience, but this would take too much room. And beside, you would hardly believe what I should state, although it would be true, so I will confine myself to Lowell, the place where operatives are used as well, I think as any place in New England. I do not wonder at your surprise that the operatives were worked in the summer season, from five in the morning till seven in the evening. Especially when you had been previously informed that we worked but ten hours per day. But 'tis true, we do all this, and against our wishes too. I know scarcely an operative, who would not have it otherwise if they could. But they do not wish their wages cut down, for they have barely enough to live on now. The time we are required to labor is altogether too long. It is more than our constitutions can bear. If any one doubts it, let them come into our mills of a summer's day, at four or five o'clock, in the afternoon, and see the drooping, weary persons moving about, as though their legs were hardly able to support their bodies. If this does not convince them, let them try their hand at it a while, and they will find the thing demonstrated at once. In fact there is nothing more common amongst operatives, than the remark that "their legs ache so, it seems as though they would drop off." Now if they desired to work so long, they would not complain in this way. I have been an overseer myself, and many times have I had girls faint in the morning, in consequence of the air being so impure in the mill. This is quite a common thing. Especially when girls have worked in the factory for considerable length of time. We commence as soon—and work as long as we can see almost the year round, and for nearly half the year we work by lamp light, at both ends of the day lighting up both morning and evening. And besides this, from November till March our time is from twenty minutes to half an hour too slow. So you see instead of getting out of the factory at half past seven o'clock in the evening, it is *really* eight. And more than this some of the clocks are so fixed as to lose ten minutes during the day and gain ten minutes during the night, thereby getting us into the mill five minutes before five in the morning and working us five minutes after seven at night. As to wages, the proprietors do not calculate the average wages of females, to exceed one dollar fifty cents per week, exclusive of board. Notwithstanding those "stray Yankees," state to the contrary. But I am taking up too much room, perhaps you may hear from me again in time.

Yours for the right,   R.

Voice of Industry, March 26, 1847

Lowell Girls—Standing at the Gate

It came to pass in the month of April 1847, that there went forth a new decree from the Cotton Lords of Lowell, that there living machinery should have forty-five minutes in which to leave their work, partake of their meals, and return back again. Now this decree was well pleasing to the friends of Humanity who had been striving for a long time to obtain a reduction in the hours of toil in the pestilential air of the cotton mills. For they understood well how for many years the girls had been shut up thirteen hours per day to the destruction of health and life, while the Cotton Lords had been waxing fat upon their blood and sinews! It came to pass in those days that when this decree took effect the great gates were all shut until the ringing of the second bell, (which took place just *thirty-five* minutes from the time they were closed, instead of *forty-five* as *was decreed*,) that many *foolish* girls were seen standing at the gates *waiting* for admittance. Now this being rumored abroad the query arose in the minds of some, why is this! Have they common sense, or any *minds* at all? If so, why are they seen wasting their precious moments, standing by hundreds before the gates? Have they been so long accustomed to watching machinery that they have actually become dwarfs in intellect—and lost to all sense of their own God-like powers of mind—yea, more, *have* they *any* minds more than the beasts that perisheth? If so, why are they not in their rooms storing their minds with useful practical knowledge which shall fit them high and noble stations in the moral and intellectual world? Why, instead of being seen waiting at the gates for the bell to strike, the *gates* should wait for *them* after the bell gives the summons! Ten minutes twice a day in one week gives two whole hours per week, eight per month and 104 hours per year or eight days and two thirds of a day, twelve hours long! Think of this ye that waste your time thus foolishly and blush unto repentance not to be repented of! Is life so long, or of so little worth that it should be thus squandered? What, has a beneficient Creator bestowed upon us faculties and powers of mind which are capable of being improved and cultivated *ad infinitum,* and which if trained aright assimilate us to God and to Angels, and shall we suffer them to *wither* and *perish* for lack of proper time and attention on *our* part? Forbid it righteous God! Let it not be said of us here in this land of boasted liberty and equal rights, that thousands are bound down in *ignorance* and worshiping at the altar of the god of mammon! Awake! daughters of America to a realization of the evils which follow in the train of ignorance and selfishness! Awake and arise from the low grovelling charms of *dollars* and *cents,* to a knowledge of your own high and holy duties and destinies! Awake and resolve from this time forth to *live,* not merely to gain a bare subsistence, but to live for nobler, worthier objects. *Live,* not to wear out and exhaust your physical energies in obtaining a few more paltry shillings, but to adorn and beautify the minds and intellects which a kind Father hath confered upon you. Whosoever hath ears to hear, let him hear, what saith the *'first chronicle?'*

JULIANA

Lowell, May 4.

Voice of Industry, May 7, 1847

The Premium System

This 'premium system' is a curse to us[20]—it ought not to be tolerated, and will not be by Christians or Philanthropists. I have worked under this plan, and know too well the base treatment of overseers in many instances.—Often have girls been denied of receiving their friends, and been so afraid of the "Old man" they dare not ask to go out when sick; for they knew he would have a great deal to say. "The work must not be stopped, and if you are not able to work you better stay out all the time."

Some girls cannot get off as much cloth as others; such ones are apt to be treated unkindly, and often reminded by the "old man" that "Sally and Dolly got off several cutts more the last four weeks; they come in long before the speed starts up; and do their cleaning, and if you don't get off more next month I will send you off." 'Tis sometimes asked "why is it that the girls come to the gate before 'tis opened, if they are not willing to work so many long hours?" The premium is offered, the girls drove up, and they want to keep the "old man" good natured if possible. No overseer ever dared use the whip, but they give looks and words, sometimes, quite as severe.

This plan of giving overseers premiums, reminds me of what a fugitive Slave said in an account of her escape. "Massa gives de drivers a drink and reward if he gets the most work done, and then massa gives us all a Jubilee." Here the poor slave got her freedom so it seems these jubilees are most fortunate to slaves; but those got by the premium money will never elevate the operative, or meliorate their condition.

The principle of giving premiums to overseers, and getting up the party, seems to savor very strong of the above incident. Could my fellow operatives see this principle, they would despise an overseer who would be made a tool of, to serve the interests of a Corporation. "Gentlemanly individuals" indeed! I should like to see liberality and generosity from the directors of the Stark mills, towards my sister operatives—should like to see it extended to some subjects of misfortune crushed by their machinery; for instance to the girl who but a few months ago, broke her arm in two places, in one of their weaving rooms; and I am told this day, in connection with scraps on the party, that "the poor girl never had received a mill from the Corporation."

I am heartily glad when anything is done to elevate that class to which it is my lot to belong. We are a band of sisters—we must have sympathy for each other's woes. It is woeful indeed that we are obliged to toil on, without time to improve our minds, and take our food properly.

An Operative

Voice of Industry, January 8, 1847

There Must Be Something Wrong

When earth produces free and fair
   The golden waving corn;
When fragrant fruits perfume the air,
   And fleecy flocks are shorn;
Whilst thousands move with aching head,
   And sing the ceaseless song—
"We starve, we die; oh, give us bread,"
   There must be something wrong.

When wealth is wrought as seasons roll,
   From off the fruitful soil,
When luxury, from pole to pole,
   Reaps fruit of human toil;
When, for a thousand, one alone
   In plenty rolls along,
And others only gnaw the bone,
   There must be something wrong.

And when production never ends,
   The earth is yielding ever,
A copious harvest oft begins,
   But distribution—never,
When toiling millions work to fill
   The wealthy's coffers strong,
When hands are crushed that work and till.
   There must be something wrong.

When poor men's tables waste away,
   To barrenness and drought,
There then is something in the way
   That's worth the finding out;
With surfeits one great table bends,
   Whilst numbers move along;
While scarce a crust their board extends,
   There must be something wrong.

Then let the law give equal rights
   To wealthy and to poor;
Let freedom crush the arm of might
   We ask for nothing more.
Until this system is begun,
   The burden of our song
Must be, and can be, only one—
   There must be something wrong.

Factory Girls' Album, Exeter, N.H., February 15, 1847

Factory Life—Romance and Reality

Aristocratic strangers, in broad cloths and silks, with their imaginations excited by the wonderful stories—romances of Factory Life—which they have heard, have paid hasty visits to Lowell, or Manchester, and have gone away to praise, in prose and verse, the beauty of our "Factory Queens," and the comfort, elegance and almost perfection, of the arrangements by which the very fatherly care of Agents, Superintendents, Overseers, &c., has surrounded them. To these nice visitors everything in and around a Lowell Cotton Mill is bathed in an atmosphere of rose-colored light. They see the bright side of the picture, and that alone. They see the graceful form, the bright and speaking eye, the blushing cheek and the elastic motions of "Industry's Angel daughters," but they fail to see that these belong not to Lowell Cotton Mills, but to New England's country Homes.—There the fair cheek, kissed by the sunlight and the breeze, grew fresh and healthful. There the eye borrowed its brightness from stream and lake and sky, and there too the intellect received the culture which enabled the "Factory Girls" to astonish Europe and America with a LOWELL OFFERING. There a FARLEY, a CURTIS, a HALL and a LARCOM[21] received the impress which made them what they are in their various departments of effort.

These lovers of the Romance of Labor—they don't like the *reality* very well—see not the pale and emaciated ones. They see not those who wear Consumption's hectic flush. They think little of the weariness and pain of those fair forms, as they stand there, at the loom and spindle, thirteen long hours, each day! They know not *how* long these hours of toil seem to them, as they look out upon the fields, and hills, and woods, which lie beyond the Merrimack, steeped in golden sunlight and radiant with beauty—fields and woods which are to them what the Land of Promise was to Moses on Pisgah,[22] something which *they* may never enjoy. They have no time to ramble and climb the hill-sides. Six days shalt thou labor and do all thy work, and on the seventh thou shalt go to church, is the Commandment as improved by the mammon worshiping Christianity of modern Civilization. The factory girl is required to go to meeting on Sunday, where long, and too often unmeaning, word-prayers are repeated, and dull prosey sermons "delivered," and where God is worshiped, according to law, by pious Agents and Overseers, while the poor Irishman is blasting rocks for them in the Corporation's canal, that the mills may not be stopped on Monday. It would be very wicked, of course, for the "mill girl" to go out upon the hills, where she might worship in the great temple of the universe, without a priest, as proxy, to stand between her and her Maker.

These lovers of the Romance of Labor—here, have much to say of the moral and intellectual advantages by which the operatives are surrounded. These may be over-rated or they may not be, it matters not. It is true there are Churches and ministers "in any quantity," with many good influences, and with some that are at least questionable.

There are lectures of various kinds, some of them *free,* and others requiring only a trifling fee to secure admission, to all who wish it. Then there are also libraries of well selected books, to which all can have access.

Those who recollect the fable of *Tantalus* in the old Mythology,[23] will be able to appreciate the position of a large portion of the population with respect to these exalted privileges. They are all around them, on every side, but they cannot grasp them—they continually invite to the soul-feast, those who, tho' they hunger and thirst, cannot partake. Do you ask why they cannot partake? Simply from physical and mental exhaustion. The unremitted toil of thirteen long hours, drains off the vital energy and unfits for study or reflection. They need amusement, relaxation, *rest,* and not mental exertion of any kind. A really sound and instructive lecture cannot, under such circumstances, be appreciated, and the lecturer fails, to a great extent, in making an impression.—"Jim Crow" performances[24] are much better patronized than scientific lectures, and the trashy, milk-and-water sentimentalities of the *Lady's Book*[25] and *Olive Branch,*[26] are more read than the works of Gibbon,[27] or Goldsmith,[28] or Bancroft.[29]

If each factory girl could suspend her labors in the Mill for a few months each year, for the purpose of availing herself of the advantages for intellectual culture by which she is surrounded, much good might be derived. A few can and do thus avail themselves of these advantages; but the great mass are there to toil and toil only. Among these are some of earth's noblest spirits. Theirs is Love's *willing* toil. The old home-stead must be redeemed,—a poor sick mother or an aged and infirm father needs their little savings to keep them from that dreadful place, Civilization's only guarantee, the "Poor House," —or a loved brother at Dartmouth or Harvard, is to be assisted in his manful efforts to secure an education; so they must not think of schools and books for themselves. They must toil on, and they do toil on. But day by day they feel their over-tasked systems give way.—A dizziness in the head or a pain in the side, or the shoulders or the back, admonishes them to return to their country homes before it is too late. But too often these friendly monitions are unheeded. They resolve to toil a *little longer*.—But nature cannot be cheated, and the poor victim of a false system of Industrial Oppression is carried home—*to die!* Or, if her home is far away and disease comes on too rapidly, she goes to the Hospital, and soon, in the Strangers' Burial Ground may be seen another unmarked grave! This is no fancy of mine—no studied fiction—(would to God it were) but sober truth. There are now in our very midst hundreds of these loving, self-sacrificing martyr-spirits. They will die unhonored and unsung, but not unwept; for the poor factory girl has a *home* and *loved ones,* and dark will be that home, and sad those loved ones when the light of her smile shines on them no more.

Voice of Industry, December 3, 1847

NOTES

1. Albert Brisbane (1809–90), son of a prominent New York landowner, went to Europe in the late 1820s and came under the influence of Charles Fourier. In 1840 Brisbane published *The Social Destiny of Man,* presenting Fourier's ideas and program, after which he founded the association movement in the United States. Between 1842 and 1844 he presented his views at workingman's meetings and in a regular column in the influential New York *Tribune.* He called for a reorganization of human society along the lines of the phalanxes organized in Fourierism, in order to eliminate the evils of industrial society.

2. Miss Bagley's letter was published in the *Lowell Advertiser* of July 10, 1845. "We have received the following from Miss Bagley," the editor wrote in an introduction, "the publication of which she considers due to herself as showing the manner in which she was forced to make the assertions she did in defence of herself and the factory girls present at Woburn. So far as we can learn there was general disposition on the part of the operatives to let the Offering alone, and the subject was only alluded to when introduced by an injudicious friend of the corporations."

3. William Schouler had owned the *Lowell Offering* for a year, and continued to print it after ownership was turned over to Miss Curtis and Miss Farley in the middle of 1843.

4. The *Lowell Advertiser* absorbed the *Patriot,* but its masthead still read *Advertiser.*

5. Miss Farley is referring to a statement by the editor of the *Advertiser* introducing Sarah G. Bagley's letter: "We never supposed that the editress of the Offering was conscious that her publication was made use of by the corporations to produce any erroneous impression in the community as to the effects of the manufacturing system. We are pretty much convinced that such an idea would be spurned by her with contempt. . . . There are, however, conflicting opinions existing in the community with respect to the system which should be adopted in this country in regard to factory labor; and in its connexion with the system the Offering can hardly escape being dragged into the arena of discussion,

although such was not its original intention" (*Lowell Advertiser,* July 10, 1845). However, the *Lowell Advertiser* itself had criticized the *Lowell Offering* for failing to speak out against corporation abuse of the operatives (see issue of June 27, 1845).

6. Lydia Maria Child (1802–80), famous for her *An Appeal in Favor of That Class of Americans Called Africans* and other antislavery writings, as well as popular writings on many subjects, and editor of the abolitionist weekly, *National Anti-Slavery Standard.*

7. George Ripley (1802–80), literary critic and social reformer, editor with Margaret Fuller of the *Dial,* organizer and leader of the famous Brook Farm experiment in Fourierism, and editor of the *Harbinger,* a magazine of the Fourier movement.

8. Michael Walsh (1815–59), Irish-American publisher of the *Subterranean,* a labor paper started in New York City in 1843, who merged it with the *Working Man's Advocate,* published by land reformer George Henry Evans in 1844. Walsh and Evans split after three years, and the former went into politics and became an anti-abolitionist demagogue.

9. The reference may be either to *Vox Populi,* published in Lowell, or *Voice of Industry,* then published in Fitchburg, Massachusetts.

10. This is an extract from the only copy of the *Journal* in existence, located in the Fall River Public Library. On May 5, 1842, the *National Anti-Slavery Standard* announced the appearance of the first issue of a *Journal* whose "name presents no beauty to the eye and no music to the ear," but would be edited by Frances Harriet Whipple for the factory girls. Miss Whipple's "spirited and oftentimes beautiful poetry has given her deserved popularity," it noted, and quoted from the "Prospectus" the statement that the *Journal* would cry out against wrong wherever it saw it, "whether it be making a woman a toy, or a chattel; whether it be flattering or flogging her; whether it be raising and dragging her away in chains to the southwestern market, or ruinously training her under the forced culture of our fashionable boarding-schools, and drawing-rooms, for the HOME-MARKET."

11. This appears to be a slightly modified version of an article under the same title published in *The Factory Girl* (New Market, N.H.) of March 1, 1843. The earlier article opened: "The females in the Mills are required to devote fifteen twenty-fourths of every working day to the corporations, being thirteen hours of incessant toil, and two hours devoted to meals and preparations." It closed: "If that step is taken, let the tyrants tremble."

12. William Cowper (1731–1800), English poet.

13. A textile mill in Lowell.

14. A mill in Manchester, New Hampshire.

15. Laws adopted in the southern states to assure domination of white masters over their slaves.

16. The reference is to a review of Henry A. Miles, *Lowell as It Was and as It Is* (Lowell, 1845). In his book the Reverend Mr. Miles presented a glowing picture of life in Lowell, insisting that the operatives worked only ten hours a day, stressing the magnanimity of the corporations and the "moral police" system whereby the girls kept themselves free of any taint of vice. In the review, published in its issue of September 18, 1845, the *Voice of Industry* particularly attacked Miles's assertion that the factory girls came voluntarily to the mills and left when they wished. "A slave too goes voluntarily to his task, but his will is in some manner quickened by the whip of the overseer. The whip which brings laborers to Lowell is NECESSITY. They must have money; a father's debts are to be paid, an aged mother is to be supported, a brother's ambition is to be aided, and so the factories are supplied. . . . Everybody knows that it is necessity alone, in some form or other, that takes them to Lowell and that keeps them there."

17. A mill in Lowell, established in 1835.

18. A mill in Lowell, established in 1839.

19. The first cotton mill in Lowell, established in 1828.

20. Under the premium system bonuses were granted to overseers and second hands who were able to get more work out of the operatives.

21. Harriet Farley, Harriot F. Curtis, Lucy Larcom, and Lydia S. Hall. All were associated with the *Lowell Offering*, and Lydia S. Hall was also co-editor of the *Operatives' Magazine*.

22. Moses did not go into the promised land himself. He was permitted to go only to Pisgah, the mountain range east of the northern end of the Dead Sea.

23. A king in Greek mythology who for his crimes was condemned in Hades to stand in water that receded when he tried to drink; the fruit hanging over his head also receded when he reached for it.

24. Identified as originally a Negro slave and stable hand in Louisville, whose song and dance were mimicked by the minstrel Thomas D. Rice, "Jim Crow" is used here to mean minstrel shows. But it came to be used to designate Negroes in general, and to be associated with all policies for excluding blacks from contact on an equal plane with whites.

25. *Godey's Lady's Book,* edited by Sarah Josepha Hale, was published in Philadelphia.

26. The *Olive Branch* was published in Boston from 1830 to 1860.

27. Edward Gibbon (1737-94), English historian, author of *Decline and Fall of the Roman Empire.*

28. Oliver Goldsmith (1728–74), English poet, dramatist, and novelist.

29. George Bancroft (1800–1891), historian, author of *History of the United States* and *History of the Formation of the Constitution of the United States.*

Part 3

The Female Labor Reform Associations

Constitutions, Rules, Regulations, Resolutions, Reports, Speeches, Social Gatherings, Correspondence

In her first signed editorial in the *Lowell Offering,* Miss Farley had struck the main theme of the genteel factory operatives, a theme which made the magazine so respected among the corporations and their allies. Speaking of the operatives, she wrote: "We should like to influence them as moral and rational beings. . . . Our field is a wide one. . . . With wages, boards, etc., we have nothing to do—these depend on circumstances over which we have no control." Not so, cried the factory operatives, and they demonstrated that they meant what they said by organizing the first unions of female factory workers, the Female Labor Reform Associations.

The most important Female Labor Reform Association, organized in Lowell by twelve factory operatives, all of them workers in the cotton mills, began operation in January, 1845. Six months later, its membership had grown to 500, and it was growing steadily.

The constitution of the Lowell Female Labor Reform Association provided that every member should pledge herself "to labor actively for reform in the present sytsem of labor." The association conducted a tireless campaign to convince the public of the need for reform in the mills. A regular "Female Department" was conducted in the *Voice of Industry,* and in 1846 the association was able to buy this labor journal. At the same time, it organized fairs, May parties, and social gatherings. The association also protested speedup in the

99

mills, and sponsored a pledge which factory girls signed refusing to tend four instead of three looms.

The association exerted its influence in the political field as well. When a committee of the Massachusetts state legislature reported adversely on the demand for a ten-hour law, it attacked William Schouler, its chairman, as "a corporation machine or tool," and announced that it would campaign against his re-election. The campaign was successful, and after the election the association published a resolution expressing their "grateful acknowledgements to the voters of Lowell" for "consigning William Schouler to the obscurity he so justly deserves."

In March, 1845, Sarah G. Bagley, president of the Lowell Female Labor Reform Association, represented the association at the convention of the New England Workingmen's Association, which came into existence in the fall of 1844 to give support to the crusade for a shorter work day, particularly the ten-hour day.

Representatives of the Lowell Association attended mass meetings of female factory operatives in Manchester and Dover, New Hampshire, and in Fall River, Massachusetts. In each of these cities Female Labor Reform Associations were organized.

On May 22, 1846, in an editorial on the New England Workingmen's Association, the *Voice of Industry* observed: "We would also, say to the Female Association, that they are *entitled* to a representation, and that it is very desirable that they should give their voice in favor of Labor Reform at this session of the meeting. Let no *false* delicacy prevent you from being present, and taking part in the plans for future progress and improvement." As this section makes clear, the Female Labor Reform Associations gave more than one "voice in favor of Labor Reform."

Of the factory operatives associated with the Female Labor Reform Associations, three were the most important: Sarah G. Bagley, Huldah J. Stone, and Mehitabel Eastman. Huldah J. Stone, a Lowell mill operative, ran the Female Labor Department of the *Voice of Industry* for the Lowell Female Labor Reform Association and was the labor paper's traveling correspondent. She was elected recording secretary of the New England Workingmen's Association in March, 1846, and also served on important committees for the association. Mehitabel Eastman, a Manchester, New Hampshire, factory operative, and a leader of the Manchester Female Labor Reform Association, became co-editor of the *Voice of Industry* and its traveling correspondent. Secretary of the New Engand's Workingmen's Association, Miss Eastman was active in the battle for the ten-hour day. □

A Leaf from My Sketch-Book

In Dec. 1844, a few humble individuals were seated in a badly lighted room, reviewing the past, and looking into the fearful future.—Sadness added to the gloom, and a storm raged without, that would have affected a cheerful company, but still they consulted measures for the future. They met again, the number had lessened, for threatenings and fear had taken possession of their roving minds, and altho' they saw the right, those lacking moral courage could find an excuse to desert a cause, where there was little prospect of any compensation, except that afforded by a consciousness of having done something to improve the condition of those with whom they associated. But there were some of the number who would not abandon the right and went on.—The little band chose for a motto, "Try again," and they succeeded.

They organized and their number afforded them two members more than their board of officers.

They met again; two years had passed over them,—their history is briefly told. They had labored industriously and perseveringly. They had preserved their motto, and been guided by its teachings. The barren waste had become a garden and the desert had blossomed by their efforts, and still their motto is, "Try again." Their number has increased to six hundred, and the future shall bless the efforts of that little company of five, who selected for a motto, "Try again."

JULIET

Voice of Industry, April 3, 1846

Report of the Lowell Female Labor Reform Association to the New England Workingmen's Association

The Report of the Female Labor Reform Association of Lowell, was called for. It was moved that the Delegate from Lowell, be requested to read said Report, which is as follows:—

REPORT OF THE F.L. REFORM ASSOCIATION

We are happy in being able to impart cheering and hopeful intelligence to the laborers and operatives of New England, through our report before this convention. Our prospects were never more flattering—our faith in the final and complete success of this humane and righteous enterprise, never more strong or well grounded than at the present time. Public attention is being thoroughly awakened—*deep* thought is struggling for utterance—philanthropy is kindling a brighter flame, in the hearts of all who have souls to feel, or powers to act. Our opposers are making the discovery that we *are in earnest* in this great,—this mighty Reform! that there is *talent,* integrity and a *true,* laudable zeal in our ranks, which *will not be looked down,* or thwarted in its noble designs, to elevate humanity—to assert and maintain the rights of a Republican people.

The Press is manifesting a more active interest in the subject of labor's rights, all over the land. The Clergy are beginning to throw off the shackles which have so long crippled their efforts for good, and like their master are pleading in behalf of humanity's rights. There is a spirit abroad in the wide world, which will not rest, until Justice shall be established on every hill—until Righteousness, with its peaceful, regenerating streams shall flow through every vale —until a union of interest, a bond of brotherhood, shall make in *deed* and in *truth, all one* in the great family of man.

Let no one disregard the holy, benevolent promptings of this heaven-derived spirit in the soul; but, rather heed its kind warnings, and obey faithfully its imperative commands! We believe this spirit is in our midst, prompting to action—to duty, and to radical reform. To aid on the cause of human improvement and intellectual culture, our Associations have established an Industrial Reform Lyceum, in the city of Lowell, which will be addressed by the wisest and best men our country affords, from week to week, thereby giving all who will, an opportunity to learn our views and aims; and also to assist in carrying forward the all-important Labor Reform movement. We have also a Press, now owned entirely by our Association, through which to communicate with the world around us, having none to molest, or at least none to make us afraid to speak the *truth boldly!* And God granting us *wisdom* we shall endeavor so to do. We shall continue to labor unitedly, and untiringly to establish again on this sin-polluted earth, the reign of Justice, equity and love.

Let us all be true to ourselves, mentally, morally and physically, and the blessings of high heaven, will crown our labors with abundant success. Our pathway through life will be strewn with flowers which never fade—our hearts retain the freshness and vigor of youth until the last sands of life have run, and death like a kind friend, shall give us a welcome passport to the joys of heaven—to the *home of Angels!*

S. G. BAGLEY, *Pres.*

H. J. STONE, *Rec. Sec'y.*
The report was accepted with much applause.

Voice of Industry, April 10, 1846

May Party

The FEMALE LABOR REFORM ASSOCIATION will give a Party on the evening of May 1st, at the City Hall. The hall will be splendidly illuminated, and decorated with mottoes and flowers; eloquent speakers and choice singers will be present. The "ROGERS FAMILY," also Bond's well known BAND, to discourse music. Rev. WM. H. CHANNING, JOHN ALLEN,[9] and others from abroad, will speak on the occasion.

Our friends from Manchester, Worcester, Boston, Woburn, Lynn and other places, are invited to be present.

There will be no refreshments served, but an intellectual entertainment, such as every lover of good speaking and singing will appreciate.

Per Order

Voice of Industry, April 24, 1846

Try Again

Try again! try again!
Never mind the clouds or rain!
Let the mind be up and stirring—
Chide the sinful, turn the erring,
    Try again! try again!

Try again! try again!
When should the spirit shrink or quail?
See! a glorious day is dawning;—
    Try again! try again!

Try again! try again!
Heart and hope should never wane;
Fear ye not the bold aggressor,
Heed ye not the stern oppressor;—
    Try again! try again!

Try again! try again!
Never fear the slanderer's stain;
Blush ye not at "infidel"—
Fear ye not the doom they tell;
    Try again! try again!

MARY

Voice of Industry, May 8, 1846

"You Cannot Unite"

We are met with this argument at almost every step. But we say to you we can, we have made an experiment and it has been successful. Some two months since, a plan was proposed by the Massachusetts Corporation, to have the weavers tend four looms and reduce the wages one cent on a piece. Some of their number thought as a protection had been given to industry, that their employers had not applied, they would take the liberty to see to the matter themselves.

A meeting was called and a President and Secretary appointed to carry out the proposed measure of "protective industry." Next in order, a Committee of three was appointed to draw up a pledge,—it was presented and unanimously adopted. It reads as follows:

"In view of the rapid increase of labor without a corresponding remuneration, therefore, we the weavers of No. 2, Massachusetts Corporation, resolve, that we will not allow ourselves to be physically taxed again, to add to the already overflowing coffers of our employers,—that we will not work under the proposed reduction, embracing a fourth loom and receive a cent less per piece.

Resolved, That we will not tend a fourth loom, [except to oblige each other] unless we receive the same pay per piece as on three, and that we will use our influence to prevent others from pursuing a course which has *always* had a tendency to reduce our wages.

This we most solemnly pledge ourselves to observe, in evidence of which, we hereunto affix our names.

Resolved, That any one giving her name, and violating this pledge, shall be published in the "Voice of Industry," as a traitor, and receive the scorn and reproach of her associates."

It has the signature of every, or nearly every job weaver on the corporation, and has been kept inviolate.

The operatives *can* unite and they will yet give evidence to their employers, that "Union is strength."

Voice of Industry, May 15, 1846

Preamble and Constitution of the Lowell Female Labor Reform Association

Whereas we, the Operatives of Lowell, believing that in the present age of improvement nothing can escape the searching glances of reform; and when men begin to inquire why the Laborer does not hold that place in the social, moral and intellectual world, which a bountiful Creator designed him to occupy, the *reason* is obvious. He is a slave to a false and debasing state of society. Our merciful Father in his infinite wisdom surely, has not bestowed all his blessings, both mental and moral on a favored few, on whom also he has showered all of pecuniary gifts. No! to us *all* has he given minds capable of eternal progression and improvement!

It now only remains for us to throw off the shackles which are binding us in ignorance and servitude and which prevent us from rising to that scale of being for which God designed us.

But how shall this be done? How shall the mass become educated? With the present system of labor it is impossible. There must be reasonable hours for manual labor, and a just portion of time allowed for the cultivation of the mental and moral faculties and no other way *can* the great work be accomplished.

We know no employment is respectable only as long as these employed are such, and no farther than they are intelligent and moral, can they merit the companionship and esteem of their fellow-beings. It is evident, that with the present system of labor, the minds of the mass *must* remain uncultivated, their morals un-improved and our country be flooded with vice and misery!

Shall we, Operatives of America, the land where Democracy claims to be the principle by which we live and by which we are governed, see the evil daily increasing which separates more widely and more effectually the favored few and the unfortunate many, without one exertion to stay the progress?—God forbid! Let the daughters of New England kindle the spark of philanthropy on every heart till its brightness shall *fill* the whole earth!

In consideration of which we adopt the following Constitution:

ART. 1st. This Association shall be called the Lowell Female Labor Reform Association.

ART. 2d. This Association shall be governed by the following Officers:—President, two Vice Presidents, a Secretary, Treasurer and board of Directors, consisting of eight in number.

ART. 3d. It shall be the duty of the President to preside at the meetings of the Association and board of Directors, and call especial meetings whenever any three members of the same shall request it.

ART. 4th. It shall be the duty of the Vice Presidents to preside in case of the absence of the President.

ART. 5th. It shall be the duty of the Secretary to be present at all meetings of the Association, and be prepared to read the proceedings of the last meeting, if requested.—Also, to keep a correct account of the business of the Association.

ART. 6th. It shall be the duty of the Treasurer to receive all money paid into the treasury, and keep a correct account of the same also, to pay all bills presented by the Association, and signed by the President and Secretary.

ART. 7th. It shall be the duty of the Directors to present all plans of operation to the Association, and to assist in all the labors of the same.

ART. 8th. Any person signing this Constitution, shall literally pledge herself to labor *actively* for Reform in the present system of labor.

ART. 9th. The members of this Association disapprove of all hostile measures, strikes and turn outs until all pacific measures prove abortive, and then that it is the imperious duty of every one to assert and maintain that independence which our brave ancestors bequeathed us, and sealed with their blood.

ART. 10th. This Constitution may be altered and amended by a vote of two thirds of the members present, provided the amendment be proposed at a previous meeting.—It shall be the duty of the Board of Directors to revise the Constitution at the time of the Annual meeting for choosing Officers, which shall be holden on the first Tuesday of January.

The following Officers were chosen Jan. 1846.

SARAH G. BAGLEY, *President*
HANNAH C. TARLTON,   *Vice Pres.*
MARY EMERSON,
HULDAH J. STONE, *Rec'g. Sec'y.*
SARAH A. YOUNG, *Cor. Sec'y.*
MARY A. K. TARLTON, *Treasurer.*
CLIMENA BUTLER,
MISS GILMAN,
ABBEY KEMP,
CATHERINE MAXEY,   *Directors.*
MARY J. ROBINSON,
ELIZA SIMPSON,
ELIZABETH L. TRUE,
ELMIRA B. STONE.

To the Friends of Reform

The *"Female Labor Reform Association,"* believing all has not been done that may be in behalf of ourselves and humanity generally; propose to hold a *"Social Gathering,"* on Monday evening, (17th of the present month,) to obtain funds, for the further diffusion of the principles of labor reform.

We most earnestly invite all the friends of the *"Ten Hour System,"* or those who are in favor of any other method of labor reform, to aid us by their assistance in preparing a collation, or any donation however small, it will be gratefully received.

We ask you to be present at our gathering, and speak a kind word, or give us a look of approbation and encouragement, and the blessing of those ready to perish shall be upon you. We would say that we intend to have a rich intellectual treat, with a few songs of a more amusing character.

Mr. Fuller has consented to be present and favor us with one of his original comic songs. Also, Dr. D. G. Robinson, (the "Reformed Drunkard Player,") with Mike Walsh, and many others.

We trust that our friends from abroad will come in season to be present at our gathering and cheer us with their presence and rich sentiments.

In behalf of the Association,

S. G. BAGLEY, *President*

Lowell, March 6 1845.

Those papers friendly to the Reform will please copy.—
Lowell Reformer.

The Awl, Lynn, Mass., March 15, 1845

Report of the Female Labor Reform Association of Lowell to the New England Workingmen's Association[1]

The ladies of Lowell having formed an association auxiliary, to the Mechanics' and Laborers' Association, the convention voted that they be invited to take seats with us and participate in the proceedings. For the past few months, the Association have been most indefatigable and perserving in the good-work of reform, and have accomplished much by the agitation of the question of labor, particularly with reference to the condition of the operatives employed in the factories. A delegation from the association, headed by its able and public-spirited President, Miss S. G. Bagley, appeared before the Committee of the Legislature, to whom was referred the petitions for the Ten Hour System, and ably defended the same. The Female Association has proved a valuable auxiliary to the cause, and their influence is yet destined to tell with tremendous effect for the final success of Humanity and human rights. By the request and vote of the Convention, the Association presented the following

REPORT

Believing that some effort on the part of female operatives was necessary in order to effect a change in the present system of labor, we have endeavored to cast in our mite of influence, and are trying to gain a well numbered association. Though we are yet few, we trust the interest now manifested in the community will not soon be lost, and that ere long the name of every operative and all who care for the amelioration of the laborers' condition will be enrolled among the list of reformers. We can now better say what [by the blessing of God] we hope to accomplish, than what we have done, as we have been but little more than two months organized. It occurred to some few of us that such an association might be formed with a tendency to excite an interest in the cause, and perhaps ultimately result in much good. A committee was therefore chosen to draft a constitution, also one to choose officers. We had several [caucus] meetings, and the first week in January organized our association and adopted our Constitution. We then had two members besides our officers, which are thirteen in number, viz; a President, two Vice Presidents, Secretary, Treasurer, and eight Directors. Since that time we have been gradually increasing, and now number three hundred and four.

S. G. BAGLEY, President

P. D. GREELY, *Secretary*

The Mechanic, Fall River, Mass., April 2, 1845

Sarah G. Bagley's Speech at the New England Workingmen's Association, May 27, 1845

REMARKS OF MISS BAGLEY.—Friends of the Association: the usages of society are such that those before whom we appear on this occasion may expect an apology, and yet we are not disposed to offer one directly. To those accustomed to pursue the same avocation as we are, and have seen so much oppression, and have heard so many cries of hopeless misery, it would seem extravagant to hear us say anything that has the least resemblance of an apology. After congratulating the society upon its prospects, Miss Bagley continued: For the last half a century, it has been deemed a violation of woman's sphere to appear before the public as a speaker; but when our rights are trampled upon and we appeal in vain to legislators, what shall we do but appeal to the people? Shall not our voice be heard, and our rights acknowledged here; shall it be said again to the daughters of New England, that they have no political rights and are not subject to legislative action? It is for the workingmen of this country to answer these questions—what shall we expect at your hands in future?

Will ye not be the recording angel who shall write on the walls of those who refuse to protect your daughters and sisters, as the angel did on the walls of Belshazer.[2]

Let your future action be peaceful, but firm and decided, lest the silent statue of the immortal Washington, (which has been permitted to keep sentinel at the doors of your Capitol) utter a severer reproof than the thundertones of his voice were accustomed to when the inspiration of other days fired his soul and beamed from his eyes.

We came here to-day as the Representatives of the Female Labor Reform Association of Lowell, and in their behalf we present you this simple but sincere token of their fidelity to the cause in which you are engaged. We give it as a token of their strong confidence in ultimate success. We give it as a motto, around which you may safely rally; and if any discordant spirits shall be found in your ranks, that they may be hushed by the warning implied in its motto—"*Union, for Power*"— and may no minor differences ever arise to check the great work so well commenced.

We do not expect to enter the field as soldiers in this great warfare; but we would like the heroines of the Revolution, be permitted to furnish the soldiers with a blanket or replenish their knapsacks from our pantries.

We claim no exalted place in your deliberations, nor do we expect to be instrumental of any great revolutions, yet we would not sit idly down and fold our hands and refuse to do the little that we may and ought to. We expect to see the revolution commenced, recorded among the revolutions of the past, and the name of a Channing,[3] Brisbane, Ryckman,[4] Ripley, Owen,[5] Walsh, and a host of others, recorded with that of Franklin, Jefferson and

Washington, on the pages of History. We do not expect this banner to be borne away by the enemy as a trophy of our defeat, but although the conflict may be long, our preseverance will overcome all obstacles that might seem to stand in our way, and a victory worthy a severe contest be ours. If Oberlin[6] with a few of the peasantry of his country, could cut his way through one of the mountains of Switzerland, shall we abandon our enterprise with an army like the one before us, or like those of which these are only the representatives? No! let your course be onward, ever onward, and adhere here strictly to your motto, Union for Power. Learn to bless humanity and you shall bequeath a lasting blessing to our race and a complete victory crown your efforts. APPLAUSE.

Voice of Industry, June 5, 1845

Report of the Lowell Female Labor Reform Association to the New England Workingmen's Association

The following report was read to the meeting by Miss Bagley of Lowell:

REPORT OF FEMALE LABOR REFORM

Lowell, May 25, 1845

Since the last meeting of the Workingmen's Convention at Lowell, Mass., our numbers have been daily increasing, our meetings generally well attended, and the real zeal of the friends of equal rights and justice has kindled anew. Our number of members is between four and five hundred, but this we consider a small part of the work which has been accomplished. The humble efforts of a few females united in the holy cause of human rights and human equalities, could not be expected to move the world in a day. But God be praised! we have moved the minds of community to think and to speak on the subject. This is truly encouraging. For when we can arouse the minds of men and women to a sense of their own individual rights, and cause them to think for themselves, then will they begin to act for themselves! The true nobility of the land—the laboring part of the community, have too long been looked down upon with haughty scorn and cold contempt, by the more prospered few, as being unworthy a place on a level with them. We would not seek to bring them down, (God knows that all such are already low enough in the scale of moral excellence) but we would seek to elevate, to ennoble, to raise higher the standard of moral excellence and human attainments. "Excelsior" shall be our motto; and let the spirit of the word thrill every heart!

> "Act—act, in the living present,
> Heart within, and God o'erhead!"

S. G. BAGLEY, Pres't

H. J. STONE, Sec'y

Voice of Industry, June 12, 1845

Report of the Female Labor Reform Association in Lowell

Since our last meeting at Boston, our cause has advanced beyond the most sanguine expectations of its friends. Not that our numbers have been greatly increased, but a general interest has been manifested in behalf of the principles for which we contend. All whether directly interested or not, are beginning to enquire whether there is not some cause of complaint on our part. Not only are *friends* interested, but those who would hush our enquiries, and leave us to the mercies of our taskmasters,—are anxiously watching our movements and questioning our motives. The press too, takes every occasion to slander our efforts, and ridicule our operations.

These are *all* indications, that our labor has not been wholly in vain,—that our influence is felt and feared.

Our light has not gone out on the altar, nor our exertions abated, and by the blessing of Heaven, we mean to fight on till a complete victory crowns our efforts.

SARAH G. BAGLEY, Pres't.

H. J. STONE, Sec'y.

Voice of Industry, September 18, 1845

Report of the Lowell Female Labor Reform Association to the New England Workingmen's Association

The following Report from the Lowell Female Labor Reform Association, was here presented, and read by the Secretary; to which the meeting responded by a vote of acceptance.

REPORT OF THE FEMALE LABOR REFORM ASSOCIATION

Since our last Convention at Fall River, a new interest has been awakened among the toiling Females of this City. Many who were ignorant of our Association meetings, and the organization even, have come out fearlessly and joined our ranks. Others not a few, have given the warm, friendly pressure of the hand with a hearty "God bless you in your noble enterprise" to cheer us on in the great struggle for *right* against *might*. Our *cause* is a righteous one— one which every *philanthropist must,* and will take a deep interest in. It is a reform which will effect not only the Laborer but the whole entire community. Its great and leading object is to give the laborer more time to attend to his or her mental, moral and physical wants—to cultivate and bring out the hidden treasures of the inner being—to subdue the low, the animal nature, and elevate, ennoble and perfect the good, the true and the God-like which dwells in all the children of the common Parent.—With this *high* and *holy aim* ever in view, we *shall go on!* Doing whatever our hands *find* to do with all our might. Humble though it may be, yet shall all our influence and exertion be given to the raising up and strengthening the bowed down and to the enlightening and instructing the un- willingly ignorant, kept thus by circumstances over which they as yet have no control. To all who are engaged in this great and hu- mane cause with us, whether Associated, or working individually, in the boundless field, we would say, be firm, be vigilant, be true to the sympathies and emotions of pity which a God of Infinite Love has implanted in every human soul, and cease not your exer- tions, until complete success shall have crowned your every laudable effort.

SARAH G. BAGLEY, *Pres.*

H. J. STONE, *Sec.*
Lowell, Oct. 30, 1845

Voice of Industry, November 7, 1845

Report of the Lowell Female Labor Reform Association

Since our last meeting in Lowell, particularly within the last six weeks; a deeper and more thrilling interest has been manifested in our "Association," than at any time heretofore. We have had some talk about a "Declaration of Independence," providing all the mea- sures now under consideration should fail; and many have expressed a willingness, provided the minds of the operatives shall be pre- pared; "to take the work into their own hands, and declare their Independence, on the *fourth of July* next." Another pleasing symp- tom in our Association, is a great increase of liberal feeling. They do not regard this measure, (the reduction of the hours of labor) as an end, but only as one step, towards the great end to be attained. They deeply feel, that their work will never be accomplished, until slavery and oppression, mental, physical and religious, shall have been done away, and Christianity in its original simplicity, and pristine beauty, shall be re-established and practiced among men. "ONWARD" is their watchword, and "WE'LL TRY AGAIN;" their motto; and they are resolved to "try again" and again, and yet again, until the work shall be accomplished or their work on earth shall cease.

HANNAH TARLTON, *Vice Pres't.*

M. EMERSON, *Sec. pro. tem.*

Voice of Industry, January 23, 1846

Social Gathering

The Ladies belonging to the "Female Labor Reform Association" of this city are making preparations for a grand and useful "Gathering," on the eve of the 13th of next month, (St. Valentines eve) at the City Hall, which bids fair to excel, in rational pleasure, any thing of the kind, recently enjoyed by our citizens. Eminent and distinguished speakers, will be in attendance from abroad to interest and instruct—a band of music, together with singing, will be there to gratify the lovers of harmony, and a rich treat of fruits and other *eatables,* will not be wanting; making in all a "feast of fat things," for the sum of 25 cts. only; the proceeds of which, will be appropriated to the cause of *Labor Reform.* Friends from Boston, Lynn, Woburn, Fitchburg, Worcester, Waltham, Andover, Newton and Manchester N.H., and all the adjoining towns, together with all others, are invited to be with us, and aid the cause.

Voice of Industry, January 30, 1846

The "Social Gathering" of the Lowell Female Labor Reform Association

Last Friday evening was a glorious time for the operatives and workingmen of Lowell. At an early hour the City Hall was splendidly illuminated and vibrated with the sweet strains from the "Lowell Brass Band," who generously volunteered their services for the occasion. Long before the hour arrived for the services to commence, the Hall was thronged with gladsome hearts and joyous countenances. The Tables looked beautiful, ladened with fruits of the earth and the ingenious preparations of ladies' domestic arts. Indeed we came nigh fancying ourself in a "better land" where sin and oppression were unknown, everything looked so smiling and happy.

Mr. George W. Hatch, President of the evening, made some very appropriate remarks on taking the chair, and then introduced Mr. Potter of Manchester, N.H., editor of the "Democrat," who spoke in a very spirited and energetic manner upon the present system of factory labor and the prospect of procuring the "ten hour system" in New Hampshire.

Mr. White of Watertown, made a pertinent speech in his usual able manner. He was glad New Hampshire was engaged in factory reform, and wished also to see her divorced from southern slavery. He closed by an eloquent appeal to the operatives of Lowell to press forward in the great reform in which they were engaged.

Mr. Campbell of Boston spoke at some length with his usual zeal.

Mr. Healback of Boston, also made an interesting address; but the joyous mirth of the happy throng prevented us from getting a distinct idea of his remarks.

After the refreshments were served out, Mr. Cluer[7] indulged in a few humorous remarks which as usual brought a response from the people.

The intervals between speaking were occupied by the Band, the songs of Mr. French and two young pupils of Lowell, and the Messrs. Reads of Reading, two honest workingmen, who serve the labor reform movement, by their sweet voices as well as their able heads and hands.

The evening passed away with but little to mar the pleasures of the occasion. The "Valentine Offering" published for the occasion,[8] was circulated, and added much to the usefulness of the gathering. The "Valentine" Post Office must be productive of much good if the sentiments there issued, were akin to the following addressed to the "Voice of Industry" by some unknown factory girl, and we sincerely hope it may fall into the hands of every apologizer of the long hour and short life system in christendom.

> "Ah! leave my harp and me alone,
>   My grief thou may'st not share,
> Responsive to its plaintive tone
>   Will flow refreshing tears.
>
> Far from the factory's deaf'ning sound,
>   From all its noise and strife,

> Would that my years might run their rounds
>> In sweet retired life.

> But, if I still must wend my way,
>> Uncheered by hope's sweet song,
> God grant, that, in the mills, a day
>> May be but *"Ten Hours'" long.*

Lowell, Feb. 14, 1846,"

Much credit is due the Ladies' "Labor Reform Association" for the good order and taste which was manifest throughout the entire arrangement; and the general satisfaction manifested by all. Our space will not admit of further comments at this time.

Voice of Industry, February 20, 1846

A Card

The Ladies of the Female Labor Reform Association would take this opportunity to return their most sincere and unfeigned gratitude and thanks, to those gentlemen who so kindly and untiringly lent their aid in getting up the Social Gathering. Also, to Mr. Emery of the Merrimack House for his kind wishes and gentlemanly liberality.

> May they be blest in basket and in store,
>> H. J. STONE,
>>> in behalf of the Association.

Voice of Industry, February 27, 1846

A Card

The members of the Female Labor Reform Association most cheerfully avail themselves of this opportunity to acknowledge their indebtedness and gratitude to those ladies who served in the capacity of officers during the past year, with fidelity and faithfulness to the cause of labor reform. They would assure those true hearted sisters that although some of them are far away from our busy city—meeting with them no more in their social, happy circles, that they are not forgotten—that their labors of love, when the Association was in its infancy, struggling against every kind of opposition and the strong tide of popular prejudice, are still bright on memory's clear page. Will they not be with them still in spirit, and make glad their hearts, now and then, by words of encouragement and of hope! Forget not, where'er fortune may cast your lines, to *plead* for oppressed, down-trodden humanity! May kind Providence shield from all evil, and give you all that peace and serenity which ever flows from purity of motive and rectitude of conduct.

H. J. STONE, *Sec'y*

Voice of Industry, March 20, 1846

Female Efforts

The spirited ladies of the Female Labor Reform Association, of this city, have purchased the Press and Type belonging to the "Voice of Industry" office, and have made the first payment. Their labors for the cause of the oppressed, demand the sympathy and encouragement of all true friends in the elevation of mankind; and any person able to render pecuniary assistance to the cause of substantial reform, cannot find a more worthy object.

Voice of Industry, March 6, 1846

Report of the Lowell Female Labor Reform Association to the New England Workingmen's Association

EVENING SESSION SECOND DAY.

President in the Chair.

Miss Stone presented the following report of the Lowell Female Labor Reform Association, was read and adopted by an enthusiastic response of hundreds who crowded the Hall.

REPORT OF THE LOWELL FEMALE LABOR REFORM ASSOCIATION

It will not be expected by this Convention, that in the three short months, any great or important changes should have occurred in our humble Association. All truly noble and beneficial reforms have ever moved with slow, but sure and permanent steps. Plans have been well matured, in sober, candid, consciencious minds, before being reduced to practice. The spirit of true benevolence and human sympathy, has, and ever must, give to reform, its impetus and success! Benevolence, having for its sole object, the exaltation, perfection and happiness of the progressive race of man. Sympathy, one of the holiest and most blessed emotions, with which Nature's God has endowed all his creatures—going out into every part of creation—encircling in its universal arms, every suffering, sorrowing and oppressed child of humanity, and longing, O, how ardently, to relieve, comfort, elevate and bless all who bear the impress of a hand Divine! But these two handmaids of Reform, have had other and not less efficient spirits to co-operate with them in every good cause.

Self-Sacrifice, patience, perseverance, union, integrity, firmness, unyielding faith in the good to be attained, and a host of others, which might be named, have been the companions and never failing friends of each and every true Reformer in the world! *Let us learn from the past,* and be guided by *principle within,* which all the honors, bribes or jeers of a world, cannot lead or turn aside from the path where lives duty to ourselves, to humanity, to God!

S. G. BAGLEY, President.

H. J. STONE, Rec. Secretary.

Voice of Industry, October 2, 1846

To the Members of the L.F.L.R.A.

The time of annual meeting for choosing officers for the coming year, is near at hand. It has been thought advisable by the Board of Directors, that a new Preamble and Constitution should be prepared, which will be presented to the meeting for discussion and adoption next Tuesday evening, Dec. 15th when it is hoped every member will be present; also every female who is desirous of aiding a cause which has for its object the *improvement* both mental, moral and physical, of the operative of Lowell.

H. J. STONE

Sec'y
Lowell, Dec. 10th, 1846.

Voice of Industry, December 11, 1846

Letter to the Operatives of Manchester from the Secretary of the Lowell Female Labor Reform Association

Sisters in the cause of human improvement and human rights—to your sympathies—to your sense of duty and justice, would we at this time appeal. You have now manifested a good degree of zeal and interest in the work of "Labor Reform," and we hope and trust that you will continue to investigate the subject and take such efficient measures as shall assist in accomplishing the great object of this our noble and philanthropic enterprise, viz:—The elevation and promotion of the real producers of our country to that station and standing in society which they were by a beneficent God designed to occupy! Too long have the virtuous poor been looked down upon as a lower race of beings, while vice and crime of the darkest hue, rolled in luxury and splendor through our streets—too long have our females been treated like as many senseless automatons in the kitchens of the purse-proud aristocrats of our Republic—and as a *part* of the machinery in our manufacturing towns and districts throughout the Union. It is now for the working men and working women of the United States to say whether this state of society which debases the masses to a level with the serfs of old countries shall continue; or whether a new and brighter era shall dawn on the republican shores, giving to all equal rights and true liberty. To effect this glorious work of reform we believe a complete *union* among the worthy toilers and spinners of our own nation so as to have a concert of action, is all that is requisite. By organizing associations and keeping up a correspondence throughout the country, and arousing the public mind to a just sense of the claims of humanity, we hope to roll on the great tide of reformation until from every fertile vale and towering hill the response shall be echoed and re-echoed:—*Freedom—freedom for all!*

Operatives of Manchester, you have begun well, may God grant that you persevere united, faithfully, triumphantly! You have now an Association organized and consisting of a goodly number already, and hundreds more are ready to join your ranks, I doubt not, if you prove active and vigilant,—true to yourselves and faithful to the noble enterprise in which you are now engaged. We shall be extremely happy to correspond with you and meet with you in your meetings as often as possible. Let us seek to encourage and strengthen each other in every good word and work.

If discouragements arise as they surely will, will you yield to despair and falter? God forbid! Rather take the simple motto of your sister Association of Lowell, and let its spirit fire your every heart with NEW ZEAL and unwavering hope—*"We'll try again!"* Let us aim in all that we do, to increase the intelligence and knowledge of all—to raise higher the standard of moral and intellectual worth among us—then shall we become stronger and stronger, throwing around us that protecting power which is, and ever will be invincible, the power of knowledge!

Let your regular meetings be fully attended. Do not leave all the duties resting on the association, to be performed by a few who are spirited and zealous enough to be at their posts whether tempests frown or sunshine gilds the horizon. No, we beseech you to "act well your parts," for on this your success depends.

We have now a paper owned and edited in and by our associations, devoted entirely to the Laborer's cause—the cause of humanity and human rights, which it is only necessary to say is emphatically the workmen and women's paper, in order to have every one who feels the least interest in the cause, subscribe for and support. Just forward one dollar to W. F. Young,[10] Editor, Lowell, Mass., and you will receive it one year free of postage. Communications, also, for the paper from any who shall feel disposed to write will be thankfully received. Shall we not hear from Manchester, often, of your success and perseverance. Let *Excelsior* be the motto, which shall serve us on to the conquest.

In a word, let us be active, firm and united in every good work, until righteousness shall be established throughout the length and breadth of Columbia's land.

Yours until death in the cause of Labor Reform.

Manchester Democrat, December 16, 1845

To the Female Labor Reform Association in Manchester

SISTER OPERATIVES:—As I am now in the "City of Spindles," out of employment, I have taken the liberty to occupy a few leisure moments in addressing the members of your Association; and pardon me for giving you a few brief hints of my own experience as a Factory Operative, before proceeding to make remarks upon the glorious cause in which you are so arduously engaged. It would be useless to attempt to portray the hardships and privations which are daily endured, for all that have toiled within the factory walls, must be well acquainted with the present system of labor, which can be properly termed slavery.

I am a peasant's daughter, and my lot has been cast in the society of the humble labourer. I was drawn from the home of my childhood at an early age, and necessity obliged me to seek employment in the Factory. Different objects, from what many possessed, prompted me to toil. It was to quench that ardent thirst for knowledge, which I have always possessed. Disappointment and misfortune have blasted my hopes, and, when taking a retrospective view of the past, I sigh for the return of those halcyon days, which I have enjoyed.— But I will not repine at fortune or circumstances, or suffer myself to despair; but my motto shall be, "Hope on, Hope ever!"

I will now give you a sketch of the wrong impressions I had received from others, in regard to the state of society in our manufacturing establishments. I found there was much injustice done to the character of the operatives; that much prejudice existed, and that their condition was considered degrading. I did not wonder at this so much, for experience and observation, too plainly told me of the evils that existed; and that the long and tedious hours of labor, fatigued both body and mind, and debased them from the blessed privilege of intellectual culture. A few evenings since, I was conversing with a young lady, who was an operative, and takes an active part in reform movements. With tears, she spoke of her toilsome condition, and limited means of improvement, and of the oppression and wrong, that had so long existed in the system of factory labor. She never spends her evenings like many others, in the reading of fictitious works, or in attending parties of pleasure; for said she, "I feel that our moments are too short, and time too precious, to be misimproved." When her day's work is completed, you find her alone, deeply employed in reading history, or the biography of some distinguished individual, or penning down some useful ideas, which she has received from her books, and in this way, she daily strives to improve her own mind, and the mind of others. Her example is worthy of imitation, and many such acquaintances have I formed; friends whom I love and esteem; and who are possessed of morals and intellectual minds, far superior to many of our aristocratic Misses, who throng our cities and villages; who spurn the factory girl's society, and think it derogatory and contaminating to associate with the individual who works for a living. I pity a character of this grade, and thank heaven that I am enabled to resist a spirit which strives to destroy unity, and harmony, among brethren.

A few words in conclusion and I close. I have heard with the deepest interest, of your flourishing Association of which you are members, and it rejoices my heart to see so many of you contending for your rights, and making efforts to elevate the condition of your fellow brethren, and raising them from their oppressed and degraded condition, and seeing rights restored which God and Nature designed them to enjoy. Do you possess the principles of Christianity? Then do not remain silent; but seek to ameliorate the condition of every fellow being. Engage laboriously and earnestly in the work, until you see your desires accomplished. Let the proud aristocrat who has tyrannized over your rights with oppressive severity, see that there is ambition and enterprise among the "spindles," and show a determination to have your plans fully executed,—use prudence and discretion in all your ways; act independently and no longer be a slave to petty tyrants, who, if they have an opportunity will encroach upon your privileges.

Some say that "Capital will take good care of labor," but don't believe it; don't trust them. Is it not plain, that they are trying to deceive the public, by telling them that your task is easy and pleasant, and that there is no need of reform? Too many are destitute of feeling and sympathy, and it is a great pity, that they were not obliged to toil one year, and then they would be glad to see the "Ten Hour Petition" brought before the Legislature. This is plain, but true language.

Probably you meet with many faithless and indifferent ones. If you have a spark of philanthropy burning within your bosom, show them the error of their ways; make them understand it; tell them that it is through the influence of the laboring community that these things are to be accomplished; engrave it upon their hearts; impress it upon their minds in a manner which can never be effaced.

Read and patronize the "Voice," and circulate the "Ten Hour Petition" among all classes, and may God strengthen you in your efforts; may you continue on in courage, and perseverance, until oppression and servitude may be entirely exterminated from our land, and thus, do honor to yourselves, and good to your country.

A LOWELL FACTORY GIRL

Voice of Industry, April 17, 1846

Extracts

Extracts of a letter received by a member of the Female Labor Reform Association in Manchester:

"I am highly pleased to hear from your interesting Association. I rather hear of a 'few in number manifesting intense interest,' than a great number manifesting little or no interest. I trust your number will increase in the spirit of Reform."

"To-day a friend from Manchester said to me, 'Labor Reform is not popular; you don't see any great folks talking about Labor Reform.' I say 'tis popular according to the definition. First pertaining to the common people, suitable to the common people, familiar, plain, 'easy to be comprehended.' So I convinced him it was indeed popular."

You will ask who was this man? I will describe him.

A rich man, who had 3 dollars a day, and 'roast beef,' to give away; drinks his brandy every day, and his bills, the *Laborer* has to pay. These kind of people will oppose, you can plainly see.

I long to see Factory Girls elevated, and still more, to see them have time. The ten hour system would be a happy thing to the majority of the operatives.

I suppose you do, most, if not all your writing on the Sabbath. I think you do, from the fact of seeing, one Sabbath evening, 40 girls in a short time, come to drop their letters into the Post Office. This was in the city of Lowell. Is it not so in Manchester?

Some people make remarks about the ignorance among Factory Girls. I wish they would consider that they have no time to read, write or think.

Go on with your good work, without fear from innovation, or fear from those whom you must expect will oppose all measures tending to get the ten hour system.

I like the Voice of Industry. Do not most of the operatives encourage this better than they did their Magazine?

Is there any place where I shall not have to work but ten hours? if there is, I shall come to the Factory and be numbered among that class, whose name, says Dickens, "is legion."

I heartily bid you farewell, and may the blessings of God rest abundantly with you.

Yours in the cause,

MARY ANN

Concord, May 9th, 1846

Voice of Industry, May 22, 1846

Report of the Female Labor Reform Association at Manchester, to the New England Workingmen's Association

Miss Eastman presented the following report from the Manchester Female Labor Reform Association, which was accepted for publication.

The female members of the Labor Reform Association, are happy to meet again their friends in a Workingman's Convention, and present to them our Report.

We do this with increased confidence in the truth and importance of our views, and with a strong hope of success in bringing about the Ten Hour system; we present this, too, with a conviction that our efforts have not been in vain.

We are happy to say our cause is steadily advancing, and increasing in power, if not so much in numbers.

Since the last Report the Male and Female Associations have met together, instead of separately as heretofore. We find this the best way as we can devise plans together, to better advantage, seeing men can do nothing without us, and we cannot do much without them.

We have met every Monday evening, and feel that we do something every evening to promote the great object of our Association. We have had some spirited discussions upon the importance of having more of the "Voice" devoted directly to the subject of a reduction in the hours of labor, and the best way to bring this needful plan about.

Original communications have been furnished most every evening, read and sent to Editors favoring our cause. There has been some additional members. The present number is three hundred. We have frequent cause of regret that so many of our sisterhood are afraid of "The old man," (as the first overseer is called,) and men dare not move in our cause, from fear of being "discharged."

Since our last report, we have sent into the Legislature, a huge petition; the result you have known; but we are not to be discouraged by one trial. We hope the next Legislature will be made of such men as shall look to our wants, more than to serve the monopolist and abuse our petitions.

We regret, bitterly that there are some acting as Editors, who undertake to make an inconsistancy in our advocating the Ten Hour system. We think such are afraid of loosing "Loaves and Fishes," furnished them by their masters. We say to such beings, for the sake of thousands of unfortunate females, for God's sake and the sake of your own souls, be "Come-outers" of such evil doings, and be saved.

To Editors who have advocated our cause, we feel an inexpressible degree of gratitude, and hope for more of your help in gaining our desired object.

In conclusion, of my more than a report as was not intended when I began, it best be said we are grateful to Miss M. Eastman, for her faithful services are Secretary. She now resigns her office to one who makes out this report, and hopes to follow the example of her predecessor in the discharging of her duty.

May our cause be upheld and exalted; may it pervade the whole land—be as unrestrained and defusive as the winds of Heaven, with the blessings of the Lord Almighty upon us, in all our efforts to elevate the human family.

SARAH RUMRILL, President

M. EASTMAN, Secretary
Voice of Industry, October 2, 1846

Extract

The following is an extract from a letter to the Female Labor Reform Association of Manchester.

DEAR FRIENDS OF REFORM: I promised to write to you, and let you know of my enjoyment away from the "city of spindles." I reached "sweet home" in safety, and was welcomed with joy, as many of you no doubt have experienced.

Here I shall remain a few weeks, in the retirement of a country residence, to enjoy a short season of freedom; and amid this pleasant repast I do not forget you. Forget! no, never shall I forget the band with whom so many evenings have been pleasantly and profitably spent. We have pressed through storms and difficulties to be present at our meetings, helping along the glorious cause, which will in time unloose the chains of oppression, which are binding so many of the human family in servitude to a certain class who think their hands are too good to work. They seem to think their brother man is too mean to associate with if he is "only a laborer." Friends, think not while surrounded by the green fields, feasting my mind with their beauties, that I do not cast a sympathising thought to the many shut up in the mills, constantly toiling, without time to look abroad upon the face of nature, and "view the glorious handworks of their Creator." Often I wander to the banks of our river, and watch its course as it wends its way to meet the beautiful Merrimack, listening to merry songs of birds, sending forth their joyful notes. Too soon I am awakened from this pleasing revery, and led to think of the evils growing up in the present state of society, which must undermine all glorious scenes with "her thousand votaries of art."

Let me say to you, press on, in the work of Reform, till the hearts of the world are turned "from mammon to the God of justice;" and "may the God of heaven look down and approve while angels smile," is the wish of thy absent sister in the good cause.

J.R.

Voice of Industry, October 9, 1846

Report of the Manchester Female Labor Reform Association to the New England Workingmen's Association

EVENING SESSION. Miss M. Eastman, a delegate from the "Manchester Female Labor Reform Association," presented the subjoined Report, which was received with applause and ordered to be recorded with the transactions of the convention.

FOURTH REPORT
OF THE FEMALE LABOR REFORM ASSOCIATION
IN MANCHESTER

It is with pleasure we present to this convention our 4th report since its organization. The past ones with this give its true state and prosperity to the present time.

In the brief period of 3 months not much can be expected from our young Association. There has been but few meetings since the last Report. A few volunteers added to serve the constitution; what has come have given good testimony of their ability and interest in our work of Reform, which is greatly needed both for our Physical and Mental benefit. In carrying on our work we labor under great disadvantages and obstacles. One of the greatest is a fear of the employer and their combined power, in case of a discharge from work. We wish with all our hearts we might be taught how to remove or overcome these things, and we believe we should have hundreds where we have now tens.

At our last meeting, which was the annual meeting for the choice of officers, a goodly number were present. An entire new board of directors were chosen consisting of eight, and other officers according to our constitution.

We have about three hundred members.—We have had some opposition to contend with, something of the kind unparalleled in the annals of history. We allude to the denial of the City Hall to citizen laborers to hold a meeting! The city government—a fine set of men calling themselves Whigs. Does this look like "equal rights and equal privileges to all men?" This Anti-Republican, Anti-Christian act is chronicled on earth and in heaven against the first city government in our own granite state.

The Premium System party has attracted some notice, but we have no fears from such a thing, as its object is understood. "A good name is rather to be chosen than great riches." The former is wanting, the latter obtained; and parties got with money given to 1st and 2nd hands to drive up us factory girls, in making a bad matter worse. Too much like "massa gives de Drivers a stint for us, and when this is done massa give us all a jubilee."

As an expression of our feelings we offer the following Resolutions.

Resolved, That we, the operatives who are members of this Association, do dread the sad effects of the Premium System upon the minds and health of our fellow operatives. It has our utter abhorrence; viewing the Premium System party with indignation, deeply regretting the participation of so many who must have been entirely thoughtless what they were encouraging by partaking of an entertainment bought with the sacrifice of health of hundreds of our associates in factory life.

Resolved, That we will not tolerate these things; if we do, we shall soon find ourselves working all the year round under the Premium System, and we will not suffer these things to be without our testimony against them.

Resolved, That in this age of improvement in the arts, especially in Cotton Factories, those great men whose pretended philanthropy denies us, the producers of their wealth, equal rights, giving us no time for eating and mental improvement, fitting man for anything rather than what God designed he should be. We feel sensible of the ignorance and vice accumulating under the present system of labor, therefore we should be vigilant, united and actively employed in making efforts to elevate ourselves.

Resolved, That we will attend to the interest of our Newspaper, which is the great interest of our Association, and our cause in general; for without this or some other organ, we can do little or nothing. This if rightly managed will promote widely our cause.— Therefore, 'tis our greatest duty to make efforts in behalf of our "Voice of Industry."

Resolved, That we need the aid of all Editors, and earnestly hope and expect help from such as feel a disposition to favor the many instead of the "favored few." We most respectfully solicit the aid with a hope that none of the editorial corps will be lacking in gallantry, patriotism, philanthropy, and christianity towards us in the attainment of a plan to elevate labor.

E. KIDDER, *President*

M. EASTMAN, *Sec. pro tem.*

Voice of Industry, February 12, 1847

Labor Reform Pic-nic

"The Ladies Labor Reform Association" of Dover, N.H. were to hold a Social PIC-NIC on last evening. Doubt less they had a pleasant and profitable time—they full deserve all they enjoyed and much more, which we hope they will enjoy after the New Hampshire Legislature reduces the Hours of Labor, in June next.

Voice of Industry, April 9, 1847

Resolutions Passed by Dover Female Labor Reform Association

The following Resolutions were passed by the Dover Female L. R. Association, and accepted by the League:

Resolved, That we, the members of the Female L. R. A., tender thanks to John Turner for his liberality and interest manifested by sending a Delegate from Boston to our Convention, and inasmuch as our ability will allow, assure him his advice shall be followed to protect our rights and advance the interest of our fellow operatives; and may the body of working men throughout the United States concentrate their forces to bring about a more desirable state of things among us Factory Girls, having the spirit of Democracy extended to us in place of Cottonocracy and Aristocracy.

Resolved, That we hail with joy the notice extended to our Petition in the Legislature, with a hope that Massachusetts may follow the example of her sister State, for the benefit of our sisterhood in its large manufacturing cities; and may the spirit of Democracy still shine upon us, giving us freedom from the insolence of Overseers and Agents, protecting us from being perfect drudges to Cottonocracy, and finally bring about the Ten Hour System.

Resolved, That we tender thanks to those persons who came from a distance to attend this League meeting, the object of which we feel an interest, and regret that the Town Hall should not be filled with town's people, and more so the forgetfulness on the part of the man who let the Hall to inform the officers of the gentlemen's Association the fact of its engagement to hold a Court, and fear 'twas too true that our friends came and being told that there was "no meeting" went away.

Voice of Industry, July 30, 1847

Letter from a Member of the Manchester Female Labor Reform Association

The following Communication was read at the meeting of the Labor Reform League[11] in Dover, July 14, and accepted by the meeting:

This is the 4th Convention of the N. E. Workingmen which it has been my pleasure to attend. I am a member of the Manchester Female Labor Reform Association, but delegated and favored with means to come here by the generosity of John Turner, of South Boston, who says "nothing would give him so much pleasure as to attend your League meeting, but by an engagement made previous to the appointment of the League, cannot be present, but will send you as a delegate on my own responsibility," and goes on to say we Factory Girls must be vigilant, we must act for ourselves and push these matters along. No Reform, and in particular this, can progress without your co-operation. Remember, you are entitled to "Equal Rights and Equal privileges" with those whom you give fat Dividends. I have been much pleased with those articles in the Voice from Eloisa, Juliana and others. It has been a query with me sometimes whether there were not some favored slaves among your number who have written in favor of their masters more than for their fellow operatives, being careless of their liberty and happiness. I am told there are men who have been thus guilty, but I have a better opinion of your sex than to believe you would be bought with dollars and cents.

Men and women should act independently in order to gain their liberty. Come out and expose the wrongs of those Cotton Lords, some of whom seem to possess more of the cotton spirit than that of Philanthropists.—Don't fear the "Black List,"[12] for no man in this nation has a right to say "you shall work for me." The time is not far distant when you will have more time to read, reflect, and learn who extended the helping hand to ameliorate your condition. I have of late learned facts from an operative who has had an experience of years within a factory prison, and it is my opinion that females are the greatest sufferers. In little time mind and health are prostrated. This must not be suffered to be so; there must and will be a remedy for this evil. These industrious factory girls are entitled to respect and our protection; they will have the protection of every genuine Republican and Christian. The operative is far more to be appreciated than those gay butterflies who fly through our Boston streets in pursuit of some vanity to adorn their person, or gain some knowledge of Paris Fashions, and as like as not, they are supported by the profits from your mill labor.

I look for a time to see the working men doing more for themselves, finding out the true cause of the poverty among producers and immense wealth among the consumers.—Be careful not to get too many subjects mixed up with the great object which must be kept in view. The true condition of matters and things among the working class is unjust and unnatural; but it may be remedied if they will not sleep under the system of labor existing at the present time, and which will be growing worse if we are silent on this subject. Get knowledge, disseminate it, 'tis of paramount importance, 'tis the sovereign remedy, with other things, for the oppression at the North as well as at the South. I want to see more of Democracy, and less of Cottonocracy and Partyocracy.

Give my respects to the Ladies of the Labor Reform Association in Dover, assuring them they have my sympathy and hearty cooperation in their undertaking, hoping at some future time to meet them in a Convention being truly for the rights of labor.

Voice of Industry, July 30, 1847

The Factory Tracts

In a letter to the Lowell Female Labor Reform Association, published in the *Voice of Industry* of November 21, 1845, George Henry Evans, editor of the *Working Man's Advocate* and *Young America,* and leader of the National Reformers, a movement which sought to abolish capitalism and wage slavery and achieve a new social system through land reform, wrote: "I have no doubt that the National Reformers of New York will aid in the circulation of your 'Factory Tracts.'" The reference is to one of the most important activities of the Lowell Female Labor Reform Association—the publication of a series of "Factory Tracts," which were "to give a true exposition of the Factory system and its effects upon the health and happiness of the operatives." Only the first number has been preserved, and this is included below in its entirety, along with an extract from the second number. □

Factory Tracts

It is pretty generally known that the Female Labor Reform Association, of this City, are publishing a series of Tracts, the object of which is, to give a true exposition of the Factory system and its effects upon the health and happiness of the operatives. The articles are nearly all written by those who are, or have been employed in the Mills, and reflect much credit upon the authors. The second number, will be ready for distribution and sale in a few days.¹³ Let our friends in various sections of the country, use their efforts to give them circulation.—Orders addressed to the Female Labor Reform Association, will meet with immediate attention.

Voice of Industry, November 7, 1845

Factory Tracts No. 1:
Factory Life As It Is

INTRODUCTION

Philanthropists of the nineteenth century!—shall not the operatives of our country be permitted to speak for themselves? Shall they be compelled to listen in silence to those who speak for gain, and are the mere echo of the will of the corporations? Shall tyranny and cruel oppression be allowed to rivet the chains of physical and mental slavery on the millions of our country who are the real producers of all its improvements and wealth, and they fear to speak out in noble self-defence? Shall they fear to appeal to the sympathies of the people, or the justice of this far-famed republican nation? God forbid!

Much has been written and spoken in woman's behalf, especially in America; and yet a large class of females are, and have been, destined to a state of servitude as degrading as unceasing toil can make it. I refer to the female operatives of New England—the free states of our union—the boasted land of equal rights for all—the states where no colored slave can breathe the balmy air, and exist as such;—but yet there are those, a host of them, too, who are in fact nothing more nor less than slaves in every sense of the word! Slaves to a system of labor which requires them to toil from five until seven o'clock, with one hour only to attend to the wants of nature, allowed—slaves to the will and requirements of the "powers that be," however they may infringe on the rights or conflict with the feelings of the operatives—slaves to ignorance—and how can it be otherwise? What time has the operative to bestow on moral, religious or intellectual culture? How can our country look for aught but ignorance and vice, under the existing state of things? When the whole system is exhausted by unremitting labor during twelve and thirteen hours per day, can any reasonable being expect that the mind will retain its vigor and energy? Impossible! Common sense will teach every one the utter impossibility of improving the mind under these circumstances, however great the desire may be for knowledge.

Again, we hear much on the subject of benevolence among the wealthy and, so called, *christian part* of community. Have we not cause to question the sincerity of those who, while they *talk* benevolence in the parlor, compel their help to labor for a mean, paltry pittance in the kitchen? And while they manifest great concern for the souls of the *heathen* in distant lands, care nothing for the bodies and intellects of those within their own precincts? Shall we esteem men honest in their pretensions to piety and benevolence, who compel their help to labor on the Sabbath day or lose their situation? Have they made their regulations hold up to the world a large amount of piety, and a great desire that those in their employ shall be religious—so much so that they have made a corporation law, that "no one shall be retained in their employ who is not a constant attendant on public worship." Will those who are obliged to hear the noise and confusion caused by some fifty or more men, with teams of oxen, and all the noise consequent on such occasions, together with splitting and blasting of rocks, to their great annoyance while *in* their places of worship—will these be deceived by such hypocritical pretensions of piety, and love to the moral interests of the community in which they live? What *is* and must be, the tendency of such examples on those who are familiar with such violations of the day called the christian Sabbath, but to throw off all restraint and make the Sabbath a pastime, or a day in which the weary operatives may attend to their own private business? Such examples *have already* produced such results, and the end is not yet.

As philanthropists and lovers of equal rights, we address our readers; and before we close this series of tracts, (which will consist of some three or four numbers,) we intend to give a fair exposition of the regulations of the "factory system," its operations and abuses, the *grand* results of protection given to industry, including the low price paid for board and wages—the long hours of labor, with its effects on the health of the operatives, and some other facts for the million, &c. &c.

AN OPERATIVE

The Evils of Factory Life

NUMBER ONE

Among the first which we shall notice, is the tendency it has, at the present time, to destroy all love of order and practice in domestic affairs. It is a common remark, that by the time a young lady has worked in a factory one year, she will lose all relish for the quiet, fireside comforts of life, and the neatness attendant upon order and precision. The truth is, time is wanting, and opportunity, in order to cultivate the mind and form good habits. All is hurry, bustle and confusion in the street, in the mill, and in the overflowing boarding house. If there chance to be an intelligent mind in that crowd which is striving to lay up treasures of knowledge, how unfavorably it is situated. Crowded into a small room which contains three beds and six females, all possessing the "without end" tongue of woman, what chance is there for *studying?* and much less for sober thinking and reflecting? Some lofty, original minds, we will allow, have surmounted all the obstacles of a factory life and come out, like gold, refined from all the dross of baneful society and pernicious examples, but they are cases of rare occurrence. But few have the moral courage and perseverance to travel on in the rugged paths of science and improvement amid all these and many other discouragements. After thirteen hours unremitting toil, day after day and week after week, how much energy and life would remain to nerve on the once vigorous mind in the path of wisdom? What ambition or pride would such females possess, to enable them to practice good order and neatness! They are confined so long in close, unhealthy rooms that it is a greater wonder that they possess any life or animation, more than the machines which they have watched so unceasingly!

Let us look forward into the future, and what does the picture present to our imagination! Methinks I behold the self same females occupying new and responsible stations in society. They are now wives and mothers! But oh! how deficient in everything pertaining to those holy, *sacred* names! Behold what disorder, confusion and disquietude reigns, where quiet, neatness and calm serenity should sanctify and render almost like heaven the home of domestic union and love! Instead of being qualified to rear a family—to instruct them in the great duties of life—to cultivate and unfold the intellect —to imbue the soul in the true and living principles of right and justice—to teach them the most important of all lessons, the art of being *useful* members in the world, ornaments in society and blessings to all around them,—*they*, themselves, have need to be instructed in the *very first principles* of living well and thinking right. Incarcerated within the walls of a factory, while as yet mere children—drilled there from five till seven o'clock, year after year— thrown into company with all sorts and descriptions of mind, dispositions and intellects, without counsellor or friend to advise—far away from a watchful mother's tender care, or father's kind instruction—surrounded on all sides with the vain ostentation of fashion, vanity and light frivolity—beset with temptations without, and the carnal propensities of nature within, what *must,* what *will* be the natural, rational result? What but ignorance, misery, and *premature decay* of both *body* and *intellect?* Our country will be but one great hospital, filled with worn out operatives and colored slaves! Those who marry even, become a curse instead of a helpmeet to their husbands, because of having broken the laws of God and their own physical natures, in these modern prisons (alias palaces), in the gardens of Eden! It has been remarked by some writer that the mother educates the man. Now if this be a truth, as we believe it is, to a very great extent, what, we would ask, are we to expect, the same system of labor prevailing, will be the mental and intellectual character of the future generations of New England? What but a race weak, sickly, imbecile, both mental and physical? A race fit only for corporation tools and timeserving slaves? Nobility of America!—producers of all the luxuries and comforts of life! will you not *wake up* on this subject? Will you sit supinely down and let the drones in society fasten the yoke of tyranny, which is already fitted to your necks so cunningly that you do not feel it but slightly,—will you, I say suffer them to rivet that yoke upon you, which has crushed and is crushing its millions in the old world to earth; yea, to starvation and death? Now is the time to answer this all-important question. Shall we not hear the response from every hill and vale, "EQUAL RIGHTS, or death to the corporations"? God grant it, is the fervent prayer of

JULIANNA

Lowell, October, 1845

Some of the Beauties of Our Factory System—
Otherwise, Lowell Slavery*

For the purpose of illustration, let us go with that light-hearted, joyous young girl who is about for the first time to leave the home of her childhood, that home around which clusters so many beautiful and holy associations, pleasant memories, and quiet joys; to leave, too, a mother's cheerful smile, a father's care and protection; and wend her way toward this far famed "city of spindles," this promised land of the imagination, in whose praise she has doubtless heard so much.

Let us trace her progress during her first year's residence, and see whether she indeed realizes those golden prospects which have been held out to her. Follow her now as she enters that large gloomy looking building—she is in search of employment, and has been told that she might here obtain an eligible situation. She is sadly wearied with her journey, and withal somewhat annoyed by the noise, confusion, and strange faces all around her. So, after a brief conversation with the overseer, she concludes to accept the first situation which offers; and reserving to herself a sufficient portion of time in which to obtain the necessary rest after her unwonted exertions, and the gratification of a stranger's curiosity regarding the place in which she is now to make her future home, she retires to her boarding house, to arrange matters as much to her mind as may be.

The intervening time passes rapidly away, and she soon finds herself once more within the confines of that close noisy apartment, and is forthwith installed in her new situation—first, however, premising that she has been sent to the Counting-room, and receives therefrom a Regulation paper, containing the rules by which she must be governed while in their employ; and lo! here is the beginning of mischief; for in addition to the tyrannous and oppressive rules which meet her astonished eyes, she finds herself compelled to remain for the space of twelve months in the very place she then occupies, however reasonable and just cause of complaint might be hers, or however strong the wish for dismission; thus, in fact, constituting herself a slave, a very slave to the caprices of him for whom she labors. Several incidents coming to the knowledge of the writer, might be somewhat interesting in this connection, as tending to show the prejudicial influence exerted upon the interests of the operative by this unjust requisition. The first is of a lady who has been engaged as an operative for a number of years, and recently entered a weaving room on the Massachusetts Corporation; the overseers having assured her previous to her entrance, that she should realize the sum of $2.25 per week, exclusive of board; which she finding it impossible to do, appealed to the Counting-room for a line enabling her to engage elsewhere but it was peremptorily refused.

The next is of a more general bearing, concerning quite a number of individuals employed on the Lawrence Corporation,[15] where the owners have recently erected and put in motion a new mill, at the same time stopping one of the old, in which said persons were employed. Now as they did not voluntarily leave their situations, but were discharged therefrom on account of suspension of operations by the company; they had an undoubted right to choose their own place of labor; and as the work in the new mill is vastly more laborious, and the wages less than can be obtained in many parts of the city, they signified their wish to go elsewhere, but are insolently told that they shall labor there or not at all; and will not be released until their year has expired, when if they can *possibly* find *no* further excuse for delay, they *may* deign to bestow upon them what is in common parlance termed, a "regular discharge;" thus enabling them to pass from one prison house to another. Concerning this precious document, it is only necessary to say, that it very precisely reminds one of that which the dealers in human flesh at the South are wont to give and receive as the transfer of one piece of property from one owner to another. Now, reader, what think you? is not this the height of the beautiful and are not we operatives an ungrateful set of creatures that we do not properly appreciate, and be highly thankful for such unparalleled generosity on the part of our employers?

But to return to our toiling Maiden,—the next beautiful feature which she discovers in this *glorious* system is, the long number of hours which she is obliged to spend in the above named close, unwholesome apartment. It is not enough, that like the poor peasant of Ireland, or the Russian serf who labors from sun to sun, but during one half of the year, she must still continue to toil on, long after Nature's lamp has ceased to lend its aid—nor will even this suffice to satisfy the grasping avarice of her employer; for she is also through the winter months required to rise, partake of her morning meal, and be at her station in the mill, while the sun is yet sleeping behind the eastern hills; thus working on an average, at least twelve hours and three fourths per day, exclusive of the time allotted for her hasty meals, which is in winter simply one half hour at noon,—in the spring is allowed the same at morn, and during the summer is added 15 minutes to the half hour at noon. Then too, when she is at last released from her wearisome day's toil, still may she not depart in peace. No! her footsteps must be dogged to see that they do not stray beyond the corporation limits, and she *must*, whether she will or no, be subjected to the manifold inconveniences of a large crowded boarding-house, where too, the price paid for her accommodation is so utterly insignificant, that it will not ensure to her the common comforts of life; she is obliged to sleep in a small comfortless, half ventilated apartment containing some half a dozen occupants each; but no matter, *she is an operative*—it is all well enough for her; there is no "abuse" about it; no, indeed; so think our employers,—but do we think so? time will show. Here, too, comes up a case which strikingly illustrates the petty tyranny of the employer. A little girl, some 12 or 13 years of age, the daughter of a poor widow, dependent on her daily toil for a livelihood, worked on one of the Corporations, boarding with her mother; who dying left her to the care of an aunt, residing but a few steps from the Corporation—but the poor little creature all unqualified as she was, to provide for her own wants, was *compelled* to leave her home and the motherly care bestowed upon her, and enter one of these same large crowded boarding-houses. We do but give the facts in this case and they need no comment for every one *must* see the utter heartlessness which prompted such conduct toward a mere child.

Reader will you pronounce this a mere fancy sketch, written for the sake of effect? It is not so. It is a real picture of "Factory life;" nor is it one half so bad as might truthfully and justly have been drawn. But it has been asked, and doubtless will be again, why, if these evils are so aggravating, have they been so long and so peacefully borne? Ah! and why have they? It is a question well worthy of our consideration, and we would call upon every operative in *our* city, aye, throughout the length and breadth of the land, to awake from the lethargy which has fallen upon them, and assert and maintain their rights. We call upon you for action—*united and immediate action*. But, says one, let us wait till we are stronger. In the language of one of old, we ask, when shall we be stronger? Will it be the next week, or the next year? Will it be when we are reduced to the service conditions of the poor operatives of England? for verily we shall be and that right soon, if matters be suffered to remain as they are. Says another, how shall we act? we are but one amongst a thousand, what shall we do that our influence may be felt in this vast multitude? We answer there is in this city an Association called the Female Labor Reform Association, having for its professed object, the amelioration of the condition of the operative. Enrolled upon its records are the names of five hundred members—come then, and add thereto five hundred or rather five thousand more, and in the strength of our united influence we will soon show these *drivelling* cotton lords, this mushroom aristocracy of New England, who so arrogantly aspire to lord it over God's heritage, that our rights cannot be trampled upon with impunity; that we will no longer submit to that arbitrary power which has for the last ten years been so abundantly exercised over us.

One word ere we close, to the hardy independent yeomanry and mechanics, among the Granite Hills of New Hampshire, the woody forests of Maine, the cloud capped mountains of Vermont, and the busy, bustling towns of the old Bay State—ye! who have daughters and sisters toiling in these sickly prison-houses which are scattered far and wide over each of these States, we appeal to you for aid in this matter. Do you ask how that aid can be administered? We answer through the Ballot Box. Yes! if you have one spark of sympathy for our condition, carry it there, and see to it that you send to preside in the Councils of each Commonwealth, men who have hearts as well as heads, souls as well as bodies; men who will watch zealously over the interests of the laborer in every department; who will protect him by the strong arm of the law from the encroachments of arbitrary power; who will see that he is not deprived of those rights and privileges which God and Nature have bestowed upon him—yes,

> From every rolling river,
> From mountain, vale and plain,
> We call on you to deliver
> Us, from the tyrant's chain:

And shall we call in vain? We trust not. More anon.

AMELIA[14]

*TO THE FEMALE LABOR REFORM ASSOCIATION.—The preceding article, with the accompanying note, written for the Lowell Offering, and rejected by the Editress, is at your disposal. If you deem it worthy a place in the Tracts you are about to publish you are at liberty to use it.

Yours,

AMELIA

MISS FARLEY:—Having been solicited to contribute to the pages of the Offering, the following article is respectfully submitted to your consideration and that of your readers generally if the views and opinions therein expressed are such that it be deemed advisable to give it entire without restriction or qualification whatever, you will please insert the same—if not, you are requested to return it immediately through the Office. Yours respectfully.

The Summons

> Ye children of New England!
> The summons is to you!
> Come from the worship and the field,
> With steadfast hearts and true.

Come, fling your banner to the breeze,
  For liberty and light;
Come, like the rolling of the seas—
  The tempest in its might.

Aye, with a voice of thunder come;
  And swear 'fore tryanny,
Thy vows are registered on high,
  To perish or be free.

Hear ye the groans from foreign lands,
  Ruled by despotic powers?
From Spain's bright shores, from Gallia's strand,
  And England's stately towers?

In costly, splendid luxury
  Each royal board is spread;
While thousands in their streets may die
  For lack of daily bread.

And turn to our own boasted clime,—
  What scenes before us lie?
Aye, want and woe and care and crime,
  Still greet the tearful eye.

'Tis mockery in the sight of God,
  To say that land is blest
Where millions bow beneath the rod
  Of tyranny oppressed.

For bread, where famished children cry,
  And none their want supplies—
Where toiling thousands live and die
  In ignorance and vice.

Then in the name of God come forth,
  To battle with the foe;
Nor stay ye till your hands have laid
  Each proud oppressor low.

Aye, come, and blessed shalt thou be,
  By millions yet unborn.
Whom thou hast saved from misery,
  From insult and from scorn.

Yea, be thou strong—there yet remains
  A promise sure to thee,
That God will break the oppressor's chains,
  And set the prisoner free.

> That righteousness and truth shall reign,
> Through all the peopled earth,
> And heaven repeat the exulting strain,
> Which hailed creations birth.

AMELIA

Factory Tracts No. 1, Boston Public Library, Rare Book Room

Extract from Factory Tracts No. 2

The second number of the "Factory Tracts" is out, and for sale by carriers and at many of the periodical stores. Will our friends in other sections of the country see that they are widely circulated. The following extracts from the present number are worthy of special notice.

The subject of factory labor and the regulations by which the operatives are governed, is a subject in which our country is ignorant. By our country I do not mean New Orleans and Texas alone, but will include Massachusetts. It is not unusual to hear a citizen of Boston, Salem, or Lynn, inquire about our regulations, and express their surprise at them.

I would not be understood as contending against system, or good regulations. I believe them to be for the good of all concerned— but when they conflict with our rights as rational beings, and we are regarded as living machines, and all the rules made subservient to the interest of the employer; then it would seem that we have a right to call them in question, and regard them as arbitrary, and call for a reform.

I refer particularly to the rule which compels all who work for the companies, to board in their houses. There has been some difference of opinion, or of words on this regulation. Some contend that it is no "abuse" of power to compel the Operatives to leave the quiet fireside of a friend and board with the mixed multitude congregated in a large boarding house. Others think that the time and labor only, are bought by the employers, and the Operative has no right to be dictated as it regards the duties he owes to himself or those of his friends, providing they do not interfere with the duty he owes to his or her employer.

We are told by those who contend for corporated rules, that the Operatives of Lowell, are the virtuous daughters of New England. If this be true, (and we believe it is with few exceptions,) is it necessary to shut them up at night, six in a room, 14 by 16 feet with all the trunks, and boxes necessary to their convenience; to keep them so? Are they not qualified to procure a place for themselves, that suits their own taste or convenience?—have they no judgement of their own that this interference is made? Is it not a violation of our principles of christianity, which says:—"as we would that others should do unto you, do ye even so unto them," and we think that every superintendent of Lowell would justify us in saying that they would think themselves grossly insulted if the directors of the companies should make and enforce such rules for them, as they make for others.

Such kind reader, are the accommodations for improvement and cultivation. Those who keep the boarding houses do all in their power in most cases to make the stay of the girls pleasant, and much credit is due to them. But the means are inadequate to meet the wants of the operatives, and too many are made to occupy the same sleeping and sitting apartment.

Another objection to this rule, is the impossibility of personal cleanliness and frequent bathing so necessary to health; it would be expressing a doubt of the good sense of our readers to contend for a sufficient amount of accommodation to allow every girl ample time and room to bathe once in each day.

We shall be justified by every physiologist in saying, that every operative who is compelled to room with five others, is thereby compelled to violate the physical laws of God, and so sure as these laws are immutable, so sure disease and premature decay must be the consequence.

There may be as many long stories told about the good health of the operatives, and factory labor being so conducive to health and intelligence as would reach from Georgia to Maine, and an intelligent community will not believe them when we tell them the girls are obliged to violate all the laws of health every day, and every night by sleeping, from six to sixteen in a room, and this is no exaggeration.

Philosophy has gained the ascendancy, and the physical laws are regarded as the laws of God, and a strict obedience to them is enforced, and those who would make the world believe that they can be suspended to suit the convenience and interest of the manufacturers, are either grossly stupid or dishonest. I leave the reader to judge in this case.

AN OPERATIVE

Voice of Industry, November 14, 1845

The Female Department of the *Voice of Industry*

The most widely read and influential labor paper of the 1840s was the *Voice of Industry*. It began publication on May 29, 1845, "by an association of workingmen," under the editorship of William F. Young. In November it was combined with two other labor papers and moved from Fitchburg, Massachusetts, to the mill city of Lowell. Here it was issued by a publishing committee of three, consisting of Young, Sarah G. Bagley, and Joel Hatch. The paper welcomed to its columns all factory operatives dissatisfied with the genteel utterances of the *Lowell Offering,* and when the *Offering* ceased publication the *Voice* urged the young women in Lowell and other factory towns to make its columns their medium of communication and to regard it as their paper.

In response to this invitation, a "Female Department" under the supervision of the Lowell Female Labor Reform Association began to occupy an important place in its pages. Directed by Sarah G. Bagley, the "Female Department" featured articles and poetry on a wide variety of subjects of interest to women. The words "As is Woman, so is the Race" appeared under the department's heading. The department carried articles and poetry by men, but the bulk of the material was written by the operatives themselves.

In this section are selections from the "Female Department." Other material from the department relating to such issues as the ten-hour day have been transferred to the sections dealing with these issues, but what follows is representative of the department in many ways. Included are selections from the "Valentine Offering," described as "a beautiful little sheet," issued by the Lowell Female Labor Reform Association on the occasion of a special gathering it sponsored on St. Valentine's Day, 1846. Notifying the public of the gathering, the "Female Department" also carried the notice that the "Valentine Offering issued especially for the occasion, under the direction of 'St. Valentine,' will be for sale." ☐

Female Efforts

By reference in another column, it will be seen that the spirited ladies of the Female Labor Reform Association, of this city, have purchased the Press and Type belonging to the "Voice of Industry" office, and for which they have made the first payment. Their labors for the cause of the oppressed, demand the sympathy and encouragement of all true friends to the elevation of mankind; and any person able to render pecuniary assistance to the cause of substantial reform, cannot find a more worthy object.

Voice of Industry, March 6, 1846

Female Department

As is Woman, so is the Race.

NOTICE

The Female Labor Reform Association, will meet every Tuesday Evening, at 8 o'clock, at their Reading Room, 76 Central Street, to transact all business pertaining to the Association, and to devise means by which to promote the common interests of all the Laboring Classes. Also to discuss all subjects which shall come before the meeting. Every *Female* who realizes the great necessity of a *Reform* and improvement in the condition of the worthy, toiling classes, and who would wish to place woman in that elevated station intellectually and morally which a bountiful Creator designed her to occupy in the scale of being, is most *cordially* invited to attend and give her influence on the *side* of virtue and *suffering humanity.*

HULDAH J. STONE, Sec'y

Lowell, January 9, 1846

INTRODUCTORY

In the "Prospectus" to the "Voice," it was asserted that there would be a Female department. As there has been no part of our paper assigned to female writers, although there have been some few communications which have been written by them; it has been deemed advisable, by the publishers, to have in future a portion of our paper devoted to the females of our country and through which they shall be heard. We would say to those who may chance to see this scroll as an introductory, or as an invitation, that it is intended as an urgent appeal to you, to contribute something for the benefit of our readers.

We are not exclusive in our views nor would we be willing to reject an honest opinion, offered by another, although it might not correspond with our own. Truth loses nothing by investigation, and whoever shrinks from investigation suspects his own cause, and should be suspected of others.

Our department devoted to woman's thoughts will also defend woman's rights, and while it contends for physical improvement, it will not forget that she is a social, moral, and religious being. It will not be neutral, because it is female, but it will claim to be heard on all subjects that effect her intellectual, social or religious condition.

It will make an effort to soften down the prejudices that exist against her as a reformer, and show those who read candidly, that she has a great duty to perform to herself and her race. It will have communication from the operatives of our city, and other places.— Manchester will give us occasional contributions; and we hope to hear very soon from our Pittsburgh and Allegheny friends. We will not promise our readers too much, but will try to do what we can to make our department useful and interesting.

S.G.B.[16]

Voice of Industry, January 9, 1846

Extracts from the "Female Department"

STANZAS

Rise, sisters, and your banner raise;
Will ye look for brighter days?
Hope ye mercy still?
What's the mercy slaves can gain?

> Behold it on the southern plain!
> Go view it o'er the eastern main!
> From Russia's serfs oppressed most vile
> To the servile sons of Erin's isle;
> No, not for mercy will we sue,
> But, ask we now our own just due.
> Great and glorious is our cause,
> Commanded by our Maker's laws;
> Those laws which elevate mankind
> Command us to enlarge our minds,
> To cultivate our mental powers,
> And, thus endow these minds of ours.
> TIME, for this is all we claim,
> Time, we struggle to obtain
> Then in the name of freedom rise,
> No rest, till we obtain the prize.

ALMIRA

Lowell, Mass.

Voice of Industry, February 6, 1846

The Universal Brotherhood

"Do unto others, as ye would that they should do to you," is a great precept, given to us by our great Teacher, as a rule and guide of action, towards all mankind. The Savior gave this for *practice;* he well knew what course of conduct would insure the greatest amount of happiness, to his creatures. And why has the world so long neglected to accept of this great lesson fraught with so many blessings if practiced. Where do we find a nation acting from this principle, toward other nations? where do we find any political body, sect, or community that have for their aim the accomplishment of this maxim? They not only neglect to make it the "chief corner stone," the foundation of all their proceedings; but it is left out of sight altogether; and hence arise all the evils in society; yes! misery, in all her forms. What but the neglect of this great principle, has brought into the world all this confusion, this disorder, this isolated state of interest, between man and man; all this monopoly and competition in business? And think you if all had "done unto others, as they would that they should do to them," if every man had "loved his neighbor as himself," that slavery would ever have existed, or oppression in any form? It could not have been.

And when will the world learn that humanity and christianity, are twin sisters? yes! more than this—that they are inseparable.

ADA

Lowell, Jan. 27.

Voice of Industry, February 6, 1846

From the Valentine Offering

OUR CAUSE

See! the rays of morn are dawning!
    Lo! freedom sheds her mellow light;
The glorious sun breaks on the morning,
    And hope's bright star illumes the night;—
And shall we idly waste in dreaming,
    Our senses and our lives away—
    Willing slaves to oppressive sway—
E'en while liberty's light is beaming?

Hark! the liberty bell is pealing
    Loud and clear its accents fall;
Tyranny beneath its chime is reeling,—
    Arouse! enslaved ones, at its call!
Behold our banner proudly waving!
    Come! join ye to this worthy band,
    And drive oppression from the land:—
Our cause a world is saving.

Come, brothers! then to the rescue come!
    Sure, heaven will your efforts bless;
Come, sisters! all to the rescue come!
    UNION is sure to bring success.
Come, stay oppression's withering blight,—
    Yes! rise, and break the galling chains,
    Where'er on earth the tyrant reigns;
Then the enslaved shall have redress.

ADA

Lowell, Feb. 13th.

Voice of Industry, February 20, 1846

From the Valentine Offering

VALENTINATORY

DEAR LOVERS:—Our visit among you, this long famed eve is an errand of love. We have long desired to have an interview with you upon this all important subject. Nature teaches us to love—on the morrow, (according to ancient mythology,) her feathered minstrelsy consummates this highest aspiration of their instinctive powers. Love is divine—it causes the snow to whiten the face of the earth, and the frosts to congeal them into a happy union. Love causes the clouds to weep tears of joy, and melt away the snow into the bosom of the earth, from which the flowers spring up as tokens of their more perfect affection. Love sends down the dews of heaven to cold sweet communion with the verdure of earth, and love in return, throws back a sweeter fragrance to seal the floral bond. Love causes the stars to dwell in concord above and gaily smile upon the sons of toil. Love overshadows the vale with darkness, brings peaceful repose to the slumberers, and bathes the hills in morning light. Love uplifts the down trodden, bears consolation to the afflicted, and smooths the pillow of the sick. Love "breaks the yoke of the bondman, and lets the oppressed go free"—gives bread to the hungry and *fresh water* to the thirsty. Love does good to an enemy and does violence to none. Love chimes on the breezes, and invites the faint and weary to the fountains of health and rest. Love gives "every good and perfect gift," reigning supreme throughout the works of creation, and centering in the great fountain of all love— "GOD IS LOVE."

But, dearly beloved, Love does not fill the land with wars and tumults causing bloodshed, devastation, and ruin. Love does not enslave men physically, morally, or mentally. Love does not adorn this beautiful earth for a favored few to monopolize and enjoy its blessings, while the many *stay* in want and misery. Love does not give stones when bread is asked for, or serpents when fish is wanted. Love does not turn the blessings of Heaven into curses for men— the bubbling waters are full of love, but with the engines of oppression which degrade humanity, love has no fellowship. Love never builds factories where beauty and health are sacrificed upon the altar of mammon—where her own fair household is plundered of many of its fairest jewels by the ruthless hand of avarice. The luxuriant harvests are never converted into *liquid death* by love. When the stately oak which adorns the forest, is hewn down and reared into the hideous, heathen monster *Gallows*—love is not there. Love knows no evil and knows no ill. And now, dear lovers, we present you this little "Offering" on this joyous eve, in manifestation of our love for you. We frankly and hopefully ask your *"hands and hearts"*—on your decision rests all that is lovely, great, and good. Do not disappoint us, but may we soon be united in the holy Heavenly bonds of *Love*—love to God and love to man.

ST. VALENTINE

DIALOGUE BETWEEN TWO YOUNG LADIES

Miss A. Well Harriet, I am glad you have finally resolved to attend the Social Gathering with me.

H. Indeed you are. I assure you it is much against my own will that I do so. Had not my dear father requested me to go, I would much rather stay at home. I do not like to be jostled in such a crowd; and then only think of the company!—the factory girls, house girls, and working men, are all that compose it! It is astonishing that father will persist on my attending!

A. Why, my dear? I am more astonished to hear you talk thus. One would suppose that you thought yourself better than they, merely because a kind Providence had placed you in more prosperous circumstances, whereas the reverse of that is true, for all real goodness consists in active usefulness. And in our republican land it should be *merit,* not station that makes any distinction. Surely, my friend, you could not be in earnest in what you said.

H. Ada, you mistake my character much if you suppose I intend to disgrace myself by associating with the lower classes who labor in our kitchens and factories for a livelihood. Nothing can be farther from my ideas of respectability than this. Let them be a class by themselves, and not presume to mingle in the higher circles of the wealthy, and refined. Only think of our condescending to visit and associate with the *common people*—the illiterate and uncultivated who throng our city at the present day! Why we should lose our caste in society at once.

A. Well, I for one, am willing to become unpopular for such reasons. Thank heaven, there is enough of the patriotic blood of my brave *ancestors* coursing through my veins, to enable me to spurn this mean, this contemptible, aristocratic spirit and custom which has been the Upas in the social communities of the Old World, and which threatens to destroy all harmony and good feeling in the New. What can be more ridiculously absurd than the feeling of prejudice which exists against the laboring classes—those classes, too, which supply us with all the comforts and luxuries of life. It does seem to me H., that they are the only people under heaven that deserve the esteem and respect of the entire community.—And if, as you say, they are illiterate and uncultivated, the more need have we to mingle with, and seek to improve and enlighten with our superior wisdom and refinement.

H.J.S.[17]

An Appeal to the Worthy, Toiling
Females of New England

Sisters in toil and deprivation, you who have heads to think and hearts to feel, give heed one moment, I pray! Are you desirous of improving the condition and elevating the thousands around you to that station in the world which the God of Heaven designed them to occupy and honor. Do you wish to see the virtuous poor protected and their rights maintained, against purse-proud aristocrats and the growing evils of the present systems of labor which are filling the coffers of the rich and making the real producers poorer—compelling them to wear out existence in merely obtaining the necessaries of their physical being leaving the mind, that noble gift of God, to perish for lack of cultivation. Would you aid the great cause of humanity and true reform in our midst—lend your name, your influence, your all in support of that "Voice," which shall speak ever in behalf of human rights and human equality. Its columns will be open for each and every individual to make known their wrongs, their deprivations and their grievances. Through the *"Voice,"* they may speak to the hearts of the generous —the brave, and the true of our country.

"A word to the wise is sufficient."

JULIANA

Voice of Industry, February 20, 1846

Beauty

BEAUTY is a captivating, but fading flower, which often leads its youthful possessor into many dangers, many distresses. Happy is it for those who are distinguished for their outward charms that they are sheltered under the parental roof. Happy for them that the watchful eye regards them with rigid circumspection. Few in the early periods of life are insensible to flattery, or deaf to the voice of adoration. Beware of the flatterer; be not deceived by fair speeches. Be assured the man who wishes to render you vain of your outward charms has a mean opinion of your sense and mental qualifications. Remember, too, that a young girl, whose chief study and employment is in the decoration of her person, is a most contemptible character, and that the more you are distinguished for the charms of your face and the traces of your form, the more you are exposed to danger.—The rose is torn from its parent stem in the pride of beauty; the jassamine is scarcely permitted to blossom before it is plucked; and no sooner are the beauties faded, than the merciless hand which was eager to obtain them, throws them away with contempt; whilst the primrose, the violet, the lily of the valley, and the snow-drop, less exposed to observation, escape unhurt and uninjured by the spoiler's hand.

Learn fair daughters of beauty, from the primrose, that your best security can be found in retirement. If you wish to be admired, be seldom seen; and if you are desirous of having a sincere lover in your train, let virtue, modesty, sweetness, be the only lures you make use of to ensnare.

You may then, perhaps, by your good qualities, retain the heart, which was at first captive to your beauties, and when time has robbed you of the graces and the innocent cheerfulness of youth, secure a sincere and tender friend, to console you in the hours of affliction, and watch over you when deprived of those charms that first made him solicitous to obtain your love.

Repine not, my young readers, though your virtues be concealed in a homely form. If you have secured the virtues of the mind, you need not envy others the beauties of the face. And ye, who are decorated with outward grace, be not vain of such fading externals, but tremble lest they should tempt the designing to lead you into error.

Neglect not, then, in the giddy hours of youth to make your mind a fit companion for the most lovely. Personal charms may please for a moment; but the more lasting beauties of an improved understanding can never tire. We are soon weary at looking at a picture, though executed in a masterly style; and she who has only beauty to recommend her, has but little chance of meeting a lover who will not grow indifferent to a mere portrait, particularly when its colors are faded by the subduing hand of time. Then it is that modesty and sweetness of temper are particularly observed; and the loss of beauty will not be regretted by him it first made captive.

Voice of Industry, February 20, 1846

The Young Lady's Choice

Give me the man that's learned without pretence,
Blest with good nature and with common sense;
Whose noble, generous, understanding heart
Disdains to act a mean, dissembling part;

Who once from virtue's path has never strayed,
Deceived no fair one, nor a friend betrayed;
Where virtue rules with an unbounded sway.
Then sense and reason prompts one to obey.
Such be the man with whom I'd stand my life.
Or never let me own the name of WIFE!

Voice of Industry, February 27, 1846

From the Valentine Offering

Lowell, Feb. 13, 1846

DEAR ANGELIC GIRL:—You may be surprised that I should dare to address your angelic goodness, being almost an entire stranger to you; but be assured I have long known and adored you. Who that has a soul capable of appreciating true worth and real goodness, could behold so much shrouded in a form divinely fair, and not become entangled in the criss-cross net of love, his heart bleeding at every pore, pierced with Cupid's mortal darts? Do not be angry, and cast this letter from you with disdain; but I pray you condescend to hear me graciously.

Dear girl! on your answer will my future happiness (and perhaps life) depend. To make a long story short, I am head and ears over in love with your own dear self, and cannot, nay, will not, attempt to conceal it. Perhaps you would like to know something of my standing and occupation in life, before you give me an answer. Well, my father is a wealthy manufacturer—lives in the most aristocratic style—keeps a number of white servants, who are never allowed to see the front door, or speak unless when some question is put to them; it being decidedly vulgar for servants to presume to converse on any subject except their work. As to myself, I am a gentleman—I spend my time in talking politics, smoking cigars, dressing and dancing. A merry life you see for me. All that is wanting to complete my happiness is a wife. Now my dear creature, I will pop the question. Will you marry me? Please answer immediately.

Yours, until death—
    if it comes in tolerable season,

JONATHAN KEEZER

Lowell, Feb. 14, 1846

MR. GENTLEMAN KEEZER,—Sir:—I would take the first opportunity to answer your very kind and very interesting letter of the 13th. As to marrying a gentleman, bless my stars! I have never even presumed to think on such an act for one moment. What could I do with a gentleman? I could not live on cigars and politics, and dance the rest of the time. I have been instructed by my poor but honorable parents, to make myself useful to others, by acting well my part in the great drama of life—and not like an idle drone, live on the hard earned goods of the worthy laborer. I could not if I would—nay, I would not, if I could—love a man who thus lived, though he possessed the riches of Golconda,[18] or the talents of an Oberlin! This, then, is my frank and decisive answer. *No, I will not!* P.S. I will just say that if you would complete your happiness, do it, not by marrying, but by reforming in your vicious habits, and seeking to make yourself worthy of the name of MAN. This advice is given gratis, by one who wishes well to all.

PEGGY GREEN

Voice of Industry, February 27, 1846

Letters from the Child of the Hills

Fort Hill, Lowell, Oct. 5th, 1846

DEAR MR. VOICE: I am but a child; yet I always read the Voice when I can get it; it makes me feel sad sometimes, too, when you tell about the factory girls and boys how long they work and how little money they get for doing so, yet I know it is true, for some of them come over to where I live, and then I hear them speak of just such things as I read in your paper, and they tell about their homes a great way off, their fathers and mothers, brothers and sisters, and how happy they were when they were with them, and some of them sit down upon the grass and weep, and then I stop my play and cry too. I think it is very wicked Mr. Voice, to make them so unhappy; and I read and hear that the people are rich that make them work so long and hard; and that they send men all over the country who tell wrong stories, and get the girls to come here; and when they get here they find out how much they have been cheated; but a great many of them are too poor to get back to their homes and so they have to stay and work in the mills, and then they get sick and die, some of them. I should think their parents would grieve very much when they hear of it, for poor people love their children as well as the rich, although the way the rich treat them, would lead one to think they did not. Do the rich people, Mr. Voice, ever put their children into the factories? I should think they would if they are such *nice healthy* places as they tell off; and how proud and grand they would feel to know that they were doing something useful; but I don't think they do, for I never heard of it, and I have been here a *great long* time. I hope it will be but a little while before these rich folks that have so much money, will put a stop to their working such a long time; but are you sure, Mr. Voice, that ten hours a day is not too long? It must be very dull to work all the time. I should not be such a merry thing if I were to be shut up all the time and kept from running in the green fields chasing the butterfly and gathering harebells and buttercups; and then you know you can listen to the pretty singing birds, and the music of the winds and waters, for they sing me to sleep very often when I get tired and lie down to rest among the bright, sweet flowers; oh! every thing is very beautiful up here and I am so happy.

I am afraid you will get tired of my prattle, Mr. Voice, but I thought I must write you a few words to let you know that children were made glad by the kind words you speak in the poor man's cause, and that they pray God to bless you. Perhaps I may write again if you would like to have me, (for I have some stories to tell which I have heard on the hillside, as told by some factory girl when she has strolled from her work to view my home—Some of them are sad, Mr. Voice, but others are real funny and would make you laugh.) and about some things which happened a great while ago, long before they built factories or houses here, or before the white man came to this country. So good bye—I am afraid you will think this too long a letter from

THE CHILD OF THE HILLS

Voice of Industry, October 9, 1846

Fort-Hill, Lowell, Nov. 8th, 1846

DEAR MR. VOICE:—I see you have printed the letter I wrote to you, a short time ago; and now I am going to write another. It seemed queer at first to think you should take so much notice of me as to print my childish sayings; when there are so many, who know so much, and can write so well about things all over the country, and who do so much good by telling of the wicked things done by people who enrich themselves, by making the poor work so many hours in the day, and then not pay them half they earn. But I have a story to tell you Mr. Voice—it is a sad one—it is about a young girl who came to work in the mills; her mother was dead, and her father used to drink strong drinks which made him cross; and then he treated her ill, and folks thought she had better go and work in the factory, and she did. When she went in, her cheeks were red as roses, and her eyes bright and beautiful, and she would laugh and romp like a little mad thing. I used to follow her sometimes on the "hill side;" for it used to make me feel glad, to see her so very happy. She had not worked there but a short time when she left the Mill looking very pale; and she coughed dreadfully. I used to see her every little while, and she kept growing poorer and weaker, and at last I missed her altogether. Then I used to linger near the house where she lived, and listen to hear some sound that would tell me she was there; for I loved the little girl that was so good and kind, and knew she would soon be an Angel, in Heaven. One day, they lifted her up to the window, where I could see her, it made me weep to look at her, for though she smiled as sweetly as ever, I knew she was dying. I thought she was praying, to, for she clasped her little thin hands, and turned her eyes toward Heaven—her lips moved—then there came a strange look across her face—she didn't move again. They took her away and I knew I should never see her more. In two days after, they buried her in the cemetery, near "my home;" and after they had all gone, I went and gathered some of the flowers I knew she loved best, and laid them on her grave, and as fast as they wilt I get fresh ones for I love to do it, Mr. Voice, altho' it makes me feel sorrowful; and I think she would thank me, if she could. There are a great many who die just as she died; and I wish the folks would not make the girls work so long in the factories; for I think that is the reason why so many die! Perhaps Mr. Voice, you can convince the rich folks, that it is not right to oppress the poor; if you can I think it will make you feel happy. But I must say good-bye for the present.

Your little friend,
THE CHILD OF THE HILLS

NOTES

1. The New England Workingmen's Association, largely the product of the activities of the mechanics of Fall River, Massachusetts, for the ten-hour day, was organized at a convention in Faneuil Hall, Boston, October 16, 1844, attended by 207 delegates. Mechanics from the New England towns made up the vast majority of the delegates, but there were delegates present from Brook Farm and from the land reform movement. In addition to calling for the freedom of public lands, endorsing Fourierism, and urging the establishment of producers' cooperatives as the method for putting an end to "the present system of labor" in which capital secured the reward which should only belong to the laborer, the convention adopted a resolution calling for a ten-hour law and organized a permanent association of New England workingmen to press for legislation that would prohibit any corporation from employing any person more than ten hours a day.

At its second convention, held in Lowell on March 18, 1845, the association adopted a constitution. The membership of the association was to consist of delegates from all local associations who were to pay twenty-five cents into the general fund. Representation was as follows: one delegate for up to fifty members; one for every additional fifty up to 500; and thereafter, one for every 100 members. Article 9 of the constitution read: "Female Labor Reform Associations shall be entitled to all the rights, privileges and obligations secured by this Constitution."

2. The son of Nebuchadnezzar II and the last king of Babylon, who was warned of his downfall and death by the handwriting on the wall.

3. William Henry Channing (1810–84), nephew of William Ellery Channing, leading Unitarian, and a Unitarian minister and reformer who was associated with the Fourieristic colony at Brook Farm.

4. L. W. Ryckman was a delegate from Brook Farm who was elected president of the New England Workingmen's Association at the second convention in Lowell, March, 1846.

5. This could refer either to Robert Owen (1771–1858), British Utopian socialist and founder of New Harmony, a cooperative community in Indiana, or to his son Robert Dale Owen (1801–77), who came to the United States with his father in 1825, was associated with the utopian and labor movements in this country, and was elected a member of Congress from Indiana in 1843.

6. Jean Frédéric Oberlin (1740–1826), Alsatian Lutheran priest and philanthropist, famous as educator of workers. Oberlin College in Ohio was named for him.

7. John Cluer was an English weaver who became a well-known radical orator in this country. He spoke frequently on behalf of the ten-hour movement and utopian socialism, and in opposition to the corporations and such "vested interests" as the church. Schouler's *Lowell Courier* launched a campaign against Cluer, accusing him of being a liar, a drunkard, a bigamist, and a man who had obtained money under false pretenses.

8. For extracts from the "Valentine Offering," see pp. 146–47.

9. John Allen was one of the editors of the *Voice of Industry*.

10. William F. Young founded the *Voice of Industry* in Fitchburg, Massachusetts, in 1845, and edited the paper after it was transferred to Lowell until the spring of 1846, when he fell ill. He returned as editor in November and remained in that post until October, 1847, when he sold out to D. H. Jaques. Young spoke frequently at labor meetings and was active in various aspects of the work of the New England Workingmen's Association.

11. The Labor Reform League of New England was the revised name of the New England Workingmen's Association, adopted at the association's Nashua

convention on September 17, 1846. One of the main reasons for the change in name was to concentrate on the reform in working hours, rather than on utopianism.

12. As early as the 1830s the mill owners adopted a blacklist system which made it impossible for any factory girl to obtain work with a new company if she did not bring with her a "regular discharge" from her former employer. A "regular discharge" was given only to those who had worked a full year and were not guilty of "insubordination." Any girl "dishonorably" discharged from one mill could find no employment in most other mills. The names of trouble-makers were placed in the hands of factory agents, and such lists were kept constantly up to date.

13. No copy of the second or of any other number of the *Factory Tracts* appears to exist. However, an extract from the second number was published in the *Voice of Industry* of November 14, 1845, and is reprinted here.

14. Amelia is undoubtedly Amelia Sargent, whose article on Miss Farley may be found above, pp. 68–73. "The Summons" was originally published in the *Voice of Industry*, November 7, 1845.

15. A mill in Lowell.

16. Sarah G. Bagley.

17. Huldah J. Stone.

18. A source of great riches, as a mine.

Part 4

Three Pioneer Women Labor Leaders

Sarah G. Bagley

Sarah G. Bagley was the first leader of the Female Labor Reform Association of Lowell, a pioneer woman labor editor and labor leader. Yet knowledge of her background and early life is scant. She was a native of Meredith, New Hampshire, and taught school before arriving in Lowell around 1836 or 1837. According to her own testimony, given in February, 1845, before the special committee investigating petitions for the ten-hour day, she had worked eight and one-half years in the Lowell Mills—six and one-half in the Hamilton Corporation and two in the Middlesex. In her December, 1840, *Lowell Offering* article, "Pleasures of Factory Life," she described herself as "having been engaged as an operative the last four years." In the *Voice of Industry* of May 15, 1846, she described herself simply as a "common schooled New England female factory operative." It is known that for four of the eight years when she worked in the mills, she conducted a free evening school for her fellow female factory operatives.

Miss Bagley contributed considerably to the labor press and the daily press on issues involving the factory girls. It thus was not surprising that in May, 1846, Miss Bagley was selected as the logical person to take charge of the *Voice of Industry* when its editor, William F. Young, had to give up his work because of ill health. She edited and published the paper from May 15 through May 29, 1846. Her editorials are included below, as well as her other writings.

Miss Bagley's last piece of writing appeared in the *Voice of In-*

dustry of October 2, 1846. After the issue of September 25 her name disappeared from the masthead of the paper, and no further mention of her was made in the labor reform movement. It was reported that Miss Bagley had suffered a breakdown. Actually, she was still active as the first woman telegraph operator in the United States, as well as in other activities.

Like those of the two other women pioneer labor leaders included in this section, some of Miss Bagley's writings appear elsewhere in the volume, under specific subjects. Here her (and their) writings cover the more general aspects of the causes in which they were engaged. □

Voluntary?

Whenever I raise the point that it is immoral to shut us up in a close room twelve hours a day in the most monotonous and tedious of employment, I am told that we have come to the mills voluntarily and we can leave when we will. Voluntary! Let us look a little at this remarkable form of human freedom. Do we from mere choice leave our fathers' dwellings, the firesides where all of our friends, where too our earliest and fondest recollections cluster, for the factory and the Corporations boarding house? By what charm do these great companies immure human creatures in the bloom of youth and first glow of life within their mills, away from their homes and kindred? A slave too goes voluntarily to his task, but his will is in some manner quickened by the whip of the overseer. The whip which brings us to Lowell is NECESSITY. We must have money; a father's debts are to be paid, an aged mother to be supported, a brother's ambition to be aided, and so the factories are supplied. Is this to act from free will? When a man is starving he is compelled to pay his neighbor, who happens to have bread, the most exorbitant price for it, and his neighbor may appease his conscience, if conscience he chance to have, by the reflection that it is altogether a voluntary bargain. Is any one such a fool as to suppose that out of six thousand factory girls of Lowell, sixty would be there if they could help it? Every body knows that it is necessity alone, in some form or other, that takes us to Lowell and keeps us there. Is this freedom? To my mind it is slavery quite as really as any in Turkey or Carolina. It matters little as to the fact of slavery, whether the slave be compelled to his task by the whip of the overseer or the wages of the Lowell Corporation. In either case it is not free will, leading the laborer to work, but an outward necessity that puts free will out of the question.

S.G.B.

Voice of Industry, September 18, 1845

To E.R.L.

Sir:—Your request to ascertain the exact number of *female* operatives, who are stockholders in the mills of Lowell, has been attended to and the result was as I had anticipated. You are probably aware that all the stockholders' names are returned to the assessor's office, on or before the first of May, on account of taxation. I have examined the books, and find that there is not a female's name upon the book that *is* or *ever was* an operative. The truth is that those who would bolster up a system of labor that is destructive to health, and fatal to mental and moral cultivation, would make such unfounded assertions, that the female operatives own the mills in Lowell or at least that they have large investments here, is not very strange. Even in our own city, with the facts staring them in the face, that the operatives are poor with few exceptions, they are prepared to publish stories as untrue as the one to which you allude.

One story which went the rounds of the papers, all over New England, was, that there was an operative here in Lowell, who had worked nineteen years here and had been married and had a family in the time, and had *saved* besides supporting herself and children, or child, two thousand dollars, invested in a farm, and eleven hundred and fifty had been given to poor relation.

Strange as it may appear to you, I was somewhat sceptical on the subject; and as I had worked in the same room and knew something of her history, I thought I had a perfect right to satisfy my own curiosity.—The facts as I gathered them from her were as follows:

It had been something more than eighteen years since she first went into the mill; but she had been absent six years in the time, on long visits; besides being absent a number of times for two or three months at a time.

So much for the years; and next the sum she had made:

She paid $950, for the two thousand dollar farm, and had been *very* kind to her poor relatives; but not to the extent of the sum of $1,150. Nor is this all; you may have some curiosity to know why her husband has not supported her, and her children. One of the best reasons that can be given is, that she *has not yet* been married.

Another fact, in this remarkable woman is, that she has not been a subscriber to a newspaper, nor a patron to any library, or had a seat at church, or a dress suitable to appear at church, in all the nineteen years; and yet she is sent out through the press as a sample of factory girls. Now, bad as the state of mental and moral cultivation is, she is not a fair representative of the female operatives of Lowell, or any other place. Most of the operatives dress well, and a large proportion of them read in their leisure time, which is *very* limited.

The question you proposed, on wages being raised, the past year, is that the companies do not pay more for the *same amount* of work; but the operatives do more work than formerly. A few years ago, no girl was required to tend more than two looms. Now they tend four, and some five; and because they make a few cents more than they did on two, it is trumpeted all over the country, that their wages have been raised. This is a true statement of the case, as it exists in our midst; and, yet, men here have the audacity to send out statements, as false as they are, to the interest of the operative;— and Heaven knows that is false indeed.

Your inquiry on the state of morality and religion shall be attended to next week.

You will pardon me for answering your inquiry through the press when I assure you that these questions are put so often that to answer them through the "Voice" would save the trouble of answering them many times by letter.

I am yours very respectfully,

S.G.B.

Lowell, April 22

Voice of Industry, April 24, 1846

To E.R.L.—No. 2

Sir: In compliance with your request, I will continue the subject of factory life; and in this letter give you some of the facts you desired to obtain. You enquire "what is the state of morals among the factory operatives?" I can assure you it is just what any reflective mind would expect of seven thousand females thrown together under a great diversity of circumstances and with all kinds and no kind of cultivation.

There are many female operatives here, who have been educated by their parents or under their direction who are now orphans, and are an ornament to the society in which they live. There are a much larger class, who are the children of intemperate parents, who have had no advantages of education, and who have had little means for improvement.

Many of them have been put out to service as soon as they were old enough to scrub or take care of children, and have had no kind sympathy to warm and expand the affections or make them kind and courteous to others. This, to my mind, is more a misfortune than a fault. That they attend church as much—nay more than could be expected, under all the circumstances. If they should not go to church at all, they would be quite excusable, and if at the day of retribution the operatives of our country should be found guilty of a want of religious devotion, how *much more* will the *teachers* of religion have need of repentance and forgiveness for their sanction of the system which disqualifies them to attend church and cultivate the spirit of the gospel.

It will be said, that we are infidel to offer an apology for a neglect to attend church? We are aware that the operatives are rapidly verging to infidelity to the religion that lays heavy burdens upon their shoulders, that it will not remove with one of its fingers. Is it strange that the operatives should stay away from the churches where they see the men filling the "chief seats," who are taking every means to grind them into the very dust, and have no sympathy with them, and look upon them only as inanimate machines, made to subserve their interests?

These things are felt by the more intelligent and reflective, and it has its legitimate effect upon them. We do not allude to this state of feeling, but with painful emotions. We deeply regret that in our democratic country, the rights of all, both civil and religious, should not be respected. We are sad to see the interests of the employer and the employed so far removed from each other. The examples of the employers, are *not* of the most moral kind; you will see the superintendent in the factory yards and shops on each Sabbath, giving orders to the men employed by them to work on their machinery, or lay foundations for new mills, and as soon as the church bell rings, hasten to the house of worship, while the workmen are left to fulfill their orders.

Sir: Is there any power in example? Is there any one, not well trained at home, that would not in *some* degree be affected by such examples? I leave you to draw your own conclusions, and close by saying that there are many of our number, who under all such influences and such disadvantageous circumstances adhere to the right, the good and the true, and are in all respects an ornament to the society in which they live. May Heaven grant that the number may increase, is the prayer of

S.G.B.

Lowell, April 28th

Voice of Industry, May 6, 1846

To E.R.L.—No. 3

You enquire, what is the physical condition of the operatives? There can be but one opinion on this subject, although there may *seem* to be many.

There is not a man in community who would not blush to say in view of the physical organization of the female operative, that the laws of health are *necessarily* and *unavoidably* violated by them every day, in various ways. The long hours of labor, the short time allowed for meals, and the large number who occupy the sleeping and sitting apartments, all go to prove that physical inability must be the result. There is no time or accommodation for bathing in their sleeping apartments, a practice that has been deemed as necessary to health, as food or sleep, by the physiologists of our day.

With but the few moments of time allowed to take their food, which is swallowed without being half masticated, and the pores of the skin being encrusted, or nearly so with cotton dust, it is not strange that so many of their number fall a prey to consumption, and find an early grave.

The social condition of the operative is a subject that should not be overlooked. It is presumed by the observer, that these free spirits, who come here from the hills of the "Old Granite State,"[1] and the mountains of Vermont, who have had free and innocent access to every department of society, and have never seen a division into grades, according to wealth or circumstance, it is quite natural for these, to seek for social intercourse, and what, you enquire, is the result? Do they find admittance into the families of the rich? Certainly not! They are "factory girls." No matter how virtuous or intelligent, or how useful an operative may be. She may be a member of the same church with her employer and the teacher of his children in the Sabbath School, or the tract distributor of the ward in which he lives, she may gain admittance to the sitting room to enquire after her pupil, or leave a tract; but if a Party is to be given and the aristocracy of the city is to be present, she cannot gain admission; her occupation,—nay her usefulness excludes her.

Such is the state of society; such its arbitrary rules; and I would return the question proposed by you,—what is the result? These children of toil have no home, which they may cluster around and find sympathy and affection; no watchful eye of maternal love to give direction to their steps; no consoling voice of a sister or brother to lighten their burden of sadness or soothe them in the trials of their weary pilgrimage. This is the life of an operative, and this their social condition.

Those who are most sensitive are most affected and those who are the most susceptible feel most the want of a place, where the highest and most beneficent gifts of our nation may find gratification, and their wants supplied. I have endeavored to answer your enquiries as briefly as possible, and if there are any points overlooked, if you will inform me I will give them all the attention in my power. Accept my gratitude for your kind indulgence and believe me ever the friend of human progress.

S.G.B.

Voice of Industry, May 8, 1846

To the Editor of the Voice, and Ourself[2]

The chair Editorial is vacant. The Voice of its editor is silent. A late number contained his adieu for the present. No longer will the dusty labor field, or the dingy work shop, be cheered by his weekly presence. Devolving, as does his task hereafter, upon the weaker sex, much of patience, much of charity, much of allowance, must be made, for the discrepancy, in interesting matter that shall find its way to the columns of the Voice, under the Editorial control of a common schooled New England female factory operative. In one thing however we pledge ourselves, to our numerous readers on the start: what we lack in Editorial ability, in rhetorick, or historical research, be assured we will make up in heart. Our heart, yea, our whole soul, is wrapped up in the cause of the oppressed—of the down trodden millions throughout the world—We ourselves, long, long, even now, a sufferer among the unwieldy yet mighty mass.

The task we have undertaken, is one of great responsibility. Long a contributor to the columns of the Voice, of course it is needless almost, to say its principles and general policy will be the same. Yet new minds will find new modes of expression, to obtain the same end. Our end, aim, and soul's wish, is the improvement of the condition of the laboring masses. The division of labor consequent upon the introduction of machinery, while it has enhanced the general stock of human production, and thereby benefited the general weal, has at the same time entailed terrible calamity—unutterable woe. Famishing want, among large classes of operatives, starving Ireland, oppressed Leeds, Manchester, and Liverpool, the cries of the oppressed from every other land, and the murder of the Chartists, shot down in cold blood,[3] by order of a woman,[4]—the millions at the same time appropriated for the support of Prince Albert's wet nurses,[5] and Lord Chamberlains, wrung from the brow of labor, all come as a warning voice, terrible as the thunder of Almighty God, *that we too, are in danger.*

As occasion shall offer, to the best of our ability will we point out in detail, our dangers, and the remedy. Of one thing friends, rest assured, on ourselves alone rests the great responsibility of reforming or permitting errors in a system, to fasten themselves upon us. The great evil that accrues from the introduction of machinery, and division of labor, is the *caste* it gives to society.—Two great principles must be introduced as a basis for the organization of the factory system in this country, or the same results are to flow in here that have caused such crying anguish in the old world. *Capital must not be permitted to demand so much of labor. Education of the mass, must be made to possess an individual certainty, past escape.* To our mind these two are the fundamental principles to be inculcated and established, to avoid the maelstrom already in motion, with a moral certainty to engulf us.

Operatives, friends! to effect the great objectives we have in view, will require your active vigilant unceasing aid. We must all begin by being good ourselves. "Cast the beam first from our own eye."—purify ourselves from wrong or unjust complaint. Thus we hope to make our start. In our course we shall perhaps be somewhat more plain, more direct to the point, and personal in its application than we have heretofore been. Truth shall be our guide; we will do no wrong—tell no falsehood knowingly. But oppression however slight, abuse of trust however trivial, insolence from whatever source, and whether from the agent, the overseer or petty tender, in the capacity of under clerk, from the Bank managers, men in authority of the city government, or gentlemen of the professions, whether Doctor, Lawyer, or Priest, we will punish as it merits, without stint or reserve; as for example: an agent in Lowell, the last week, called up one of the young ladies employed under him, and reprimanded her for employing her leisure hours in assisting in the organization of our "Labor Reform Association"—notified her she must desist, or suffer the consequence. "For all past offences we say a truce; but a repetition in any form, we will punish." What! deprive us after working thirteen hours, the poor privilege of finding fault—of saying our lot is a hard one. Intentionally turn away a girl unjustly—persecute her as men have been persecuted, to our knowledge, for free expression of honest political opinions! We will make the name of him who dares the act, stink with every wind, from all points of the compass. His name shall be a by-word among all laboring men, and he shall be hissed in the streets, and in all the cities in this wide-spread republic; for our name is legion though our oppression be great. Our sympathies are for the sailor and soldier, as well as the citizen. We war with oppression in every form—with rank, save that which merit gives.

To one more subject, fair readers, let me call your particular attention. The standard of virtue in Lowell, is far above that of any other city of its size in the Union; pray God it may so remain. How can I find language to warn all my sisters, of the sacredness, the high charge devolving upon us in this respect? With us and us alone, rests the great responsibility of *the standard of female virtue in Lowell*. This must be preserved at all and every hazard, or all of our labors are as sounding brass. Never, never, in the name of heaven, permit Lowell to boast her "nymphs of the pave." At the dance, upon the street, at the social gathering, in church, or by your own fireside shrink as from the abyss of infamy, from the steady gaze or stealthy touch of the *fiend* in human form, who for a paltry momentary job, would rob you of bliss for life, and destroy a lone girl's happiness, away from friends and home. Give us the name of all such, even making the attempt, and the scorching memory of their crimes shall follow them. Not Lowell only, but the dark walls of the prison-house, shall find for him no companion; for even there, the lone girl in Lowell, driven by poverty or misfortune, from her mother's home, to seek shelter under the task master's rod, will find sympathy, even in his stony heart.

Voice of Industry, May 15, 1846

A Pledge

It has been suggested to us, by those in whose judgment we have perfect confidence, that a series of articles should be prepared for the Voice, giving in detail the most exact account of the every day life of the operatives, the manner by which they are procured, by the runners in the employ of the companies; together with the *modus operandi* of the whole system. We promise our readers that we will enter upon this department of the operatives' organ forthwith. We pledge ourselves that our statistics shall be those gathered from our own experience, or observation, and entitled to perfect confidence. We will not give a onesided view, but show the bright spots in the existence of the operatives; and we will dwell upon the green sunny spots in a life so toilsome, as does the weary traveller upon the oasis of the desert. We will not enlarge upon the proposed plan, lest the reader expect too much. We hope to give the first chapter next week. Shall we have statistics furnished from responsible sources—and will our city subscribers send the papers to their friends in the country.

Voice of Industry, May 15, 1846

How the Corporations Procure Help

CHAPTER I

In commencing this series of articles, I am aware of the difficulties to be encountered, and the many objections to be met. I shall confine myself to the facts which are of so common occurrence, that it will be impossible to find any one to gainsay what shall be given to the public.

It is a notorious fact that the Corporations here have been in the habit of sending out agents to procure help ever since 1836. In that year James Cook, then superintendent of the Middlesex Corporation,[6] went to England, to procure help and brought back quite a number. I am acquainted with some of them and have had the story of the deception used to procure their services, from those upon whom it was practiced.

There have been agents out in the country, for several years past, a part of the time; and of this we do not complain, but why do they talk of the *voluntary* choice of the operatives, and send abroad false impressions about hiring help? Do they not send out men of questionable veracity? Have not there been very serious difficulties from the promise of a large compensation, when they knew it would not be realized? One case that occurred about a year since, as an illustration:—An agent went out and hired all that would count one, without respect to age or condition. He hired one, who was *not* fifteen years of age, and could not be employed by the Company, without a violation of the Statute providing for the education of children. There were no objections made to her, or her parents on account of age, until after she arrived in the city. The agent who hired her informed her then, that she must tell them at the count-ing-room, that she was sixteen years old, or she could not get work; and she could not go back alone,—of course the girl gave her age to suit the circumstances. She had been promised $1.00 per week and board, and went to work. It was a five weeks payment, and when she received her pay, she had but *ten cents* left, after paying her board; or two cents per week. She had a friend in the city, who interfered in her behalf and compelled the company who employed her, to send her back to her friends, or pay the fine imposed by the laws of Massachusetts, for hiring a child under fifteen years, without a certificate of having attended school three months in the year.[7] That the company *is* responsible for such violation of truth is quite evident, from the fact, that the same man is kept out, most of the time, and if they did not approve of his course, they most assuredly would not employ him. This is not a solitary instance, there are scores of them; and we might write not only a column of a paper, but a volume of such frauds.

The agents who hire the girls, often find it necessary to pay their expenses. A case of this kind came under our observation a few days since. Our informant was in company with the girls in ques-tion, and gave the facts as follows:—"Five girls were hired, and an agreement made to pay their expenses. They started in company with a girl who had been in Lowell before, and the agent went in another direction, after giving them the 'needful' for their journey. He told them he had arranged to give them a ticket from a given place on their journey, through to Lowell. They bought the ticket, as directed, and it took every farthing they had, and they rode from Lower Canada to Lowell without eating or drinking, except a little cake furnished by their friends. They had not means to buy lodging, and were furnished with it, by the benevolence of some passengers who would not let them sit up for want of a bed."

We press the enquiry: are not the men who send out such agents, responsible for their violation of truth and honesty?

The names of all the persons alluded to, are in our possession, and will be given if requested.

Voice of Industry, May 22, 1846

The Introduction into the Mill

CHAPTER II

It will be seen by the by-laws in the preceding chapter, that "those in the employ of the companies, are required to be constant in their attendance at some *regular* place of worship, and those who neglect this regulation, will not be employed."

As it is not the design of these chapters, to enter into a discussion of the claims on the sympathies of the operatives of the different sects, who allow wickedness in *high places* to go unrebuked in our midst, we shall confine ourselves to the evil effects consequent upon the long hours of labor, and the want of time. Can it be reasonably supposed that those who are called to their task every morning at half past five, and kept there until seven at night, will have sufficient energy to be constant in their attendance at church on the Sabbath? The reader can judge.

One objection which is kept out of sight, is, that *no washing* is done by those who board the operative for them except their mill dress, consequently there is much additional labor in keeping their wardrobe in church-going order, which falls upon them, and which they have *no time* to perform.

Another objection arises from the fact, that our Agents and the aristocratic class to which they belong, have ordained fashions in dress and equipage, which the operative is unable to follow, and they must at any rate *ape them,* or they will be wanting in self-respect.

Those who have been in Lowell but a short time, and venture out to church, with their plain country dress, are stared almost out of countenance—and unless they have an unusual amount of independence, they will not venture again, until they have a new bonnet of the most "approved style," and "other things to match." These causes are a *sufficient* apology for the neglect of attending church.

But we would not be understood, as giving these reasons, with a design to lend our influence on the side of a neglect of religious cultivation. We would thank God most devoutly, if there could be found a house of worship in Lowell, where the gospel, as preached by the ancient disciples, could be heard by every operative, and those who are not of this class also,—where it would not be "binding heavy burdens," that those who minister "will not move with one of their fingers." We hope for the future!

Voice of Industry, June 12, 1846

To the "Circle" for Mutual Agreement

By an appointment made by the Union Association, the duty of an introductory address to this "Circle for mutual improvement" devolves upon me.[8] I sincerely regret that you had not selected some other member, who had not spoken so often and freely to you, upon the subject of mutual improvement. It can hardly be expected that I can give you any new thoughts, after having urged this subject so often upon your attention. You will therefore pardon the repetition which is quite unavoidable, under the existing circumstances.

The duty we owe to each other, and above all, to ourselves, makes such a circle absolutely necessary. Can we be satisfied with ourselves, and make no progress in writing? Can we sit down after a wearisome day's toil and not find a new thought upon which the mind may rest for a brief space? I am aware of all the obstacles to be encountered, and the difficulties to be met. I know them, as most of you know them, by painful experience. I feel disposed to speak kindly and charitably to you, and yet I cannot but urge you to the duty of self-cultivation. And whatever sacrifice it may cost, let it be made cheerfully. Do not say "I have no time," we are all aware of the fact; but let your frequent communications testify to the circle, that your resolves are omnipotent, and will not be defeated by any circumstances, however unfavorable.

The advantages to us, as social beings, should not be lost sight of. In whatever light the subject of Social Reform, and Improvement may be viewed by others, to me there is but one method—that is, social intercourse, and an interchange of thought. There is no stronger evidence to my mind, of the progress of any cause, than the free expression of thought upon the subjects embraced by its advocates.

One of the objects of this Circle, is, to give an opportunity for free expression; and we trust no one will lose so good a chance to utter his or her thoughts freely. As there is a great variety of tastes and opinions, let there be as great a variety of subjects, presented.

We are in no danger of infidelity or fanaticism, by free discussion; and he who would shut up a free soul, within the narrow limits of a creed, in these days of Progress and Reform, has yet to learn, that the mind of man is greater than all parchment, and will not be driven into dark caverns by any theology save that written by the Great Architect, on the blue arch of heaven.

The duty of self-instruction to us all, should urge us to this duty. Those who have time and means to educate themselves, might neglect to meet us here; but we, whose time and opportunities for cultivation, are so very limited, can find no possible excuse for neglecting this duty, which we owe to ourselves and this circle.

Let no one say they cannot contribute for want of ability. This excuse is just such a reason as ought to be given *for* writing. We might assign such a reason for refusing to learn to sing, or learn any other science. In writing as in every thing, "practice makes perfect," and those who refuse such discipline are untrue to themselves and may never expect to be better qualified than they now are, to interest or instruct us.

Finally, let us meet promptly, and be determined that we will bring something to amuse or edify those who are present, and we shall make our meetings not only pleasant but profitable; and shall be enabled to send out an influence which shall be felt and approved, by all within the range of our example.

S.G.B.

Voice of Industry, May 29, 1846

The Improvement Circle

At our last meeting I took occasion to make a communication to you on our social relations. The engagements of the hour allotted me to furnish something for your amusement and instruction, were such that I but glanced at the subject. I shall be pardoned, therefore, if I allude to it again and again. Much of our happiness, nay, *every thing,* depends upon our *social* existence. Make us rich and give us no social intercourse and what will it avail us? Make us wise and shut us out from society and the world will not be instructed from our stores of wisdom. Make us happy and remove us from those we love and the smile is followed by a tear. Make us devotional, and the soul cannot approach the bosom of its God, and be obliged to leave its cherished object behind. Our *whole* life is interwoven with each other, and our happiness made to depend upon each other, in a greater or less degree.

Such are our relations to each other, that while we are unhappy we spread gloom on all around us. I would enquire if these things are not so? How important then that we feel sensibly our true relation to each other. How often should we stop and think before speaking, lest we inflict a wound we have no power to heal. There is enough of sorrow mingled in our cup of existence, without one pang being carelessly or wickedly added.—There are thorns, too often found in our pathway, to need any addition made by envy or mischievous hands.

Then let *us* as *real* lovers of the good, the beautiful, and the true, live not for ourselves alone, but for each other, and the good of our race; remembering at all times, that if we would be happy we must confer happiness, for, "it is *more* blessed to give, than to receive."

S.G.B.

Voice of Industry, June 12, 1846

Some Incidents of My Journey

For the *Voice of Industry*

Mr. Meriam:

In compliance with your request to give you some incidents of my journey to the old "Granite State," I would say that we had a pleasant ride, allowing for the extreme heat. We passed rapidly through the "magic city" of Manchester, and found ourselves at the "American House," Concord, N.H., otherwise called "Gass' Hotel." Well, as riding always makes one disposed to eat, I could not resist the impression that we had one of Gass' "best," and every body knows, that ever finds himself there, that that is good enough for a prince.

I found myself seated before some of the friends of home, and received from them the warm grasp of friendship. I could not but feel sad as the stage left for my early loved home, that I must be deprived the pleasure of receiving the cordial greeting of a dearly loved father and mother, and other friends most dear. I took my pen and gave them a few lines to atone in part for my return without seeing them.

My first call was upon our worthy friend, N. P. Rogers.[9] I found him very sick, and learned that his case is very doubtful. My next visit was to the State Prison. I carried a letter of introduction to the keeper, Hon. J. Berry, from the State Attorney, Hon. L. B. Walker. He received us with the greatest civility and gave us every possible attention. We went through every department of the prison and found the most perfect neatness and system throughout. We made particular enquiry about the hours of labor, and found them less than what the operatives work, by about two hours. They leave their cells at 5½ in the morning and take breakfast at 6½, having three quarters of an hour. Take dinner at 12 o'clock, having one hour; and leave off at 6 o'clock at night. This is what the Judges of our Courts call "hard work," in pronouncing the sentences of the law.

We would ask the fathers and brothers of the operatives to think of their loved ones, who work at this season of the year, two hours a day more than they do who perform work as a punishment for a crime. In the winter they never "light up" their work, but leave at dark.

Among the prisoners, we saw an old man mending clothes. The keeper gave me leave to ask him any questions I might desire. In answer, he informed me he was 83 years old; had been sentenced to nine years imprisonment, had four years and five months to stay; said his health is perfect and expects to serve his time out and get a release.

Among the other prisoners was a man of much beauty. A full, round, well developed head—a keen black eye, and straight, genteel figure. What a pity, thought I, that you did not make a more judicious selection for the practice of rascality. You might have selected some game equally dishonest, that would not have exposed you, but have made you looked up to, as a man of wealth, and, therefore, to be respected without regard to the means by which it was procured. You might have performed some "hocus pocus" means of robbery, without forgery, and passed as an Appleton, a Lawrence,[10] or an Astor[11] in society. Foolish man! Let others learn wisdom by your folly, and then the little petty thieves and robbers will cease their small games, and take to wholesale plunder, and not only escape the prison, but have a ticket to the circles of the "upper ten thousand."

I am warned that I am extending my letter too long, and will close by saying that my next visit will be to the Insane Asylum, of which you will hear on my return.

I am very respectfully yours for universal emancipation.

Concord, N.H., September 7, 1846.

Voice of Industry, September 11, 1846

To W.E.B., Correspondent to the *Dundee (Scotland) Warder*

Sir:—Our attention has been called to a communication published in the "Warder" of a recent date, giving an account of a visit made by you to Lowell, on the 9th of June last. There are several things[12] mentioned in your letter, which in our judgment are incorrect, and deserving notice. . . .

You inform the readers of the "Warder," that the state of religion in Lowell is highly prosperous. "That there are twenty-three churches." This is probably correct. You might have given them some specimens of the *practical* religion of the manufacturers, had you remained in Lowell during one of *our* Sabbaths. You might have seen workmen employed by hundreds, in shops and canals. You might have seen teams moving gravel, and building materials into the factory yards to be used in the erection of new mills. You might have seen a train of cars coming in from New Hampshire, at early dawn, loaded with workmen to forward the work of completing a new canal, and returning at sun down. You might have heard the reports of stone blasting, that would shake the foundation of the "twenty-three churches," and drown the voice of the man of God, who was dispensing the word of life to the agents under whose directions the work was performed.

It is true you might have seen a by-law, making it obligatory on the *females* employed by the company to attend church and pay five dollars per year for a seat, but it would cost you no more pains to find 14 men who were employed by one company, where you visited, who were discharged from their employ for refusing to work on the Sabbath.

This is the *real, actual, practical* religion of the corporations, a very different thing from profession. It looks well on paper when the piety of the manufacturers of Lowell is sent abroad, especially in a country as distant as Scotland.

We should rejoice as sincerely as any one could, if they were deserving all that has been said in their behalf; but they are not—and truth is better than falsehood—and if they will justify such exaggerated stories, they ought to be exposed.

Another item of your communication will show you the impossibility of procuring a correct idea of the merits or demerits of a factory city, by a visit of a single day.

You say, "No rags, no poverty, no drunkenness, no rioting," &c., &c. We would say, but not without the deepest regret, that there are four hundred places in Lowell, where intoxicating liquors are sold. A population of 30,000 make them sufficiently profitable to warrant their existence.

We are happy to believe that our condition as operatives is more fortunate than those of the old country, in some respects. But still, we are convinced that the same causes which have produced such fearful results there are at work here; and unless they are speedily remedied will assume the same horrid features.

We are sure that the public mind is directed to the subject of the long hours of labor among the operatives. The Manufacturers are unwilling to own how much feeling there is in society, upon the subject.

The time is not far distant when a man would be regarded as a monster, who would exact thirteen hours labor in a day, from females. Public sentiment is taking a right direction, and will work a change, in spite of the avarice of the employer.

They are ashamed to own that England is in advance of "the land of the free and the home of the brave," in its improvement in the hours of labor.[13]

Such we blush to say is the fact. Our "Democratic Government" we trust will awake to the subject soon. Till then we shall labor for its consummation.

Very respectfully yours, for the operatives of Lowell.

SARAH G. BAGLEY

MR. EDITOR:—In compliance with your request to give some account of our visit to the Insane Asylum in this town[14] we would like to give a description of the place to your ten thousand readers; It is situated on a beautiful elevation west of Main Street. One of the most admirable spots that could have been chosen was selected and every means has been put in requisition to beautify and render it attractive by trees and shrubbery. The most perfect neatness and arrangement is observed throughout every department of the domain. The kitchen as well as the parlor was in the most perfect order, and were illustrative of the good system which is observed. We were received by Doct. McFarland and he visited the different wards with us. The worst form of insanity was to us most deplorable —human beings, with reason prostrated and they turned like madmen, as they are, into a ball to protect them from the violence of their own hands. One female patient had her hands confined by bands of leather about her waist to prevent her from committing suicide, which she had attempted the day previous, with a pair of scissors.—She made a slight wound in her throat, and would have succeeded, undoubtedly, had she not been discovered.

The most imperfect mildness and kindness was manifested by those in charge. If a correct opinion in some slight degree could be formed, the Asylum is a great blessing to the unfortunate inmates. The truth of the science of Phrenology was never so forcibly impressed on our minds as at the Asylum.—The peculiar developments of the religiously insane were particularly prominent. Marvelousness was the most striking, and in some heads amounted to deformity.

The insane who are in a state to read are furnished with papers received on exchange for the paper published there.

We saw one evidence of the want of respect to the keepers of the Asylum which we are constrained to mention. It was two men assisted by the Doctor, purifying the door steps from tobacco juice, with acid, which had been left there by visitors.

We never felt so truly grateful for the gift of reason as when we left, nor were so fully satisfied of the benefit derived from a visit with the unfortunate and sick.

There are 99 patients now, one left the day before our visit, for the "Valley of Peace." There were about an equal number of the sexes.

Very respectfully yours for the
Morally and Physically Insane.

S.G.B.

Concord, N.H., Sept. 10, 1846

Voice of Industry, September 18, 1846

Huldah J. Stone

Mill operative Huldah J. Stone, secretary of the Lowell Female Labor Reform Association, was another of the pioneer women labor leaders of the 1840s. During most of the life of the *Voice of Industry,* she had charge of its Female Department. She attended all the meetings of the New England Workingmen's Association, participating in the discussions and serving on important committees. At the Manchester convention in March, 1846, she was chosen recording secretary, with a man as her assistant.

Miss Stone toured New England for the *Voice of Industry,* soliciting subscriptions by speaking at meetings of unions of male mechanics, and describing her experiences in letters to the labor paper. She also helped during her tours to organize Female Labor Reform Associations in several communities. Although less militant in her writings than either Sarah G. Bagley or Mehitabel Eastman, she was a steady influence in the organizations of the factory operatives during the mid-1840s. When she was appointed a regular correspondent of the *Voice of Industry* by the Female Labor Reform Association, that paper said of her in its issue of July 31, 1845: "Miss Stone is an able writer, and conversant with the evils which affect the laboring classes, especially the operatives in our manufactories—their privations and requirements, and will lay them before the community through our columns. . . . This will be a valuable acquisition to our paper and we feel deeply indebted for this generous aid and *acting* interest. . . ." And on June 25, 1847, the *Voice of Industry* announced: "Miss H. J. Stone, a lady favorably known to many of our readers, will visit Methuen, Exeter, Haverhill, and other towns in that vicinity, to solicit subscriptions to this paper. We trust her labors will be well rewarded." □

A Letter from the Secretary[15]

Lowell, July 24, 1845

Mr. Editor:—At the last meeting of the Ladies Labor Reform Association in this city, it was voted that "we appoint some Lady of this Association, a Correspondent of your valuable paper, who shall furnish articles herself, and receive them from others who may feel disposed to contribute to the support and interest of the same, by giving interesting items and facts, which may come under their observation." Miss H. J. Stone was accordingly chosen to act in the capacity of correspondent from this Association. She will endeavor in the future to furnish an article herself, for every paper if desirable, and obtain as many others as may be. Her influence will ever be given on the side of equal rights, and the just claims of humanity whether black or white, living at the North or South, whether friends *smile* or *frown* on her humble efforts! She feels that there is a great work to be accomplished through the humble instrumentality of means, ere our Nation is elevated to that high and sublimely glorious pinacle of fame, which it is her privilege, nay, her *imperative duty* to attain! Believing as she does that each and every individual has some duty to perform, some mission to accomplish, for the great good of all, and the elevation of the mass, to a position worthy of our far famed and republican Nation, she will gladly contribute her "two mites" to strengthen that *"voice"* which has been heard above the roar of elements, and the discordant sounds of human degradation and woe, that it may be enabled to speak in tones which shall cause the flinty heart to quake, the stubborn knee to bow, before the mighty and all conquering power of Eternal Truth and Justice!

God speed thee in thy holy mission gentle *"voice,"* mayest thou speak comfort to the despairing—whisper *Hope* to the ear, and pour balm into the heart lacerated and festering with the cankering cares of life—reclaim the wandering, sin enslaved, wretched and lost ones of Our Father's family, and invite them into the bonds of fraternal love and union—thus shalt thou be a blessing in thy day and generation! And when thy "voice" shall be hushed in death, its soothing tones, and encouraging words, shall thrill through every heart, while life or being lasts!

Voice of Industry, July 31, 1845

Our Real Necessities

Is it really necessary that men and women should toil and labor twelve, sixteen, and even eighteen hours, to obtain the mere sustenance of their physical natures? Have they no other wants which call as loudly for satisfaction as those? Call ye this *life*—to labor, eat, drink and die, withuout knowing any thing comparatively speaking, of our mysterious natures—of the object of our creation and preservation and final destination? No! 'tis not *life*. It is merely existing in common with the inanimate and senseless part of creation. "Life *is earnest!*" Not to obtain the perishing things which pertain to the outward; but *earnest* in procuring the riches of enduring, unfading and *ever increasing* goodness and true wisdom. Goodness and wisdom are among the *real* necessities of life! In truth there can be no life without them—all is darkness and *death* where these are wanting. True wisdom will lead us to cultivate all our faculties in that way and manner which shall most increase our own usefulness—add to the good of our fellow creatures and honor the great Creator. In order to increase the former, a portion of time must be devoted to moral and intellectual culture corresponding with the importance of the object. When I hear people say they have no time to read—O, how does the thought come home to my heart—"in Heaven's name what do they live for." No time to read! What in mercy's name do they do for thoughts, for the ever active and restless mind to feast upon from day to day! What do they do with that starving intellect which is ever crying give, give, as the wonders and sublimities in the vast creation unfold themselves to view and which requires *knowledge* to satisfy its unbounded wishes. Is it possible that *any* can be satisfied to exist only in a physical sense, entirely neglecting the cultivation of the noblest powers which God has given them? Rather *we* say, let the old tabernacle of clay be clothed in *rags,* and enjoy but two meals per day, than suffer the intellect to dwindle—the moral and religious capacities to remain uncultivated—the affections unfurnished, the charity limited—the mind contracted with blind bigotry and ignorance! Oh! toiling fellow mortal, if thou by hard and un-

remitting labor eight hours out of the twenty-four, canst not provide for thy physical wants—resolve from this time hence forth and
ever, to give thy influence on the side of Labor Reform!

Voice of Industry, September 18, 1845

Our Cause

Many things have transpired of late to give new courage and
hope to every heart. The good effects of establishing a paper devoted
entirely to the cause of *human right* is already being realized and
appreciated by a large portion of community. That one item of
the business transactions of the last convention in Lowell will, we
confidently believe, be productive of great and lasting good to the
cause of Labor Reform. An independent press, one from which
truth clear and irresistible, shall ever shine forth—truth which shall
cause the moneyed tyrants to desist from their accursed work of
grinding the face of the poor, and keeping back Ananias[16] like, a
part of the real hire—truth which shall raise up the bowed down,
and show every workingman and woman, their true position in
society—their abject state of slavery to capital and capitalists under
existing circumstances.—Truth which shall not only portray the
great and alarming evils of society, but prescribe an effectual
remedy. Let the "Voice" of truth be hailed at the fire-side, in the
work-shop, and in the public mart, by every son and daughter of
New England: Let it go forth, bearing precious seed, which shall
take deep root in the mental soil, and bring forth fruit abundantly!
We do sincerely hope that every individual, within whose breast
glows one spark even, of true philanthropy will lend their aid,
both pecuniarily and mentally in extending and supporting this
messenger of good to the toiling millions of our country. It is to
the general diffusion of knowledge alone, that we look for
success, and triumph over the present evils and abuses which now
flood our nation with crimes, misery, and unholy oppression.
Public opinion must and will be changed. Man must be made to
feel that he is not an isolated being, placed here merely to
gratify his own selfish desires, regardless of the wants or rights of
his fellow man, but that all are indeed and in truth, of one great
family bound together by the strong ties of human sympathy and
love.

We have unbounded confidence in the power and omnipotence
of correct principles diffused into the minds of men—those princi-

ples which are founded on eternal justice and impartial goodness! The National Reform movement we believe to be based on this sure foundation, and we pray God to strengthen and greatly increase its numbers of active and efficient friends—until our country shall be free indeed. Every man who earns his daily bread honestly, and who is sufficiently enlightened on this subject, will if he has any humanity or love of country, give his whole influence on the side of this great National Reform! The signs of the times are truly encouraging. Men, (and women too,) are beginning to realize the great truth which has been so oft sounded in their ears. "All men are created free and equal;" not free to starve, or work for a mere pittance, but free to work reasonable hours and receive a reward proportionate with the real production of the labor performed. They are beginning to see that they are as perfect slaves to a false state of society, as are the poor black and white negroes of the South, to the will and caprices of their inhuman masters. 'Tis true we are not exposed to public sale or liable to be beaten without mercy, but we *are* liable to be treated like as many idiotic females not knowing their right hand from their left, if perchance we condescend to make ourselves really useful, by assisting to prepare the common nutriments of life in some pious minister's family! Awake then awake fellow mortals and spurn from your midst these gross and anti-republican practices! They are a libel on the name—a disgrace to humanity.

There seems to be a general waking up on the subject of Labor Reform[17] throughout the country. Only get the working classes wide awake, so that they are no longer dreaming of Eldorado's and Elysian fields, and they will very quickly command, and it shall be done. Then shall man recognize his brother man beneath the most lowly garb, and virtuous deeds be the only badge of honor.

H.J.S.

Voice of Industry, January 30, 1846

A Word to Philanthropists

We come before you, kind readers, at this time, to speak of our hopes, our prospects, our determinations and our wishes. Our hopes are bright, and our prospects cheering. Our determinations are to persevere in the good work now commenced, until every mountain of evil and oppression shall be brought low—every valley of privation and want be filled with *justice* and *equality*. Our wishes are, that every *well wisher* to human improvement, and the elevation of our race, as a mass, should lend a helping hand in this our holy cause. The Female Labor Reform Association, consisting, for the most part, of operatives now actively engaged in the mills, have purchased of Mr. John Scism, of Fitchburg, the printing press and fixtures belonging thereto, on which the "Voice of Industry" is and ever has been printed. They have made their first payment, which was one hundred dollars; the next will become due in three months, in six, nine and twelve months the remainder. They will be grateful for the smallest donations, from individuals disposed to aid in this, their novel enterprise. We feel that if there is a place in the wide universe where true liberty and freedom should be enjoyed—where the *press* should be untrammelled—and where woman should take her proper place and standing in society, as a rational intelligent being—a fit *companion* and *friend* of man, not a *slave*—it is in the United States of America! *Cultivation* alone, is what our necessities demand; and cultivation it is, which will give to woman that true dignity and moral worth which nature, reason and christianity proclaim to be her high exalted privilege, her sublime destiny! Too long has she been considered an inferior being, merely capacitated to bask in the sunshine of fashion and prosperity contributing to the happiness of those around her, by offices of kindness and labors of love. Her mind and intellect suffered to dwindle, through lack of cultivation and improvement—her sphere of action, being exclusively domestic, she rarely presumed to think or act independently or clearly, on any subject.—Those days thank heaven have passed, and a new era in the life of women, has dawned upon her hitherto prescribed and limited sphere of action! Men are beginning to realize that woman is blessed with an *intellect,* which if rightly trained and expanded, will be productive of incalculable blessing and real advantage to the world, as well as the pure, ever active affections, which flow forth, shedding life and joy almost like heaven's around the sacred altar of domestic love.—They are no longer willing to commit the destinies of the young and rising generation into the hands of the uninformed and inefficient, knowing that it is in childhood, *correct principles* and a *love of knowledge,* must be implanted in the soul. This has been styled an age of improvement, and why should the advantages which accrue therefrom, be confined to the *lords* of Creation alone? Why should not woman seek to improve, elevate and raise higher her standard of moral and intellectual worth, in order to keep pace with the age in which she lives? We surely can see no impropriety in such aspirations and exertions. And until we are convinced that it is unfeminine and out of place to labor and toil for the *best good* of all our race, we shall devote a portion of the time which heaven may allot us here, to this great—this all important work; and we would most earnestly and cordially invite all who take any interest in the progress of our race—in the cause of "Labor Reform," or the elevation of the mass from ignorant servitude, and blind devotion to the god of this world, to high table-lands of promise where *universal* brother and sisterhood shall encircle in its charitable arms, all the families of the earth—to lend us their aid—if not in a pecuniary point, let us have an encouraging word, or an approving look even, to cheer us on our way! Philanthropists, have we spoken in vain? Will you not feel for us, as did the good honest quaker—in your *pockets?*

H.J.S.

Lowell, March 2, 1846

Voice of Industry, March 6, 1846

Letter to the *Voice*

Dear Voice:—When last I addressed you I was in Claremont: left there on Tuesday for my own mountain home. Arrived in Cabot, Wednesday eve—found friends blest with health and ready to greet me; but there was one familiar face which I was wont to see beaming with affection's holiest smile, and ever ready to embrace me in the arms of love, which came not forth to welcome her child: her voice fell not in rich cadence, on the listening ear, telling of undying love and trust and watchful care. No tender loving mother was in that *dear old home,* but methought, unseen, her blest spirit hallowed each loved, familiar spot. There, in the very room, on the very table lay the old family Bible in which she so often looked for counsel, wisdom, and strength to bear her on through the deep waters of affliction—over which so many fervent prayers had been offered up to the Father of spirits for my happiness and welfare in life—for the happiness of all her offspring and friends, (enemies she had none). There sat the old arm-chair in which her venerable form had so oft reclined—all—all was the same as in days of childhood met the eye—save that fond mother's presence. Thanks to heaven for remaining blessings and comforts! O how much have we to be grateful for—how much to weep over and lament? How much to cheer us on in the path of duty to one another—to our God.

In Cabot, as well as other places, I found brave hearts and true, alive to the cause in which we are engaged. God bless your labors in behalf of humanity's rights—persevere undaunted in the noble work of elevating and assisting to make industry what it should be, *"honorable and attractive,"* is the language of every sympathetic soul. The cry of *Infidelity* there, as here, salutes the ear. If it is infidelity to plead for justice and right—in God's name we are willing to be branded with the title—we fear little the *name* and much less the influence which such unchristian epithets will have over the minds of a thinking community. Unholy "mysteries" and *infallible* clergy have kept the *laboring classes* too long in awe, compelling them to pay for preaching which instead of raising and enobling their views and conceptions of God, served only to give them false and pernicious ideas of his government, character, and attributes—of their own relation to that best of Beings and to the whole brotherhood of man. It is *time* to leave mysteries to the moles and the bats, and commence studying the beautiful—the sublime, volume of Nature, if we would learn of God aright. We must know him through his works. They are ever before us—ever the same. Infinite skill and wisdom is stamped on their every feature. Harmony and grandeur conspire to fill the soul with emotions of deepest reverence and love toward the Great and Mighty Architect! We must all be students in the great laboratory of Nature—acquaint ourselves with the laws which govern throughout her variegated realms—with the beauties and utilities which meet us in every department of vast creation, if we would live as rational, intelligent beings, and enjoy the rich and glorious feast of soul which wisdom and true knowledge ever yields. That all who listen to thy words and understand well their import, dear "Voice," may become such *indeed;* that science and *true* christianity may walk among us hand in hand, causing the waste places around us to become gardens of truth's own planting, in which shall flourish the unfading flowers of virtuous friendships and human sympathies, is the constant prayer and doubtless hope of your unchanging friend *for the right.*

H.J.S.

Voice of Industry, May 8, 1846

Take Courage!

Take courage, faithful "Voice", thy words are heard and their true import appreciated in the "Granite State." Her sons and daughters are cheerfully coming to thy aid. We have everything to hope, and with *union, nothing* to fear! The cause is onward. The true spirit is abroad, and the pure breezes of heaven, are wafting it o'er hill and dale, sounding abroad the notes of freedom and right, which shall yet cause the moral and intellectual deserts to blossom as the rose.—Slavery of any kind cannot exist for any length of time, in fair New England's clime. Intelligence and morality will destroy and uproot its unholy branches from our land.—*"God speed the Right." "Industry, not servitude!" "Excelsior."* These are our mottos. Heaven grant that the spirit of each may fire every heart! O could the toiling millions of our country, feel that great truth, "Union is power," and act accordingly, how soon would the mighty chariot of reform, sweep through this republic! They would need only to speak the work and lo! tyranny, oppression, and crime, even, would be annihilated almost entirely.

What but tyranny, causes oppression? and what but oppression produces crime? Want it is, which drives man from virtue's flowery paths, into the howling wilderness of sin and misery. Want of the common comforts of life—of right and wholesome instruction, for the human soul—want of sympathy and friendly feeling, one toward another, in community—these and many other wants, are the direct source of all the growing evils around us. Let there be an immediate and complete union among all producing classes; and the interest of one become the interest of all, and we shall soon see "a better time coming" without "waiting a little longer." Many may be ready to ask, how shall this union be accomplished? Answer! By the industrious becoming well informed, on all subjects which pertain to the interests of that class. Knowledge is power, also, as well as union. Ah yes! and too well is this fact known and appreciated by the capitalists generally! They look upon an *intelligent* laborer, or operative with distrust and misgivings. They fear that their craft will be in danger, if general intelligence, and right cultivation should prevail among the working men and women of our country. They know, that with them and their unrighteous exactions, ignorance is the power which holds them in "durance vile." The long hour system of labor is just adapted to this grand scheme of holding them in servitude and ignorance. It appeals to the very lowest capacities of our natures, viz., the gratification of the senses, without giving one noble impulse to the better—the inner—the God like capacities of mind! Money, that which has been truly styled as the root of all evil, is with many the *summum bonum* of existence. Regardless of everything which elevates and humanizes—of all those tender sympathies which if allowed to flow forth in their vivifying purity, and holy influence, fling a halo of glory, and of brightness, over the whole social and moral world, and exert a saving—a hallowing power over the frail wanderers, in sin's dark and gloomy paths—they toil on, having but one object in view, but one aim in life—money! Yes, strange as it may appear, there are beings, who walk this beautiful, this glorious earth, endowed with all the five senses, each in itself a gift which should excite eternal gratitude and praise, perfectly indifferent, and seemingly unconscious that there is aught in earth or heaven to be sought after, or prefered, before this *God of Mammon!* O debasing, humiliating reflection! That beings, created in the image of God—blest with minds capable of the highest cultivation, morally and intellectually, should thus sink to a level with the brute that perisheth! Awake, arise! fellow mortals, from this degrading state, and resolve from this day forth, to be no longer slaves to ignorance— of the earth, earthly! Let "the spirit of Divinity which stirs within," shine forth, and life-intellectual quicken anew!—Then shall man be redeemed, God glorified, and earth a paradise become. God grant it, dear Voice, is the pray of

H.J.S.

Claremont, N.H.

Voice of Industry, May 22, 1846

Social Gathering at Manchester, N.H.

We had the pleasure of being present at this gathering, and can therefore speak confidently. In company with a few friends from Lowell, Mr. Albert Brisbane of N.Y., Mr. Allen of Roxbury, we took the cars at Lowell, or car rather, as they could not afford two, we were squeezed and crowded into that one, until there were few, if any *"standing* up *seats"* left unoccupied! However we picked ourselves out as best we could, and soon found our way to the Town Hall, which was at an early hour well filled with youth and beauty, enjoying the sweets of social, friendly interchange of thoughts and feelings—smiles and greetings. The Hall was very tastefully decorated with evergreen—with mottos, and a "Post Office" in the far distance, was just visible among the shrubbery. The tables were neatly laid with those things which please the animal taste.

The Manchester and Lowell Brass Bands were in attendance, to cheer and animate the souls of all who had any music in them. It is unnecessary to speak of the rich treat they gave, for is not their praise among the people? Then too, we listened to the sweet, harmonious, soul-elevating notes of the *"home branch"* of the Hutchinson Family. O, how did that rich, spirit-moving piece, "Excelsior" breathe forth the holy prophecy of GOOD to our cause. We gazed at the noble motto o'er their heads, "Excelsior," and listened, as to a voice from God out of heaven, speaking to us one and all, through those, his humble messengers. Higher and yet higher, let us aim! Let us not think our work half done, until the spirit of that motto, shall *elevate* and *redeem* the *masses,* from all servitude, degrading ignorance, and vice of every kind! Faithful souls, must struggle and toil on, after hoping against hope—meeting with cruel ingratitude and indifference from the very beings, which their labors are calculated to bless; but let none of these things move you in the least.

We were extremely happy to witness the perfect unanimity of spirit which prevails among the Associations, and God grant it may continue to bind them together, with a two fold cord which cannot be broken.

On the whole, we think this Gathering a good one, and calculated to do much good for the Labor Reform movement. We know of no better way of spending a social hour, or one in which all the laboring classes can meet and become acquainted with each other, than this. May others go and do likewise. Shall we not have the pleasure of attending one of a similar character at Nashua, ere long? It serves a double purpose, by bringing the masses, together, and thereby enabling them to become acquainted with each other, creating a union of feeling and sympathy which otherwise could not be felt, and also to raise funds with which to carry on the Reform. Brothers and Sisters in this noble enterprise, in heaven's name, persevere! Every day brings tidings which speak of encouragement to our ears. The *great heart* of community beats in unison with our humble efforts to bless humanity. Let every philanthropist exert all the powers God hath given to circulate the "Voice" in every nook and corner of our land. Do not forget, that in order to be *free* indeed, we *must* sustain a *free* paper. Let us all individually act as

Agents for the paper, wherever we may be. Let us be up and doing whatever our hands find to do with all our might.—"EXCELSIOR."

H.J.S.

Lowell, June 10, 1846.

Voice of Industry, June 19, 1846

Looking on the Surface

People are too prone to look only on the surface of things. Especially is this the case when looking at the subject of the evils of the factory system as now progressing in New England. Many are ready to say, there is as much intelligence among the operatives in our manufacturing towns, as there is among any other class, as a whole; and there they stop—not even doubting but what they have overturned one of the main pillars of Labor Reform. Let us see! Grant there is intelligence among the spindles; how came it there? Was it acquired by bending in unnatural positions thirteen hours per day over machinery, whose clatter is sufficient to confuse the clearest head, and cause the whole intellectual machinery to run out of gear? No, far from this! They gathered their intellectual treasures among the green hills and fertile vales, of their own loved mountain homes, where the pure air of heaven, gave life and animation to the whole being—where earth's variegated beauties and harmonies, all combined to fill the soul with rapture and peace! But this is merely talk—it does not enter deep into the soulless, heartless System, of which we are speaking. The great question is, can a factory population, such as will ere long grow up here in America, like Jonah's gourd, become an educated, intelligent people, a people worthy that country which stands pre-eminent among all the Nations of the earth? That is the question to be solved, more anon.

H.J.S.

Voice of Industry, September 25, 1846

On the Road for the *Voice*

Methuen, June 28, 1847

BR. YOUNG:—

It is with feelings of real pleasure that I now address you. Since I left Lowell, Wednesday eve, I have been more successful in circulating our faithful Voice than I anticipated. That fact has given me *new* courage to act in the cause of human elevation, since it teaches me that the *"masses"* are beginning to co-operate with those, who have been bearing the burthen and heat of the day of combined wealth, against the poor laborer, in our country—I have not conversed with an individual on this subject who does not see and acknowledge the importance and righteousness of the principles which the Voice lays before the public from week to week. Very few refuses to subscribe except those who are already taking four or five weekly papers.—I called on Agent Davis[18] of this Village, and gave him a polite invitation to assist us in publishing a paper which should be filled with the most useful and instructive matter, as the working men and women had so little leisure to devote to reading, we think it all important that *their* paper should be liberally sustained, in order to enable the publisher to make it such as should meet the hearts of the laboring classes, &c. Said he I take about twenty now, and that is more than I can get time to read. But sir said I, will you not give us some little encouragement in this righteous cause which has for its object the elevation and improvement of our race? *"If"* said he "it *is* a *good* cause I wish you God speed!" I thanked him for his good wishes and told him I should be labor with more courage if I knew that the *good* and *great* of earth wished well to our cause. He very politely gave me leave to pass into the cloth room with my paper, but no farther. I find the same overbearing tyranical spirit bears sway here in this beautiful little village, which holds so many in "durance vile" in our own, otherwise, pleasant City.

Here as well as in Lowell, a man who works for the Companies, is little better than the machinery which he conducts—he must go to *the* church (which by the way is the Calvinist church), and vote the "ticket" or take up his quarters somewhere else. I rejoice to learn however, that there are spirits here, true to themselves, and to the world, who will not, and do not submit to such anti republican rules and requirements. God grant the number of such may increase daily in New England! What? shall it be said of men born and educated here in this our free and democratic nation, that they will submit to be deprived of the last vestage of liberty bequeathed them by our brave ancestors! Forbid it heaven!! Working men of N. England, will you sit calmly down and suffer these things so to be? Will you not rather raise your voices in one long, loud cry to heaven— "LIBERTY OR DEATH!" Will you yield inch after inch to the aggressor until driven off the footstool of God? Or, will you be MEN the true

NOBILITY of the earth, and as such, claim your right to the soil—to the air of heaven—to the running stream, and the bright sunshine of God and to the fruits of your own industry. Let *immediate action* answer these all-important questions! Let *your* "voice" workingmen be heard speaking in the clear, steady, persuasive tones of justice and mercy, from the rivers to the end of the earth. Would you see principles diffused thro' community, on which, rests the beautiful temple of freedom, support *your* "Voice" liberally, that it may discouse in rich and varied notes of melody to every ear. Would you have that "union for *power*" among the working classes, which shall "bless humanity" give your influence on the side of that "Voice" which is and ever has been the true friend of the laborer— let it be heard in every man's dwelling and its truths sink deep in every heart! What might not that "Voice" become, did every man and woman too, for whose interests it is pleading, give it their countenance and support? Why, we should then have the largest and best paper in the world! We have only to speak the word and *'tis done.* Who among us cannot give 1.25 per year for this *noble* enterprise? Is there one? We hope not. Nobility of the earth wake up to your own interests, and be no longer degraded in your own and the eyes of the world! This is not idle speculation—or visionary imaginings of a disordered brain, but sober truth—truth too which is being brought home to every rational mind from day to day— there is no avoiding it—it *is* truth which he that runs even now, *may read* and understand! But I must close this scrawl for this time.

In haste,   I am &c.,

H.J.S.

Voice of Industry, July 2, 1847

On the Road for the *Voice* (Continued)

Lawrence, June 30, 1847

BR. YOUNG:—Since I last wrote you I have met with one gentleman whose noble, philanthropic heart is so expanded with that *charity* which *thinketh no evil,* that I cannot in conscience, pass him over in silence. Besides, my sisters who are laboring in this holy cause of elevation with me, will be very grateful to know that we have men who are willing to allow woman to have some rights in this age of improvement as well as the gentlemen. But to the point. The above gentleman shall be nameless, suffice it to say he is "*Bossee*" in the Machine Shop on the Essex Corporation, over some part of the work. After conversing some time with me on the present evils which affect the working men and women of our country, and admitting that there must be a change in these things or times would continue to grow worse and worse, said he, "but if I wished to take that paper ever so much I *would not,* if it was presented to me by— *a female!!*" There, my sisters, now will you not hang your heads in disgrace, and abandon the cause of equal rights at once and forever? "Why," said he, "no man that has any *influence,* or that is of any use to the cause will take it. Females are out of *their place* while soliciting names to a working man's paper." Only think of it, girls, how very unfeminine and "out of place" it would have been in this gentleman's eyes, had he lived in Christ's day, for Mary to have gone alone to the sepulchre where none but *Jesus* slept. No *ladies* there? Why in all probability he would not have received the news of the glorious resurrection from her lips had it been what his soul was panting to hear; for, O shameful to relate, a *female* had dared to presume to know for herself somewhat of that blessed "truth" which was to elevate and make good and happy the race, and had even stepped out of *her place* (the *back kitchen* I suppose he meant) so far, as to go out and ascertain whether Christ was indeed risen, and to proclaim the glorious news to her friends and her kindred! From my very soul I *pity* such a man—one who holds the female sex in such low estimation as to make such an assertion as the above. His associates in former days must have been of rather uncertain characters, or else he made the statement to attempt to throw impediments in the way of a cause which, if it prospered, might possibly take a few dollars and cents out of his pocket. I suppose he is one of those who would wish to have "the *woman*" a domestic animal, that is, know just enough to cook his victuals, mend his feetings, rock the cradle and keep the house in order; and if she wished for any further information, why she must ask her Lord and Master! An *equal* she must not be. She must not engage in any great and noble enterprise to benefit her own and the other sex, *even* if she could accomplish *twice* as much as a man, for she would be "out of place." She must not dare go forth among her own friends and in a virtuous, upright, *christian* community to labor in order to sustain a paper devoted entirely to the interests of the thousands of females who are toiling beyond any thing which their physical natures can endure, in close, unhealthy atmospheres, and to hard working laborers who receive just enough to keep soul and body in the same latitude, for fear of getting out of place!— Lord, forgive, pity and *enlighten* the understandings of all such, if any more there are! I, for one, shall labor for the rights of *all,* so long as God shall permit me to live and possess my faculties entire. Thank heaven we live in a land blessed with Gospel light and freedom, where there are no distinctions; all are *one* in Christ. More anon.

H.J.S.

Voice of Industry, July 13, 1847

Mehitabel Eastman

Mehitabel Eastman was a Manchester, New Hampshire, factory operative and one of the organizers and prominent leaders of the Manchester Female Labor Reform Association. After Miss Bagley left the *Voice of Industry,* the name of Miss Eastman appeared on the masthead as co-editor. She contributed to the paper, and also went out on tours seeking subscriptions to keep it alive. Her letters to the labor paper from various villages she visited, written in a sprightly language, tell us much about her courage in overcoming existing prejudice against women speaking in public and becoming involved in public affairs. It is interesting that she obtained the greatest encouragement from workers and the most opposition from professionals as well as spokesmen for the employers. Her letters offer interesting insights into American social affairs in the late 1840s.

The section opens with what is, so far as is known, the first published piece by Miss Eastman, a challenge to Harriet Farley to prove that the *Lowell Offering* truly represented the factory operatives. ☐

Rejected by the *Courier*

The following article, written for the "Courier," but refused publication until inspected by Miss Farley, who was absent from the City, was handed us by the author, with a request to publish.

We comply with the request without entering into the controversy. The reason of its rejection by Schouler, is evidently its
impartial reflection upon the Offering as a factory girls magazine.

Mr. Schouler; Sir:—In reply to the communication in your paper
of the 30 ult., from the man who "fell into conversation with me,
from motives of mere curiosity," I will say to the public, there is
no "mistake" on my part, and that his curiosity was gratified, by an
assertion from me that the Offering was "written by Factory Girls,"
(nothing being said by either of us about the number of writers.)

"The Offering is not written by Factory Girls."

Then comes Mr. Moulton's challenge, "If you will produce twelve
original articles, in the three last Nos., from Factory Girls, I will
give you twelve dollars."

It is hoped and believed, that Miss Farley can gratify this man
of "curiosity," by "bringing forward twelve writers," though the
number of writers was not questioned. If Miss Farley cannot produce
"twelve," I am very sorry, and rejoice that such a thing is dis-
continued.

Give this a place in your columns, and oblige "quite a talker."

M. EASTMAN

Tuesday Evening, Dec. 30.

Voice of Industry, January 2, 1846

To the Public

In coming before you as one of the Publishers of this paper, I
am disposed to submit a few remarks. The great reason why shall be
given. A desire to give the paper a wide circulation, in view of the
importance of having one organ through which factory girls and all
laborers can speak, telling their wrongs, asking the world to help,
when help is wanted, in many things that should not be. The world
should know the sufferings of *The Factory Girls* from crowded
boarding houses, short time allotted for meals, the "Black List" and
many other evils accumulating under the present system of labor in
the mills. In short we are impelled from a sense of duty, not for
profit or pleasure.

Experience is said to be the best teacher, and an experience of
years in factory life has taught me its sad effects on mind and health.

Knowledge cannot be acquired under the present system of labor. It is by the enlargement of the mind that all evils may be checked, and it seems to me, prevented. Therefore its diffusion should be encouraged among laborers. Our country cannot be secure without it. It must be among factory girls, in counting rooms, in the boarding houses and indeed everywhere.

How are we to get information and keep knowledge? Give us time to read, for social intercourse, for amusement. Let us work less hours. Let us have the hearty co-operation of the many, and there will be great good done to the toiling sons and daughters of New England—to the country, for knowledge is more powerful and important than dollars and cents.

Here I respectfully ask the assistance of all, having faith to believe much will be given to help us along in this great undertaking, as soon, and as far as is practicable. I shall come in person to ask many to take my paper—shall hope for a hearty welcome and a cheerful subscription of $1.25 for one year.

Thanks to the city of Manchester for what they have done in the beginning. We will try to send our paper promptly, and hope its contents will be acceptable. Much gratitude to the donors.

Those who purchase single copies we hope will soon send in their names as subscribers.

Friends and patrons of Manchester with whom we have spent the past year, we bid you adieu for a little while.

MEHITABLE [*sic*] EASTMAN

Voice of Industry, February 12, 1847

Correspondence from Dover

MR. EDITOR:—My last letter from this place was on the 12th inst. Since that time I have seen and spoken with a large number of Dover folks of all descriptions, Lawyers, Doctors, Merchants and a few Mechanics, thinking I would leave the latter class for her who is to take my place in procuring subscribers; for they seem to be much interested in the paper, and I think they will sustain it. I am heartily glad you have secured a Factory Girl to act as a travelling agent, but I sincerely hope she will not be taxed with "taking advantage of the gallantry of Dover gentlemen," or "making a League with either political party, to bring about the Ten Hour system."

Yesterday I paid the "Fathers of the Town" a visit. I found them very busy in looking over "the list of voters in Dover," but then they laid all this by to attend to my list. I told them our motto was, "Equal Rights and equal privileges to all men," and we Factory Girls do want the privilege of an hour to dinner and ¾ to breakfast.

"Let us subscribe for the paper; her argument is not unreasonable," said one. The others seemed "dead set;" because it proposed "Legislation to restrict the hours of labor."

The next call was upon a Dr., an Englishman. "He was rejoiced to see a movement to ameliorate the condition of operatives, and would do almost anything to favor us in our undertaking; his practice as a physician had convinced him of the need of a reduction of hours in labor."

Next I called at the splendid U. S. Hotel, kept by F. G. Whidden, His guests speak of this house in high terms. The gentlemanly Landlord done us a great favor, and I should be glad if our friends would favor him.

Many of our friends are desirous to have our next Convention held here of Newburyport, and seems to me to be a good place.

I have visited one of the Agents. He was not inclined to patronize this; and I felt sorry he declined to purchase one single number.—By his permission one was left on his desk, and we hope he will be disposed to aid in means to elevate labor, he convinced that the present system does not tend to the acquirement of knowledge. We ought to have the co-operation of agents, proprietors, and operatives.

Yesterday was spent in distributing the Voice to my subscribers, who seemed to think "it was planned out to be the very best," as it was in its first introduction. I was very sorry I could not supply all with single numbers.

To-day I have made calls upon the Editorial corps. I cannot but think the Gazette men in our favor; for "by their fruits we know them." One of the fraternity seemed crusty and I am fearful that my call was an annoyance.

Thanks to patrons and friends of Dover; to whom I must soon say adieu.

M.E.

Voice of Industry, April 23, 1847

Looking through Corporation Spectacles

MR. EDITOR:—A variety of reasons not a little unreasonable have been given for declining to subscribe for the Voice of Industry and to show the world how easy a matter it is to suit all, we give some of the most important.

"Your object is a good one and I have tho't for a long time I should be a subscriber, but do dislike the manner it treats *our* Mexican War.[19] The man who speaks against this is directly against his country and should not be encouraged; then you meddle too much with Slavery, taking sides with those Whig Abolitionists."[20]

"Your editor is too much of a Loco[21] for me. He ought to come out on this cursed Mexican war, he is quite too silent on this subject which ought to occupy a large space in every paper, especially, one circulated so extensively among laboring men as yours. Working men have got to support this war and this ought to be all shown to them."

"Away with your Free Trade principles and the foolish idea of calling on the Legislature to restrict the hours of labor. Don't you see the Corporations are doing the things right of themselves?"

"You dont give the glorious War news I want to hear all about the war, who's killed and whose going to be. Your editor don't seem to take a part. Dont see a word in this paper. Here's 71 volunteers going to start tomorrow and I mean to take some paper that will give news about them. Young is one of these comeouters[22] and a Four-year-ite."

"Don't seem to be but few deaths and marriages, accidents, and such kinds of news. Telling so much about these old factories, folks in other countrys will think we are slaves and tis true in some measure but then who wants to have it told, cause we can't mend the matter."

"This Ten hour plan will ruin the Factory's. Just so sure as the Legislature passes that bill just so sure we shall all be thrown out of employment. You have got the time lengthened out, and now what do you want to fuss for? If a man had come into my establishment with your paper, I would have ordered him out. You being a lady I am in duty bound to let you pass."

"Too much of Whig spirit. 'Tis not neutral in politics. The editor is a Partisan.—Why don't he come to the point? A reform in the present system of labor, let Texas,[23] Mexico and Slavery at the South alone."

Now for a clergyman's reason called a Universalist.[24]

The principles of your paper are visionary. Here I see what you "Labor For." "The Rights of man to himself; to a Choice of Industrial pursuits, to an equivalent to what he produces." There's so much selfishness in the world that it is utterly impossible to bring about such things. That Working Men's Protective Union[25] is of no particular benefit to laborers. I tell you all these things tend to create a spirit of discord accomplishing no good and will ultimately fall through.

For illustration a man is in the river, on a plank; he sees a log yonder and instead of going ashore on the plank he strives to get on the log, and he falls into the river and is drowned."

This Rev. seems to me he has been looking through Corporation spectacles.

Saturday I took the last train of cars for Manchester, where I enjoyed one day in business more profitable than pleasurable.

The ladies of the Manchester Association have in contemplation a Picnic to come off in June. At a meeting last Saturday evening, there seemed to be an unusual degree of interest in reform movements.

In this place I have done far better than I expected.

There is to be a petition circulated and a Whig Representative told me he would hand it in.

M.E.

Nashua, May 4th

Voice of Industry, May 7, 1847

A Renegade

MR. EDITOR: To-day my business in this place will be done. My subscribers have all paid in advance, with a few exceptions which is decidedly the best way and the only way to carry on business right.

Those who have subscribed for six months think they will continue for a year, and promise to inform you if they "wish to discontinue."—Most of your patrons here are workingmen and friends to the cause, and by their request I will give some note of my success among the Representatives. All seemed amicable but one, whom his constituents call Capt.—whose name means "a pledge on pawn" and who by promise to go for the Ten Hour System was elected, he now says "he never was in favor; and that his constituents misunderstood him. He cannot take the Voice because it goes for Legislature on labor to limit the hours to ten! Corporations had got the power and would keep it, for all what could be done by the cry of the Voice, and he would rather I would not circulate the paper in his shop as it was not time to discuss the subject."

Since the late arrangement he has denied his men the privilege of going out to supper, being importuned to do so by the Corporations. This seems to show how much he goes for reducing the hours of labor, but I suppose he don't care, he will get his "two dollars per day and roast beef," but his constituents in his employment "can't go out to supper."—

Thanks, and a good-bye to friends and patrons, of Nashua, on the 7th day of May 1847.

M.E.

Voice of Industry, May 21, 1847

Correspondence from Boston

DEAR READERS:—According to promise you shall have some letters from me during my sojourn here. Having but little time or talent for writing, you will not receive much improvement from what may be told from time to time in these letters, but may answer my fellow operatives whom, I am in hopes, take an interest in our little sheet, which is called here "The Factory Girls Voice, far better calculated to improve the condition of operatives than the one coming monthly, purporting to have been written by themselves."

I made my debut in this place Thursday, beginning with the name of the President of the Workingmen's P.U. [Protective Union] Division, No. 5.—Thus far my visits have been to the workshops, with the exception of a few, one of which shall be told:—

Having occasion to call upon a cold street named Winter, and seeing the name of one on a door well known to me in my native place, methought it would be well to "drop in," and found by the waiter that they were at dinner though 'twas 3 o'clock, P.M. Thinks I to myself I have got into the "wrong pew," and sure enough when the Dr. made his appearance he was a stranger to me and more so to my cause. In answer to my appeal he says, "I have more books and papers than my house will hold, and wish you would take some away." I assured him I would come for the books. "What is the object of your paper?" He was told its object. "The laborers have their rights and live like kings, and I don't see any need of this contention for rights." Having enquired what day I should call for the books, "I am too busy to attend to you," and away he went leaving me alone, giving me no chance to say good bye, sir. When I get the books I shall send them to the "Improvement Circle," and the freight will be paid by Dr. R———, the donor. One more notion from the "man in black" whom we met under the "Liberty Tree" on the Common.[26] This man came from the "Sunny South," he told me about his plantation and Slaves, how contented, how happy they were before the "crazy Abolitionists" meddled with that which would, if finally carried out, dissolve our happy Union, and was inclined to think our paper was tending to create a discontent, keeping up a kind of commotion among the Factory Girls; you are sowing the storm and will reap the whirlwind. I am sorry to see you thus spending your time in vain. It is true you have slavery here, but then such always has been and always will be, and your Voice will not be noticed among those who have all the power.

Truly this is a "city of notions," containing notionists in an abundance. Some entertain a notion that I am an imposter, calling on me to produce my certificate of Agency. This brings to mind the importance of presenting our Prospectus, and has been of more avail than a certify of my good name, signed by all the clergy of Lowell.[27] Then comes a train of interrogations: How long since this began?—How do corporations like it? Who's W. F. Young? and who's this Eastman? I can answer all but the latter. We don't understand by your paper that you advocate the tariff, if you mean to carry out what you have just read from your Prospectus as strong as this paper (handing me a paper which has been called the "lieing Atlas") urge the tariff principles.

My success so far has been as good as can be expected, in consideration of "hard times," which I hear more about there than elsewhere. I must not forget our obligation to J. J. Mitchell for much favor of a list of workingmen and their places of business. Should we get one third of them it will be doing well.

With the advice of several friends I have engaged Bela Marsh, 25 Cornhill, to deliver our papers, being assured by his customers that he will be reasonable in his charge, and that he is decidedly in favor of our principles and the welfare of our sheet. In short I am told by many of my patrons here that he is a "whole souled" man. We hope he will be extensively patronized by congenial spirits.

I am told I must call on the "lions in State street," and if I can summon courage enough their wishes shall be gratified and yours, by an account of my success in their quarters.

Sabbath morn we took a walk, and coming past the Post Office saw men selling newspapers, our guide said the sale of penny papers on the Sabbath was common. You shall hear from me again, till then good by.

Truly yours in the good cause.

M.E.

Boston, May 24

Voice of Industry, May 28, 1847

Selling the *Voice* to Mill Hands

DEAR VOICE: I arrived in this place last Monday morn. Every one knows this is a manufacturing place and very much like all others where wealth is concentrated in Cotton Mills. There are five large Mills in this place and I understand there are nearly 2000 operatives, and learn from the Agent they have great privileges and would not consent to work ten hours per day. By the way, it must be said, Mr. B. the Agent gave us something towards helping along "the good cause," I told him I was going in to look about, and as 'tis said "silence gives consent," very soon I was offering our paper to the inmates of the mills, they manifested an interest in the cause and no one made me afraid by looks or words, but when I came to enter a lower weave room there was a lord who molested me, but could not make me afraid, though his appearance was very much like the feline species. He ordered me out of his room, but "Bill" could not extend his authority any further and I went on with my business and was well treated throughout the premises. My stay in this place has been very pleasant and profitable, could I remain I have no doubt my list would soon number one hundred.

There is but one small paper published in this place, but this I understand is well supported. An attempt was made to start a workingman's paper in this place a short time since, but not quite sufficient encouragement was given to warrant its projectors a good living. Our Voice was particularly welcome at this time, and they say we shall have their support if it is true to the cause of the Workingmen.

In closing this communication I cannot but mention the Great Falls Hotel, kept by A. Staples. This is strictly a Temperance House elegantly furnished throughout—there are one hundred rooms, any one stopping at this house cannot but be made happy during their sojourn. No more for this time, and this in haste.

M.E.

Great Falls, July 24

Voice of Industry, July 30, 1847

To the Readers of the *Voice*

With the present number, our connection as publishers of this paper ceases. The ill health of the editor, with other circumstances, not necessary here to detail, render such a step advisable. We are happy, on retiring, in being able to state to our friends and the public, that THE VOICE OF INDUSTRY is in a more prosperous condition, than at any period of its existence, and that the growing interest in its behalf and the righteous cause it advocates, warrants us in the belief, that it is permanently established. We also congratulate the friends of Labor Reform on being able to announce the name of Mr. D. H. JAQUES—a man of strong devotion to human progress and elevation, and of acknowledged ability as our successor. In this change we feel quite sure our patrons will sustain no loss and we bespeak for Mr. Jaques a continuation of their aid and sympathy, believing they will be rewarded an hundred fold. To our friends— those who have generously aided us in our arduous and sacrificing labors, we return many thanks. To our enemies, or the enemies of our cause, we would entertain that degree of charity, which becomes beings liable to human frailty. With these brief remarks we take leave of our readers and the public.

W. F. YOUNG
M. EASTMAN

Voice of Industry, September 3, 1847

To the Friends of the *Voice*

It may not be out of place to make some remarks, in addition to those of last week, relative to the dissolution of my proprietary relationship to this paper. I connected myself with the paper from a sense of duty towards others; and my connection ceases, in some measure, from a similar cause. There is much pleasure in the view of the past, having met with success far beyond the expectations of many who pronounced the undertaking as "impracticable and unwise."—The paper is now on a good foundation, having a greater number of subscribers than at any time since its commencement, and little, if any, doubt is entertained of its continued existence; and none need fear but our successor will do justice to the cause—making the paper an advocate to the cause of the working classes. It is hoped he will receive their aid in his arduous undertaking.

The principles advocated in this paper are received more favorably than heretofore, which must impart encouragement, and I look forward with undoubting confidence to a time when labor will be made more attractive, especially factory labor. Eight long years of experience has convinced me of the need of Reform. The present system is drudging indeed, and it is the duty of every one to try to effect a change. This has been my constant pleasure for the seven months past, in which time many new friends have been made, and many favors received which will always remain on memory's page, and for the encouragement of any of the sisterhood let me say that the utmost courtesy has been extended. In visiting five hundred places of business, mostly workshops, but few unkind looks or words are within memory.

A few words to a gentleman of immense wealth, in Cotton Mills, who read this paper for several weeks, but could "not encourage it longer, as its tendency seemed to be to make the operatives discontented with their lot," is respectfully reminded of his promise to "give in black and white further reasons why the Voice of Industry should not be encouraged."

Thanks to patrons and friends—a kind and grateful remembrance of all will ever be cherished. May those tokens of favor and regard be extended to the present proprietor, is the wish of

M.E.

Boston, Sept. 6, 1847

Voice of Industry, September 10, 1847

"Voice of Industry Girl"

SOUTH BOSTON, Oct. 4th, 1847

MR. EDITOR:—My business is done here for the present, and it is hoped your patrons will like the paper so well as to render it unnecessary to send for a renewal of their subscription. More than one hundred names have been booked in this vicinity, three hundred copies distributed gratuitously, and some sold;—in short your paper has been thoroughly introduced into every work-shop with the exception of three, viz.; Geo. Thomas's, Alger's, and Gray's. These establishments will not even permit those called "fair sex," "weak vessels," &c., to enter for the purpose of getting subscribers to a newspaper, designed to ameliorate the condition of "Factory girls!" The most of the subscribers were obtained at the Old Colony Machine Shop, Union Works, Plough Factory, Chair Factory, and Mr. Coney's establishment. "This Voice of Industry Girl" is exceedingly grateful to the gentlemanly working men, proprietors, and foremen of the above establishments, from whom so much encouragement has been received not only in pecuniary point of view, but by kind treatment which made the task more agreeable and easy. One who chose to give another man's name instead of his own, causing no little confusion, is informed that no papers will be sent him, and he must be forgiven "as he did not know any better."

My visit to the celebrated Locomotive Establishment of Hinkley & Drury was very pleasant. Here I saw several of those Iron Horses, whose shrill whistle and loud bell will soon be heard on the roads. Mr. H. and the gentlemanly clerks in the counting room seem to be interested in your paper, but "could not give a permission to go in to solicit subscribers," however a plan was suggested to introduce the paper at the Counting room on pay day, and a large number of copies have been left with the following preamble:

To working-men in the employment of Hinkley & Drury.

According to the rules of the establishment I cannot come into the shop with the Voice of Industry but am pleased to present the paper in this way for your subscription, one year, six months, or three, at $1.25 per year delivered at your door weekly, and in proportion for less time.

We need and expect your aid, for which we shall be grateful.

I am, truly yours in the cause of Labor Reform.

The result remains to be seen. Mr. Child is a True Reformer and though a high salaried clerk, is not afraid to maintain his principles.

My calculations are now to go to Portland, and on return shall visit Roxbury, East Boston and Worcester.

The generosity of A. A. of W., Ct., is appreciated by me and if possible I shall avail myself of it, for good offers should always be accepted.

To friends and patrons of South Boston I am sorry to say good bye.

M.E.

P.S. Seven men, who recently left the amiable and gallant Capt. of the late Legislator-Ship launched from Nashua, N.H., are here at work in "first rate shops, for higher wages and less hours." They said they were "going to send Capt. ——— up Salt River," guess he would do more good up there than in the Legislature, so his constituents say, and added he is not entitled to our confidence or respect and cannot have our votes again.

Voice of Industry, October 8, 1847

Some Reasons for Encouragement

Roxbury, Nov. 20th

MESSRS. EDITORS:—I have spent one day in this city, in behalf of your paper. You have reason for encouragement, if I am to judge by my success among the gentlemen, in the employment of Hunnaman & Co., with whom there seems to be an enjoyment of Equal Rights and equal Privileges, and all seem generous and gallant. The neatness and order of the several shops speaks volumes in favor of the workmen. They are no strangers here to the principles you promulgate, for they talked Democracy, and would encourage it whenever an opportunity offered. They did not like so much of this "special privilege;" and it seemed to them, there was too much of that commodity in the Cotton City, and too little of Justice, Equality, and Natural Rights. Then it seems unwise in the Legislature to create so many corporations without proper restrictions. Many other good remarks were made which have been partly forgotten.

My next visit, was to the New England Cordage Factory, under the supervision of Webber & Son, who encouraged me with a subscription, and admittance into the establishment. Next came a place called "Hard Scrabble," and the inmates called themselves "Hard cases," but they seemed generous and good natured, and would "Subscribe after payday."

I have had a list of names made out, by a member of the W. P. U., a greater part of whom reside at "Grab Village," and my next letter shall be from this place.

M.E.

P.S. A gentleman by the way of advice, presents the following sentiment, with a "here, print this in your paper."

M.E.

"If truth does any where manifest itself, seek not to smother it with glossing delusion, acknowledge the greatness thereof, and esteem it thy best victory when the same doth prevail over thee."—*Hooker.*[28]

Friend, we thank you for the hint. "Them's our sentiments." EDS.

Voice of Industry, November 26, 1847

Good News from a Wrongly-Named City

Grab Village, (Roxbury,) Dec. 29, 1847

MESSRS. EDITORS:—Permit me to tell your numerous friends in this city, of my good success in this wrongly named village. It should not be called by such a hideous name. The Valley of Industry would be much more appropriate and creditable.

Early on one of the coldest days last week, I started for the above named village, and as it was my wish to get to the "line" as soon as possible, I ventured into a lane called Water Street, but on a warm day it might be more properly called Mud Street. On a sign was written in capital letters, "Dangerous passing, this way not chargeable upon the city." With assurance from an Irishman that if I kept to the "right, there would be no danger from the foot-holes," having observed strictly the direction just given, I found myself on the "Grab Village line."

My next adventure was in a "Ball Alley" which was mistaken for a work-shop. However, the Voice of Industry was presented, and carefully examined by the young man who had charge of the establishment, and some copies were presented to the German boys who had come, so early in the morning, "to set up the pins." Each took off his cap, and thanked me very modestly, and would "read till somebody came in to roll." On enquiring why they were there, they replied: "Our folks are poor, and we can't get anything else to do." The young man present said they had an easy time and it was not a bad place as I supposed. It was on the Temperance plan[29] and a place of innocent amusement. There were a great many paintings hung around the hall—General Taylor in the centre, and the battles he had fought[30] with pictures of opera dancers of several foreign countries. These "were selected to please customers," according to the taste of such folks as frequent "ball alleys."

A few steps beyond, the scene was changed. Here, in the shop of Messrs. Chubbuck & Campbell, were a set of men at work, industrious, intelligent, and if I made no mistake, by their physiognomy —good, at least, good looking. They had expected me, and the cash was ready—they would have me know that they would do more than any other shop in the city for the Voice of Industry, and true, they did. Next came Day & Sewell's establishment. Here the hands followed the example of their "worthy predecessors," and I came home well satisfied, wishing there were many more of the "same sort."

About one hundred names have been booked, nearly all paying in advance. Two hundred copies have been distributed gratuitously. All seem to be satisfied with the paper except some few of the most wealthy and sectarian. "Your paper has a tendency to set the poor against the rich, pull down churches, establishing a kind of feeling no better than infidelity—we are puritans, and we like puritanical papers."

My visit to this city has been pleasant and profitable, and indeed, my travelling tour must impart knowledge more minute and accurate than could otherwise be obtained; and I sincerely wish for the sake of your paper and the good of the many, that some of those who are so well qualified, would undertake to solicit subscribers. They would be often times greatly edified and as often amused, would learn some things and unlearn others, they would see development among the mechanics—not in words so much, but in things—they give symbols which cannot but be valued by the improved mind.

And now I must leave Roxbury friends with pleasant recollections, that would induce me to go again on the same mission, should you require my services to renew subscriptions. *Until then, Good Bye.*

M.E.

P.S. To one thousand persons whose names I have procured for the Voice of Industry since last January, I will at this early period, wish them "A Happy New Year."

M.E.

Voice of Industry, December 31, 1847

NOTES

1. New Hampshire.

2. In this editorial Sarah G. Bagley informed the readers of the *Voice of Industry* that she was taking over the editorship of the paper because of the illness of William F. Young. Although she held the position only briefly, Miss Bagley thus became the first woman labor editor in the United States.

3. The Chartist Movement in England derived from the People's Charter, drawn up by six members of the Working Men's Association and six radical

members of Parliament. The Chartists asked for universal manhood suffrage, equal electoral districts, the vote by ballot, annual parliaments, no property qualifications, and payment for Members of Parliament. The movement, stirring great enthusiasm among the workers in the cities, resulted in a monster petition with a million and a quarter signatures; it was presented to Parliament in 1839 and rejected. In November of that year troops fired upon Chartists at Newport, killing ten and wounding fifty; leaders were arrested and several transported. Despite the merciless repression, the movement produced another petition in 1848 signed by over five and a half million people, but was once again rejected.

4. The reference is to Queen Victoria, who ascended to the throne in 1837.

5. Prince Albert, the Queen's husband.

6. A mill in Lowell.

7. The law, passed in 1833, imposed a twenty-five dollar fine for violation of the provisions.

8. Although there were a number of improvement circles in Lowell which had been in existence for several years, the one mentioned here appears to have been organized by the militant factory girls and to have had as one of its aims the provision of material for the *Voice of Industry*, especially the "Female Department."

9. Nathaniel P. Rogers, editor of the *Herald of Freedom*, published in Concord, New Hampshire; a militant abolitionist and land reformer, as well as a supporter of the ten-hour movement. Strangely, however, a study of the *Herald of Freedom* reveals that while Rogers, unlike many abolitionists, was concerned with improving the conditions of wage workers (or wage slaves, as they were sometimes called), his paper never contained a single article about the struggles of the factory girls, or about their Female Labor Reform Associations; further, there was never an article by one of the factory girls of New Hampshire, even though Rogers's paper was published close to Manchester, Dover, and Nashua.

10. The Appleton and Lawrence families had been founders of the textile industry in Lowell and grew wealthy from the mills.

11. John Jacob Astor (1763–1848), fur trader, financier, and New York real estate operator, who had acquired the largest fortune in the United States when he retired.

12. One of these "things" referred to by Miss Bagley related to the petitions for the ten-hour day; these were ignored in the account published in the Scottish paper. "At the commencement of the last session a petition was presented by 5,000 operatives of Lowell," Miss Bagley wrote. "There was about 15,000 in all thro'-out the State. These are the facts in the case." For the petitions to the Massachusetts legislature and the outcome, see below, pp. 229–42.

13. Although Tory England did not pass a ten-hour law until 1847, the three decades of intensive agitation for the ten-hour bill, led by shorter-time committees of workers, reduced working hours in the British factories below the level existing in Democratic America. See below, pp. 218–19.

14. Miss Bagley was in Boston as a delegate to the American Union of Associationists, having been recently elected vice-president of the Lowell Union of Associationists. This is her last letter to appear in the *Voice of Industry*. For background on treatment of the insane in the United States, see Karl Michael Wielgus, "Emerging Care for the Insane in America, 1750–1820" (Ph.D. dissertation, Columbia University, 1972).

15. Although unsigned, the letter is undoubtedly from Sarah A. Young, corresponding secretary of the Lowell Female Labor Reform Association.

16. A liar who dropped dead when Peter rebuked him.

17. Labor reform was the term used in the movement both for shorter working hours and better working conditions and for the movements for basic changes in American society, such as those put forward by the associationists,

land reformers, and advocates of producers' cooperative. The term was revived after the Civil War by the postwar labor movement.

18. The manager, who lived at the site of the mill and was in charge of production.

19. The Mexican War began in April, 1846, and ended in September, 1847. It was opposed by the *Voice of Industry* as a war for the extension of slavery that should not be continued. In taking the position that American troops should be withdrawn from Mexico, the *Voice of Industry* was in keeping with the stand taken by the New England Workingmen's Association: at its meeting in Boston that organization deeply deprecated the "unhallowed war now being waged with such inhuman results" and called upon workers to oppose the scheme to "plunder Mexican soil for the United States officers, slaveholders, and speculators to convert into a mart for traffic in human blood and human rights" (see *Harbinger,* June 20, 1846).

20. The *Voice of Industry* condemned Negro slavery but also supported the view that wage slavery was either the same or worse than chattel slavery. For the position of the factory girls on the slavery question and criticism of their stand by the *Voice of Industry,* see below, pp. 276–83, 290.

21. An abbreviation for Locofoco. Locofocos were the radical wing of the New York Democratic party in the 1830s; firm advocates of equal rights, the group had its base in the working class. The designation was given in 1835 at a meeting in Tammany Hall, where the radicals struck friction matches, called locofocos, to keep the room lit after the regular Democrats tried to cut off radical proposals by turning off the gaslights and dissolving the meeting. By the mid-1840s the Locofocos were no longer a political force, but they had left behind a radical tradition.

22. Come-outers was the name assumed by the abolitionists, mainly supporters of William Lloyd Garrison, who denounced the subservience of the church toward slaveholders and called upon congregations to join them in "coming out" of a degenerate church.

23. The *Voice of Industry* expressed opposition to the annexation of Texas as a scheme for the extension of slavery.

24. Universalism was a liberal religion which insisted that people were too good to be damned. It had a large following in New England rural areas.

25. On October 6, 1845, a group of Boston mechanics set up the first Working Men's Protective Union. This association, soon to become the model for hundreds of similar organizations, had as its main purpose the purchase, at reduced price, of necessities for its members. It also included mutual benefit features, such as provisions for sickness and old-age insurance. The *Voice of Industry* ran a series of weekly educational articles on the subject of "Protective Unions," both for consumer and for producers' cooperatives, and played a big part in the spread of the movement.

26. The tree before which the Sons of Liberty had convened during the American Revolution and pledged their efforts in the cause of liberty.

27. The prospectus of the *Voice of Industry,* dated Lowell, February 1, 1847, and signed by W. F. Young and Mehitabel Eastman, was a lengthy statement. It announced that the *Voice* was "The People's Paper and the organ of the 'New England Labor Reform League,'" that it was "devoted to the elevation and improvement of the industrial classes, and the final and permanent emancipation of labor from the present suicidal, competing and depressive tendencies." The paper would be "conducted upon strictly *Independent Principles,* opposing all prominent evils, social, political or ecclesiastical, with that spirit which knows no fear or favor, while in the path of duty, and advocating all cardinal truths with perseverance and sincerity of purpose." It called for the support and sympathy of "true friends to the Race—the honest Philosopher and Statesman, the untram-

meled and devoted Teacher, the hardy Farmer, the Mechanic and Artisan—
and last, but not least; the toiling Operative at the Loom and Spindle," and
urged all such to join with it in putting "their shoulders to the car-wheel of
Labor Reform, for as mind is practically made superior to matter, and Man, to
wealth and external circumstances,—poverty, ignorance, crime and intemperance
will disappear." The terms for subscribers were $1.25 per year, paid in advance,
for single copies, and $5.00 for five copies sent to one address.

28. Thomas Hooker (1586?–1647), early liberal Congregational minister and
author of "Fundamental Orders of Connecticut" (1639), the first written constitution in America.

29. See below, pp. 287–88, for discussion of temperance.

30. Zachary Taylor (1784–1850) defeated the Mexicans at Palo Alto (1846)
and at Buena Vista (1847). He was elected twelfth president of the United States
on the Whig party ticket in 1848.

Part 5

The Ten-Hour Movement

The Demand for the Ten-Hour Day

The issue which more than any other led to the formation of the New England Workingmen's Association and the various Female Labor Reform Associations and which united working men and women in the 1840s was the struggle for the ten-hour day. Many mechanics had gained the ten-hour day during the 1830s, but the New England workers had not shared the gains of the shorter working-day movement of the preceding decade, and the vast majority of workers, mechanics, and operatives alike still worked twelve to fourteen hours each day. In other sections, too, factory workers experienced the same oppression; some mechanics had been forced during the depression years to return to the "sun-up to sun-down" system familiar to the agricultural areas around the mill towns.

The ten-hour movement of the 1840s was advanced by the magazines and periodicals issued by or in behalf of the factory operatives. These publications carried articles and letters from the operatives to justify the demand for the ten-hour day and to win public support. In general they stressed that the physical and mental effects of the existing hours of labor were so demoralizing that the average worker could not expect to live long or hope to devote his energies to anything but unceasing toil. They also stressed that the community would definitely stand to gain if the working class was enlightened but this was impossible so long as the hours of labor were not shortened to ten a day.

215

Some ten-hour advocates regarded the lessening of the hours of labor as "the primary social step" toward the achievement of a new social order. As the workers became more enlightened they would grasp more clearly the necessity of putting an end to the present economic system and join eagerly in the crusade for a cooperative society. □

Is It So?

"You can't make the Ten Hour System go in Fall River,"—remarked a gentleman of property and standing, the other day, while conversing with a friend of the cause. This, I think, is a bold assertion. I would ask the ladies of the Ten Hour Association, if they believe it? I anticipate the answer will be given in that little monosyllable, NO! What, say they, are the rights of our husbands, fathers, and brothers to be wrested from them so easily, if we can prevent it? *Never.* Woman did much when our fore-fathers were struggling for equal rights, and the Mechanics of Fall River will see that they are still true to their interests. True, we have few, if any, of the wives and daughters of the rich and noble among our number,—*noble*, did I say? Pardon me, riches can never confer true nobility. We will not upbraid them for their contemptuous sneers at our efforts; but hope that they may never be engaged in a worse cause.

This is a subject in which *mothers* should feel a deep and thrilling interest. There are few mechanics in our community whose children are not obliged to engage in a species of labor as destructive to the physical as it is crushing to the intellectual energies of their nature. And where is the mother of such a family whose heart has not ached for her little ones, as she calls them at early dawn, while they plead for a little more sleep. But no. The bells have rung and well she knows, if not there in season, they will either be discharged or in some way abused by their despotic overseer. O, the appearance of squalid wretchedness which these poor factory children present might well soften any heart in which avarice and selfishness are not the ruling passions. I ask any of those who are so much oppressed to a reduction of the hours of labor, to station themselves for one morning at the entrance of one of the manufacturing establishments and view these operatives, who toil from sunrise to sunset, during these long, long summer days, and if there be one spark of humanity in his bosom, he will use his influence in favor of the ten hour system.

I could say much on this part of the subject, but forbear for the present, and conclude by saying to the mechanics, fear not, your cause is just and must triumph. Be strong, be united, and be assured that

> Woman is upon your side,
> Full armed for moral fight,
> For brother's aye, and sister's wrongs,
> For God and human right.

A Ten Hour Woman

The Mechanic, Fall River, December 28, 1844

The Ten Hour System

There is not, we believe, a press in the whole country, that has urged a single reason against the adoption of the "TEN HOUR SYSTEM." The New York Mirror, alluding to the recent petitions of the Lowell Operatives to the Legislature, praying for the enactment of a law to prevent the corporations in that city from working the laborers in their employ more than ten hours, says that Russia, with her serfdom system, requires only eight hours per day, and that the labor is not very excessive; and quotes an article from Hunt's Merchant's Magazine, showing that the serfs of Russia are better fed, clothed, and generally more comfortable than the factory operatives of England, even than many of the poor in Christian America.—The labor of the southern female slave is neither so hard, or so wearing upon the constitution as the burdens imposed upon the factory operative of the north.

Even so, in many of the manufacturing villages in the south part of Massachusetts, in Rhode Island and Connecticut the English system is fast gaining ground. No men are employed but those having families—the larger the better. Those that are employed must trade at the corporation store, live in the corporation house, and patronize the corporation tavern—But little money is paid to them, and but few years elapse ere they are bound, body and soul, wife and children; at the command of the agent, forced into the mills at an early age, sold, as it were body and soul, to a corporation who will always keep them enslaved.

But the time must soon come when a change will take place in the condition of the laborer either for better or for worse, (Heaven grant it may not be the latter), when the laborer will arise and throw off the chains which bind him claiming an equality, at least, with capital; or when he will cease to exert himself to become other than the slave of the corporation which holds him.

J.I.B.

The Literary Wreath and Factory Girl's Garland, Exeter, N.H., July 10, 1845

The Manufacturing Establishments of New England

During the last winter a petition was presented to the Legislature of Massachusetts, by eight hundred and fifty "peacable, industrious and hardworking men and women," declaring that they are confined from thirteen to fourteen hours per day in unhealthy apartmenst, and are hastening through pain, disease, privation, down to a premature grave, and praying the State to inquire into their condition and to restrict the number of hours of labor in Factories to ten per day,—This, and other similar petitions, were signed by two thousand one hundred and thirty-nine persons, chiefly females.

The operatives in England are prohibited, by act of Parliament from being employed more than at a rate of eleven and a half hours per day. They work sixty-nine hours per week; 12 hours on the other days, and nine on Saturday. They have six holidays in a year.

The operatives in Lowell work

In January,	11 hours 24 min.
In February,	12 hours
In March,	11 hours 52 min.
In April,	13 hours 31 min.
In May,	12 hours 55 min.
In June,	12 hours 45 min.
In July,	12 hours 45 min.
In August,	12 hours 45 min.
In September,	12 hours 43 min.
In October,	12 hours 16 min.
In November,	11 hours 46 min.
In December,	11 hours 24 min.

To this must be added in each instance thirty minutes, at least, for going to and from the mill, at morning and evening. They go to and return from breakfast in thirty minutes, to and from dinner in thirty minutes, for about eight months in a year; and the other four months they are allowed forty-five minutes.

From this it will be seen that in New England the operatives work on an average of the whole year, more than twelve and a half hours per day, exclusive of going to and from their work. We have placed side by side with the above table, the brief spaces allowed them to go for food, eat it, and return. A woman in a Factory in New England, works one hour and some minutes longer, every day in the year, than a woman in a British Factory—They are allowed four days as holidays; the English are allowed six. First it must be apparent that the hours allowed for labor are too many.

Second, that the minutes allowed for them to take their food are too few.

Third, that these causes are sufficient to impair health, induce disease, premature old age, and death.

Fourth, that these causes, conjointly with the bad effect of close and heated air,* acting upon so large a number of females assembled in the manufactries of New England, must in time affect the physical condition of the people of New England. To say nothing of the intellectual degeneracy which must necessarily result from the want of mental recreation and cultivation.

Fifthly, that no reason can be given why these evils should not produce the same terrible effects here, as in England, where their full results are developed.

Sixth, that as the British Parliament, from motives of humanity and public policy have been compelled to interfere in behalf of the operatives, prudence and mercy call upon our legislators to do likewise.

Seventh, that the example of this State would be followed at once throughout New England.

A Committee of Factory Girls

*In one room, in Lowell, no less than two hundred and ninety-three small lamps and sixty-one large ones are kept burning when evening labor is required.

Voice of Industry, June 26, 1845

The Hours of Labor in Lowell

We are moved to write this by erroneous reports concerning the hours of work under which we operatives in Lowell labor.

The operatives are allowed ten minutes in morning and ten at noon in going from their boarding house to the mills, which deducted from the time the wheels are in operation, leaves *twelve hours and ten minutes,* the actual amount of time the operatives are required to labor for day's work, the shortest days in December, *exclusive* of the time required in going to and from their daily task.

Many who board near the mills, commence work as soon as the gates are raised, consequently make out *twelve and a half* hours of real service during the shortest days in the year.

We are informed by those engaged upon the Middlesex, (Woollen) that the mills on that corporation run still longer, and the goods finding a ready market at great profits, every means is resorted to by the manufacturers to produce the largest possible amount. On no corporation in Lowell, do the mills operate less than twelve hours per day, at this season and in the longest days of Summer they run thus:

Commence in the morning 10 minutes before 5, gates shut down for breakfast, at 7 o'clock, commence again 20 minutes past 7. Gates shut down at half past twelve; commence again 5 minutes past 1; gates shut down for supper at 7; making *thirteen hours and fifteen minutes* between the ringing of the bells, thirty minutes of which is allowed the operatives in going to and from their meals, leaving *twelve hours and forty-five minutes,* of actual service in the mills.

During the month of April, the factories run more hours than in any other month of the year, which is, according to Mr. Miles,[1] thirteen hours and thirty-one minutes. On Saturdays from the 20th of September till about the 20th of March, the operatives are released soon after dark, which will take off upon the average, about one hour per week, during that time.

From the foregoing facts, it will be seen that much deception has been used in reporting the hours of factory labor by self interested men who wish to aggrandize themselves by courting the favor of the manufacturing power of this country. It will be seen, that, at no season of the year, less than twelve hours is considered a regular days work in the Lowell factories and that they range from about twelve hours and ten minutes up to thirteen hours and thirty one minutes, and should the time spent in going to and from the mills be taken into the account, as it ought, the longest days labor, would exceed fourteen and a half hours, and the shortest, never fall below twelve and a half.

A Committee of Lowell Factory Girls

Voice of Industry, December 26, 1845

Untitled Verse

Ah! leave my harp and me alone
  My grief thou may'st not share,
Responsive to its plaintive tone
  Will flow refreshing tears.

Far from the factory's deaf'ning sound,
  From all its noise and strife,
Would that my years might run their rounds
  In sweep retired life.

But, if I still must wend my way,
  Uncheered by hope's sweet song,
God grant, that in the mills, a day
  May be blest, *"Ten Hours"* long.

Voice of Industry, February 20, 1846²

The Ten Hour System

This is well understood, its need universally confessed, and 'tis infinitely important that immediate measures should be taken to bring about so desirable an event to the laboring classes, especially those who are shut up within the "Prison walls of a Factory," where we are continually inhaling cotton-dust, lamp smoke, and away from wholesome, pure air. Then the jar from machinery is enough to tire in less than ten hours; it must be considered too that mill labor has no attraction, the scenery is always the same, 'tis work, work, fourteen hours per day, the year in and out, we are tired of the same routine of duties and singing the song of the fourteen hour system, worn out and cast down by the long hours of labor in the mills, which for the above reasons seem tedious and longer than elsewhere.

There must be a reform in the factory system, because the operatives are "dying off" by inches. Every operative can testify to this appalling fact.

There are many who know no other home than that which industry in the mills give, who do not look for relief by a reduction of hours in labor and anticipate the time not far distant when health will be regained, spirits restored, so a "dance or a sing," can be enjoyed "about the mills," hoping to be most as free as the birds of the air.

We have great reason for gratitude to Patriots, Christians, and

Philanthropists, who have taken our part by wielding the pen to convince capitalists in these manufacturing establishments that he is causing the lives of thousands "in the prime of life" to be sacrificed for mammon in "temples of brick and mortar."

I speak from sad experience upon the effect of work in the mills, having been an operative more than ten years, the consequences were felt in less than two years, and was often admonished to leave, but the homestead was not redeemed and duty to unfortunate parents bound me. The desired object was accomplished and with it the loss of health.

My present employment is under the ten hour system by a Corporation—health has improved, spirits restored, and knowing the great number of applications by the mill girls for situations in this branch of business, tells plainly they would rather work less hours, even if they must have less money.

In advocacy of the reduction of labor in the mills, no one can tax me with political party spirit, but I *try* to go *strong* for a very large party called "Factory Girls" feeling for such, ardent sympathy, with a wish that we may be united in the cause of Reform and the ten hour system be adopted by the virtue of the next Legislature, is the prayer of an operative.

E.M.

Manchester, Sept. 6th, 1846

Factory Girl's Album, Exeter, N.H., September 12, 1846

The Ten Hour System and Its Advocates

There is no subject that agitates and interests us as a people more than the subject of a reduction of the hours of labor. All who oppose it, agree in saying it is just and right. But instead of removing obstacles, they are raising up more barriers, and creating insurmountable difficulties. We will not charge these *professed* friends with dishonesty, nor insist that they do not believe all they say—but we are quite certain they have taken a one-sided view of the subject and need only to see it in all its bearings, to become its advocate. We would not venture an opinion that those who oppose the labor reform movement, are less humane, than others; but we insist that those who oppose it on account of dollars and cents, have low and sordid views of human existence, or they do not represent *themselves* truly.

We are fully aware that *none,* be they ever so wise can realize the weary tediousness of the life of the operative. We have heard many give expression to their own worn-out and debilitated physical strength, but it falls far below the reality.

It is truly painful to hear the complaints of this unfortunate class. As the day dawns upon them, they regret that it is not past, and as the evening closes, and they retire, they wish that it would not so soon be morning. Is there a *human* heart that would destine the fair daughters of New England to such an existence? Is there a man in *our* city, nay; is there a man in this universe that would perpetuate such a state of things? We are sure there is not. Avarice and familiarity with such a life of toil, may blunt his feelings on this subject, and his own condition and that of his children may give him a sort of assurance that he nor they shall suffer such a life of toil and privation; But amid all this security there are times when conscience speaks in thunder tones, and its voice, *must* be heard whether we will or not. It is then we see this subject in its true light—and he who had looked calmly and indifferently, takes, a more correct view. He sees the weary toiler as the child of some fond parent, whose affection is as strong and pure as his own; who watches the slow moving hour-glass, and counts the minutes when they shall return, wearied and depressed with toil. He stops amid his plans for future gain and listens to hear the prayer that goes up from the family alter; and as blessings are invoked, upon the absent children who are doomed to toil on, amid the croud, he sees their wasted forms, and like the gibbering of a ghost it haunts his quiet by day and his dreams by night. We are fully aware that if a reduction in the hours of labor were to take place, everyone whether capitalist or agent would feel a great degree of satisfaction. It is not in the human heart to love misery; and when the question shall be fairly settled, (as it surely will be) the bright and joyous hearts and happy faces will more than compensate for the trifle that capital may lose. We will not follow this subject farther at this time but take it up in our next number and give some of the reasons why we should labor to bring about so desirable an event.

S.G.B.[3]

Voice of Industry, December 26, 1845

The Ten Hour System and Its Advocates (Continued)

As we promised to give some of the inducements, to labor for the Ten Hour System; we will consider, some of the objections before entering directly upon the subject. One of the strongest reasons urged by those who oppose it is; that the time allowed to the operatives, would be spent in vicious indulgence, and annoying the *peaceable* citizens of our city. Now to me, it seems somewhat contradictory, to hear those who contend long and loud, that we have a "moral police," so vigilant that it is hardly possible for an operative to be vicious, (if she is kept upon the corporation day and night,) talk about the "virtuous and puritanical daughters of the New England farmers," being kept within the walls of a cotton mill, longer than is consistent with their physical or intellectual condition, to keep them virtuous. Think you the *benevolence* of the "powers that be" ordained the "all day system" of labor? was it not rather their avarice? Ye sticklers for decency and propriety—why do not they give the operatives a few minutes more for their meals; they would not stay from the corporation, and this would be doing something to improve their condition. How miserable such evasions of the real system of labor looks to one who has examined its relative claims to the morality of the masses.

At one time, they tell us that our "free institutions" are based upon the *virtue* and *intelligence* of the American people, and the influence of the mother, form and mould the man—and the next breath, that the way to make the mothers of the next generations virtuous, is to enclose them within the brick walls of a cotton mill from twelve and a half to thirteen and a half hours per day. How is it about the intelligence? Do not overlook that part in the premises, lest you come to wrong conclusions. There cannot be found an individual who claims for himself common observation, who will admit that the operatives of our country have a suitable portion of time for improvement. No man will allow his own children the education of a machine tender and expect her to read French or Latin, or be skillful in mathematics. He takes the child from the mill, and sends her to school, if he wishes her to be educated. The reader is ready to enquire how the operatives spend their "leisure hours?" we will take it for granted, that the enquirer is a lady.

Let me remind you (for you know) of the duty the young woman owes to herself in the way of personal appearance. The factory girl has to wash and iron every article of clothing used by her, except her mill dress. Her pocket handkerchief, collars, hose, &c., &c., are to be washed nearly every week, if she attends church and an evening lecture, and no one would suppose for a moment, that *one short* evening in the week, would be sufficient time to consume in that department of taking care of one self. But let us enquire how much time the operative has to look after herself. She has no time in the morning, for she is called from the table to the mill. She has no time at noon,—thirty minutes only are allowed her to go to her meals—eat and return to her work. How is it at night? The lamps that have been burning from 30 to 50 minutes in the morning to assist the weary operative to labor before the morning light,—is again relighted, and she must toil on until seven and a half, or according to Boston time, within ten minutes of eight o'clock. You would not expect her to go to her boarding house and take her evening meal in less than thirty minutes and according to Lowell time, it would be eight o'clock and still later by the Boston time. Now taking into the account, the duties, the operatives owe to themselves in taking care of their clothes, doing their own sewing, knitting and repairing, where do you find their "leisure hours?"

(continued next week.)

S.G.B.

Voice of Industry, January 16, 1846

The Ten Hour System and Its Advocates (Continued, II)

It may be well, to inform those who do *not* know the fact that the operatives labors *is* hard,—that it requires great physical exertion in almost every department. We are aware that Mr. Miles says it is *not* laborious. But we do not hesitate in the *face of his testimony,* and add to it, that of Mr. French, (formerly agent of the Boott Corporation,) as given in the report of the committee on the reduction of the hours of labor, page 18. "The amount of muscular strength which a girl is required to exert in any department, is very small."[4] Page 24, he says, "the girls make periodical visits to recruit their *wasted* energies,—and prepare if need be for another campaign."[5]

Now we do not know which of these testimonies, he expected the world to believe, but they may be assured of one thing,—that the operatives of Lowell will not believe the former, although it come from the man whose calling should have entitled him to their respect and confidence. Every operative who is required to tend four looms, making an average of 160 yards of cloth per day, has a sufficient amount of common sense to know whether she can perform such an amount of labor as is necessary and *unavoidable,* without *more* than "a very small amount of muscular strength." But Mr.

Miles and French were not writing for the operatives, but for those who are ignorant of the facts in the case, and those who would not disbelieve what any man might say who has Rev. attached to his name. We would not reproach any *honest* opinion offered by any man, whether he be clergyman or otherwise, but when a man descends from the sacredness of his calling as a moral teacher, and gives sanction to a system *not sanctioned* by Him, whose follower he professes to be, it will not be expected that the operatives, whose condition he misrepresents, will keep silent.

One would be induced to believe that every minister of the gospel would labor to bring about the ten hour system, as a "means of grace." How many operatives stay away from church, on account of want of time, to keep their clothes in suitable order to appear at church. Then add to this, the number who stay away on account of fatigue, and then add to these, those who stay away to perform some little job of sewing that they have not found *time* to do, during the week, and the number would not be small. Now if attending church is necessary for the spiritual growth and perfection of the operative—we put the question, whether the clergy of our city are doing all their duty, by removing *all* obstacles, in the way of spiritual improvement and perfection.

We do not appear as an apologizer for a neglect of attending church, and yet we doubt whether those who would condemn them would give any better examples, if they were in like circumstances; especially if we take into the account, the constant violation of the Sabbath, by the corporations for whom they work.

We regret such a state of things, and it is for this reason we have laid some of the reasons, which induce us to labor for a reduction of the hours of labor, believing that many of the evils would find a remedy in such an event.

In the next number, we will give some of the positive benefits, to be derived from a reduction of the hours of labor.

S.G.B.

Voice of Industry, January 23, 1846

The Ten Hour System and Its Advocates (Continued, III)

The "Ten Hour System" recommends itself to every Patriot, and lover of his country, as a means of security against a monarchial form of Government, being introduced into the boasted land of the free. It is admitted by *all,* that the intelligence of our country have made our political institutions what they are. Take from the masses, the opportunity of cultivation, and if causes produce their own effects, what will be the results? Our young men will go to the workshop, at sixteen or eighteen years of age, with a good common school education, perhaps—but, is he educated in the political history of our and other countries. He has had but little access to libraries, and needs much time, for general reading, and information, and where will he find *that* time under the present long hour system? He must remain in the condition in which he commences his apprenticeship. We have heard many young men give as an excuse for not buying a share in the library, that they have no time to read—they drop to sleep with the book in their hand. This is a lamentable state of things, but it is what every one knows to be true, who has worked under the present regulation of time.

Fathers of our own happy, free New England! Do *you* sanction this long hour system? Are you willing that your sons, aye, and your daughters, too, shall thus go out into the world? Are you the sons of those who fought so nobly the battles of freedom? Are you the sons of the fathers of '76? If so, let your voices be heard in thunder-tones, and your hands be stretched forth to save us from the same evils that threatened us when they declared themselves free from a foreign power.

The ten hour system commends itself to every philanthropist. Can a man be in *reality* a benevolent man, and see his brother starve while he has the means to feed him? Can he see him mentally or morally hunger, and shut him up in a prison, and raise an everlasting barrier that shall prevent him from drinking from the inexhaustible fountain of knowledge? Every one must answer in the negative. Then why box up your benevolence and send it across the Atlantic or to Louisiana? Can you find nothing here in our own city or State, to improve? Has custom sanctioned the present state of things, so that you would not enter a protest against it lest you find yourself on the unpopular side of the question?

How much of this kind of philanthropy we find in our midst, and yet, no object worthy a Howard or an Oberlin, is manifested by their boasted benevolence. Can we not find this sort of philanthropy in existence, in Louisiana, and across the Atlantic, where we are so willing to send ours? They are as free to denounce our inhumanity, as we are theirs.—Then let us see that we do not look so eagerly after the comet, that speeds his fiery course in the heavens, that we heed not the poisonous serpent that lies at our feet, ready to destroy us.

It would seem to many, that the religious part of community should be the *first* to engage in the work of improving the operative, physically. Has the Master left no examples for your imitation? Has he never taken upon himself, the improvement of those with whom he labored? Has he fed the hungry, clothed the naked, and had compassion on those who were out of the way? Has he anointed to preach the gospel to the *poor,* and undo the heavy burdens of those who were bound?

Who are his followers practically? "By their fruits ye shall know them."

S.G.B.

Voice of Industry, February 6, 1846

The Battle for the Ten-Hour Day

There was a difference of opinion among the ten-hour advocates as to the methods to be employed to secure the shorter working day. Some advocated legislative enactments only and called for the launching of a huge campaign to convince legislators that incessant toil was inconsistent with the health, happiness, and liberty of the laborer and with the welfare of the community. In accordance with this principle, laws had to be passed restraining employers from hiring workers for more than ten hours a day. Others believed that groups of workers should concentrate upon achieving an agreement with their employer and establishing the ten-hour day in their own shop or factory. Still others favored the adoption of methods used successfully by workers in England in their struggle for shorter hours. This plan of action was popularized in America by John C. Cluer, an English weaver and labor organizer who had come to this country early in the 1840s and became associated with the ten-hour movement. It included three points: first, a convention to be called of workers and manufacturers to discuss and agree on a program for the reduction of working hours; if the convention failed, a petition campaign to the legislatures should be instituted; and finally, if that method also failed to bring results, a general strike, or, as it was popularly called, a Second Independence Day should be initiated. The general strike would take place on July 4, with all New England workers declaring "their independence of the oppressive manufacturing power."

Cluer outlined his plan at a meeting of the Lowell Female Labor Reform Association and was "enthusiastically received" (*Lowell Advertiser*, December 13, 1845).

In the main, however, the movement for the ten-hour day depended upon legislative action. When petitions for a ten-hour day were forwarded to the Massachusetts legislature from mill workers in 1842 and 1843, the legislature took no action on the requests. But in 1845, sparked by the *Voice of Industry* and the Lowell Female Labor Reform Association, fresh petitions were circulated through the mill towns and thousands of signatures, most of them from women, were obtained. When the committee of the House of Representatives assigned to hold hearings on the ten-hour petitions met, it had as its chairman William Schouler, proprietor of the *Lowell Courier* and an important backer of the *Lowell Offering*.

Upon receiving the petitions, Schouler informed the petitioners that since most of them were women, they would have to appear and testify in defense of the ten-hour day, "or we shall be under the necessity of laying it aside." Evidently he was convinced that maidenly modesty would keep the militant factory girls from appearing in public before a legislative committee in the state house in Boston, but he quickly discovered that he had underestimated their militance. When the committee hearings opened on February 13, 1845, Sarah G. Bagley and other operatives were on hand, and their testimony provided a valuable picture of the working life of a female factory operative. While no record of the verbatim testimony was kept, the statements of the women witnesses were summarized in the committee's report—incorrectly, according to Sarah G. Bagley. These hearings before the legislative committee were significant in still another way, for the committee was one of the earliest governmental investigating committees to inquire into U.S. labor conditions. (A committee of the Pennsylvania Senate investigated hours of labor in textile mills in 1838.) The very fact that the investigation was referred to the committee on manufacturers indicates how little attention was paid to labor conditions in this period, although the enormous amount of interest aroused by the great petition crusade undoubtedly was the prime reason why the committee on manufactures, before holding these hearings, changed its name to special committee to investigate labor conditions.

Despite the witnesses' overwhelming evidence of the pressing need for a ten-hour day, the report of the investigating committee, written by Schouler, was averse to any ten-hour legislation. The report insisted that "a law limiting the hours of labor, if enacted at all, should be of a *general nature;* that it should apply to individuals or co-partnerships as well as to corporations." It conceded that there were abuses in the factory system but expressed confidence that these could be eliminated without legislation, for "here labor is on an equality with capital, and indeed controls it, and so it ever will be while free education and free constitutions exist." The report concluded by asking that "the petitions be referred to the next General Court."

When the report was made public, Harriet Farley timidly rebuked the committee. Calling the petition to the legislature both "proper and dignified," she concluded that it was not possible to expect the ten-hour system to be introduced "in the present state of things" (whatever that meant), but then asked, "might not an arrangement have been made which would have shown some respect to the petitioners, and a regard for the ease and comfort of the operatives" (*Lowell Offering*, April, 1845, p. 96). Neither the *Lowell Advertiser* nor the *Voice of Industry* was so restrained. The *Advertiser* charged the committee with inconsistency in conceding the existence of abuses but at the same time insisting that it was not up to the legislature to deal with them. As for the statement that labor was on an equality with capital, it asked, "Why do not laborers reform the abuses of which they complain, instead of applying for protection to a Legislature that tells them they are abused, but that the Legislature can't help them? Why does capital take the Lion's share and compel the laborer to put up with the Jackal's? . . . Capital is the Lion! and the terms he imposes *must* be submitted to" (*Lowell Advertiser*, September 2, 1845).

The *Voice of Industry* and the Lowell Female Labor Reform Association charged that the only reason the petitions had been rejected was that the committee had been sought out by the corporations. When Schouler ran for re-election for the legislature following the release of the report, the Lowell Female Labor Reform Association urged the male workers to defeat him. When the returns were in and it was clear that Schouler was defeated, the *Lowell Advertiser* disclosed that it had warned Schouler that he could not possibly win in the face of the campaign waged by the Lowell Female Labor Reform Association, for even though the female operatives could not vote, they would effectively line up the workingman's vote against him (November 10, 1845).

While the campaign had been going forward in Massachusetts for a ten-hour law, the factory girls in Pittsburgh were so angry at legislative stalling that they decided to take matters into their own

hands. In Sepember, 1845, the Pittsburgh female operatives conducted a month-long strike for the ten-hour day. In the Battle of
Blackstocks, described below, the Pittsburgh operatives gained na-
tionwide renown as the "Amazons" of the working class. Just as the
male workers had helped the Lowell female operatives defeat
Schouler in his reelection bid, so the male workers in Pittsburgh
helped the women strikers by functioning as a male auxiliary to
protect them from the police. The strike was broken when the employers convinced the female operatives that they could not institute the ten-hour day so long as their competitors in New England
mills continued to operate on a thirteen- or fourteen-hour basis.
The Pittsburgh operatives turned to their sisters in New England
and urged them to intensify their fight for the ten-hour day. There
was some talk of a general strike for the ten-hour day on July 4,
1846, to unite the factory workers in New England and Pennsylvania, but it never went beyond the talking stage.

The petition crusade for ten-hour laws continued in Massachusetts, but in 1846 the legislative committee to which petitions of
the factory girls and others were referred refused to recommend
the legislation requested. The Senate committee appointed to consider the petitions again advanced the principle that a ten-hour law
applicable only to corporations would be unjust. Admitting that
the legislature had the power to define the number of hours that
should constitute a day's labor, the committee insisted, nevertheless,
that it "could not deprive the citizen of his freedom of contract."
Furthermore, any restriction on business would hit the workers most
severely, for "you injure business, and the result will be, the laborer
is sure to suffer" (General Court, Senate, *Senate Document* No. 81,
1846, pp. 19–21).

The female operatives denounced the report and vowed to continue the struggle. In Nashua, New Hampshire, a struggle took
place against the "lighting up" of the work rooms. With the beginning of autumn, mill workers could look forward to six months
during which they would be working by artificial light for several
hours both morning and night. When a group of female operatives
refused to work by candlelight, they were locked in by the overseers. This led to a huge demonstration in behalf of the imprisoned
operatives and for the ten-hour system.

The petition crusade for ten-hour laws was successful only in
New Hampshire, where the Female Labor Reform Association
joined forces with the male operatives and mechanics to carry on a
militant campaign through mass meetings and petitions. The ten-

hour law adopted in New Hampshire, however, infuriated the mill workers because it included clauses which permitted employers to draw up special contracts with workers for more than ten hours. Employers' attempts to force workers to sign such clauses or go jobless led to new demonstrations in New Hampshire. ☐

Rebellion among the Operatives

TURN-OUTS. There are symptoms of rebellion among the operatives in all quarters. At Lowell, Pittsburgh, Philadelphia, Chicopee, and elsewhere, outbreaks follow each other among different classes of mechanics. They are attended by processions, that are in imitation, if not "as terrible as any army with banners." The evils of which they complain, are, the order system, by which they are subjected to extortionate prices for articles of necessity, or to ruinous discounts for cash, which is indispensable for many purchases; and in some cases, they are oppressed by a decrease of wages and an increase of labor. This was the cause which led to the glorious turnout of the fair operatives in the factories at Chicopee. They formed in solemn column, arrayed in their best bibs and tuckers, and marched to the music of the drum and fife through the streets, and waved their kerchiefs to the girls in the other mills to join them. Failing to enlist reinforcements, they returned to their places. A few days afterwards they mustered their forces again, with as little success as before, and to add to their discomfiture, when desirous of turning in a second time, they were turned out by their employers. Processions and martial music are now the usual accompaniments of strikes.

New York State Mechanic, May 18, 1843, reprinted in John R. Commons, ed., *A Documentary History of American Industrial Society* (Cleveland, 1910), VIII, p. 219

Turn-out in Chicopee

April 28

The girls in the Factories started on a turnout yesterday and have kept up the spirit of 76. They held a consultation and determined to turn out. They sent for Mr. Carter but he told them they must work out their notice or he would give them no settlement as the cuts would remain the same until the first of June.

May 2

The girls in the factory show a great deal of uneasiness and threaten to turnout

May 3

Great turnout among the girls. The weavers met last night at . . . and were advised ? ? but what I do not know. But after breakfast this morn. a procession preceded by a painted window curtain for a banner went round the square, the number sixteen. They soon came past again with Mr. . . . They then numbered 44. They marched around awhile and then dispersed. After dinner they sallied forth to the number of 42 and marched down to Cabot under the direction of Mr. . . . They marched round the streets doing themselves no credit. Messrs. Mills and Dwight are up from Boston.

May 4

Girls on the turnout. They had a meeting at C. last night and were ably addressed by Hosea Kenny Esq. This morning after breakfast they came out and marched round the square numbering 22 and after dinner they were to come out under the direction of Hosea. He went down all dressed in uniform but the girls would not be led by him. Soon the old leaders came on dressed with "Gewgaws" and around him they rallied. After they had formed a procession they marched to Cabot. but it did no good.

May 5

The girls had no turnout today.

May 6

The girls have got over their excitement in some degree.

Taylor Diary, April 28 *et seq.*, 1843, quoted in Vera Shlakman, "Economic History of a Factory Town: A Study of Chicopee, Massachusetts," *Smith College Studies in History*, XX (1934–35), 121–22

The Banner Room

We understand that the young ladies employed in the Spinning Room of Mill No. 2, Dwight Corporation, made a very quiet and successful "strike," on Monday. The spinning machinery was set in motion in the morning, but there was no girls to tend it. They had heard the rumor that their wages were to be cut down, upon which they determined to quit. They silently kept their resolve, and remained out until Tuesday afternoon, when they were requested to return to their employment, with an addition to their previous wages of fifty cents per week. The Ladies connected with the other Mills ought certainly to present them with a banner, as a tribute of esteem for thus volunteering as pioneers in the march of increasing recompense. . . .

We think the girls have acted rightly, and by way of encouragement, and stirring up their minds by way of remembrance, we say "stick to your text," and pursue a steady course, with a determined spirit, and you will come off victorious.

Cabotville Chronotype, reprinted in *Voice of Industry*, November 21, 1845

Ten Hours, Ten Hours!! Sign the Petition!

We have forwarded to some of our friends in different towns of Massachusetts, petitions asking the Legislature to prohibit incorporated companies for employing one set of hands more than ten hours per day. We hope our friends will be active in circulating them for signatures and have them all returned to the office of the *Voice of Industry*.

Lowell Female Labor Reform Association

Voice of Industry, January 15, 1845

Petition to Massachusetts Legislature

We the undersigned peaceable, industrious and hardworking men and women of Lowell, in view of our condition—the evils already come upon us, by toiling from 13 to 14 hours per day, confined in unhealthy apartments, exposed to the poisonous contagion of air, vegetable, animal and mineral properties, debarred from proper Physical Exercise, Mental discipline, and Mastication cruelly limited, and thereby hastening us on through pain, disease and privation, down to a premature grave, pray the legislature to institute a ten-hour working day in all of the factories of the state.

Signed

John Quincy Adams Thayer
Sarah G. Bagley
James Carle
and 2,000 others mostly women

Voice of Industry, January 15, 1845

Reply to Petition

Boston, February 6, 1845

To J. Q. A. Thayer, S. G. Bagley and others:

A petition relative to a reduction of the hours of labor has been referred to the Committee on Manufactures, of which I am Chairman. By a resolution passed by the House, instructing said Committee to send for such persons and papers as may be necessary to make an investigation of the claims of said petitioners to an interference in their behalf, I would inform you that as the greater part of the petitioners are females, it will be necessary for them to make the defence, or we shall be under the necessity of laying it aside.

WILLIAM SCHOULER, *Chairman*

Voice of Industry, February 12, 1845

Reply to Schouler

To Wm. Schouler, Esqur., Chairman of the Committee on Manufactures:—

Sir:—We received your note of the 6th inst., and would inform you, that we hold ourselves in readiness to defend the petitions referred to at any time when you will grant us a hearing.

I am very respectfully yours, for the Operatives of Lowell.

S. G. BAGLEY

Documents Printed by Order of the House of Representatives of the Commonwealth of Massachusetts during the Session of the General Court A.D. 1845, Number 50 (Boston, 1845), p. 2.

Commonwealth of Massachusetts Report

House of Representatives, March 12, 1845

The Special Committee to which was referred sundry petitions relating to the hours of labor, have considered the same and submit the following

REPORT:

The first petition which was referred to your committee, came from the city of Lowell and was signed by Mr. John Quincy Adams Thayer, and eight hundred and fifty others, "peaceable, industrious, hard working men and women of Lowell." The petitioners declare that they are confined to "from thirteen to fourteen hours per day in unhealthy apartments," and are thereby "hastening through pain, disease and privation, down to a premature grave." They therefore ask the Legislature "to pass a law providing that ten hours shall constitute a day's work," and that no corporation or private citizen "shall be allowed, except in cases of emergency, to employ one set of hands more than ten hours per day."

The second petition came from the town of Fall River, and is signed by John Gregory and four hundred and eighty-eight others. These petitions ask for the passage of a law to constitute "ten hours a day's work in *all corporations* created by the Legislature."

The third petition signed by Samuel W. Clark and five hundred others, citizens of Andover, is in precisely the same words as the one from Fall River.

The fourth petition is from Lowell, and is signed by James Carle and three hundred others. The petitioners ask for the enactment of a law making ten hours a day's work, where no specific agreement is entered into between the parties.

The whole number of names on the several petitions is 2,139, of which 1,151 are from Lowell. A very large proportion of the Lowell petitioners are females. Nearly one half of the Andover petitioners are females. The petition from Fall River is signed exclusively by males.

In view of the number and respectability of the petitioners who had brought their grievances before the Legislature, the Committee asked for and obtained leave of the House to send for "persons and papers," in order that they might enter into an examination of the matter, and report the result of their examination to the Legislature as a basis for legislative action, should any be deemed necessary.

On the 13th of February, the Committee held a session to hear the petitioners from the city of Lowell. Six of the female and three of the male petitioners were present, and gave in their testimony.

The first petitioner who testified was *Eliza R. Hemmingway*. She had worked 2 years and 9 months in the Lowell Factories; 2 years in the Middlesex, and 9 months in the Hamilton Corporations. Her employment is weaving,—works by the piece. The Hamilton Mill manufactures cotton fabrics. The Middlesex, woollen fabrics. She is now at work in the Middlesex Mills, and attends one loom. Her wages average from $16 to $23 a month exclusive of board. She complained of the hours for labor being too many, and the time for meals too limited. In the summer season, the work is commenced at 5 o'clock, A.M., and continued till 7 o'clock, P.M., with half an hour for breakfast and three quarters of an hour for dinner. During eight months of the year, but half an hour is allowed for dinner. The air in the room she considered not to be wholesome. There were 293 small lamps and 61 large lamps lighted in the room in which she worked, when evening work is required. These lamps are also lighted sometimes in the morning.—About 130 females, 11 men, and 12 children (between the ages of 11 and 14,) work in the room with her. She thought the children enjoyed about as good health as children generally do. The children work but 9 months out of 12. The other 3 months they must attend school. Thinks that there is no day when there are less than six of the females out of the mill from sickness. Has known as many as thirty. She, herself, is out quite often, on account of sickness. There was more sickness in the Summer than in Winter months; though in the Summer, lamps are not lighted. She thought there was a general desire among the females to work but ten hours, regardless of the pay. Most of the girls are from the country, who work in the Lowell Mills. The average time which they remain there is about three years. She knew one girl who had worked there 14 years. Her health was poor when she left. Miss Hemmingway said her health was better where she now worked, than it was when she worked on the Hamilton Corporation.

She knew of one girl who last winter went into the mill at half past 4 o'clock, A.M. and worked till half past 7 o'clock P.M. She did so to make more money. She earned from $25 to $30 per month. There is always a large number of girls at the gate wishing to get in before the bell rings. On the Middlesex Corporation one fourth part of the females go into the mill before they are obliged to. They do this to make more wages. A large number come to Lowell to make money to aid their parents who are poor. She knew of many cases where married women came to Lowell and worked in the mills to assist their husbands to pay for their farms. The moral character of the operatives is good. There was only one American female in the room with her who could not write her name.

Miss Sarah G. Bagley said she had worked in the Lowell Mills eight years and a half,—six years and a half on the Hamilton Corporation, and two years on the Middlesex. She is a weaver, and works by the piece. She worked in the mills three years before her health began to fail. She is a native of New Hampshire, and went home six weeks during the summer. Last year she was out of the mill a third of the time. She thinks the health of the operatives is not so good as the health of females who do house-work or millinery business. The chief evil, so far as health is concerned, is the shortness of time allowed for meals. The next evil is the length of time employed

—not giving them time to cultivate their minds. She spoke of the high moral and intellectual character of the girls. That many were engaged as teachers in the Sunday schools. That many attended the lectures of the Lowell Institute; and she thought, if more time was allowed, that more lectures would be given and more girls attend. She thought that the girls generally were favorable to the ten hour system. She had presented a petition, same as the one before the Committee, to 132 girls, most of whom said that they would prefer to work but ten hours. In a pecuniary point of view, it would be better, as their health would be improved. They would have more time for sewing. Their intellectual, moral and religious habits would also be benefited by the change.

Miss Bagley said, in addition to her labor in the mills, she had kept evening school during the winter months, for four years, and thought that this extra labor must have injured her health.

Miss Judith Payne testified that she came to Lowell 16 years ago, and worked a year and a half in the Merrimack Cotton Mills, left there on account of ill health, and remained out over seven years. She was sick most of the time she was out. Seven years ago she went to work in the Boott Mills, and has remained there ever since; works by the piece. She has lost, during the last seven years, about one year from ill health. She is a weaver, and attends three looms. Last pay-day she drew $14.66 for five weeks work; this was exclusive of board. She was absent during the five weeks but half a day. She says there is a very general feeling in favor of the ten hour system among the operatives. She attributes her ill health to the long hours of labor, the shortness of time for meals, and the bad air of the mills. She had never spoken to Mr. French, the agent, or to the overseer of her room, in relation to these matters. She could not say that more operatives died in Lowell than other people.

Miss Olive J. Clark.—She is employed on the Lawrence Corporation; has been there five years; makes about $1.62½ per week, exclusive of board. She has been home to New Hampshire to school. Her health never was good. The work is not laborious; can sit down about a quarter of the time. About fifty girls work in the spinning-room with her, three of whom signed the petition. She is in favor of the ten hour system, and thinks that the long hours had an effect upon her health. She is kindly treated by her employers. There is hardly a week in which there is not some one out on account of sickness. Thinks the air is bad, on account of the small particles of cotton which fly about. She has never spoken with the agent or overseer about working only ten hours.

Miss Celicia Phillips has worked four years in Lowell. Her testimony was similar to that given by Miss Clark.

Miss Elizabeth Rowe has worked in Lowell 16 months, all the time on the Lawrence Corporation, came from Maine, she is a weaver, works by the piece, runs four looms. "My health," she says, "has been very good indeed since I worked there, averaged three dollars a week since I have been there besides my board; have heard very little about the hours of labor being too long." She consented to have her name put on the petition because Miss Phillips asked her to. She would prefer to work only ten hours. Between 50 and 60 work in the room with her. Her room is better ventilated and more healthy than most others. Girls who wish to attend lectures can go out before the bell rings; my overseer lets them go, also Saturdays they go out before the bell rings. It was her wish to attend 4 looms. She has a sister who has worked in the mill 7 years. Her health is very good. Don't known that she has ever been out on account of sickness. The general health of the operatives is good. Have never spoken to my employers about the work being too hard, or the hours too long. Don't know any one who has been hastened to a premature grave by factory labor. I never attended any of the lectures in Lowell on the ten hour system. Nearly all the female operatives in Lowell work by the piece; and of the petitioners who appeared before the Committee, Miss Hemingway, Miss Bagby, Miss Payne and Miss Rowe work by the piece, and Miss Clark and Miss Phillips by the week.

Mr. Gilman Gale, a member of the city council, and who keeps a provision store, testified that the short time allowed for meals he thought the greatest evil. He spoke highly of the character of the operatives and of the agents; also of the boarding houses and the public schools. He had two children in the mills who enjoyed good health. The mills are kept as clean and as well ventilated as it is possible for them to be.

Mr. Herman Abbott had worked in the Lawrence Corporation 13 years. Never heard much complaint among the girls about the long hours, never heard the subject spoken of in the mills. Does not think it would be satisfactory to the girls to work only ten hours, if their wages were to be reduced in proportion. Forty-two girls work in the room with him. The girls often get back to the gate before the bell rings.

Mr. John Quincy Adams Thayer, has lived in Lowell 4 years, "works at physical labor in the summer season, and mental labor in the winter." Has worked in the big machine shop 24 months, off and on; never worked in a cotton or woollen mill. Thinks that the mechanics in the machine shop are not so healthy as in other shops; nor so intelligent as the other classes in Lowell. He drafted the petition. Has heard many complain of the long hours.

Your Committee have not been able to give the petitions from the other towns in this State a hearing. We believed that the whole case was covered by the petition from Lowell, and to the consideration of that petition we have given our undivided attention, and we have come to the conclusion *unanimously,* that legislation is not necessary at the present time, and for the following reasons:—

1st. That a law limiting the hours of labor, if enacted at all, should be of a general nature. That it should apply to individuals or copartnerships as well as to corporations. Because, if it is wrong to labor more than ten hours in a corporation, it is also wrong when applied to individual employers, and your Committee are not aware that more complaint can justly be made against incorporated companies in regard to the hours of labor, than can be against individuals or copartnerships. But it will be said in reply to this, that corporations are the creatures of the Legislature, and therefore the Legislature can control them in this, as in other matters. This to a certain extent is true, but your Committee go farther than this, and say, that not only are corporations subject to the control of the Legislature but individuals are also, and if it should ever appear that the public morals, the physical condition, or the social well-being of society were endangered, from this cause or from any cause, then it would be in the power and would be the duty of the Legislature to interpose its prerogative to avert the evil.

2d. Your Committee believe that the factory system, as it is called, is not more injurious to health than other kinds of indoor labor. That a law which would compel all of the factories in Massachusetts to run their machinery but ten hours out of the 24, while those in Maine, New Hampshire, Rhode Island and other States in the Union, were not restricted at all, the effect would be to close the gate of every mill in the State. It would be the same as closing our mills one day in every week, and although Massachusetts capital, enterprise, and industry are willing to compete on fair terms with the same of other States, and, if needs be, with European nations, yet it is easy to perceive that we could not compete with our sister States, much less with foreign countries, if a restriction of this nature was put upon our manufactories.

3d. It would be impossible to legislate to restrict the hours of labor, without affecting very materially the question of wages; and that is a matter which experience has taught us can be much better regulated by the parties themselves than by the Legislature. Labor in Massachusetts is a very different commodity from what it is in foreign countries. Here labor is on an equality with capital, and indeed controls it, and so it ever will be while free education and free constitutions exist. And although we may find fault, and say, that labor works too many hours, and labor is too severely tasked, yet if we attempt by legislation to enter within its orbit and interfere with its plans, we will be told to keep clear and to mind our own business. Labor is intelligent enough to make its own bargains, and look out for its own interests without any interference from us; and your Committee want no better proof to convince them that Massachusetts men and Massachusetts women, are equal to this, and will take care of themselves better than we can take care of them, than we had from the intelligent and virtuous men and women who appeared in support of this petition, before the Committee.

4th. The Committee do not wish to be understood as conveying the impression, that there are no abuses in the present system of labor; we think there are abuses; we think that many improvements may be made, and we believe will be made, by which labor will not be so severely tasked as it now is. We think that it would be better if the hours for labor were less,—if more time was allowed for meals, if more attention was paid to ventilation and pure air in our manufactories, and work shops, and many other matters. We acknowledge all this, but we say, the remedy is not with us. We look for it in the progressive improvement in art and science, in a higher appreciation of man's destiny, in a less love for money, and a more ardent love for social happiness and intellectual superiority. Your Committee, therefore, while they agree with the petitioners in their desire to lessen the burthens imposed upon labor, differ only as is the means by which these burthens are sought to be removed.

It would be an interesting inquiry were we permitted to enter upon it, to give a brief history of the rise and progress of the factory system in Massachusetts, to speak of its small beginnings, and show its magnificent results. Labor has made it what it is, and labor will continue to improve upon it.

Your Committee, in conclusion, respectfully ask to be discharged from the further consideration of the matters referred to them, and that the petitions be referred to the next General Court.

For the Committee,

WM. SCHOULER, Chairman

Massachusetts General Court, House of Representatives, *House Documents, No. 50,* 1845, pp. 1–6, 15–17

Resolutions Denouncing Report of Committee by the Female Labor Reform Association

Lowell, April 1, 1845

To the Editor of the New England Mechanic:

At the meeting of the "Female Labor Reform Association," this evening, April 1st, the following resolutions in reference to the report of the Committee "to whom were referred sundry petitions relative to the hours of labor," were unanimously adopted:

The two following were offered by Miss E. K. HEMINWAY:—

Resolved, That the Female Labor Reform Association deeply deplore the lack of independence, honesty, and humanity in the committee to whom were referred sundry petitions relative to the hours of labor—especially in the chairman of that committee; and as he is merely a corporation machine, or tool, we will use our best endeavors and influence to keep him in the "city of spindles," where he belongs, and not trouble Boston folks with him.

Resolved, That we are highly indignant at the cringing servility to corporate monopolies manifested by said committee in their report; as in that document the most important facts elicited from witnesses relative to the abuses and evils of the factory system are withheld, truth violated, and the whole shaped to please their aristocratic constituents. May never again the interests of the oppressed, downtrodden laboring classes be committed to their legislation.

The following by Miss S. G. BAGLEY:—

Resolved, That this Association, in their next petition to the Legislature, ask them to extend to the operatives the same protection they have given to animals, and our condition will be greatly improved.

Resolved, further, That the Special Committee are guilty of the grossest dishonesty in withholding from the Legislature all the most important facts in the defence made by our delegates; and that we regard them as mere corporate machines, and if there are any honorable exceptions they are entitled only to the same sympathy extended to "poor Tray," who was chastised for being found in bad company.

One by Miss A. SKINNER:—

Resolved, That if the Representatives of the State of Massachusetts have no higher aim than that of competing with the pauper labor of Europe, and for that reason refuse to grant the prayer of the petitioners, they are unworthy of a seat in the halls of legislation.

Resolved, That "intelligent" and shrewd as the Committee have styled the laborers of Lowell, it would illy become us to overlook so prominent a feature in the character of the report as the false coloring and sad perversion of truth which they have so indelibly stamped on its pages as to merit our united disapproval.

Resolved, That the Committee who made out the report acted unfairly and ungentlemanly, leaving out those points which bear with force on the subject, and supplying their own compositions, so as to involve the witnesses who appeared before them in unavoidable falsehood, asserting what they never said and never could have thought of saying.

Voice of Industry, January 9, 1846

What Was Omitted in the Report

MR. CLUER—*Sir:*—I received your note of January 2nd, requesting me to give you some of the evidence of the operatives *not given* in the report of the committee to whom the petition was referred, relative to the abridgement of the hours of labor, of which William Schouler, Esq. of this city, was Chairman.

Sir—you say in your note, "not given in the report," as though much or at least a part of it had been given verbatim—which I would say is not the case. I am not prepared to state that there is not *one* original sentence given by those who appeared before the Committee. But I am prepared to say that whatever was given, was so changed in its connection or removed from its original positon that it *was* made to say what we never said, or thought of saying. It will be impossible for me to do justice to your request within the limits of a letter—but I will give you a few incidents in the investigation at this time, and if there are any other enquiries you wish to make, I will answer them to the best of my ability.

The Chairman of the Committee manifested a great desire to bring out everything that would look bright and beautiful upon the side of manufactories. Now to this I do not object—but I do object to his wish to conceal the deformities of which we had a right to complain, as he most assuredly did make strong efforts. For example, a gentleman by the name of Herman Abbot, who worked on the Lawrence Corporation, appeared as a witness. After he was notified, he went to the Counting Room and told Mr. Aiken that he had been notified, and asked him what he (Mr. Abbot) must do about going down. "You must go" said Mr. Aiken, "but you must say as little as possible." We learned this fact while Mr. Abbot was being examined—and as leave had been given a number of times to the witness to ask questions, leave was obtained to put a question to him, when the following question was proposed: "Mr. Abbot, did you have an interview with Mr. Aiken, after you were notified to come here as a witness?" The Chairman looked daggers at the enquiry, and told the witness that he should not answer such enquiries, it was a wish to implicate his testimony. The enquirer assured him that he had no such motives—but he was strenuously refused, until the Committee ruled that the question be put—and Mr. Abbot answered affirmatively. Also giving the instructions as above mentioned. Now to my judgment, Mr. Aiken ought to have had not only a hearing before the Committee, but before the House through the report.

The report says that I was out of the mills last year a third of the time; but does not say why; but the testimony that I gave them, said being unable to work from ill health, the only thing worthy of mention in that part of the testimony. The report says that I had taught evening school four winters and it had injured my health. I said in reply to a question put by the Chairman, "would the operatives spend the time, if it should be given them, in the cultivation of their minds?" I stated that I believed most of them would. A reason was called for—to which the reason assigned was—that I had very often written letters for those who could not write, and had taken some few girls to my own *sleeping apartment* and instructed them in the simplest branches of education, and learn them very imperfectly how to write, without any compensation except that of improving that unfortunate class of which I was a member. This was termed teaching school *four years*—and if that be a true definition, I have not yet had a vacation, nor do I *hope* for one, until I can do nothing to improve the condition of those with whom my lot is cast.

There are many other things that I would like to mention, but my sheet is nearly full. You ask me if all the ladies who appeared as witnesses, were present at the time the resolutions relative to the report were adopted: I answer they were; all with one exception presented a resolution; a copy of which published in the "Boston Mechanic" you have received. The lady who did not present a resolution, voted for the adoption of those presented, and expressed her entire approbation of them.

You will excuse the length of this letter, with the assurance that I have strong reasons to believe that our petition referred to the next Legislature, (or the one about to commence its session,) will have a candid hearing from the fact, that all the "Corporation Machinery" has been labelled and directed to Lowell.

SARAH G. BAGLEY

Lowell, January 7th, 1846

Voice of Industry, January 9, 1846

On the Defeat of William Schouler

We are requested to publish the following Resolution, unanimously adopted by the "Female Labor Reform Association," at their last meeting, as a token of respect and esteem, for the services of Mr. Schouler, in behalf of the operatives of this city.

Resolved, That the members of this Association, tender their grateful acknowledgements to the voters of Lowell, for consigning Wm. Schouler, to the obscurity he so justly deserves,[7] for treating so unjustly and ungentlemanly, the defence made by the delegates of this Association; before the special committee of the Legislature, to whom was referred petitions for the reduction of the hours of labor, of which he was Chairman.

Voice of Industry, November 28, 1845

Capital against Labor, Ten-Hour Strike in Pittsburgh

FACTORY STRIKE AT PITTSBURGH—ATTEMPT TO END THE STRIKE
DEFEATED—THE LAW AS USUAL, COMING TO THE AID OF CAPITAL

If ever the principles of the Declaration of Independence shall be put in practice, by securing to men all their inalienable rights, (as I believe they will be,) when that day comes it will be a matter of astonishment that men of America should ever have tolerated a state of things that compelled thousands of their daughters to leave their homes and their natural protectors at a time of life when above all others they ought to be under the paternal roof. The astonishment then will be, not that these daughters of the Republic petitioned their Lord for a Ten Hour instead of Twelve or Fourteen Hour System of drudgery, but that a race of men qualified to cast a vote or shoulder a musket ever consented that their offspring should be immured in the Factory Bastilles as hirelings for any number of hours under any system. The whole Factory Scheme, as at present in operation, is a libel on Humanity, and a disgrace to the Republic, and yet only so as an effect of the omission to establish the fundamental right essential to "life, liberty, and the pursuit of happiness," the Right of Rights, the right to use the earth to obtain the means of existence.

The justice of the demand of the Factory Girls, that they should not be compelled to work more than Ten Hours a day, is so obvious, that the papers of all parties have loudly asserted it, and many of them have even condemned the Factory Lords for not at once acquiescing in the demand; yet the moment that distress forces some of the turn-outs to resume work, and the others, in self defence, to restrain them, then, immediately the "Law and Order" cry is raised, and the girls, they say are all in the wrong, although they know that there was no other possible means by which to obtain their object. The "law" has made the parents of these poor girls landless, and thus thrown them in the Factory stock-yards homeless, destitute, and dependent, and Republican editors have not a word to say against this operation of the law; but if these poor girls use the only means that the law has left them to prevent their being worked to death, oh what virtuous reproofs flow from the pens of these Republican editors! What a respect and veneration they have for the majesty of the law whenever it can be wielded for the advantage of capital!

These remarks have been elicited by the progress of the Factory Strike at Pittsburgh, as detailed in the following articles:

FROM THE PITTSBURGH *Journal*

THE FACTORY GIRLS.—GOING TO WORK.—There was a great excitement among the girls on Monday morning. A portion of them, "moved and instigated thereto," most probably, by necessity, determined to go to work. The rest—the real out-and-outers, determined to prevent their refractory sisters from doing so. A large number of them collected around Blackstock's Factory, and began hooting and hissing at those who were going to work. Notwithstanding this, however, a few persisted; although the majority were, no doubt, deterred from their purpose by the violence of the others.

The mayor was sent for, who attempted to remonstrate with them. They would not listen to him patiently, however, or even respectfully; although he spoke to them in his usual amiable and conciliatory manner. They accused him of being in favor of the employers, and he had to leave without accomplishing any thing. The Amazons then proceeded to the upper cotton factory, and commenced a similar assault upon the recusants in that quarter. Mr. Moorhead came out among them, but was rather roughly treated. After sufficiently expressing their dissatisfaction, they returned in increasing numbers to Blackstock's. The police were called; and the mayor and Squire Campbell were on the ground. The girls drew up in front of these two, who were standing on the steps and commenced telling them their notions of matters and things in general, and of the ten hour system in particular.

It was all in vain for the two to attempt remonstrance. At length the mayor crossed over to the opposite side of the street, and left Mr. Campbell to face the storm alone for a few minutes. "He's no 'Squire,' " screamed one of the girls; and a general shout reiterated the sentiment. "Give him a cent," said another, and four or five stepped forward to offer him that liberal reward for discharging his duties. "Now, ladies," said the squire, "let me inTREAT"—whack! went a handful of mud, missing his squireship's head by an inch or two. "Let him alone, didn't you hear him say he was going to treat." "Really now, I"—and here the Squire's harangue was interrupted by another handful of dirt; this time hitting him in the face. He brushed it away, and taking off his hat, wiped his face, without a word. This forbearance appeared to have more effect than all he could have said, for after a few more shouts and cheers, they dispersed.

The return to work has not been, by any means, a general one. Perhaps not two in a hundred have gone to work; and from the almost ferocious determination exhibited by the others, we are induced to believe that no reconciliation will be effected for sometime.

The Allegheny Police were on the ground; the mayor did all in his power; and too much credit cannot be given to Mr. Campbell for his forbearance, under such provoking circumstances. (We have seen several rows in our time, but really this mob of women is the most formidable that ever came under our observation.) You can do nothing with them; if you attempt to reason with them, they can speak two words to your one. What are the police to do?

AFTERNOON.—It used to be considered that dinner settled discontent: In the case of our factory girls, however, it seemed as though they had hardly swallowed that natural meal, before they were ready for a renewal of hostilities on a still more extensive scale. Their efforts in the morning had not been sufficient to stop work in the factories. The engines still puffed to their great dissatisfaction, and worse than all, the recreants were still employed. It was not to be borne. The tocsin was again sounded, and the petticoated legions once more advanced—this time to a complete victory.

The first object of assault was the Union Cotton Factory. After some struggle they were successful. The doors were thrown open; the girls at work came out, joined their comrades, and the works stopped. The Hope was the next point of attack. The garrison appeared, at first sight, disposed to make some defence, but overawed by superior numbers, they surrendered at discretion; and the invaders received another addition to their ranks.

The new factory owned by Messrs. Gray and Fife, was the next object of vengeance. It shared the fate of the others.

They were now in full force. A whole legion of men and boys accompanied them, as auxiliaries, to be used in case they were required. Thus prepared, flushed with conquest, and confident in numbers, they marched for the scene of the great struggle—a struggle which we will christen the "Battle of Blackstock's Factory."

On their arrival, they saluted the enemy with three shouts of defiance, and an universal flourish of sticks and bonnets. After a minute or two spent in a reconnoitre, they moved forward in a solid column of attack, on the principal gate of the fortress—that is, the pine gate of the yard.

In a moment the gate was forced open. But the defenders were determined on a heroic defence, and the assailants were thrown back and the gate again closed. A second time the assault was made with a similar result.

Both parties now took time for breath, and opened negotiations. The Factory girls demanded the instant expulsion of the girls at work. The people inside obstinately refused the terms, and both parties again prepared to decide the matter by the uncertain chances of the field.

"They say they won't—let's try again;" and encouraging each other with loud cries, the legions marched to the "imminent breach." For a moment, the combat was a doubtful one. The garrison made a stubborn resistance—but what could you expect from pine boards? Can bits of plank half an inch thick withstand the "might that slumbers in a peasant's arms?" The idea was absurd! Progressive humanity won the day, over clerks, proprietors, pine boards and all. The gate gave away—"hurra! hurra!" and in a moment the yard was filled, the fortress was taken by storm, and the garrison were prisoners of war.

Of course, resistance was now out of the question—how can a man resist "when the foot of the conqueror is upon his neck!" There was no help—and with sullen resignation the girls employed were escorted to the door, and given in charge of their overjoyed companions, now half frantic with exultation and success.

The moment, however, that they gained their point, all violence ceased. There certainly were shouts which could not have been particularly agreeable to the vanquished: but nothing outrageous.

They afterwards repaired to the Temperance Ark, where the money, collected for their use, was distributed.

AT NIGHT.—A very large meeting was held in the Old Court House, on this side of the river. A number of addresses were delivered. The meeting finally broke up in good order and in good spirits, apparently.

FROM THE SAME

THE MANUFACTURERS AND THE ALLEGHENY POLICE.—We are informed that the manufacturers have expressed a great deal of dissatisfaction with reference to the conduct of the Police, on Monday, during the disturbances. It seems to us that this is unjust. It was utterly impossible for any ordinary police force to have maintained order. There were hundreds of the male friends of the operatives standing around—ready to interfere whenever it should be necessary. The first appearance of violence or a disposition to use force, would have brought on a struggle, in which the Police would have been instantly overpowered, and a general riot would have ensued. Consequences much more serious must have occurred, had any attempt been made to coerce the Factory Girls into a more peaceful course of proceeding.

As for Mayor Nixon, we did not really see what was in his power, to do more than he did. He exposed himself to insult and ill-usage; did all he could, in connection with Mr. Campbell, to quiet the disturbance. His Police were on the ground, but helpless. In short, we do not think he should be blamed.

What were the Police to do? You would not have them rush in with their maces, and hammer away on the heads of the Girls? It is too much to expect of men, and besides they would have found themselves in a situation anything but pleasant if they had attempted such a course. "Let 'em hit one of them gals if they dare— and we'll fetch them out of their boots!" said a grim double-fisted fellow in our right, while they were breaking open Blackstock's.

FACTORY GIRLS

Calm in Allegheny. The girls appear satisfied with their victory on Monday, and the manufacturers are doubtless maturing some system of defence. We shall see sights in a few days, we expect; in the meantime the champions on both sides, appear confident.

WARD MEETINGS IN BEHALF OF THE FACTORY GIRLS.—Meetings were held on Tuesday night, according to appointment. They were, we learn, very well attended: and a strong determination evinced to sustain the girls. Committees were appointed to take measures for raising funds. Steps are also taken for the establishment of Societies, having for an object an organizing system of support in cases of "strikes."

THE FACTORIES

The disorders of Monday have had the effect to deter all operatives from going back to work, and yesterday the factories were again idle.

We learn that some of the manufacturers have instituted legal proceedings against the male rioters. This is all right; but we hope it is not true, as alleged, that these proceedings are directed as well against innocent men as the guilty.

(Of course, "legal proceedings" should be instituted against all who had the hardihood to succor the oppressed. By all means let us have another Delhi tragedy! Perseverance will work wonders.)

*Young America*8, October 18, 1845

We Are Confident of Ultimate Victory

We have been asked whether we do not intend to give up the effort to introduce the ten-hour system since the operatives have returned to work on the old terms.[9] Certainly not. We see not why we should hesitate one moment. True it has been proven, as we feared from the first, that the rich manufacturer, even in this great country of ours, can compel his poor operatives to work just as many hours as he pleases, or starve, if the community will countenance and aid him in doing so; but we do not believe that the infamous means employed to array the community against the operatives and their friends will succeed again. We believe in the omnipotence of a good cause, we believe that every mechanic and laboring man is interested, and can be made to see it, in the establishment of the system; that the humane of all classes will yet join us in endeavoring to introduce it; (and that we shall not always be regarded as a demagogue and meddler for endeavors to secure justice to woman). Men who look only to interest—who think that it is of more importance that trade shall flourish than that justice be done—may be swayed by the selfish appeals which for a time have checked this movement, but the wise and good of all classes have been led to think, and we are satisfied that the apparent defeat will be found a victory for our cause.

Woman is wronged in every occupation and condition of life. She labors but for a pittance in the workshop or as a domestic servant. She is debarred from every means of righting her own wrongs by her present social position. She must have others to plead for her, and if the high and mighty and talented will not speak in her behalf, we shall face calumny and misrepresentation to do what we can for her.

Though professing Christians denounce us—though a Christian preacher of this city says we should not meddle with the world, it is a bad world, and we should get along as comfortably as possible till we are ready to leave it for heaven! (we wonder what he preaches for?)—we think it our duty to do all we can to improve the condition of man. (For that reason we are a Temperance man, an Anti-slavery man, and an advocate for Social Reform.) We have no more interest than others have in any of these movements—we have not been a drunkard, nor a slave, nor a factory operative—but because fellow beings have been, are, and more may be, we feel bound to warn them—to meliorate their condition. It does not appear to us that any right of refusal to act against evil is left—we must do what we can or be criminal. Perhaps we might become habituated to that kind of non-committalism which always looks to make a safe leap for popularity and we dislike to be frowned on by old friends, but conscious would ever and anon be reminding us that we had shaken hands with the devil only to learn to despise ourself; and neither he nor the world can tempt us to that folly.

We labor not only in hope, but in confidence of ultimate triumph, in the ten hour movement. We have made arrangements for continuing the warfare by meetings, associations, &c.; a correspondence will be opened up with the operatives eastward; a publication devoted to the cause is projected; and we have received the first number of a monthly tract commenced by the Lowell operatives, since the strike took place here.

They are blind who do not see that we have every reason to

stand fast, and be confident of triumph. The manufacturers will not risk another five weeks' suspension for a slight consideration. They have lost three hundred and forty hours by the suspension—more than half a year's loss, at two hours per day.

Pittsburgh Spirit of Liberty, reprinted in *Young America*, November 15, 1845

Report from Manchester

GREAT MEETING AT THE TOWN HALL—THE TEN HOUR SYSTEM—OPPOSI-TION—ITS RECEPTION—THE MANCHESTER FACTORY GIRLS, AND THEIR SPIRITED ORGANIZATION, ON FRIDAY NIGHT LAST.

By request from our Manchester friends we found ourself, together with some of the *fair invincibles* of Lowell, making our way towards the manufacturing emporium of the "Old Granite State," with the characteristic speed of old "Mars," after devouring a half cord of "hard pine," and a hogshead or two of the Merrimack to wash it down.

We arrived at the Manchester depot, about two o'clock, P.M.—found the Scotchman, (J. C. Cluer;) awaiting our arrival and "looking queer," (pleased) to see us on the ground for the evening meeting.

After enjoying a luxurious half hour before a flaming New Hampshire fire, and receiving many congratulations upon the interest felt by the operatives and workingmen of Manchester in the cause of industrial reform, we strolled about the beautiful and thriving village, which has risen Phoenix like, from the Sandbanks of old Derryfild, until the hour arrived for the contemplated meeting to commence; and a more glorious one never convened, where rests the remains of New Hampshire's honored Stark.

Notwithstanding a great effort was made by the Corporations and their tools to prevent the operatives from attending the meeting, more than a thousand were present in a short space of time after the ringing of the factory bells.

The spacious Town Hall was filled to overflowing and hundreds, we are told, went away, being unable to get in, and a more attentive orderly and interesting audience, it has not been our fortune to witness.

Mr. Cluer addressed the meeting with his usual pathos and ability, urging the necessity of united action on the part of the operatives and the workingmen of this country, to protect themselves against the great system of organized capital and commercial feudalism which are waring upon the industry of the American operatives and fast reducing them to want, dependence and circumstantial slavery.

He administered a scorching castigation to Warland, editor of the corporation organ of that place, who had resorted to all means to defend and uphold the "darling system" of legal robbery against the truths which Mr. Cluer had poured out upon it during his lectures in that place. He even professed to be very religious, and a great advocate of *temperance,* for the purpose of working upon the prejudices of the people by accusing Cluer of being an infidel and a falsifier, because he had stated, that he had admired the republican sentiments expressed in "Paine's rights of Man,"[10] and that Warland was not entitled to much regard, as a true friend to virtuous industry, being a man of intemperate habits. Mr. C. showed him up to be an enemy to true religion, temperance and the prosperity of our people as a Christian and Republican nation. His remarks were warmly applauded by the audience, showing that they appreciated the truth of his sentiments and justice of the cause.

After Mr. Cluer sat down we were called upon and detained the meeting a short time in urging the necessity of *action* and organization among the producing portion of the country.

In the course of our remarks, we introduced the following resolution:

"In view of the alarming increase of the evils of factory labor, as it now exists, the tendency of which is to gradually subvert the republican institutions of our country and fill the land with a dependent, overworked and much oppressed populace, and spread disease and poverty among our people, therefore RESOLVED, That we, the operatives of Manchester, do fully and heartily concur with the plan proposed by our friends of Pittsburgh and Allegheny city, and adopted nearly throughout the manufacturing country; that the Fourth of July 1846, shall be the day fixed upon by the operatives of America, to declare their INDEPENDENCE of the oppressive Manufacturing power, which has been imported from Old monarchial England, and now being engrafted upon the business institutions of our country; provided the manufacturers shall *practically* signify an unwillingness to mutually adopt the Ten Hour System."

The vote on this resolution was put in Mr. Cluer's peculiar style, and the universal demonstration in its favor, altogether exceeded our most sanguine anticipations; hands, muffs, and handkerchiefs, a perfect ocean of them, were raised by the *real* operatives of Manchester in manifesting their approval of the plan which it proposes.

The resolute determination of the Manchester factory girls, is worthy of commendation and gives the lie to the arguments of those who contend that the operatives are contented with their present condition, and would not have the time of labor reduced if they could.

Although the hour was now quite late, no signs of weariness were manifested by the audience. A committee of gentlemen having been chosen to draft a constitution for a workingmen's association, the male portion of the meeting were requested to withdraw while the females organized their Association, but what did leave, went away with great reluctance and finally the remaining were requested to be seated while the ladies proceeded with their business, with which they cheerfully complied.

Miss Bagley of Lowell presented a constitution, for their acceptance, accompanied with some remarks, characterized throughout for their candor, truthfulness and beauty and evidently made a powerful impression upon those present. The constitution was adopted and the necessary officers chosen with energy and dispatch, showing that there was no scarcity of *materials* among the Manchester factory girls, for any such event. We shall publish the list of officers next week. Notwithstanding the lateness of the hour (nearly eleven) about sixty names were immediately subscribed to the constitution and hundreds of others stand ready as soon as a favorable opportunity presents itself—the meeting then adjourned.

Thus ended one of the most rational and enthusiastic meetings ever held in New England,—it did honor to the producing sons and daughters of Manchester, and may God bless their future efforts and crown their labors with abundant success.

Voice of Industry, December 19, 1845

Demand for Perseverance

> Laborers, to the GREAT CAUSE plighted!
> Firm of limb and high of soul!
> Shall it e'er be said, united
> We were forced to brook control?
>
> What though broad petitions moulder,
> In yonder Legislative Hall?
> Let not hearts, or hopes grow colder—
> Perseverance conquers all.

Voice of Industry, April 10, 1846

Legislative Report on the Ten Hour Petitions

It is well known to most of our readers, that petitions signed by nearly *five thousand* operatives and citizens of Lowell and by about *ten thousand* petitioners in other towns in the State, have been presented to the Legislature during its present session, asking that body to *practically* carry out the professions it has long boastingly made about having great solicitude for the welfare of LABOR, and the laboring classes. That the public may be fully acquainted with the grounds taken by the petitioners, and thereby better enabled to appreciate the contradictory and sophistical defence made by the committee in their Report upon this subject, we publish the Memorials, as signed by the above fifteen thousand workingmen and women, of Massachusetts, and which read as follows:—

To the Senate and House of Representatives of the State of Massachusetts:

We, the undersigned, Operatives and Laborers of Lowell, in view of the alarming effects of the present number of hours which the Operatives in our Mills are required to labor, upon their health and happiness; and believing this system of tedious and protracted toil to exist, in a great degree, by virtue of legislative enactments, in opposition to the great principles of justice, equality and republicanism, laid down in the Declaration of Rights, so essential to the moral, mental and physical well-being of society and the existence of a free and virtuous people; therefore in justice to ourselves, to our fellow workers, and to posterity, we anxiously and hopefully invoke your aid for legislation preventing private companies from employing one set of hands more than ten hours per day.

That the present hours of labor are too long, and tend to aggrandize the capitalist and depress the laborer, is admitted by the good, the wise and philanthropic of the world; and we trust by every consideration of duty to your highly severed State, and the prosperity of her industrious population and as just and righteous legislators, you will be induced to grant this reasonable petition; thereby saving our country from many of the calamities which have visited all people who suffer wealth and monopoly to feed upon the natural rights of the working classes.

Your petitioners would also call your attention to an article in the "Factory Regulations," which is the cause of much injustice and oppression on the part of the corporations, and which reads as follows:

"All persons entering into the employment of the Company are considered as engaged for twelve months, and those who leave sooner, or do not comply with these regulations, will not be entitled to a regular discharge."

The effects of this regulation are becoming every day more grievous, giving to the manufacturer great power over the operative, and leading to monopoly and wrong. Your memorialists firmly believe that this combination is entered into to destroy the independence of the operatives, and place their labor within the control of the manufacturers—an illustration of which we briefly subjoin:— Mary A—— engages to work for the M—— Company, in the city of Lowell; according to the regulation she is considered engaged for one year; but for some good reason, perhaps ill treatment from her overseer, she wishes to leave, and applies for a "regular discharge"— it is refused, and her name is immediately sent to all the other Corporations, as being upon the "black list;" and should she apply for work she is denied, no matter how destitute her condition. Thus, we consider a "people's Legislature" in duty bound to interfere for the protection of the weak and defenceless against the combined strength of capital and organized power.

The petitions from Lowell, Holliston, and North Chelmsford, were presented by Mr. Huntress, of Lowell, who we have been credibly informed, gave some of the petitioners to understand, that he would use his influence in their behalf, which we regret to believe he has not done.

The several petitions were referred as the "Joint Standing Committee on Manufactures" which Nathaniel D. Borden of Fall River, was Chairman.

Voice of Industry, April 17, 1846

The Cause Is Onward

Truly, we have reason to thank God and take courage! Courage, ye toiling ones! the God of Right and Justice, is raising up friends on every hand, to speak boldly and manfully in behalf of the wronged and oppressed of our countrymen and women.

Workingmen and women, do you realize sufficiently your own true worth and dignity, as God's imitators—God's last and noblest, of all his works? Do you take your places in society among the intellectual and moral, which the most useful and wealth-producing part of community should occupy?

Workingmen, are your voices heard in the Legislative Halls of our country—in our courts of justice, or in our Senate Chambers? If not, in heaven's name awake! arouse yourselves to life and action, like MEN. Be no longer slaves! Suffer not the idle drones in society, longer to mock you in derision, by professing to be *your* representatives. What can they *know* of your real wants and deprivations, who have fattened from childhood, on the wealth and abundance which your hands have produced? Nothing at all! And they *care less!*

Will you, *can* you, be longer indifferent on this subject? You have had another incontestible proof, of their heartless and unmeaning words, in the entire neglect of your petitions for redress of wrongs, signed by over fifteen thousand laborers and operatives of New England, and presented at the last session of the honorable body of men, styled *your* representatives—the representatives *of the people!!* How long, O, how long, will ye suffer these things thus to be? You have the power, and will you not use it, to represent *yourselves,* and not as you now do, pay a man two dollars per day to *mis*-represent you and all your interests! Our illustrious ancestors bequeathed this *power* to redress your wrongs through the ballot box, and will you not use it? Will ye sell your birthrights as did one of old, not for a mess of pottage, but for dollars and cents? God forbid! Awake then to duty, ere it be forever too late.

> "ACT! act in the *living* present;
> Heart within, God o'er head."

H.J.S.

Lowell, March, 1846

Voice of Industry, April 24, 1846

Farewell to Colonel Schouler

Col. Schouler has left for a tour to Europe. We trust he will see Lord Ashley,[11] and imbibe some of his Democracy on the "Ten Hour Bill." It is very desirable that he should find out some means by which *Massachusetts can Legislate for Labor* and protect the operative.

Lowell Female Labor Reform Association

Voice of Industry, May 22, 1846

March Boldly On

Sisters, let us be encouraged to labor yet more abundantly! Let the thought that we are engaged in a *good* work nerve us on to duty. The battle is not to the strong, alone, nor the race to the swift—but to the righteousness of the cause. In the strength of Elijah's God, the God of Right, let us march boldly on to the conquest. Let us take no rest until the shout shall rend the earth and heavens—"Goliath is fallen!"

JULIANA

Voice of Industry, June 12, 1846

Our Petition in the New Hampshire Legislature

MR. EDITOR:—Permit me to make some remarks upon the treatment of the late Legislature on our petition for the ten hour system.

I am a Factory Girl, one of the thousands of petitioners, and a member of the Labor Reform Association in Manchester, which Mr. Clark says "was got up by lazy Devils!"

Sad experience has taught me the great necessity of reduction in the hours of labor in the mills. We have tried in vain to convince our employers of the health-destroying tendency of the present system of labor. They will not harken to our entreaties, therefore we ask the Legislature. Why should they not restrict the hours of labor, as well as regulate the sale of ardent spirits?

We rejoice that there were some men in that august body who contended for us without fear of giving offence to such as would bind us down still stronger in their employment.

The being from Manchester who so cruelly abused us, probably thinks he has gained certain temporal advantages for himself, but he has made a mistake in such a false idea. A man who has not a strict regard for truth ought not to help make laws.

Mr. Clark must be contradicted in saying "the operatives do not ask legislation," and that "Operatives in Manchester do not work 12 hours a day, except in some cases!" Let me tell him and the world, this is untrue. I work eleven and one half hours every day, most all work one and a half hours longer. Did he make a mistake, or did he mean to tell a lie?

In regard to Mr. Clark's interrogation to the House about "sustaining our brothers in college," we would sustain them with ten hours' labor every day, if we had our honest due, and we hope they would not come out "lazy devils," and lazy lawyers.

Reader, do you suppose Mr. C. judged the "men who got up the Labor Reform Association" by himself?

Should we be allowed to vote next year, Daniel will surely be kept at home, and some good true Republican fill his place.

Mr. Clark opposed us (Factory Girls) having one hour for dinner! "As such a quantity of spare time, would be occupied by the operatives in wandering about the town, and they might be dancing and singing about the mills!" In the name of common sense I would ask don't we want some time for recreation and amusement as well as the aristocratic, lazy lawyers? who go "wandering about town" "seeking whom they may devour!"

To Mr. Nesmith it must be said, he complimented one of our number, but we will give him and all others the very important information that we "operatives *are* in favor of this legislation."

We hope the House next year will be made up of men imbued with benevolent courage and love of truth, "which delivers from the fear of man."

We, the Factory Girls, who are members of the Labor Reform Association of Manchester, take this opportunity to tender our thanks to Mr. Ayer of Hillsborough, for defending our Association from the abuse of Mr. Clark.

A FACTORY GIRL,

for the female L. R. A. in Manchester,
July 21, 1846

Factory Girls' Album, Exeter, N.H., September 2, 1846

Corporation Abuse

A very large portion (about two thirds, we are told,) of the girls on the Nashua Corporation, *turned out,* on Wednesday night of last week, and refused to work evenings; and if operatives had been as plenty as they were a few years ago, one half of them at least would have been dismissed; and by the most dastardly and wicked rules of the factory companies, they could not have obtained employment in any other factory. But hands being very scarce, most of them were allowed to remain. On the Jackson Corporation, where only seventeen *turned out,* they were all dismissed at once; and to prevent them from being employed elsewhere, to gratify a mean spite and contemptible malignity which only a soulless corporation would entertain or *dare to gratify,* their names were all sent to the agents of all the Mills in Lowell and Manchester; and some of these poor girls went to Lowell, we are told, and applied for work, and were told that their names were on the *black list,* and they could not be allowed the poor privilege of earning their bread by the labor of their hands.

Nashua (N.H.) Gazette, October 1, 1846

The Ten Hour System

Thursday evening, week, a stranger in the city asked of a "factory girl" the cause of such commotion, and those torch lights on the common. The reply was in substance as follows:

"I am glad to inform you that we have a Labor Reform Association here, composed, in part, of us 'factory girls.' The male members are mechanics, honorable and industrious, who mean to try for a reduction in the hours of labor, which you and every one must know is needed. At the last meeting of our Association, it was a unanimous vote that a part of the money in the treasury should be appropriated to pay lecturers favoring our cause, and that the City Hall should be engaged, (not thinking we should be denied, as it is invariably let for everything that comes along, even the 'Man-eater,') and our purpose was to hear the Rights of Labor discussed. Our Secretary applied to the Mayor, Deacon Brown, for the use of the Hall 'For hold a Labor Reform meeting.' Well, he would see about it, and he should know if he would call in the evening."

Mr. Cushing, with others in city authority were consulted. The result and answer was, "I have laid your petition before the committee, and you can't have it."

Does this look like a republican form of Government? It seems to me like a monarchical government. Here, sir, please accept of this "Circular to the Citizens and Operatives of Manchester,"[12] and you will get more information than I am able to give you.

"Well, Miss, by your account, I am inclined to think you have been wronged by the City Government in denying the use of the Hall. I am sorry for your disappointment, especially, on the part of the Factory Girls, who seem to be taking a conspicuous part in promoting Labor Reform and contending for a reduction in the hours of Labor, so they may have time for mental cultivation. I hope you will get the Ten Hour System; you do yourselves honor by contending for your rights and all men who contend for you, honor themselves and their country. You have my best wishes, and may God bless you."

Thus ended the colloquy between a Factory Girl and a Reverend Stranger.

We think the treatment our cause has received from the City authorities deserves resolutions of censure and indignation from us Factory girls, as well as from the citizens petitioning.

Truth is our watch word, and *Justice* our motto, and we must be allowed to say, we hope the latter will be observed by the City authorities. We cannot but think the Deacon will repent and "so all things will be well" for time to come.

Editors who still persist in saying "all manner of evil against us" and our movements "must keep truth on their side," and have *Charity* for Labor Reformers who denounce sometimes, but less perhaps, than lecturers in Electioneering campaigns.

I see something in the American which seems to me to be "Disgusting Billingsgate."—viz: "Many in the State are as sick of Jared W. Williams, as a candidate for Governor, as ever a Thompsonian patient was of having swallowed a porringer of Lobelia Tea." "Cannot speak of him without such contortions of countenance, frightful writhings, which are dreadful to behold." We think Joseph did not hardly do Justice by his remarks on Labor Reform. We think the "unknown man speaking from the gate top" must have said some true things about "money power, corporation influence, and oppressed operatives." Was he too tired to take notes or remember what he said about them?—There has been misrepresentation by our opposers in regard to our Convention at Nashua, which I feel glad has been contradicted. I was there during the sitting of the Convention and can say there was a oneness of sentiment as to the principle for which our Convention was held, and an entire harmony of feeling among its friends which gave the convention a character for strength seldom equalled among any body met to discuss matters of such great importance and of so exciting a nature.

We shall still strive for the Ten Hour System, and we feel grateful to every one who lends a hand in ameliorating our condition, and may this be the last time we may have occasion to speak of injustice from the officers of the first City in the Granite State.

A FACTORY GIRL

An Appeal to the Female Operatives in the
Manchester Mills

You are aware that much has been said of late about signing the new regulation papers, which require fourteen hours to constitute a day's work, notwithstanding the law recently passed in the State Legislature, limiting the same to ten hours.[13] You are aware, too, that in that act there has been a provision made for the capitalist, allowing him to hire those who will agree to work the same number of hours as heretofore, provided they will voluntarily enter into such contracts. You are to recollect, this agreement must be made voluntarily on the part of the operatives.

Now permit me here to state, that during the few weeks past that the subject of reduction of the hours of labor has been agitated, some of the operatives have been away, and consequently have been ignorant of what was being done for the amelioration of their condition. On their return, they call on their overseer to secure a place in the mill, take a new regulation paper, being urged to do so under pretence that the name of the corporation has been changed, or that some new arrangements have been made, which render it necessary to have new regulations.

Many have done so, and others continue to place their names upon these documents without reading them, thereby signifying their willingness to work fourteen instead of ten hours. Their names are now upon the records of the corporation, purporting to signify an agreement to a contract they had nothing to do in making, against which nature and reason would have remonstrated, had they but glanced at that detestable paragraph in that article.

I know not what others may do, but for myself, my resolution is fixed. Justice to myself and fellow operatives, with whom I would co-operate by yielding my influence toward breaking off the shackles with which we are bound, compels me to make a public retraction of the agreement I so thoughtlessly put my name to. I am fearless of the result; the consequences I am ready to meet. If I am discharged, be it known, that it is not because I have not performed my duties faithfully to my employers, for this I have ever done. I respect them, and have ever been treated kindly by them, and am sorry that necessity obliges me to assume a position hostile to their expressed wishes; but it will be simply for asserting my right to think, speak, and act, according to the dictates of an enlightened and reluctant mind. This right I will never yield let those censure who may; but when called upon to defend the cause of the down trodden and oppressed, by giving my influence (though this may be small indeed) to a cause based upon principles of justice, virtue, and truth, I will fearlessly do it.

The time has now come when woman should stand in her own defence and plead her own cause. Let us then heartily and with one voice respond against the libel that is upon the female name; that would render her incapable of thinking or noting understandingly, and reduce her to a mere machine, moved only by the operating power of a monied aristocracy, which shall regulate her hours of labor, tell her how long she shall remain in their employ, and if she refuse to comply with the requisitions of said power, she must submit to the penalty of being discharged—driven perhaps from her home, and compelled to seek other employment or find a place among strangers. Shall we quietly submit to all this or shall we not rather come up in one mighty phalanx, and with one voice say we will be free—that the ten hour system shall prevail?

Charity forbids me to presume that our overseers are in fact opposed to this movement, but they dare not speak as they think. Some, indeed, there may be, who feel distinterested in regard to others, and who are actuated by entirely selfish motives, are willing to remain in the mill the same number of hours as heretofore, for the pay they receive, knowing that they can take to themselves many indulgences that common laborers cannot; therefore it may cost them but little sacrifice of time or principle to conform to these regulations, since they feel amply compensated.

Others there are who would, were they placed in other circumstances, speak and act far different from what they do. Some have local attachments from which they cannot break away. They have families depending on them for support, and they know if they advocate this measure they will lose their place, and perhaps be unable to obtain employment to advantage elsewhere. For this cause they violate their consciences, and sign the new contracts.

And others there are, who have toiled long and hard to obtain a first or second hand's place, and having but just received the regalia of that office, they feel unwilling so soon to be thrust down from a position toward which they have so long anxiously aspired, and from which they expect to derive some recompense for the long years they served to obtain it.—These are willing to throw the work into our hands; they are willing that we should unbind the yoke that now encircles their necks, for they know we can do it if we will. They know if we do not succeed, we shall all be dismissed from the corporation, assured that the fearless spirit and ever active ingenuity of woman cannot fail, in some manner, to secure employment of some kind, and in some honorable manner obtain a livelihood, without voluntarily sacrificing her health upon the altar of despotism.

By the love of our peaceful home, and the sacredness of its domestic altars, animated by the example of our forefathers, and with the dauntless spirit of the pilgrims, let us, their children, never yield the privileges they so nobly earned for us, nor sacrifice to wealth and sordid ambition the principles of our foes institutions. Let us not forget that we are reasoning and intelligent beings, and that we help compose an important part of community, and that a work is devolving upon us from which in consequence of oppression, we have too long stood aloof. But the time now is, when we dare to think for ourselves, and when our reflections may be accompanied with corresponding action; when we may unite our efforts with the few of our brethren who have dared to lift up their voices against tyranny and oppression, and assist by our influence in urging forward the mighty engine of reform, that is destined yet to bless the world and release from hopeless servitude generations yet to come.

And ye mistresses of boarding-houses upon the corporations, have ye daughters on whom the heavy hand of the taskmaster is laid?— Then discharge your duty faithfully to them, in regard to the position they occupy. Instruct them in the principles of truth and justice—justice to themselves and the rising generation. Bid them reflect what their condition now is, and what it will soon become, if despotism is allowed to pour upon them unchecked in its lava tide. Furnish them with the means of information relative to the important trust committed into their hands, and urge them on to bold and energetic action in the cause of philanthropy and self-defence.

Once again permit me to say to my fellow operatives, that they will please remember that the law requires that this contract be entered into by us voluntarily. It does not compel us to sign this document, but takes the power and places it in our own hands, to choose liberty or bondage, and invests every individual with the free use of their thinking and reasoning faculties, enabling them to act according to the dictates of reason and common sense. Then shall we abuse the power thus delegated to us, and cringe, like dogs at the feet of their masters, to the will of those who would bind us in fetters worse than the manacles worn by the southern slave, who would rob us of everything that makes life to us, could they but amass more wealth and continue in the same or still greater ratio to add to their already increasing stores?

Let our watchword be, *onward to victory.*

If we fall, let it be in maintaining our inalienable rights, nor die, except it be in the cause of Freedom.

HARRIET E. PUTNAM

Manchester (N.H.) Democrat, September 1, 1847

Ten Hour Meeting at the City Hall

THE TEN HOUR SYSTEM—TREMENDOUS EXCITEMENT
—MEETING AT THE CITY HALL

The most exciting and crowded meeting ever holden in our city, was at the City Hall on Saturday evening. During the past week the agents and overseers have been trying to induce the operatives in the various mills to sign special contracts in order to "get round" the Ten Hour Law of the last Legislature.—But up to Saturday it was without avail.—Those operatives, who have been represented by the ignorant, designing and false, as opposed to the "ten hour" movement—persons who did not "wish for legislation"—"contented with their lot," and the like, refuse to sign any such contracts. Some two or three different "regulation papers" have been presented, but all to no purpose; most of the operatives are content with the law and refuse any compromise of their rights under it. Still they would proceed with the utmost caution. It had been so often asserted that "this reform should be brought about by mutual arrangement between the manufacturers and the operatives," and that "the operatives were not proceeding in the right way," that they concluded to appeal to the manufacturers, and respectfully ask them to conform in their mills to the principles of the Ten Hour Law. Accordingly the following petition was drawn up for signatures in the Machine Shop.

To the Stockholders of the Amoskeag Manufacturing Company, at Manchester, N.H.:

The undersigned would most respectfully represent, that they are operatives in the Machine Shop of said Company, and that they would gladly be governed by the beneficent principles of the Law of the last Legislature of this State, which recognizes Ten Hours of continuous labor as a DAY'S WORK; believing, as we do, that it would be for the interest of all concerned in the labor of this establishment,—the employers, as well as the employed—that this principle should prevail:—We therefore would most earnestly request that you would so act in the premises,—that your operatives in this shop be required to labor *Ten Hours* only on each day.

Manchester, Aug. 17, 1847.

This most respectful petition was taken to the agent, its object made known, and permission asked to circulate the same among the hands in the shop. *This was most peremptorily refused.* Thus this long suggested alternative failed through the very channel proposing it, as we ever supposed it would, the proposition being a subterfuge of the enemy, to procrastinate and stave off a result they see too plainly must sooner or later inevitably follow. Such tyranny, however, instead of staying the movement only added to the propelling power. On Friday, some few minors having been discharged for the reason that their parents refused to sign the new regulations, much excitement prevailed. This was not at all allayed by the fact that a committee of the Labor Reformers were refused the use of the City Hall, unless they could say Mr. Cluer would not be present. This the Committee could not say, as they *did not know.* In the evening, without notice, and without call, Merrimack Hall was filled with operatives—met as with one impulse to deliberate.

At this meeting a committee was raised to draft resolutions to be presented for the consideration of the operatives at an adjourned meeting. The most decided and harmonious spirit prevailed at this meeting. Meantime our excellent Mayor had heard of the refusal of the Hall to the Labor Reformers, and at once said to one of their committee, *"you can have the Hall* by applying for it—it cannot be that the committee will refuse it"; and the Hall was obtained for Saturday evening—to which place the reformers adjourned. On Saturday the following hand-bill was posted;

TEN HOURS OR MORE? THAT'S THE QUESTION.

The friends of Labor Reform, one and all, are requested to meet at the City Hall, this (Saturday) evening, at 7½ o'clock, to discuss the question of their rights and duties under the Ten Hour Law of the last Legislature.

It is hoped that every friend of the laborer, his rights, his duties to himself, society, and to his Maker, will be present to co-operate in this attempt to assert his rights.

"Now or never!" is the motto that should be inscribed on the banners of Labor Reform.

The Ladies are respectfully invited to attend and give their influence in favor of the movement.

Manchester, Aug. 21, 1847.

In answer to this call, the City Hall was filled to overflowing, with the factory girls prominent among those in the large audience. Hundreds upon hundreds were obliged to leave, unable to gain admission. The committee upon resolutions, composed of representatives of male and female operatives, reported the following:

Resolved, That we hold these truths self-evident,—that man is endowed by his creator with certain inalienable rights; among which is life, liberty, the pursuit of happiness, a home on the earth, a right to labor, and the power to limit for himself, his hours of labor.

Resolved, That agreeable to the laws of New Hampshire, Ten Hours constitutes a legal day's work.

Resolved, That ten hours' labor in each day is all that a man's constitution is able to bear.

Resolved, That on and after the 15th of September next, we will not work more than the legal number of hours in each day.

Resolved, That we will sign no contracts to work more than ten hours per day.

Resolved, That to the support of these Resolutions we pledge our lives and our sacred honor.

Resolved, That a copy of these Resolutions be sent to each of the manufacturing towns in the State.

Resolved, That a copy of these Resolutions be published in the Manchester Democrat and American, and the Voice of Industry, published in Lowell, Mass.

The resolutions were taken up separately, and passed with the utmost unanimity. The fifth resolution was postponed for further consideration, till the adjourned meeting on Monday evening.

The meeting illustrates that both male and female operatives are capable of uniting effectively in a common cause. It must tell upon the manufacturers, as it will prove to them what has been heretofore most industriously denied—that the operatives want, ask for, aye demand, the shorter hour system. It will show to them also, that the operatives are united and determined upon this matter. And more than this, it will show to the operatives themselves, that they have the strength, the power, the intelligence among themselves, to keep this ball in motion—to agitate this question till humanity shall triumph over avarice, and the rights of the laborer be acknowledged and guaranteed by the employer.

Manchester (N.H.) Democrat, August 25, 1847

Ten Hour Meeting at the City Hall

THE TEN-HOUR SYSTEM—EXCITEMENT INCREASING—TREMENDOUS MEETING AT THE CITY HALL ON MONDAY EVENING, AUG. 24.

The excitement increases. At an early hour the City Hall was filled to overflowing with male and female operatives. After representatives of both groups had spoken, the following resolutions were presented and were received with enthusiasm by the audience.

Resolved, That money is not our only object in our pilgrimage on this earth, but the welfare of the rising generation is worthy of our regard.

Resolved, That justice, reason, and law, demand that we should not be constrained by promise of place, or by fear of discharge from place, to work more than ten hours in one day.

Resolved, That if ten hours of daily work fail to produce as much as is now produced by the long hour system, we ask only corresponding pay.

Resolved, That our motto is, that justice to ourselves and to our employers is clearly right, and this we are willing to give and receive.

Resolved, That the labor reform system has for its great end and object, the elevation of the laborer, the diffusion of education, and equal rights to all men, the employer as well as the employed.

Resolved, That the ten hour system is a system better adapted to carry out the principles of equal rights to all men, than any system that has ever been promulgated in any time or in any country.

Resolved, That we will ask for nothing but what is clearly right, and will submit to nothing that is wrong.

Resolved, That all political power rightfully belongs to and emanates from the people, that they are the fountain of all law, and any usurpation of rights by any person or class of persons not conferred upon them by the people, ought to be resisted and frowned upon by an intelligent community.

Resolved, That being born freemen and freewomen, we will die freemen and freewomen—detesting tyranny, we will put down oppression—loving liberty, we wage eternal war with slavery; that hoping for the best, we will not distrust the future; knowing our cause to be just, our motto shall be *"onward and upward"*—less labor and more intellectual culture—less toil and more leisure—less confinement and more air; so believing, thus will we act, and thus acting, willingly will we die when our great change comes.

The resolutions were taken up seriatim and passed with the greatest unanimity.

Manchester (N.H.) Democrat, September 1, 1847

The Turn-Out

To-day (Wednesday 15th), the ten-hour law goes into operation. "Special contracts" were some time since prepared by the corporations, and presented to the operatives for their signatures. Those who persisted in refusing to sign, we are told were discharged on Saturday night. There are many reports in circulation, as to the number of the non-signers. It is thought about one half the operatives on the Nashua corporation are at work, while many state the number at one third. On the Jackson corporation we think the number of non-signers is less, proportionately.

It is understood that the operatives are turn out to-day, Wednesday, in procession, with music and banners. On the whole, the times promise to be rather exciting.

Nashua Oasis, reprinted in *Voice of Industry,* September 17, 1847

NOTES

1. The Reverend Henry A. Miles, author of *Lowell as It Was and as It Is.*
2. The editor noted that the verses, untitled, had been addressed to the *Voice of Industry* "by some unknown factory girl, and we sincerely hope that it may fall into the hands of every apologizer of the long hour and short life system, in christendom."
3. Sarah G. Bagley.
4. The letter, dated March 22, 1844, and addressed to William Boott, made the following point: "It is always intended to adapt the employment of the hands to their age and intelligence. A contrary course, if persisted in, must inevitably result in discomfiture. The amount of muscular strength which a girl is required to exert in any department is very small. The water-wheel has nearly superseded the use of it in all cases; and where the agent cannot be advantageously used, men are employed to perform those offices which require any considerable effort" (Massachusetts General Court, House of Representatives, *House Documents,* No. 50 [1845], p. 18).
5. The entire paragraph reads: "As a general rule, the girls pass their time with great regularity,—early to bed and early to rise. The evils which constant

employment and want of amusements are calculated to produce, if persisted in too long, are to a very great extent counteracted by periodical visits to their friends. They are sustained by the certainty of obtaining the object of their pursuit, if health and life are spared, and when the time arrives, they grasp it, and immediately retire to their homes, to recruit their wasted energies, and prepare, if need be, for another campaign" (*ibid.*, p. 24).

6. This is printed as part of Miss Bagley's letter to W.E.B., Correspondent to the "Dundee (Scotland) Warder." See above, pp. 174–76.

7. "As a direct result of having alienated the Lowell Female Labor Reform Association, Schouler was defeated when he stood for the Legislature again in the fall, a remarkable circumstance when it is remembered that these women had no vote" (Hannah Josephson, *The Golden Threads: New England's Mill Girls and Magnates* [New York, 1949], p. 261).

8. *Young America* was the name of the weekly newspaper, formerly the *Working Man's Advocate*, published in New York City by George Henry Evans, leader of the land reform movement. The term "Young America" also refers to a movement developed in the 1840s which emphasized America's manifest destiny to expand.

9. The Pittsburgh textile operatives had gone back to work on the old terms after they were convinced by the employers that they could not compete with other manufacturers who still maintained the twelve-hour day. The employers left the impression that they would follow suit as soon as others instituted the ten-hour day. The Pittsburgh girls then turned to their sisters in New England and urged them to intensify their fight for the ten-hour day, assuring them that in Western Pennsylvania arrangements had been made "for continuing the warfare" (New York *Tribune*, October 31, 1845; Pittsburgh *Spirit of Liberty*, reprinted in *Young America*, November 15, 1845).

10. *Rights of Man*, published in England in 1791–92 by Thomas Paine (1737–1809) in defense of the French Revolution and democratic institutions, was suppressed and Paine himself was prosecuted. But it continued to influence lower-class struggles both in this country and in England. For its influence in England, see E. P. Thompson, *The Making of the English Working Class* (New York, 1963), pp. 19–23, 36–37; in the American labor movement, see Philip S. Foner, *History of the Labor Movement in the United States* (New York, 1947), I, 41, 45, 87.

11. Lord Ashley, Earl of Shaftesbury (1801–85), one of the greatest English philanthropists of the nineteenth century, was noted for his work in attacking the evils of the factory system and was a major force behind the achievement of the ten-hour law in 1847. Among other activities, he sponsored the famous "Stafford House Address," signed by thousands of Englishwomen. Directed at American women, the address pleaded with them to speak up for the freedom of the Negro slaves.

12. The "Circular to the Citizens and Operatives of Manchester," issued by the Labor Reform Association, informed them that the labor reform meeting to be held at the Universalist Meeting House, where resolutions were to be drawn up, could not be held. The "house was closed against us, and the people were compelled to hold their meeting in the streets, the Resolutions were not offered." The resolutions denounced the mayor and aldermen for subserving "the interests of Corporation Tyrants and Conspirators against the rights of the people" by refusing to open City Hall "to the citizens of Manchester, to discuss the wrongs and grievances of the Laboring classes"; condemned the practices of the corporations in Lowell, Nashua, and Manchester for conspiracy against labor by employing blacklists; charged that "the Corporate Factory System of the United States . . . is reducing the laboring population to a state of tenantry, serfdom, and dependency, more fearful in its character, tendencies,

and results, than the military feudalism of Europe"; asserted that slavery existed in the North as well as in the South, and that "the remedies of these evils of Slavery at the South and the North, are to be found in the adoption of the principles of Industrial Reform"; and finally resolved "That the fourteen hour system of Labor, adopted in the American Factories . . . makes the system of Factory Labor and life but little better than physical assassination, that it gives the operative no time or opportunity for improvement of the mind and heart, and is therefore the enemy of intelligence, religion, and morality, and that the least amelioration that can be asked, is that TEN HOURS SHALL CONSTITUTE A LEGAL DAY'S WORK" (*Voice of Industry,* October 23, 1846).

13. At the insistence of the employers, New Hampshire's legislature inserted into the ten-hour law passed in 1847 a provision permitting employers to draw up special contracts with workers for more than ten hours. Even before the law was passed, employers submitted these contracts to their workers and informed them that they had the alternative of either signing and continuing to work or refusing to sign and going jobless. They also threatened that the names of the workers refusing to sign would be sent to all corporations in the district so that it would be impossible for them to gain employment in other factories.

Part 6

Other Causes

Other Causes

While the battle for the ten-hour day occupied the major attention of the female factory operatives, they were also involved in other reform movements. Some believed it was a mistake to take a stand against Negro slavery in the South while ignoring the worse slavery, as they charged, in the factory of the North, but the vast majority disagreed. The factory operatives, in fact, were known as the "Pretty Friends of the Slave" (*Lowell Advertiser*, February 10, 1845). They wrote letters and poems denouncing slavery, and the Lowell Female Labor Reform Association participated officially in antislavery meetings. The association also aided the drive to bring relief to the starving peasants of Ireland during the tragic potato famine. The movement to abolish capital punishment also involved the young women, and the Female Total Abstinence Society of Lowell, a temperance organization, was largely made up of factory operatives. Finally, the female operatives became associated with the Utopian Socialist movement organized by the followers of Charles Fourier in America, and Sarah G. Bagley was elected vice-president of the Lowell Union of Association. The section closes with an item published in *The Harbinger*, official journal of the Fourier movement in the United States. □

Slavery

A great cry is raised in the northern states against southern slavery. The sin of slavery may be abominable there, but is it not equally so here? If they have *black* slaves, have we not *white* ones? Or how much better is the condition of some of our laborers here at the north, than the slaves of the south?

The laws of the southern States require of the master to support his slaves when they are past their labor. But is there any law at the north requiring those who receive the benefit of the poor man's labor to support him when he is past his labors?

It may be said that he enjoys his *liberty;* but how many of our working men, how many of the operatives in our mills, enjoy any thing worthy of the name of liberty? Such liberty is theirs as Napoleon gave the press. They could do what they chose, but if they did not espouse the cause of Bonaparte, every one should be brought to the guillotine. Freedom! the capitalist allows such as "vultures give to the lambs—feeding on and devouring them." Our laborers may work as the capitalist dictates, or not, but if they do not, they must starve! And if they do work, the capitalists derive *nine elevenths* of the products of their labor. How much better, then, we ask, is the condition of some of our *white* northern laborers, than some of the *black* southern slaves?

Manchester Operative, reprinted in *The Mechanic* (Fall River), November 2, 1844

Slavery, North and South

I, for one, have been greatly disappointed in men who have heretofore advocated the cause of humanity, but whose acts of late do not agree with their professions—men who stand up and dole out pity for the souther[n] slave, but would crush with an iron hand the white laborer of the north.

A TEN HOUR WOMAN

The Mechanic (Fall River), October 5, 1844

A Parody

Master spare the lash,
 Touch not a single slave
In anger wild, and rash:
 But oh! forbear and save—
'Twas God that gave him breath
 And placed him here with thee,

Then master, spare this death
    And let it cease to be.
The same immortal mind,
    Created by one hand,
In *black* and *white,* we find
    In every clime, and land;
Master—forbear thy stroke,
    Touch not a single hair,
This bondage must be broke
    And *pity* says *forbear.*

When he was his *own* and *free,*
    Thou stole him from his home,
From a home beyond the sea,
    In this strange land to roam,
His mother watched him there
    In his cot beyond the sea,
And say—dost thou not care?
    Oh! let the slave go free.
His heart around it clings,
    His own dear native home,
And the wild bird sweetly sings
    In the grove, where he has roamed—
Slave holders—no longer dare
    To bind him, with thy chain,
And from his friends him tare
    For the *sake of paltry gain.*

ADA

Fitchburg, Sept. 16th.

Voice of Industry, September 18, 1845

Should We Keep Quiet about Slavery?

Providence, Sept. 19th, 1845

MR. EDITOR:—Having received intimation from my friends in your place, that should I happen there while our *pro-slavery* friends from the South are visiting there, I must keep quiet on the subject of slavery, if I wish to keep in their good graces, as they do not like to hear anything against their "peculiar institutions."

Lest our pro-slavery friends should return to the South without having heard one word of anti-slavery truth, I hope thay will pardon me, if through your invaluable sheet, I should offer a few ingenuous remarks on a subject which I fear has never been very fully presented to them. Were I to attempt to move the heart of the slave holder and call forth his sympathies for those he so unjustly and inhumanly tyrannizes over,—would be folly—I can only utter what has already been reiterated throughout the length and breadth of the land, on this and the other side of the Atlantic.

There is a *depth* in *slavery* beyond the reach of any, but those who have been made the recipients of its horrors—words have not the power to express its meaning. Were we to listen to that fugitive from the galling chains and fetters of the South, Frederick Douglass,[1] whose eloquent appeals have caused the tear of sympathy to course down the furrowed and blooming cheek of thousands who have listened to the sad recital of his woes, we should see but the shadow, while the substance of slavery lies beyond the power of description, were we to imagine ourselves reduced to a level with the brutes—robbed of self, and all that elevates mankind above the lower order of creation, our very soul would shrink at the idea, and life itself appear loathsome.

Consider and contrast the condition of the slave with that of your own; while you enjoy the liberty of conscience, and possess all the natural and endearing relations of human existence, the slave who is made in the image of the God who "made of one blood all the nations of the earth," is denied the *rights,* aye the *name* of *human beings*—are bought and sold like cattle—families scattered, and hearths made desolate—infants torn from the fond embrace of a mother and sold by the pound!

A FACTORY GIRL

Voice of Industry, September 25, 1845

A Mile of Girls

It will be seen, says the Free State Rally, that the women of Lowell, God bless them, who have signed the remonstrance against the extension of slavery, if they were to join hand in hand, would stretch more than a mile. Probably not a few of them are the young women, called "white slaves" at the South, who work in the factories. They have signed the remonstrance from no selfish edification, but from pure, heaven-inspired sympathy for the oppressed slave.[2]

Stratford Transcript, reprinted in *Voice of Industry,* December 26, 1845

North and South

"For the wail of millions
Is sounding in our ears."
List ye that low and plaintive wail,
Borne on the southern balmy gale!
See Afric's wretched daughter weep,
Nor close her weary eyes in sleep.

Her wretched husband at her side,
Strives to assuage—her cares divide;
But cruel white, with lash appears,
Nor heeds his groans, nor minds her tears.

"Hie to your task—of darker hue,
What sympathetic chords have you?
Go, toil and sweat on yonder plain;
Ye were but made for white man's gain."

List ye again that plaintive moan!
It strikes the ear like childhood's tone;—
Ah, little one! thou weep'st in vain!
Thy mother toils on yonder plain.

Friends of freedom! heed the wail!
'Tis God's own cause,—ye cannot fail!
His richest guerdon will be given,—
The joy of earth—the peace of heaven.

Remember, too, that wrong is here,
And give the north one pitying tear;
Oh! let the fruits of love go forth,
To free the South and bless the North!

MARY

Voice of Industry, February 13, 1846

Lines for the *Voice of Industry*

SUGGESTED BY READING AN EDITORIAL ARTICLE IN
A LATE NUMBER OF THE BOSTON OLIVE BRANCH.

What though the clergy's tongues defame,
And brand him with a felon's name,
And boldly say, he would destroy
Christ's kingdom, and his truth alloy,—

And dare assert, he'd wrong the man,
For whom, thus far, he's spent life's span.
What's that to him?—within his breast
A higher, holier, aim will rest;
Than ever fear a scoffing world,
Or bow to priesthood bought with gold.
Go ask of Afric's fettered son
The blessed work his hand hath done;—
Who guarded, cheered, protected, fed,
As he, his toilsome journey led
From sunny South to bleaky North,
Beyond the land of FREEDOM'S BIRTH!
Who strives and toils, with heart and hand,
To wipe the stains from off our land,
That holds her sons in galling chains,
With scourge and rack, and fiery pain!
Which crushes all that's man's delight,
And sinks the mental ray in night!—
That husbands, wives, and children part,
And tears anew the bleeding heart;—
And mars the image, God hath wrought,
And makes of man, a chattel, bought.
What is religion,—but to bless,
And aid a brother in distress?
To keep the soul from sin and wrong,
And in the ways of right be strong?
And ever lend a helping hand,
To bless the wrong'd of every hand?
Thus, GARRISON hath earn'd a fame,
And black and white, will bless his name.

MARY

Lowell, April 1846

Voice of Industry, April 10, 1846

"What Is It to Be a Slave?"

Hast thou ever asked thyself
What is it to be a slave?
Bought and sold for sordid pelf,
From the cradle to the grave!

'Tis to know the transient powers
E'en of muscle, flesh and bone,

Cannot in thy happiest hour,
  Be considered as thine own!

But thy master's goods and chattels
  Lent to thee for little more
Than to fight his selfish battles
  For some bits of shining ore!

'Tis to learn thou hast a heart
  Beating in that bartered frame,
Of whose ownership—no part
  Thou can'st challenge—but in name.

For the curse of slavery crushes
  Out the life-blood from its core;
And expends his throbbing gushes
  But to swell another's store.

God's best gift from heaven above,
  Meant to make a heaven on earth,
Hallowing, humanizing love!
  With the ties which thence have birth!

These can never be his lot,
  Who, like brutes, are bought and sold;
Holding such—as having not
  On his own the spider's bold!

'Tis to feel, e'en worse than this,
  If ought worse than this can be,
Thou hast shrined, for bale or bliss,
  An immortal soul in thee!

But that this undying guest
  Shares thy body's degradation,
Until slavery's bonds, unblest,
  Check each kindling aspiration!

And what should have been thy light,
  Shining e'en beyond the grave,
Turns to darkness worse than night,
  Leaving thee a hopeless slave!

Such is slavery! Couldst thou bear
  Its vile bondage? Oh! my brother,
How, then, canst thou, wilt thou dare
  To inflict it on another!

ELLEN

Voice of Industry, January 23, 1846

The Slave's Revenge

Lend, lend imagination wings,
While yonder sun in beauty wanes;—
Soar far away to southern clime,
Where souls in cruel bondage pine.

In yonder cabin kneels a form
That slavery's galling yoke hath worn;
In broken accents hear him cry,
"Must I in bondage always sigh?"

The morning dawned in beauty bright,
And chased away the darksome night;
But yet it brought no kind relief
To him whose soul was filled with grief.

The busy crowd the market throng,
And he whose prayer to heaven hath gone,
With heavy tread reached the stand
Where men are sold in christian land.

His dark eyes flash in deep despair—
Yon little group—his all—stands there;—
Alas! deep anguish fills his heart;
With wife and children he must part.

The thought is madning—worse than death—
Of loved ones, dear as life, bereft;—
He crossed the stand with resolute air,
And whispered in the planter's ear.

"You own my wife, my children dear,"
And then he wip'd a briny tear;
"Me work for you by night, or day,
Oh! bid me off, good master, pray."

But soon advanced with haughty stride,
He who the Almighty's law defied;
The slave cast one dark, withering look,
All fear of man his soul forsook.

He raised his strong, athletic arm,
Then rose his voice in wild alarm—
"You cast my lot far far away;
Me never work for you a day."

Cease! cease these idle words, black slave!
Nor longer like a maniac rave;
The highest bid hath made you mine;
Henceforth you dwell in distant clime.

The bondman raised his eyes to heaven,
Then gazed on those whom God had given;
With frantic yell he leaped the stand,
Seized fast an axe—cut off his hand.

Then raised his bleeding arm to him
Who vainly thought the prize to win—
"Remember sir, again me say,
Me never work for you a day."

. SARAH W.

Voice of Industry, June 18, 1847

Capital Punishment

"Life belongs only to God, and that is why it is written, 'Thou shalt not kill.' When the law kills, it inflicts not a chastisement, *it commits a murder!* Can you call by the name of justice the act which renders man infamous—the act which at one blow ravishes from a human being all his rights, and even the faculty of ever possessing any rights?

"When you have converted an animated being into a handful of dust, will that dust, scattered by the winds over the face of the earth, prove a seed of good, a germ of virtue?"

We thought, when we commenced, to have written something on capital punishment worthy of being read, but the eloquence of Mennais[3] [*sic*] from whom we have stolen our text, has rendered any sermon unnecessary. The abolition of this sanguinary relic of antiquity is becoming a subject of deep interest to the philanthropy of the age. We think we can see in the reason given by its advocates, a reason for its abolition. If you ask a believer in hanging what good it does a man to hang him, he will urge several reasons which are easily shown, to be no reasons at all; and when driven to his only sermon, that answer invariably is, "He has murdered a man and *ought to die!*" This is a blood-thirsty retaliation and not a wise or merciful policy. If crime unrepented of is held to account beyond the grave, how necessary it is that all possible means be afforded to the criminal to settle his account with his maker before his death!

The Factory Girl, New Market, N.H., March 1, 1843

Capital Punishment

It came to pass on a certain evening, that a paper known as the "Prisoner's Friend,"[4] was placed in my hands. Having read and re-read its contents, my thoughts assumed a new train. I wandered in imagination, over the whole earth, to find some who had been benefited by that law, which, as a punishment, takes the life of a man; that life which they can never restore; which none but God could ever give, I asked if it improved society—lessened crime, or reformed the guilty; and the very mountains echoed, No. But to the question, will it ever be abolished, no answer came, and I retired to rest. I vainly tried to collect my wandering thoughts; but alas! over my mind there was no control, and I wandered. First, I stood beside an extensive building, near which was erected a scaffold. The hoarse creaking of the massive doors upon their hinges told too plainly, that the scene within was even more dreadful than that without. Soon three men are led out for execution. They ascend the steps. One speaks, confesses his guilt, relates the circumstances of a murder, which, it seemed, had been committed. and declared that his two friends who were to die with him were innocent.

They, also, plead not guilty. But it was of no avail, and they were together, hurled into eternity. As I turned to leave this heart-rending scene, I beheld two objects which had before escaped my observation. The one was clothed in the purest white, and on his forehead, in letters of gold, were inscribed, "They know not what they say." The other held in his hand a sword, reeking with blood, while on this brow were the words, "Kill them, kill them, they deserve it." Next I stood in a humble cottage, where it seemed intemperance had dwelt. The mother had just drawn a sword from her husband's heart, and he lay struggling in the agonies of death. The children slept on, unconscious of what had passed. The two objects of my especial notice, too, were there. The motto on the one was, "Sin shall not go unpunished." On the other, "Make more rigid the laws of the land."—

The scene changed, and I stood in a court room. The word guilty, echoed through the apartment. The solemn sentence of death passed upon her who had perpetrated the awful deed. The two stranger guests were there, and upon the brow of the one might be seen the words, "I am the prisoner's friend." Upon the other, "You killed him and we'll kill you." The former followed her to the prison, spoke words of consolation to her wounded heart, and, when at last, she hung upon the gallows, he heaved a sigh, and turned away, saying, it aught not so to be.

I was about to enquire, what were his resolutions, when this scene passed away, and I found myself wandering in search of her child. Years had fled since I had seen him. Great was the change. He stood in the "Legislative hall."

Before the house was the great question, "Shall the death penalty be abolished." In one corner of the room, reclining on a couch, was the object who had so often been seen with the sword. Near him, sat the one with garment white like snow. Powerfully the speakers "wielded the sword of argument." And when at last the question was decided, the former sank back, and, with a groan, expired.

The countenance of the latter brightened, and he said, " 'tis finished;" "let all the earth rejoice." Behold I saw, and understood not; and I said, who are thou, and who is this that now lieth dead in his bed. He answered, "has thou been so long time in the world, and yet does not know us." Immediately I understood. And he said, "be faithful." "Write, these things are true." "For he hath looked down from the height of his sanctuary; from heaven did the Lord behold the earth, to hear the groaning of the prisoner; to loose those that are appointed to death; to declare the name of the Lord in Zion, and his praise in Jerusalem."

EUNICE

Voice of Industry, May 22, 1846

To the Girls of Lowell

The thought has occurred to me to-day, while visiting the miserable hovels of the poor creatures dying with destitution, that the girls of Lowell, of whom the world has heard such honorable mention, might do a grateful thing in securing some of their sex not only from the misery but the shame of their situation. No language of mine can describe the destitution of clothing to which all ages and both sexes are reduced in this land of the shadows of death. Everything of value has been pawned for food. Thousands of women and children here are so destitute of covering as to prevent them from going out into the streets to beg. In hundreds of these hovels the living wife or child or husband has lain for days close beside the dead body of a husband, mother or wife, in order to cover themselves with the rags spread over the deceased. Now I had thought to-day, while witnessing these scenes of suffering, that the Girls of Lowell might give each a comfortable calico dress, to clothe the destitute of their sex in Skibbereen. I am sure such an example would be followed by the ladies in different towns in New England, and that tens of thousands of these poor, thin, naked, blue-lipped children would attest in favor of their benefactresses at another day. "I was naked and ye clothed me." I hope the counties of Middlesex and Essex will club together and send out a ship freighted with provisions and clothing for Ireland, and that it will embrace in its bill of lading 10,000 calico dresses, suited to every size, from the Factory Girls of the two counties.

ELIHU BURRITT[5]

Skibbereen, Poor Ireland, Feb. 23d 1847.

Voice of Industry, April 9, 1847

The Factory Girls—Heaven Bless Them!

The following brief communication will show how cordially and effectivly the factory girls of Lowell have responded to the appeals made to their feelings of sympathy and benevolence, by the distresses of the suffering poor in a foreign land. We wish that we were at liberty to make public the names of those who have been the chief instruments in this labor of love, but true charity seeks not the applause of the world, and the injunction of silence is put upon our lips.

Merrimack Corp., Lowell April, 14

FRIEND DREW:—A few evenings since we received a call from two blessed "sisters of charity," who were responding to the appeal of the Christian Citizen, by visiting every Factory boarding-house in Lowell, and presenting the claims of the suffering Irish. The enclosed list proves that their efforts were not in vain, though the result would have been far more surprising and delightful, had the response been as fervent as the appeal through the lips of these most excellent females. One small boarding-house, upon this corporation, was the focus and fountain of all the interest; and when I went in to add my mite of labor to theirs, and saw the five large boxes so nicely packed, I was astonished to see how much a few weak hands could accomplish.

Dresses,	301	Shawls,	24
White garments	252	Cloaks,	2
Men's "	116	*Hetrogeneous,*	107
Pairs of hose,	148		1,032
" boots and shoes	48		
Quilts,	44		

I believe the above statement is correct, and though I trust *our mite* will comfort some of Erin's daughters, yet how small is it to what it might and *ought to have been.*

Christian Citizen

Voice of Industry, April 30, 1847

Temperance[6]

There is no subject that should so deeply interest us and no one that is so much overlooked by those who have the means to contribute to its support as the subject of temperance. The poet dwells upon the beauties of nature, the artist paints the lovely scenes that charm the eye, and nearly all who are endowed with intellectual faculties devote their time to subjects of minor importance. Therefore the great and glorious subject of temperance must be overlooked.

The female portion of community see and suffer the effects of this baneful malady and yet they must forever seal their lips and remain silent. If they possess gifts more noble than were ever possessed by mortal man they must bury their talents in silence and hold their peace. Is it not time that the abused and sufferers should take a decided stand in the cause of liberty and truth? Male or female what is the difference if they are the ones directly concerned. Is it any excuse why the greater part of the world should hesitate to defend their rights because they are ladies and the would-be "lords of creation" say "keep silent?" I affirm it is not, so long as they are compelled to suffer from the effects of the worst contagion that ever spread over the face of the earth. How often are our hearts pained in beholding the tears of the devoted wife and mother, as they course down the care worn check, for the once affectionate and dutiful husband now degraded and despised even by those who caused his destruction. Think for a moment, O ye rumsellers, of the tears and sighs of parent and children, of the sorrowful days and sleepless nights of sisters for the crimes of an intemperate brother, and if your consciences do not condemn you in your vicious course your hearts must be callous to every sense of right and wrong. But the rumseller argues that by trafficking in ardent spirits he receives money and obtains wealth and why not continue his deadly occupation. Why is it not equally as just to employ one man to kill his brother and reward him with paltry gold as to murder him from time to time in a more fashionable way? Would it not be easier for the victim to have the chords of life sundered by a single stroke than to prolong his existence under the misery that must follow the free use of alcohol? It destroys the faculties, benumbs the intellect and deprives those who use it of all real enjoyment. Man in such a state is not to be compared with the dumb beast that grazes in the field, and I believe the drunkard is far superior to him who knowingly furnishes him with materials for his own destruction. The unsuspecting are enticed to partake of the fatal draught, while the unmerciful rumseller, with a demon like smile playing upon his unholy countenance rejoices that he has obtained a new customer. And after he has robbed him of that which the wants of his family demand, and taken him a priceless treasure, a good reputation and virtuous name, he turns him from his den of infamy and disgrace, and bids him no more come beneath his roof. In the meantime the murderer and thief, even the rumseller, is looked upon as an influential and virtuous man and is permitted to go at large destroying as he goes like the incurable disease, while those who commit smaller offences are confined within the prison walls. Is not a good name of greater worth than any worldly goods that can be taken from us? Gracious Heavens! think of this and blush at the condition of our happy New England, the land for which our fathers crossed the ocean to secure to their children a free land, little dreaming of the falling chains with which it would be bound.—Awake female sisters and let your voices be heard above the cry of the thousands who advocate the cause of sin, misery, and death. "Let no hand be idle" for it is a "great work" and will and *must* be accomplished. Heaven will aid you in your enterprise for it is a heavenly object, and He who rules all events will crown your efforts with success.

FLORELLA

Weekly Messenger, Literary Wreath & Factory Girl's Garland, Exeter, N.H., July 11, 1846

The Lowell Union of Associationists[7]

Our friends in Lowell, Mass. have organized for the purpose of carrying on the good work. They enter upon it with the right spirit, and will not fail to render a good account of themselves. More than fifty names are already attached to their constitution,— a band larger than many that have succeeded in revolutionizing the world. Let them only feel what they have to do, and lay their hands heartily to it and it will be done; but to this they need no exhortation. The officers of their society are,

JOHN ALLEN, *President*
SARAH G. BAGLEY, *Vice President*
WILLIAM T. G. PIERCE, *Secretary*
D. H. JAQUES, *Treasurer.*

They hold two meetings in the week; one on Saturday evening for social intercourse and recreation, and one on Sunday evening for lectures and discussions,—an excellent arrangement. Let Associationists unite socially, and learn to know each other not only as laborers in a common cause but as personal friends. In this way they will become more firmly united, and their efforts will be rendered more thorough and efficient.

In relation to Tracts, we will say to the society at Lowell, and to affiliated bodies elsewhere, that the Parent Society designs to prepare and publish a complete series of tracts for popular distribution, and that only the want of funds for the purpose delays its execution. This is an object which small contributions can attain. By forwarding a few dollars the publication of a new tract can be ensured, while at the same time the donors will be entitled to the value of their remittance in our publications.

The Harbinger, August 29, 1846, p. 191

NOTES

1. Frederick Douglass (1817–95), born a slave and completely self-taught, escaped to the North in 1838, joined the antislavery movement in New England, and made his first public speech in 1841. After six years as a lecturer for antislavery societies, he moved to Rochester and began to edit his own paper, *The North Star,* the first issue of which came off the press on December 3, 1847. As editor, orator, and organizer, Frederick Douglass led the black protest movement for almost fifty years.

When *The North Star* made its appearance, it was hailed by the *Voice of*

Industry: "Glad are we for a peep at the North Star. We mean a paper published and edited by Frederick Douglass, at Rochester, N.Y. It gleams and flashes all over with the light of genius. It is such a paper as Frederick Douglass would be expected to edit. . . . We cordially welcome him to the labors, so recently entered upon ourselves, and earnestly wish him the happiest success" (December 31, 1847).

2. In reprinting this report, the *Voice of Industry* praised the factory girls of Lowell for having "enlisted in the great and good cause of emancipating the oppressed slaves of the South." But the *Voice* asked why the Lowell factory girls "are so *free* to enter their names against the annexation of Texas" while they were discharged and blacklisted if they signed petitions for the ten-hour day—was there then less slavery in the factories of Lowell than on the plantations of the South?

3. Friedrich Menniuss (?–1659) was a Swedish writer opposed to capital punishment.

4. *The Prisoner's Friend* was published by Charles Spear (1801–63), a Universalist minister of Boston and advocate of prison reform and opponent of capital punishment. He helped organize the Society for the Abolition of Capital Punishment in 1844 and published the *Hangman* in 1845; the next year the title was changed to *The Prisoner's Friend,* which continued publication until 1859. The *Voice of Industry* of April 2, 1847, carried an account of a fair for support of *The Prisoner's Friend.*

5. The Irish had suffered severely at the hands of British oppressors before the 1840s, but the potato famine of 1846 was the worst blow. People died like flies in Ireland, and relief movements were organized in the United States. Over half of Ireland's working class streamed into America, with many of the immigrants coming to New England and a fair number moving into the textile mills.

Elihu Burritt (1810–79), "the Learned Blacksmith," self-instructed linguist, and leading American pacifist, organizer of the first international peace congress in Brussels in 1848, was in Ireland on a mission to mobilize support for the starving Irish.

6. Women were very active in the temperance crusade not simply because they suffered at the hands of drunken husbands, but also because through the temperance movement the women's rights advocates obtained a significant platform.

7. The Lowell Union of Associationists was founded in February, 1846, with the name of the Lowell Fourier Society. It had at its formation about ten members; their numbers had grown to fifty in May, 1847, the majority of whom were factory girls and mechanics. "Pecuniarily we cannot do much here," the Union's officers reported, "as we are mostly Operatives and Mechanics, who, under existing organizations, cannot be expected to be rich, and are less so perhaps for being Reformers." They added: "We have to contend with the almost omnipotent and omnipresent power of Corporate Monopoly. This controls the city Government, the Pulpit, the Press—every thing. But there are few here who are true to the cause of Universal Unity, whose voices will ever be raised against that system of society of which the Factory system here is a legitimate result, and who in weakness or in strength will do what they can in the cause of Human Redemption." (D. H. Jaques, President, and Mary Emerson, Secretary, in *The Harbinger,* May 29, 1847, p. 390.)

Part 7

Women's Rights

Women's Rights

In the *History of Woman Suffrage* edited by Elizabeth Cady Stanton, Susan B. Anthony, and Matilda Joslyn Gage, the *Lowell Offering*, "edited by the 'mill girls,' " is listed as one of the groups of newspapers published by women during the 1840s. No mention, however, is made of the factory magazines and papers which came into existence to challenge the views set forth in the *Offering*. Yet in its entire history of publication, the *Offering* carried only one article devoted to the issue of women's rights (see pp. 38–44), and even Harriet H. Robinson, a champion of the *Offering*, concedes that the approach in the article was a timid one. Nevertheless, when the Lowell Female Labor Reform Association announced the launching of its Female Department in the *Voice of Industry*, it pointed out bluntly: "Our department devoted to woman's thoughts will also defend woman's rights. . . ." This it did throughout its existence. So, too, did the other publications which carried the writings of the factory operatives. While these writings on women's rights varied in militancy from magazine to magazine, all of them carried articles dealing with the subject written by the operatives themselves. The three articles by "An Operative," written in answer to "Spectator," printed below, are not unusual for the factory girls, and they compare favorably with the best writing on women's rights by anyone at that time. In addition, they add a working-class point of view to the answers to men who denigrated women—a viewpoint missing from nearly all of the other contemporary articles.

293

In their letters to the *Voice of Industry* describing their experiences during their travels to various towns and villages to gather subscriptions for the labor paper, Huldah J. Stone and Mehitabel Eastman noted the fact that they spoke to audiences of male workers and were cordially received. Thus while middle-class women were finding it difficult to obtain attention and respect from men of their class, the female operatives who wrote their articles and letters in the factory magazines and the pioneer women labor leaders who addressed male workers were accorded respect and understanding. To be sure, the men had the same interest in obtaining the ten-hour day as the women, and they were fully aware of the fact that the drive by the factory operatives gave the entire campaign great impetus. Nonetheless, it is worth noting this willingness on the part of many working-class men to treat the women workers from the factories as equals both in their organizations, such as the New England Workingmen's Association, and in the local communities visited by the women serving as agents for the *Voice of Industry*.

The young women in the factories sent no delegates to the first Woman's Rights Convention held in Seneca Falls, New York, during July, 1848. But they learned of the Declaration of Sentiments adopted by the convention through its publication in the *New Era of Industry,* successor to the *Voice of Industry,* and when they read the list of impositions upon women by men, beginning with the fact that he had never permitted her "to exercise her inalienable right to the elective franchise," and the assertion by the convention that women "do insist upon an immediate admission into all those rights and privileges which belong to them as citizens of these United States," they undoubtedly felt that their writings and actions in the preceding years had helped lay the foundation for the declaration. The journal known as the "Factory Girl's Voice" declared in publishing the Declaration of Women's Rights in its issue of August 3, 1848: "Few are willing to admit the fact, and many are not aware of it, that woman in all civilized countries, is politically, religiously, and socially enslaved; but we challenge any one to deny it, after reading the following statement of her grievances, which we take from the Declaration of Sentiments, put forth by the aforesaid Convention. This Declaration, by the way, is not a parody upon our world-famed Declaration of Independence, as the (Boston) Transcript calls it, but an improved edition, the complement of that instrument. Deny the truth of the following statements who can! We rejoice in that Convention as a significant indication of the tendencies of this age." □

Marriage

No female would enter into the married state, if she could for a moment believe that the fond lover would one day be transformed into the morose and intractable husband; and anything like tyranny on the part of the husband, augurs a mind alike mean and vicious, which can thus take advantage of the position of a confiding woman, who has surrendered to you, on the faith of your honor, and from the impulse of her affection, her will, her person, and all else she possessed in the world. I am aware that there is no scarcity of bad wives; but I am at the same time sensible that in very many instances their husbands have made them so; and that much of the derangement of domestic happiness, of which we have unfortunately so many proofs, is attributable to early neglect, or positive ill usage on the part of the husband.

Some women there are, so weak and gentle by nature, that no course of treatment, however harsh, can force them to rebel or retaliate; they suffer on, and no one knows of their agony, till death closes the scene on a broken heart. But there are others made of more fiery materials, who resent neglect or ill-treatment, with a degree of spirit which ill becomes the fair sex; and which nothing, perhaps, but such a course of harsh usage, would have called forth. Their rough encounters with a morose or dissipated husband blunt the keen edge of female modesty and virtue; and when a woman once falls, she sinks to lower depths of infamy than a man would do; and demands a fearful retribution from her husband, for having made her what she is.

Surely no one who pretends to be a man, and who has a wife at all worthy of his love, can subject her to torture, such as is expressed in the lines above; and yet we know too well that it is of every day occurrence, even when the pair have started in life with all the attributes of youth and love. And somehow or other, men do not look upon it as criminal. We see men who are so amiable in the world's estimation that they will not even injure a fly, and the blood of a reptile throws them into convulsions; and yet these same gentle creatures will by coldness and systematic neglect, make their wives wish they were dead.

A Factory Girl

Factory Girls' Album, Exeter, N.H., March 14, 1846

Matrimonial Duties

Many young men seem to imagine that after they have wooed and won the affections of a loving and confiding girl, pronounced the marriage vow, and gone through with the pleasant monotony of a *"honey-moon,"* that their duties are all and fully accomplished— that their *"love-making"* is to be thrown aside *in toto,* and that she whom they vowed to love, cherish, and protect, is to be treated as a *servant* rather than as a companion, and has no greater stranger in the world. Such principles as these, when carried out, are productive of more evil than many people are aware of, and we would earnestly advise all young men, before they take this important step, to think well and long upon what they are doing and to remember that—

> The *married* man who truly loves his wife,
> Abjures his latch key with his single life—
> The *bachelor* to stay out late is free,
> But all good husbands should be home to tea.

Factory Girls' Album, Exeter, N.H., February 15, 1847

Rights of Married Women

If the thing we call marriage had not become so palpable a matter of trade or vanity, so wholly reduced from its Divine light to the base level of the senses, we should never have heard of the "Rights of Married women," which hints of that untold tale of the Wrongs of Married women.

Woman has lost her individuality, in the marriage relation, she is no longer a living soul self-centred, and responsible in a straight line to her God, but at best is Mr. Blank's wife, under whose protection she has only a secondary and limited personality, where the very kindness which is offered her by the public, is an insult. The cares of government, the managing of business, the mysteries of societies for several large, but alas unknown objects, are very tenderly withheld from her, and indeed she can well spare them, were it not that there is a covert degradation in the rejection of her.

A self-complacent arrogating of all practical wisdom to the stouter sex, is neither good sense or justice. We have felt a slight curl of the derisive lip in spite of ourself, to hear a maudling lump of conceit, whose imbecility was only equalled by his vanity, prate about the inferiority of the feminine intellect in the abstruser walks of business and thought; and our mind turned proudly to those noble women whose great souls have soared out before us, strong without grossness, doing heroic works, and women still.

Masculine and feminine are not simply temporal distinctions, belonging to the body alone, they are elementary and spiritual, running through all organic nature, and to the very soul itself. Each without the other is fragment, which can never make full harmony till blended. Man was not man till woman was created, nor the woman Woman till he was made. Their creation is simultaneous in time, their souls co-existent in eternity.—But here as everywhere, there must be wholeness of parts before a harmonious whole can be expected. Man and woman are two in form that the twain might grow the more perfectly in the electric pulses of each other.

Somewhere in their destiny, the fact of Marriage exists and must be overtaken, but it is not to be sought or resisted. The same laws which govern the stars in their orbits, and draw drop to drop in the dewey hearts of flowers, will rule in obedient hearts, and draw them into one. But we deal now with the fact as it is found, not with the methods of union.

Man, the husband of woman, is not therefore lord of woman, has no more authority over her, than woman, the wife of man, has therefore over him. The relation is equal and reciprocal. If Paul says the man is the head of the woman as Christ is the head of the Church, and believes that Christ is absolute lawgiver, higher than all appeal, and hence that man bears the same relation to woman, Paul must answer that to the whole rebel heart of Humanity, for all deny it is fact; and if he didn't mean so, let him step out of the controversy till it is known precisely what he did mean.

God made woman, a living soul, and in no block-lettered records of antique ages wrote the charter of her rights, but here and there, wherever she may be, inscribed it in the nature which she bears. The rights of soul are infinite expansion for all, and a free field for each particular individuality. One mould is not made for all. When a kind is perfect, Nature makes no more of that sort but suffers it to die out. Of all her innumerable productions it will be found she has never quite repeated herself. Indeed the very end of organism is to produce diversity, so that no person's destiny is fulfilled in moulding it by another's, or by any outward law.

When God made man he gave him a new and particular nature, which never could be fulfilled by shaping him to the law of any existing being. When he made varieties in men, he made them for the same end, to develop a new nature,—to modify the old, not to copy it. When he made woman, he gave her yet unimagined peculiarities of being, and they demand unchecked freedom to develop them. To shape her by man's law, or by any other than the internal law of her own nature, is to do violence to her being, and subvert the prime intention of nature.

We have no right to measure her duties or rights, by those of any created intelligence—she is her own measure, and just that which she can do, (restricted by the same requirement of not interfering with the natural rights of others which all are) she has a right to do. It is fool's work to say, because she is not man she may not do as man does. So far as their powers and inclinations are in the same line she is man, and their rights and duties are identical, and in everything they are at least analogous. So far as she can create a new field of endeavor and hope, she has new rights, and if at last she can do a work that no man can do, it shall offset anything of his that surpasses her. Their rights are equal, yet not of course identical, for the only measure of any one's rights is his capacity, and is summed up in one word, the right to be whole.

How vain to deny a woman's right to govern—if man has one—while we see that she can rule with all the dexterity and firmness which man shows. How idle to deny her right to use speech in assemblies, when it is found that her eloquence is deep and refined, and not a womanly trait of her most fine nature is compromised by it. Doubtless she would prove as much better moral teacher than man, as she is more successful in the early culture of youth, for her instincts are far surer than his, and while he is tangled in wordy details of metaphysical science, her surer heart leaps to the fact with an instinctive foresight—and if she may not tell you of the path, the truth arrived at may be trusted with a faith that we would scarce give to produce of wisest logic.

Man forgets his essential identity with woman, when he attempts to lower her nature into submission. He is blindly plucking the stars from his own crown, and degrading the wide soul of Humanity. Can men be free and woman slaves? nay verily. As well might the right eye be plucked out and sight be unimpaired. Man and woman are one, and the elevation of their twain parts is necessary to the elevation of the whole, and the depression of one is the loss of both. When this great fact, of their unity in diversity, is remembered in all life, the minutia of their rights will arrange themselves. Spendthrift husbands will not be suffered to waste the possessions of a woman, nor a woman be compelled to bend to the passions of a legal spoiler. Law will find no place in adjusting the marriage bond,—which can be only love and affinity,—nor shall the terror of the world's scorn bind the outraged wife to the wretch who wrongs her.

If men and women cannot walk the world as equal friends let them sever as avowed foes, or each for his own or herself live a life of heroic isolation in calm self-reliance. It were better than submission. Even downright resistance, gross and false as it is, is more noble than weak succumbing to another's will.—Away with the base admission of the old lie of inferiority; away with submitting and servility, and instead let every soul study its nature and its wants, and calmly demand right food for them, throwing off all obstructions in the right of its acquisition.

No relation is true that *makes* one soul subservient to another, none is true which does not rather tend to the elevation and equalization of both parties. The same lie which reveals itself in slavery, is at bottom of our marriage institution,—the governing of one nature to its loss by the will of another, and they must both pass under the renovating hand, now that they have been bared to the marching eye of this Age.

AN INDIGNANT FACTORY GIRL

Lynn Pioneer, reprinted in *Voice of Industry,* August 14, 1847

Female Labor

The labor of one person ought to command the same price as the labor of another person, provided it be done as well and in the same time, whether the laborer be man or woman. A thousand of type, properly set in a stick and deposited on a galley, a thousand stitches in a waistcoat, by a girl, are worth as much to a master tailor or printer, as if the work were done by a man,—and ought to be paid as well. Those who have employment fit for woman, to bestow, ought to give them the preference; for there are fewer occupants of which they are capable, and they need help and encouragement more than men.

Away with the mean prejudice and jealousy which sneer at women for trying to get an honest living. Girls deprive journeymen of employment, and the latter cry aloud in consequence. As well might the Mississippi boatmen protest against steamboats. Say, that this or that is not a woman's place or a woman's business? Has poor woman no fit place but the kitchen, or the factory? Can her hand wield no implement but the needle and the dishcloth? Is she created only, "To suckle fools, or chronicle small beer!"

Was her tongue given her only to sing or scold babes to sleep? The fit place and the proper employment, for male and female, are that employment and that place for which they are best fitted by bodily powers, character, intellect, and education.

Factory Girls' Album, Exeter, N.H., April 25, 1846

Knowledge among Females

Some persons suppose the Female mind incapable of comprehending abstruce science, because there are so few females who have attained eminence; but this is a great mistake. Notwithstanding they have been excluded from the advantages thrown open to the other sex, there are a few, who, by their own exertions, ascended high in the temple of science, and one whose name is inscribed on the roll of fame among those of the most profound Philosophers that ever lived; and when means of acquiring knowledge shall have been thrown open to them, we shall see as many learned Ladies as men.

The first Lady that rose to eminence was Hypatia, the daughter of Theon, the Mathematician, in ancient Rome, who rose to great eminence, and became the Tutoress of some of the most learned men of her age and country.

Maria Gœtena Agnesi, was actually professor of Mathematics in the University of Bologna, in 1748, and wrote the Analytical Institutes, a profound work on Algebra of great excellence; and a treatise on Curve lines, and the Differential Calculus, the best produced in that age on these most abstruse branches of profound analysis.

Caroline, the sister of William Herschel, the great Astronomer who discovered the planet bearing his name, was the constant assistant of her brother, in his bright career of science.

A lecturer in Boston, recently stated that the best Mathematician now living in our country, is a young Lady—One of the best linguists, expert in the classics, and as eminent for her Metaphysical and Mathematical skill, is a lady in this country—As close a reasoner as we ever met with, is a Lady now living.

But the prodigy of learning, who for varied attainments, in many branches, perhaps never equalled in any age or country, is Mrs. Somerville of Scotland. At the age of 15, she heard her brother demonstrate a proposition of Geometry which fired her genius; and when she returned from a tour in Europe, she had actually mastered that science, and was engaged in studying Newton's principia, which had not then been translated from the Latin, and she had to learn that language also to read it. Mrs. Somerville is now about 50 years of age—is master of every modern Scientific language besides the Latin. In the Science of Astronomy her name ranks with those of La Place of France and Bowditch of our own country, and her treatise on physical Astronomy is one of the best ever published. She has several drawers filled with Diplomas from learned Societies in all parts of the world the voluntary gifts of the great and good of all enlightened countries—is an accomplished Scientific and practical Musician, a first rate Painter in Oils, a learned Chemist, and thorough Mineralogist and Botanist; and besides is the adored Mother of a numerous and happy family.

What a theme for reflection, admiration and eulogy! Let those upstarts in Science, who take pride in denouncing the female mind as inferior to their own, but have not yet learned what has been accomplished, by the gentle sex, remain forever silent, and shrink into their own native nothingness compared with this noble Lady, who stands proudly pre-eminent—a genuis of unrivalled excellence the admiration of the learned world.

H.R.S.

Voice of Industry, August 14, 1845

Woman's Sphere of Influence

Various and novel, are some of the opinions formed of the sphere of woman's influence. All agree in its potency, and most contend, that it is lasting as the mind. Be this as it may, if it be exerted in behalf of right, then should it extend to all the departments of society.

Many fear that woman shall lose her dignity and female delicacy, if she should chance to depart from her usual beaten track of thinking or acting. If she be rich and educated, she may know all about the last novels, and the latest fashions for dress. She may play the piano and attend a party if no one from the vulgar class of seamstresses, housegirls or operatives are to be present. She may in fact, be of no use to any one, and a real drone in society, and then, she is qualified to pass for a real lady. If she be what the world calls less fortunate, she may take an active part in domestic affairs, she may educate her daughters in the common duties of a good housewife and instruct them in reading proper books, but never allow them to read a political paper, lest their good taste or manners become corrupted, and they learn something of the political history of their own state or country, which would be very unlady-like.

True it is that the good mother might allow her daughters to read the history of Greece or Rome, but to read the political history of our own country, would be another affair, and would subject them to ridicule at once. It is not at all strange, that we see so much ignorance of the commonest events of our political history when we take into consideration, the fact that to inform ourselves on these subjects, prepares us for the ridicule of a large class of very refined *sensible* persons. But we would enquire whether the real duty and influence of woman should begin and end within the narrow circle prescribed by the narrow prejudices of the past or present.

Is there any good work or benevolent enterprise to be carried forward, where she may not labor? Is there any vice that she may not rebuke? Is there any heavy burdens that she may not lighten? Is there any degraded son or daughter of vice to whom she may not speak words of encouragement and hope? Shall she not be a ministering angel at the hovel of intemperance and wretchedness; shall not her kind words and tears of sympathy recall the wanderer, and make glad the hearts made desolate by sin? These are some of the labors for woman to engage in,—these some of the imperative duties she should perform, to fulfill her whole duty as a philanthropist and a christian. Let her not wait until society is prepared to appreciate her labors of love—but be vigilant in preparing them. Let her quiet influence be at all times doing its holy and benign work, on all that shall come within its range, and she shall perform a work worthy of herself, and receive the plaudit, "well done good and faithful servant."

OLIVA

Voice of Industry, December 5, 1845

On "Woman's Weakness"

To the Editor of *Bee:*—

SIR—I have observed that it is a common practice, among Editors, to fill their papers with advice to women, and not unfrequently with ill concealed taunts of woman's weakness. It is a pity that they should so neglect their own sex, to take such exclusive care of those, who, with all their weakness, sometimes have wit enough to take care of themselves. But, taunt them not; whilst boys are left to gain what strength they may, or at least to retain what Nature gave them, almost everything that can be, is done, to enervate and weaken girls, both mentally and bodily, and strong indeed is she, who comes forth from the "fiery ordeal" unscathed. If the effort to weaken has been but too successful, let the blame rest where it is deserved. Society has a heavy debt to pay for it, nay, is paying it even now. Woman's weakness, and timidity may be pretty things to sentimentalize upon, but they often prove very inconvenient, very troublesome realities, even to those who like them, or pretend to, in theory. Marriage is almost the only *business* in which there is any chance of success, that the world (to its shame be it told) willingly leaves to women, and that certainly requires no great degree of strength or wit, if wives are weak and foolish; for strength with no field for its exercise would be intolerable misery. When it is recollected, that the motives held up to women for action, are poor and paltry,—that most of the books addressed exclusively to them, are "one weak, washy, everlasting flood" of—scarcely milk for babes; that they are taught to believe that two of the greatest misfortunes, (mental and bodily weakness) are virtues, who that is not decidedly *verdant*, would laugh, or wonder, at woman's weakness. I should as soon expect that the plant bound down by strong bands, and deprived of air and water, would grow up strong and healthy, as that women, occupying the position they do, and surrounded by such influences, should be remarkable for anything but weakness.— The only way of accounting for the fact, that there yet remains no inconsiderable degree of strength among them, is to believe that Nature is too strong to be subdued, even by a miserable education.

It may be, that most women are so dwarfed and weakened, that they believe that dressing, cooking, and loving, (to which might be added the various accomplishments of the sex, and flattery thrown in as a sort of sauce, to the delectable dish,) make up the whole of life; but Nature still asserts her rights, and there always will be those too strong to be satisfied, with a dress, a pudding, or a beau, though they may take each in its turn, as a portion of life. I speak not now of the distinguished of either sex; they form a bright relief in the otherwise dark picture. Neither do I suppose that there are no exceptions, perhaps many, to the general rule. But to the generality of men let the question be put, what have you done in return for the great advantages you possess in your position in society? merely nothing. Are you not, thousands of you, as effeminate as the veriest woman of them all? You talk of your manliness; where is it? "Alas, echo answers where." You boast of the protection you afford to women. Protection! from what? from the rude and disorderly of your own sex—reform them, and women will no longer need the protection you make such a parade of giving. Protect them, do you? let me point you to the thousands of women, doomed to lives of miserable drudgery, and receiving "a compensation which if quadrupled, would be rejected by the man-laborer, with scorn;" are they less worthy protection because they are trying to help themselves? because they have little inclination and less time to lisp soft nonsense? and you think when you have sung the praises of "lovely woman," and talked of the "ladies" with all imaginable gallantry, that you have done all that is necessary. If you would have the manliness you talk of, seek to raise those poor women from their oppressed, and too often degraded, condition; if you will not do it, go on in your old course, but prate no more of your manliness; why the very boys at play in the street, will laugh at you; they, poor fellows, are dreaming in their simplicity, that manliness includes every noble and generous feeling. Long may it be ere they awake from that pleasant dream to find that manhood is often synonymous with extreme effeminancy.

Bad as is the condition of so many women, it would be much worse if they had nothing but your boasted protection to rely upon; but they have at last learnt the lesson, which a bitter experience teaches, that not to those who style themselves their "natural protectors," are they to look for the needful help, but to the strong and resolute of their own sex. May all good fortune attend those resolute ones, and the noble cause in which they are engaged. *"She devils"* as some of them have been elegantly termed by certain persons, calling themselves men; let them not fear such epithets, nor shrink from the path they have chosen. It is, indeed, a theory one, but they are breaking the way; they shall make it smoother for those who come after them, and generations yet unborn shall live to bless them for their courage and perseverance. If we choose to sit down in our indolence, and persuade ourselves that we can do nothing, let us not censure those who are wiser and stronger than we are. It has been said that men and women are "natural enemies," which I do not believe; but if a running fight must be kept up between the two, let women have half the battle-field and fair play. The time may come when both parties will learn that they can be much better friends, when they have more equal rights.—If that bright day should ever dawn, then will the old battle, between cunning and brute force, be done away with. I see that I am writing more than I intended, but I find there is much room for thought, in a subject so

often treated with ridicule. My intention was, not so much to advocate "woman's rights," as to remind those who like so well, to
talk of "woman's weakness," that the "retort courteous" can be as
easily made, as it is richly merited; poor fellows! they never dream
that they are admirable illustrations of "Satan reproving sin." I
know that brevity is desirable when writing to editors, and I
should, indeed, expect that you would find some fault with the
length of this letter, did not your paper convince me that you
possess that desirable quality, good nature. Hoping that it is strong
enough to excuse the length, and all other imperfections, I close.

ELLEN MUNROE

Boston Bee, reprinted in *Voice of Industry*, March 13, 1845

The Rights of Women

It is natural for one animal, to exercise, if it can, domination
over another. We see this among almost all herds of animals, and
even flocks of domestic fowls. The strongest and most permanently
vindictive obtain, after repeated struggles, the ascendancy; and,
while the florescency of strength remains, most generally retain it.
The spirit of domination is not confined to the male, but extends to
the female with less power, but with almost equal tenacity. Thus in
a dairy of cows there is from the strongest down to the weakest, and
from the most vindictive down to the least pugnacious, a place of
sequency or position of yielding in a short time invariably assigned.
The least observant country boy has noticed this fact, no doubt, a
thousand times. Let him scatter the salt upon the flat stones in
summer, or the hay upon the edge of the untrodden snow in winter,
and the dominant pass from rock to rock, and from one pile of
fodder to another, select what pleases them, and, in regular order
the weaker have to give way. This is physical brute force, embittered
or ameliorated by the good or bad disposition of the dominant
animal: for even brutes have, according to their sphere of action,
and each individual according to its superior nature, all the attributes of mind, and affections of the heart. What has in a state of
ignorance been called *instinct?* a term merely used to satisfy a
superstitious feeling, and to make an absolute and essential distinction in animalized beings, so as to give man only a soul,
understanding, sense, and reason? Is reason in animals more or less
superior according to the more or less perfect organization of their
physical constitution? As man has mounted up from a savage to a

civilized state, no matter what his religion, customs, government, and laws, more or less equable and perfect, have supplied the place of violence and force; and in the same proportion, have the female sex been raised from a state of servitude and dependence. In Egypt, Greece and Rome, they attained under heathenism, all the elevation in the domestic and social relationship that ever they have in christian lands. This is a fact, which none acquainted with universal history, can consistently deny. The fact is, that it is on the *degree of civilization and refinement,* and not on the virtues of any *religion,* that female privileges depend. We are prepared to argue this point with any individual, whatever be his capacity or energy of mind, or however extensive his acquisition. We repeat, *it is on the degree of civilization and refinement to which a nation has arrived, and not on this or that superstitious faith that their privileges have depended.* In fact, if the christian faith were carried out, it, of all others would most subject the female sex to the lowest point of subjection in servile dependence on man, and implicit obedience to what he conceives his lawful commands. The Apostle commands her "to be in subjection," "to reverence her husband," "not to speak in the churches," "to keep her head covered," as an evidence of her subjection; the marriage ceremony requires what it does not on the reverse, of the husband—that she "obey her husband, as her lord and master;"[1] and Wesley,[2] the head of the Methodist church, who is by far more democratic, and who permits them to exhort, says that "the woman is *inferior* to the man," and "a sort of higher servant."

Among the Dutch and Swiss, and throughout Germany, the female is inured to the most severe and laborious manual labor, and yet, Switzerland is called the "cradle of Protestant religion," and Germany has long been one of the most free and scientific empires on earth. Where, now is the argument for Christianity so often in a bombastic inflated clerical style insisted on, as "the divine source under God, to the female of all her privileges and endeared relationships in life!" From all this will they appeal to experience? Let us then appeal to personal observation and experience, and what do they demonstrate? Why! the same demonstrable, veritable fact! She has to yield in sentiment, opinion, judgment. During the halcyon days of courtship, her judgment, taste and choice are highly commended; but no longer. No sooner is she married than the Lord Premier takes the dictatorial position, and the more ignorant his mind, and incorrect and unrefined his taste, the firmer he defends it, and with nine out of ten every vestige of anything more than servile assent, or at most, persuasive dissent is in the least degree tolerated. We all know this to be a fact. We have been in a thousand different families, sufficiently long to make all due observation. We know it to be so; and so does every man and woman of the land, worthy to take his or her stand as a person of common sense, judgement and observation. She is degraded, brow beat, cast down by a continued and resistless action on both the sentimental and intellectual parts of her constitution; educated in a childish and fantastical manner, being taught that her dancing, embroidering, drawing, and music, the delicacy of her skin, the artificial tenuity of her form, and the gracefulness of her motions, are to secure admiration and lay the foundation for her happiness for life! and then forsooth, after being thus degraded, with all the peculiar sympathies of her sex pressing upon her, she is told, "that she is inferior in mind, talent, judgement, and capacity, to man," her lord and master! Does she pretend to authorship? she is merely tolerated—subjected to the severest criticism, and has, no matter how transcendent-soever be her mind, correct her taste, refined, strong and energetic her diction, finished her style and triumphant her execution, she has to spend a life in defending what she has with an almost infinite degree of firmness and perseverance, with all these difficulties specified in the way thus, dearly achieved. In mind, we affirm the female is not inferior to the males and in delicacy and correctness of taste, she transcends him. As an evidence of this we adduce the fact that female sovereigns have had more splendid reigns, comparatively speaking, that is, we mean making a few exceptions, than any monarch on earth. Who in ancient times, surpassed Semiramis?[3] or in modern, Christina[4] of Sweden? the Catherines of Russia?[5] Elizabeth[6] and Victoria[7] of England? Who ever in the languages has surpassed Madam Dacien,[8] whose translation of Homer still stands preeminent?

Having brought the subject of our remarks, the object of our vindication fairly on the ground, we are now prepared to state simply, leaving the arguing the case to another article, what we conceive to be the rights and privileges of women, the female sex. And, in doing this, we shall encroach on no domestic duty or privilege founded on sexuality, reason and common sense. Let her as she has to be, remain the woman; and let her appropriate and specified duties be domestic, or to engage in any line of action in any calling which shall not interfere with their discharge.

Having made the reservation, we affirm, and affirm it boldly, and have ourselves ability, if we are female, to defend our position—

that females have an indefeasible and inalienable right to enjoy that mode and system of education both physical and intellectual, which shall give compass, depth and solidity, both to their habit of thought and tone of feeling—that they have an indefeasible and inalienable right to be equally respected in their sentiment, judgment, opinion, and taste, as the male sex—that they have an indefeasible and inalienable right to buy and sell, solicit and refuse, choose and reject, as have men. That they have an indefeasible and inalienable right in all domestic concerns, to have their judgment, taste, opinion, sentiment, and choice, equally, and at all times; and forever, equally respected, as the male sex. And that in the outgoings of friendship and affection, freedom of intercourse, and unrestrainedness of expression in language and address, they are on equal ground. These five distinct propositions, we are prepared to defend; and, while we have mind, talent, acquisition, ability, and a pen, we will defend them.

We shall take them up separately and successively; and make each the topic of discourse, and the subject of a separate article. We repeat, these five propositions thus limited and restricted we are prepared to defend, and while we have mind, talent, acquisition, and ability, will with our tongue defend them. "Ah! with a woman's tongue?" Yes, and the sneer too upon your own grovelling and selfish susceptibility! who will angelize the same object in sentiment and passion, and the next moment, brutalize her in intellect, reason, judgment, and in all the grand prerogatives of a high, noble, and intellectual being!

We cannot conclude this article, without exhorting those of our own sex, who read it, at once to embrace cordially its truth. You have been degraded long enough. You have sufficiently long been considered "the inferior"—a kind of "upper servant," to obey and reverence, and be in subjection to your equal, and no more than your equal! Enter, at once upon your privileges. Cultivate a clear, strong, matter of fact way of thinking, and a natural and therefore, conclusive mode of reasoning. Look upon all your accomplishments, dancing, drawing, as only the gewgaws of a youthful day, soon to be of little or no use, what the most contemptible of society, the most excel in, and pursued, only as amusements, not as qualifications. Improve the mind by solid reading, such histories as Gibbon, Hume,[9] Goldsmith, and Rollin.[10] Make yourselves acquainted with Chemistry, Geology, and especially those sciences, Phrenology and Electricity, which are calculated to unmask superstitious pretentions, and give you an intimate knowledge of your own nature, and of the constitution of man. Resolve that you will think, reason, judge, love, hate, approve, and disapprove, for yourselves, and, at your own volition; and, not at the dictation of an other. At the same time, as females and as rational beings, be wise, discreet, kind, conciliating, affectionate, benevolent, just, and virtuous. This is the line of conduct which common sense, and the eternal and immutable laws of nature, in mind and matter, distinctly prescribe, and imperiously command us undeviating by to pursue. Doing this, you will perform your part towards extending and improving the intellectual capacity of your sex, unrestricted by brute force and clerical cunning, interest and deceit and placing yourselves on the above ground of true enjoyment and self-respect.

Voice of Industry, May 8, 1846

Female Labor

It is well known that labor performed by females commands but little when compared to that what is paid to men—though the work may be of the same character. Why is this? What possible difference can it make to the employer whether he pays A or B one dollar for accomplishing a piece of work, so that it be done equally as well by the one as the other? A female generally receives but about one-half as much as is paid to a man for doing the same amount of labor. It has been urged that they are the weaker sex, and are dependent upon us for assistance, and per consequence this difference in the price of labor should be made. But this very dependence is the result of inequality, and would not exist were the proper remedy applied. There are, it is well known, hundreds of families in our cities supported solely by females, who are obliged to labor with the needle twelve and fourteen hours out of the twenty-four, to gain hardly a comfortable subsistence for themselves and those dependent upon them, so trifling is the compensation they receive. Whole families are supported in this way—not an hour can be devoted to the improvement of the mind.

Why is it that so many of the wealthy, whose whole lives are filled to overflowing with luxuries and plenty, use every possible endeavor to crush down to the lowest imaginable point, the seamstress, milliner and manteau-maker. And even though this mean and selfish spirit is so universally practised, they are very apt to think the recipients thereof owe them an everlasting debt of gratitude for such manifestation of their unbounded charity and benevolence!

The female teachers in our public schools receive but about one-third as much as those whose labors are no more arduous or responsible. If a certain amount of labor is performed, it can make no difference by any manner of rational reasoning, by whom that labor is done. It is folly to argue that labor performed by females is not in every respect done as well as by men; and there is no earthly reason why they should not receive as much. When it is considered that it requires ten and twelve hours a day, and the most strict regard to economy and industry on the part of the laboring men and our mechanics to acquire a comfortable living—so low are the wages of labor—is it not a wonder how our female laborers can succeed as well as they do with such a meagre and miserable pittance? It cannot be done but by the greatest deprivation of the common wants of nature. We are happy, however, to notice that this subject is beginning to attract the attention of the more philanthropic portion of community. This is gratifying, and it is hoped the matter will continually be agitated until the rights of woman, in this respect at least, shall be duly appreciated.

PRO BONO

Voice of Industry, April 2, 1847

A Reply to "Spectator"

MR. YOUNG:—In the last "Voice" I noticed an article signed "Spectator," which I perused with some degree of indignation. Your own comments I highly approve;[11] but trust you will permit me to review his statements still farther, and return upon his own head the guilt he has charged upon females; for there, in my humble opinion, the guilt rests.

I leave his first position, respecting the law, for those who frame laws and put them in force, and pass to notice that part relating to us females. He says, "resolve to be independent," i.e., to be rich; "to effect which it is not necessary to be mean and niggardly, only form habits of industry and economy." Now let me ask what such a resolution would effect, in our present situation? If we have not resolved to be industrious, are we not compelled to be so? Is not fourteen hours of constant, unceasing toil sufficient to satisfy the gentleman's idea of industry, and all that he thinks necessary to make us independent? Or would he have us drilled still longer in order to claim the title of industrious. And then let us economise according to the method he has marked out for us, such as adopting a uniform method of dress &c. and in five years, he says, we shall accomplish our ends, "be free from oppression, able to go to the far West and purchase farms for ourselves, without asking Government to give them to us." In my opinion, the man that could thus calculate, must either be an isolated bachelor, who knows nothing of expense, or grossly deficient in the organ of calculation; and I hope he will permit some of us who make no pretensions to a knowledge of Mathematics, just to reckon the account for him. In the first place our average amount of wages is two dollars per week; then allowing for every day's labor, without sickness, and without rest, we have, at the close of the year, one hundred and four dollars. Out of this sum, for the "preservation of health," we must be supplied with comfortable clothing, suitable for toil with constant wear and tear; not put on to merely loll upon sofas. No small amount is paid out for the mere article of shoes; for this running six times a day back and forth from the mill to our boarding houses, over stone sidewalks, takes off our *soles.* Then come rubbers, umbrellas, shawls, bonnets, &c., for every day use; and this is not all;—we are required by our corporation rules to attend church regularly, and if we comply a pew rent is added to our expenditures, of about five or six dollars. And what church is there in the city that would receive us upon their velvet cushions in our mill attire? Not one, I believe, could be found. Then comes the expense of a better suit, a Sunday garb, to appear decent in the eyes of community. And to follow it out and really not to be niggardly or mean, we must contribute to the various *professedly* charitable objects of the day.

Now, Mr. Spectator, how long do you think it would take us to become independent at this rate, go out west and buy us farms? Five years, think ye?

With the next position of Spectator, I perfectly accord; i.e., that a change is necessary in female education, and a great change too. For if "as the twig is bent the tree's inclined," and if woman is the author of all the wickedness there is on the earth—if woman makes all the warriors, murderers, pirates, slaveholders, drunkards, hypocrites, debauchees and monsters there are in the community, surely it is time for a change. I will not attempt to deny this charge, for I am well aware that early impressions are of the utmost permanent kind, and truly believe that if a right tone were given to the youthful mind, if love was inculcated by precept and example, to both friend and foe—if children were taught to regard as equal all persons, of whatever grade—to do good to all, of whatever nation or color, or situation in life—if they were taught that their own existence was for some great and wise and noble purpose—a very perceptible change would be wrought in society. And if woman is the cause of all this ignorance and wretchedness and misery and corruption, it is time for a change. But is woman the first cause of all this? I know she has been called the great transgressor, since the time of our poor old mother Eve, when Adam fell asleep and left her to fight the adversary alone; but methinks if we look behind the screen, we shall find the wire-pullers that make woman what she is, and prevents her being what her own energy of character would enable her to be. Our laws are framed for us, and we are required to yield obedience—and woman is just what man makes her, or rather allows her to be. Compare, for a moment, our opportunities of acquiring knowledge with those of the other sex, commencing at adult age, to say nothing of the neglect of our physical education before this period. Throw each upon their own resources—go out into the country, where for school teaching a female receives the small pittance of four or five dollars a month, for three, perhaps four months—amounting to twelve, sixteen or twenty dollars for a whole summer's labor; and when for teaching the same school, the same scholars, &c., a male teacher receives sixteen, eighteen or twenty dollars per month, amounting to forty-eight, fifty-four or sixty dollars. As in school teaching, so in all other business, there is an equal diversity of wages. Take these individuals to literary seminaries, and how is it there? Are expenses proportionate? No, by no means. A female pays for her board, her tuition, her books, as much as the gentleman. Then how far will her sixteen dollars carry her? let us see—for one term, board one dollar and fifty cents per week; tuition, four; books six—amount, twenty-eight dollars; then we must write her minus eight, twelve, or sixteen dollars. Now for the chances on the other side. Expenses at school, the same; leaving a balance in the gentleman's pocket of twenty, twenty-six or thirty-two dollars. Now, under these circumstances, will any man pretend to tell us we never think of preparing for anything only to get a husband, and that we know as little as the wild Arab? How does he know we never think of anything else; for if any one chances to think, does she not at the first glance behold interminable barriers in her way? Mr. Spectator says, a female can lay up more money in the mill than males. If this is true, I should like to have him show it; for while we are earning fifty cents per day, males are commanding from one dollar to two dollars and fifty cents; and why must they expend so much more than we? And then he recommends us to devote all our leisure to the cultivation of our minds. Shall we take a newspaper? then we must work from three days to two weeks to pay for it. A man can pay for the same in one day. Shall we buy ourselves books?—then we must pay as much as men. Shall we read them?—then after four-teen hours of toil, take a seat with twenty or thirty others, and your mind knows just about as much of the subject as you would if you were in a vast whirlpool, know of the depth of the current. These are some of the advantages for obtaining knowledge. And now let me ask what man or what woman does not strive for the attain-ment of the highest honor set before them? Is not man stimulated to action by honors held up before him, both classical and political? Are not the most important subjects brought before their minds for consideration and reflection? Now what are the honors placed before females? Why just this one, and this alone—to get married! to make good industrious, social, smiling, obedient wives! Then why does any wonder that every method is adopted to accomplish the end, and just such means as suit the opposite sex? And so long as man uses her as a plaything, a toy, and talks nothing but mere nonsense and trifling in her presence, and pays his attentions and requests to those who appear out most gaily dressed—just so long will woman strive to please his fancy, bedeck herself with gew-gaws, bedaub her face with paints, cover her fingers with rings, and spend her leisure time at the toilet.

Now I say, place some other attainable object before us. Give us an opportunity, time and means to cultivate our minds. Treat us as equals, and we will show you that we are not naturally more peevish, more fretful and idiotic than the other sex. In short, re-store to us our rights, and we will prove ourselves intelligent, virtuous and reasonable beings. This we should accomplish our-selves, without the benefit of being remembered in the wills of the rich. But I fully accord with the gentleman in the practicability of thus using their wealth, instead of giving it those they denominate heathen, in foreign lands.

I trust Mr. Spectator will pardon me for these remarks, and receive them as coming from one who wishes to "retrieve her lost condition"—that has long felt it, and wishes to see her sex raised to the high position it was destined to occupy.

AN OPERATIVE

Lowell, Jan. 17, 1847

Voice of Industry, January 22, 1847

A Reply to "Spectator" (Continued)

MR. EDITOR:—Will you again permit me to speak through your "Voice," to our friend the "Spectator,"[12] as in his communication he seemed to think I may again censure him for some remarks; but whether he derived this conclusion from all his other ideas of *female excellencies,* "that woman will always have the last word," or whether he believes himself really deserving, I am unable to tell; be that as it may, I have thought best again to speak, and endeavor to convince him and some others, that the "power behind the throne" is utterly powerless, while the throne itself is but an opaque body, between the power and the great sun of light and knowledge, and also so much of an adamantine nature as to be immovable.

I have no contention with "Spectator" in regard to his views of education, as I truly believe a knowledge of all he has mentioned as desirable and necessary for man's perfectability. True education is of three kinds, physical, mental and moral; and without this we are imperfect beings, and to a want of it we must plead guilty. Now will the gentleman please inform us, how we shall teach what we ourselves do not know? how we shall know without a teacher? how we can have a teacher without the means—the want of which I think I showed in my last? I speak of those who *toil*—those that give, in part, a practical education to their system, and suffer it not to become ennervated by luxury and indolence, or to rust out for want of action, and whose minds of course partake of the health of the body. Drones will always be found in every hive, but 'tis *working* bees which repair the waste places, cull the sweets from every flower, and lead the young into honeyed fields.

Look at the millions of toiling females in America, whose hands are ever busy from ten, twelve, fourteen to sixteen hours even, of the day, and realize what time there is for them to cultivate their mental organs?

Lowell, alone has about eight thousand factory girls, that are destined, perhaps, to go out into the "far West," and give a tone to the system of education and morals there. What will they teach? Physiology? What do they themselves know of the laws of health, or what advantages have they of knowing or practising them.

Can a person, with only thirty minutes' time, put on her bonnet and shawl, and go out to her meals and back to her work, think much of mastication, deglution and digestion? Can another, with hundreds in the mill, and in her sleeping apartment from six to twelve, study respiration, circulation of the blood, and the necessity of its purifications? Can another attend to the perspiratory organs, the functions of the skin, &c., surrounded by cotton dust and oil? Can any one cultivate their auditory organs, where thousands of shuttles are flying at their utmost speed, and the clatter is as if ten thousand wind mills were set in motion by a hurricane? Can they learn optics by lamp light, both morning and evening?—and with all these advantages combined, study the convolutions of their own brains or the brains of others?—improve upon their organs of benevolence, reverence, causality, comparison, order, adhesiveness and calculation, to say nothing of *combativeness?* And then ideality— what a fine opportunity for its cultivation, and bringing out noble and high sentiments, ennobling to every faculty, to watch the flying shuttle and the whirl of spindles!

There appears just about as much reason in casting all the blame for the wickedness there is in the world upon *woman,* as there would be for the slaveholder at the south to gravely tell his slaves that *"he* is just what the slave has made him, and that he, the slave, must realize that if he suffers from the bad acts of his master, that himself alone, is the cause of it." And in this *free, civilized, enlightened, christianized* America, where woman is acknowledged by all to occupy more nearly the station designed for her than in and other, but where she happens not to be yet so elevated but she is taunted as "knowing no more than wild Arabs," and more "resembling peacocks" than reasonable beings, &c., it should become the inquiry of every true and philanthropic mind, what shall be done to educate and elevate her. Will "Spectator" be kind enough to inform us how to remedy the evils he charges upon us, under our present embarrassments—when we shall look for a change—when the world will be renovated and become what it should be, by the instructions of those who have been educated in the seminaries, such as he has described? If he fails to point out to us the remedy, as well as the evils, he has done but half his duty; and we must make the same request of the male portion of community, as did Diogenes of the conqueror, when asked what he could do to benefit him, he replied, "just stand out of my sunshine."

I trust "Spectator" will realize that a war of words is not dangerous, and that all *pains* occasioned from such wounds, are easily healed, by an application of the balsam of truth acknowledged.

AN OPERATIVE

Voice of Industry, March 5, 1847

A Reply to "Spectator" (Concluded)

MR. YOUNG:—"Spectator" may have tho't from my long silence, that I had no more to say, but the subject of female duty and responsibility is quite too important to be readily passed over, and the charges he has brought against us, of too serious a nature to be hastily canvassed. He must have been aware of the commencement, that a smouldering volcano is more manageable and less dangerous than after the rubbish and smoking lava has been disturbed and given vent to latent fires to burst forth; and, if he becomes wearied in hearing woman's defence he must realise that he first roused the latent fires within her. Be sure he has nothing to fear from rocks of argument that may be hurled at him, but at least I hope to cast some small dust into the balance of justice.

His last communication[13] was written with so much candor, and with all, so much reason and trust manifested that I almost began to think he believed us possessed of higher, nobler natures than formerly, and if he had not imposed upon us a task far above the reach of human attainment, it would have appeared more like sincerity. But I would like to review the whole matter, slightly, and see what our chances are.

First, he says, "A great majority of females know as little as wild Arabs, having far less simplicity and gentleness of disposition."— "Doing as others do, perfectly heedless of consequences, and too *ignorant* to comprehend them when explained." "More resembling peacocks than reasonable beings," and then very gravely tells us to *educate ourselves.* Now if this is logical reasoning, then I do not know when the premises are correct and how to reason correctly from those premises. For how could any one under these circumstances throw off the miasma that has settled around them or soar above it? Would it not rather require some mighty power to lift them up? And then, to the operatives, one day in seven is allotted them, one day, after six long, tedious days of toil, to educate themselves in, and this too, where churches and corporations combine their united efforts to insure their attendence upon public worship *regularly,* which if they—young, inexperienced girls, away from home and friends, surrounded by strangers, relying solely upon their good names and reputation for a passport through society; if they, have moral courage enough to withstand popular usages and customs, willing to hear the odium, that may be heaped upon them, and making themselves liable, at any time, for what would be considered, an open and disgraceful discharge from employment, their names blacked at every counting-room in the city, with all the disadvantages attending a quiet study, in a boarding house, I say, with all this; if there is one that can endure this, and boldly claim the seventh day, for self-improvement—then she can educate herself.—This truly *"would be climbing the hill alone,"* and the man that imposes it upon us, in good faith, must certainly believe us "angels" and not wild animals.

Again Spectator says, "If our ministers would preach practical moral lessons &c."—And *if* said the farmer, I find the question might have been settled without an if, and *if* ministers and people and systems and society had always been, and were now what they ought to be, then *women* would not have thus been degraded and *ignorant,* as at present represented, but have occupied a higher station; she would have been a bright lamp, *beside* the "throne," casting a lively hue upon all surrounding subjects and the *throne* instead of being an opaque body would have been a sun of itself, shedding its benign rays upon the world.

But I cannot pass unnoticed the circumstance hé has quoted to prove women's power at present; as manifested in the Baltimore mob,[14] which I think, ought to convince every candid mind, that such burning lights were obtained to stand upon a candlestick and not forever to be hid under a bushel. It proves to my mind, most clearly that the lady who thus quelled a tumultuous mob, was more highly endowed by the great author of the universe with those immutable weapons that were intended to govern mankind, viz., wisdom, prudence and love, and this is by no means a solitary instance of the kind the circumstances were the same ever where man is exasperated beyond endurance, officers, law and bayonets, are equally disregarded; but let a person step forward armed with *moral courage, truth,* and *love,* and hostility ceases at once. Who quelled the mob of Philadelphia a few years since when the city hall had been demolished and vengeance was breathed out against all friends of the slave? Mary Needles,[15] a quakeress, who loved her enemies, and said if any must die, let me die. This love overcomes thousands, and no doubt is just as efficient when wielded by man as by woman. Man was destined to overcome evil with good. To conquer enemy by reason, argument and love, and not by the sword.

But I wish to show how entirely dependent woman is, upon man, for all she is permitted to be, in our present state of society, and how unjust is the charge of the guilt of the world upon us. Man forms our customs, our laws, our opinions for us. He forms our customs, by raising a cry against us, if he thinks we overstep our prescribed limits. Woman is never thought to be out of her *sphere,* at home; in the nursery, in the kitchen, over a hot stove cooking from morning till evening—over a wash-tub, or toiling in a cotton factory 14 hours per day. But let her for once step out, plead the cause of right and humanity, plead the wrongs of her slave sister of the South or of the operative of the North, or even attempt to teach the science of Physiology, and a cry is raised against her, *"of out of her sphere."* Not so with man, he can fill the chair of State, stand as the mediator between God and Men. Soar to the highest point in the scientific world, and military glory—and he can as readily descend to measuring off ribbons and tape by the yard, selling pins by the cents worth, and peddling out candy by the ounce, all alike is taken within the range of man's sphere.

Man forms our laws, and by them we must abide, although we have no voice in making them. Does he say, we must pay a tax, (in the form of duties,) to support an unholy and unrighteous war, then we must obey. Does he say for a certain offence our lives must pay the forfeit, then woman is swung from the scaffold and her neck broken; and she would be out of her *sphere* in saying aught against it! Does he say she shall be tried as a witch, then she must be placed in the scales with a Bible, or in some other way found guilty and robbed of life—as there were at one time thirty thousand under man's judicious laws! Does man say she may be set upon the auction stand and sold to the highest bidder, then what female ought to say she is not the property of her master?

Man forms our opinions, for he has the keys of knowledge in his own possession. Our colleges of education are founded expressly for him—and all offices, scientific, as well as political, military and ec- clesiastical, man fills. He directs our education—he permits us to pursue plain, practical science, for which we may, by dint of econ- omy, chance to obtain the means; and while he retains all honors to himself, selects the highest offices and gravely comes forward and points us to the object of making man what he ought to be! Would man, stimulated by no other motive, do any better than we do?

But if woman is well adapted to teach, so beautifully calculated and gifted by the author of her existence, to instruct the youthful mind, as has been represented—qualified to impress the great lessons of truth and morality, and give a right tone to sentiments—in short, capable of making man a noble being, but a little below the angels, I wish to inquire why in the name of common sense she is not per- mitted to finish the work she may have begun? Why are all the offices in public institutions of learning filled by men? Why is the child taken from under the maternal care and placed under the teachings of man? Why is every professorship usurped by man? Why not confer them upon woman, and permit her to go on with the good work? Why not bestow upon her the honors of the D.D.s, and M.D.s, and A.B.s, and stimulate her to go forward, and permit her to look upon the glorious motto of "excelsior?" Will Spectator tell?

I think I have proved that the "power behind the throne" is powerless; and I only think of a case now which I wish to relate to the contrary; it is of Mark Anthony. When once angling, and being unsuccessful, he commanded his attendants to dive and attach to his hook some large fish that they had previously caught, that he might gain the applause of Cleopatra; but she, understanding the trick, commanded her own attendants to go down and attach a large dried, salt fish, which he drew up, to his own shame and consternation, and the amusement of the company. This was a power behind the throne with a witness.

I would sincerely thank "Spectator" for marking out for us a course of study, and would be happy to pursue it, if I had the books and *time* to peruse them—but my excuse must be that I am still an

OPERATIVE

Voice of Industry, April 16, 1847

The Education of Women

We commend the following remarks we have received from a female operative in the Manchester mills.

Great injustice has been done the character of woman by the absurd notion, that her powers of mind are inferior to those of man. If nature has marked any difference between the mental capacities of man and woman, it is certainly not so great as the vanity of the former is willing to imagine. It cannot, in reason, be expected that the sexes should resemble each other in this grand particular, when their system of education is so widely different. The conversion of females is more refined and elegant than that of men, owing to the care which is taken to form their ideas;—they cannot, it is true, converse upon every subject with the fluency and learning that men can, for there are many in which they cannot be so interested as the other sex—politics for instance—man makes this subject his study, as he is directly interested in it,—but upon nearly every other topic, as far as my observation has extended, a well educated female exhibits as much intellect as a well educated male, and adorns her ideas in language which it is not in the mind of man to conceive. If the scholastic education of females was more generally and more strictly attended to, we think all doubt of their capability to compete with man in the exhibition of intellect would soon disappear. Until they are educated scholastically and physically upon an equality with the males, as is now the practice in England, the female character will continue to be under-rated by the false estimation of the female mind.

Proper attention has not been, and is not now bestowed upon the *intellectual* instruction of females, while dress, music, painting, and the like, have received undue and improper attention, and have been patronised to a degree which has nearly annihilated knowledge and worth. It would appear from the manner in which some of our young ladies are educated, (the daughters of the opulent, particularly) that they are destitute of all mind. To bestow proper attention upon dress and personal accomplishments is commendable—but to employ most of your time and devote most of your attention to those particulars and other amusements incorporated in the present day, is certainly reprehensible. The opinions of an author unknown to us, upon the education of females, are quite in accordance with ours. He says: "Such a general tincture of the most useful sciences as may serve to free the mind from vulgar prejudices and give it a relish for the rational exercise of its powers might very justly enter into a plan of female erudition. The sex might be taught to turn the course of their reflections into a proper and advantageous channel, without any danger of rendering them too elevated for the feminine duties of life. In a word, they ought to be considered as designed for *use* as well as *show* and trained up not only as *women* but as *rational creatures.*"

A Factory Girl

Manchester (N.H.) Democrat, August 18, 1847

May the Day Come

May the time soon come when females will have their proper station in society, when they will no longer be considered the plaything and slave of men. May they cease to follow every vain or foolish and expensive fashion; and that instead of being so very anxious about dress—what they shall put on, or how gaudy they can make themselves appear, may they turn their attention to the cultivation of their minds—to the acquirement of such useful knowledge, as will assist them in performing the duties incumbent upon them, with credit to themselves, and incalculable benefit to the rising generation, and may they be right examples of prudence, frugality, economy, kindness, and every other virtue which adorns their sex; and above all may they detest the prudery, duplicity, insincerity and hypocrisy so much in vogue at the present day.

Voice of Industry, August 27, 1847

NOTES

1. These doctrines of Saint Paul the Apostle were used over the centuries to justify male supremacy.

2. John Wesley (1703–91) was the British founder of Methodism.

3. Semiramis was the legendary founder of Babylon, wife of Ninus.

4. Christina (1626–89) was the daughter of Gustavus Adolphus and Queen of Sweden (1632–54).

5. Catherine I (1684?–1727) was Empress from 1725 to 1727; Catherine II, called "the Great" (1729–96), was Empress between 1762 and 1796.

6. Elizabeth I (1533–1603), Queen of Scotland and Ireland from 1558 to 1603.

7. Victoria Alexandrina (1819–1901), Queen of Great Britain and Ireland (1837–1901), and Empress of India (1876–1901).

8. Anne Dacien (1654–1720), French Hellenist and translator.

9. David Hume (1711–76), Scottish philosopher and historian.

10. Charles Rollin (1661–1741), French historian and educator.

11. "The author of the article . . . (if we mistake not), is quite a liberal minded physician of this City," noted the *Voice of Industry.* Referring to "Spectator's" discussion of "Female Education," it commented, "We have ever endeavored to impress upon the public, the paramount necessity of thorough, practical, common-sense education for females. This is one of the prominent reasons why we labor for the 'Ten Hour System,' in all incorporated establishments. For how can women be properly educated for good wives and lives of usefulness, if they are to be shut up from twelve to fourteen hours per day, until they enter upon domestic duties? What can be the use of colleges for female culture, while the mass have not the means of common school education. Although we are sorry to admit that much our correspondent has said in relation to females is too true, yet we think him rather partial—much of the guilt belongs to the other sex.—Society has made woman what she is. Man wishes her to become a 'plaything' and she consents to be one. If she spends her hard earnings for gay and useless dress, it is to please the other sex; and many a young lady who has spent the last farthing in this way, has had a gay lover complete the compliment of finery from his own scanty treasury" (January 15, 1847).

"Spectator" wrote in part: "What are the habits, feelings and education of our females at the present time. Why, a great majority never think of preparing their minds for anything only to get a husband to maintain and wait upon them. She knows as little as the wild Arab, and has far less simplicity and gentleness of disposition, totally unfit to take charge of the household affairs that belong to her. The females who work in our mills can lay up more money, with some economy than our young men who get employment in the same place, and why should they expect the young men whom they may marry to not only buy the farm and furnish it, but also to furnish her with things with which to keep house? No wonder the more prudent of our young men choose to live single; for singleblessedness with competence is far better than poverty and a peevish, fretful wife, whose bad disposition increases in proportion to the misery she has brought upon all around and depending on her" (*ibid.*).

12. "Spectator" answered the editorial criticism in the *Voice of Industry*, January 22, 1847, which also carried an editorial, " 'Spectator' Again," that concluded: "We will give him over to 'An Operative' for the present." "To an Operative" by "Spectator" appeared in the issue of February 19, 1847. He conceded that it might be argued that "the operative has no time; but do those that have nothing else to do, do any better? Hundreds of females now in this city, are employing their time to no useful purposes. If they attend school, their silly mothers are satisfied if they can dress them fine, and see appended to their names the study of Latin, or some other useless language, that tends rather to make parrots of them than reasoning beings. They never dream that they are or should be fitting them to be guides and conductors for the next generation."

13. "Spectator" commented in the *Voice of Industry* of March 12, 1847, that it was "easier to find fault, than to give good and correct advice at any time; more especially upon a subject that has been so much neglected, and which almost all avoid. I must take a little time to consider upon it." He gave his full answer to "Operative" in the *Voice of Industry* of March 19, 1847: "As you have in a former communication, laid claim to the whole six working days, necessity compels me to lay claim to some portion of the seventh. If no other time can be found in which to educate women, that whole day cannot be appropriated to a better, a nobler, or a higher purpose. This proposition may startle some; but I ask them to reflect and examine the position of things—the absolute necessity and importance of a change and an entire revolution in the nature and manner of educating females, and more especially operatives, who say they are doomed to work the whole of six days in a week and have no time but the seventh for improvement." He recommended that they be taught "Physiology, Phrenology, and every other science that would be proper. . . ."

14. "Spectator" referred to a riot in Baltimore arising from a great bank failure. He described how the mob, after destroying the homes of others responsible, came to one who "was among the most guilty, and commenced breaking the glass and thundering at the door. The wife, who was a woman in every sense of the word, rushed to the door, threw it open, and stepped outside and said to the raging multitude. 'Gentlemen, my husband is home, there is the door, if you are Baltimorians you will not go in, and I know you are!' They did not go in. The excited mass were instantly subdued by that irresistible power that every woman possesses and would display, but from a wrong education that destroys their native simplicity. They gave her three cheers and left, nor did they return" (*Voice of Industry*, March 19, 1847).

15. Mary Needles (1802–74) was a Quaker antislavery leader in Philadelphia, organizer of the Free Produce movement in that city.

Part 8

The End of an Era

The End of an Era

By 1847 it was clear that the ten-hour movement was a failure. Massachusetts had refused to pass any law for the ten-hour day, and while New Hampshire had enacted such legislation, it was crippled by the provision enabling employers to compel their workers to sign contracts agreeing to work longer. The factory workers in New Hampshire had pledged not to sign such contracts, but they were unable to maintain these pledges. The power of the corporations was too great. Workers who refused to sign were discharged, and when they went elsewhere to seek employment, they found all doors closed to them.

The female factory operatives still voiced their determination to continue the struggle, and their poetry, articles, and letters expressed this feeling. But the trend was away from militancy. In January, 1847, the name of the Female Labor Reform Association was changed to the "Lowell Female Industrial Reform and Mutual Aid Society." The aim of the organization was to appeal to the "self-love" of the factory girls and "their higher natures." Through enlightenment and education, the factory operatives, "doomed to eternal slavery," would be brought together to end a "state of society which debases the masses to a level with the serfs of the old countries."

The Lowell Society and the Female Labor Reform Associations in New Hampshire sent delegates to the New England Labor Reform League, and at a convention held in Lowell in March, 1847, several of the female delegates engaged in a heated debate over the so-called beauties of factory life. But the general tone of the discussion was on the need for enlightenment.

However, more than enlightenment was needed to cope with the power of the corporations. By March, 1848, the New England Labor Reform League, formerly the New England Workingmen's Association, came to an end. The Lowell Society and the New Hampshire Female Labor Reform Associations also disappeared about the same time. With the disappearance of the unions of factory workers, the factory magazines and the *Voice of Industry* soon ceased publication. With no organizations and publications to voice their grievances and to unite them to resist oppression, many factory girls left the mills. Some returned to their homes; others, like Lucy Larcom, left for the West; still others went to the grave, victims of brown lung, or byssinosis, a pulmonary affliction caused by inhalation of cotton dust.[1] Those who remained in the mills envied those who had escaped, but they could do little to improve their own conditions. An unpublished letter from a female factory operative in Lowell, included in this section, expresses the feeling of hopelessness of those who remained in the mills. The song "The Factory Girl's Come-All-Ye" reflects the desire in the 1850s to leave the factories and live outside the power of the overseers.

With the disappearance of the magazines and periodicals which had challenged and doomed the *Lowell Offering,* Harriet Farley attempted to regain her former audience. The *New England Offering,* her new enterprise, began publication in April, 1848, soliciting the support of the operatives for a work "to be wholly written by females who are or have been employees in mills." Probably convinced by her previous experience with the *Offering* that she could not entirely exclude material of a "controversial nature," Miss Farley opened the columns to bitter attacks by the factory girls on the evils of slavery in the South, but she still would have nothing to do with the "wage slavery" of the mills. Receiving as she did a small stipend from Amos Lawrence, one of the mill magnates, she was certainly not inclined to question the benevolence of the factory owners, and the *New England Offering* carried much material reminiscent of the earlier pieces in the *Lowell Offering* on the "Beauty of Factory Life." Only once did she venture to question the fact that Lowell might not be a "workers' paradise"—in questioning the indifference of the author of an article on "The Rights and Duties of Mill Girls," concerning the tragic effect of wage cuts for the operatives. Even then, Miss Farley assured the operatives that the depression would end shortly, and that wages would be restored by the benevolent "humanity of Abbott Lawrence, the Lowells, and others of our most influential capitalists. . . ."

Before it expired, the *Voice of Industry* carried a few pieces critical of the *New England Offering* by some of the militant factory girls. Miss Farley ignored the criticism, but she discovered by July, 1849, that her efforts to portray the "Beauty of Factory Life" met with little response from the operatives. By 1850 the *New England Offering* also ceased publication. The young women who remained in the mills and who had repudiated the *Lowell Offering,* turning to publications more attuned to their interests, were not interested in supporting a carbon copy of the original *Offering.* The operatives who replaced the Yankee women who had left the mills were mainly recruited from recently arrived immigrant groups; they were as yet not ready to challenge the power of the corporations.

The era of the magazines for and by factory operatives, and of the Female Labor Reform Associations, was over. Yet it had not all been in vain. The magazines and the associations had united the factory workers and created a tradition of organization among them. The era had not produced the ten-hour day, but in some Massachusetts factories hours were reduced from thirteen to eleven, and in New Hampshire many factories instituted a ten-hour and fifty-minute working day. Moreover, the magazines and the Female Labor Reform Association had given considerable impetus to the movement for women's rights.

The struggle for the ten-hour day was resumed immediately after the Civil War. The *Boston Daily Evening Voice,* one of the first daily labor papers in America, picked up the cause of the women in the factories where the *Voice of Industry* and the factory magazines had left it. Letters from women who had been active in the ten-hour movement of the 1840s (and still worked in the mills) were now part of the new movement of New England factory workers to secure a shorter working day, indicating that there was a continuing thread in the battles waged for a decent way of life.

These struggles gained the support of *The Revolution,* published by Elizabeth Cady Stanton and Susan B. Anthony, the pioneer women's rights leaders in the United States. Among the most interesting articles in *The Revolution* were those by Jennie Collins, a woman of working-class origins who became a settlement worker and woman suffragist in Boston. Her articles supporting the 1869 strikes of women in the mills of Dover, New Hampshire, are included in this section.

The section closes with "The Factory Girl," a song by J. A. Phillips published in the *Machinists' Monthly Journal* of September, 1895. The tone of the piece makes it clear that many struggles still lay ahead for women in the factories before they would obtain their objectives.   □

Lowell Female Industrial Reform and Mutual Aid Society

The following Preamble and Constitution having been adopted, we would most strongly urge upon every female operative, as well as others who are compelled by necessity to support themselves by their own industry, to avail themselves of this opportunity to help us in this humane enterprise: Let us unite together and protect each other. In health and prosperity we can enjoy each other's society from week to week—in sickness and despondency share in and kindly relieve each other's distresses. The young and defenceless female, far away from home and loving hearts, can here find true sympathy and aid. We do hope and confidently believe that many of our toiling sisters will come in next Tuesday, sign the Constitution, and engage heart and hand in this benevolent cause.

Our meetings will be holden every Tuesday evening, at eight o'clock, at the Reading Room, 76 Central street. The officers for the coming year will be chosen Jan. 12. Let there be a full attendance. Now is the time for ACTION.

H. J. STONE, Sec'y.

PREAMBLE

The time having come when the claims of Industry and the Rights of all, are engrossing the deep attention, the profoundest thought and energetic action of the wisest and best in this and other lands—when the worthy toiling millions of earth are waking from the deathlike stupor which has so long held them in ignorance and degradation, to a sense of their true dignity and worth as God's free men and women, destined to eternal progression and ultimate perfection, we, females of Lowell, feel that *we* also have a *work* to accomplish—a high and holy destiny to achieve. We deem it a privilege and also a *duty* we owe to ourselves and our race, to lend a helping hand, feeble though it may be, to assist in carrying forward the great "Industrial Reform" already commenced, and which is progressing with such unlooked for success, in the Old and New World. To assist in scattering light and knowledge among the people—to encourage in every good word and work, those who are devoting themselves, and all that they have, to the cause of human elevation and human happiness.

We feel that by our mutual, *united* action, and with the blessing of high heaven, we can accomplish much, which shall tell for the progress of Industrial Reform—the elevation and cultivation of mind and morals, in our midst—the comfort and relief of destitute and friendless females in this busy city.

With this high aim and these noble objects in view, we most solemnly pledge ourselves to labor actively, energetically and unitedly, to bring about a better state of society. In order the more successfully to accomplish these objects, we adopt the following

CONSTITUTION

ART. I. This Association shall be called the LOWELL FEMALE INDUSTRIAL REFORM AND MUTUAL AID SOCIETY.

ART. II. The objects of this Society shall be the diffusion of correct principles and useful practical knowledge among its members—the rendering of Industry honorable and attractive—the relieving and aiding of all who may be sick, or in want of the comforts and necessaries of life, or standing in need of the counsels and sympathies of true and benevolent hearts. Also to encourage and assist each other in self-culture, intellectual and moral, that we may be fitted for and occupy that station in society, which the truly good and useful ever should. That we may know and respect our own individual rights and privileges as females, and be prepared, understandingly, to maintain and enjoy them, irrespective of concentrated wealth or aristocratic usages of an anti-republican state of society.

ART. III. Any female can become a member by signing the Constitution and paying an initiation fee of fifty cents.

ART. IV. The officers of this society shall consist of a President, two Vice Presidents, Secretary, Treasurer and Board of Directors, four in number, all of which officers shall be members, ex-officio, of the Board.

ART. V. It shall be the duty of the President to preside at all meetings of the Society, and in case of absence, the Vice President shall fill the chair.

ART. VI. It shall be the duty of the Secretary to be present at all meetings, and prepared to read the minutes of the previous meeting, if requested.

ART. VII. It shall be the duty of the Treasurer to receive all money paid into the Treasury, and to pay all bills presented by the Society and signed by the President and Secretary; also to keep a correct account of the same.

Art. VIII. It shall be the duty of the Board to appoint a Charitable Committee the first Tuesday of each month, or oftener if necessary.

Art. IX. That Committee shall be styled the Sisters of Charity. It shall be their duty to ascertain who is needy or sick in the Society, and report the same at each meeting, that their wants may be attended to faithfully, their hearts cheered by the voice of sympathy and love. It shall also be their duty to furnish watchers for the sick so long as deemed necessary.

Art. X. Every member shall deposite not less than six cents weekly in the hands of the Treasurer, which sum, with the initiation fee and fines, shall go to make up a sick fund, which shall be appropriated no other way, except by vote of two thirds of the Board.

Art. XI. No member shall draw from this fund until she has contributed to the same three months the amount specified in article tenth; and then not less than two nor over five dollars a week, or longer than four weeks, unless the Board see fit to order otherwise.

Art. XII. Any member who shall absent herself from the meetings three weeks in succession, without a reasonable excuse, shall be subjected to a fine of thirty-seven and a half cents per week. If at the end of three months said member does not come in and pay up her fines, she shall not be entitled to any of the benefits of the sick fund.

Art. XIII. The officers of this Society shall be chosen on the first Tuesdays of January and July, two weeks notice being previously given.

Art. XIV. This Constitution may be altered or amended by a vote of two thirds of the members present, provided it be proposed at a previous meeting.

Voice of Industry, January 8, 1847

Notice

The adjourned meeting of the Labor Reform League of New England will be holden in Boston the third Wednesday and Thursday of the present month, (Jan. 19th and 20th.) It is all important that there should be a full delegation from all the different Associations throughout New England, as business of deep interest to all working classes will come before the meeting. Let every male and female who wishes well to the cause of human improvement, human elevation and the *Rights of all the People,* see to it that they are *there* and ready to *act!*

H. J. STONE, Rec. Sec.

Lowell, Jan. 6, 1847

N.B. Will the "Manchester Democrat," "Essex Banner," "Oasis," and "Farmer and Ledger," please copy the above.

Voice of Industry, January 8, 1847

New England Labor Reform League

This Association met in convention at Chapman Hall, Boston, Jan. 17th, and was called to order by the President, David Bryant.

The minutes of the last convention were listened to from Sec'y, Miss H. J. Stone, of Lowell; after which the general objects of the League were briefly and comprehensively laid before the meeting by Mr. Campbel, of Boston. Remarks were also made by Messrs. Hovey, Young and others. On motion, W. F. Young, J. Campbel, Miss M. Eastman, J. Putnam and N. W. Brown, were chosen a committee to report Resolutions and business for the convention. Voted, that Messrs. J. Campbel, N. W. Brown and J. Sterritt, constitute a committee of Finance during the sitting of the convention. The following Resolution was presented by E. W. Parkman of Boston, and sustained by some forcible remarks.

Resolved, That Protective Unions should at once be formed in every City, Town and Village through this country and the world; the concentration of the wealth of the producers in purchasing the articles they consume carries with it a power which above all others, will prove a death to tyrants.

Voted, to accept for discussion.

Voted, that the opening of the evening session be allotted for hearing reports from any Female Associations represented.

Voice of Industry, February 12, 1847

Report of the Lowell Female Industrial Reform and Mutual Aid Society

EVENING SESSION.—The following Report from the Female Industrial Reform Association of Lowell, was presented by the Secretary, accepted and ordered a place in the records of the Convention:

Since our last meeting in Convention we have accomplished little except to draft a new constitution and reorganize. We have long felt the necessity of having a constitution which should embody something more *definite*—there seemed to be too much of theory and too little of the real practical in the old one. We wished for one under which we could accomplish something now in the present time for the amelioration of the physical and mental condition of our toiling sisters, one which should appeal to their self-love, as well as their *higher* natures, and awaken a lively interest in behalf of Industrial Reform. The wants of every member under the present constitution are to be promptly attended to and relieved by the Society, so that those who have not as yet much sympathy for the Reform movement may be induced to unite with us on the ground of Mutual Aid. We most confidently believe that could there be such societies formed and judiciously managed in all our manufacturing places, they would be the means of saving from ruin, disgrace and an untimely grave, hundreds, nay, thousands of young, unsuspecting females, who are thrown upon the charities of a cold, unfriendly world, in helpless childhood, and compelled to earn their daily bread somewhere or perish in the streets! They would then know and feel that there were true and sympathetic hearts to whom they could turn for council and assistance in the day of trial and of want. Oh! how many have fallen and perished by the wayside in life's great thoroughfare for lack of sympathy and encouragement from the virtuous and good! How many in our own loved city of Lowell have sunk in ignorance and vice through that feeling of hopeless despondency which poverty and lack of sympathy ever engender in the human heart. They felt that no kind heart was interested in their well being—no one loved or cared for them in the *wide* world, and they would seek sympathy somewhere, (for that is the undying craving of every human being's soul,) and if denied the companionship and sympathy of the good, the true and the noble of the earth, they *will*, they *must* find it among the low and the degraded in community.

Again, how many are allowed to sicken, waste away and die even for lack of kind care and attention. This is another important consideration with us. The words, *Mutual Aid*, to us imply much—they are *full* of meaning and intended to call out every dormant power and put in action every benevolent and humane faculty of our natures. It is time to *awake*—to *think*—and to *act!* We must strike at the *root* of the tree of evil and oppression if we would destroy the wide spreading branches. We do hope that the friends of

Industrial Reform will continue to dig about that Upas tree until it is completely uprooted from our land and world! Let us look to Europe and take new courage and labor *on* waiting patiently for the "Good time coming." In the mean time let us *not forget* to *labor while we wait.*

MARY EMERSON, *Pres.*[2]

HULDAH J. STONE, *Sec.*

Voice of Industry, February 19, 1847

Meeting

The FEMALE INDUSTRIAL REFORM AND MUTUAL AID SOCIETY of Lowell, meets every Monday evening at 8 o'clock, at the Reading Room, 76 Central street. All Ladies friendly to the mental, moral and physical improvement of their sex, are respectfully invited to smile upon our humble efforts, by their presence.

MARY EMERSON, Pres't.

H. J. STONE, Sec'y.

Voice of Industry, May 28, 1847

Again a Factory Girl

Lowell, Sept. 7th 1846

Dear Harriet,

With a feeling which you can better imagine than I can describe do I announce to you the horrible tidings that I am once more a *factory girl!* Yes, once more a factory girl seated in the short attic of a Lowell boarding house with a half dozen of girls seated around me talking and reading and myself in the midst, trying to write to you, with the thoughts of so many different persons flying around me that I can hardly tell which are my own; but having the organ of individuality very prominent perhaps I can select a few ideas which are indisputably my own and if I succeed I shall in all probability send them to you in the shape of a long letter. I received your epistle with pleasure and was very happy to hear you were enjoying yourself so well, perhaps you would like to hear how I enjoyed my visit to Vermont. I enjoyed it well I assure you. I was gone three weeks and when I came away the vines, the bare fruit trees, & the berry bushes broken and trampled upon, showed too plainly that I had not been idle, and the scratches upon my hands and arms in plain hieroglyphics that the berries were not without their thorns; but like all happy hours these three weeks passed quickly away and I returned home to enjoy a season of rest as I supposed for my friends and my mother had almost persuaded me to stay at home during the fall and winter but when I reached home I found a letter which informed me that Mr. Saunders was keeping my place for me and sent for me to come back as soon as I could and after reading it my Lowell fever returned and come I would, and come I did, but now, "Ah! me, I rue the day" although I am not so homesick as I was a fortnight ago and just begin to feel more resigned to my fate. I have been here four weeks but have not had to work very hard for there are six girls of us and we have fine times doing nothing. I should like to see you in Lowell once more but cannot wish you to exchange your pleasant time in the country for a factory life in this "great city of spindles."

I hope you will learn to perform all necessary domestic duties while you have an opportunity for perhaps you may have an invitation from a certain dark eyed gentleman whom you mentioned in your letter to be mistress of his house his hand and heart and supposing such an event should take place then I will just take a ride some pleasant day and make you a visit when I will tell you more news than I can write—but I will not—anticipate.

I almost envy your happy sundays at home. A feeling of loneliness comes over me when I think of *my home* now far away. You remember perhaps how I used to tell you I spent my hours in the mill—viz, in imagining myself rich and that the rattle of machinery was the rumbling of my chariot wheels, but now alas; that happy fact has fled from me and my mind no longer takes such airy and visionary flights for the wings of my imagination have folded themselves to rest; in vain do I try to soar in fancy and imagination above the dull reality around me but beyond the roof of the factory I can not rise and in my disappointment I can express my feelings in no other way but in the sublime and beautiful language of the poet

> "When I was a little boy and lived by myself
> All the bread and cheese I had &c."

You probably know the rest and can sympathize with me, as you no doubt did when you fell in the Mer[r]imac[k] river. I wish you would tell me in your next letter who fished you out for it was a lucky chance for some one for you must certainly have been worth catching. You told me you had been gipsying a number of times but I hope you will not turn gipsy in imitating their wandering yet *happy* life; I say happy because any one must be happy while they are free to rove when and where they will among the green fields, by the running streams, in the depth of the forest, and in the pleasant valley with none to molest or make them afraid, so different from a city life. But enough of this now, for the very good reason that I have no room to write it; do not think I am unhappy because I cannot wish you here; far from it, but I think you are happier *there*.

I forgot to tell you that Sarah Burton has left our dress room in Old No. 2. to be married I believe she is going to reside in Maine. I have no more that you would be interested in, to write. When you receive this letter I shall expect that long one you promised me do write it wont you.

Your friend H. E. Back

Excuse all blunders for I have written it all upon a band box cover I only put this last line in to help full up do burn it wont you—is not this letter as long as you care about reading let me know wont you

Letter to Miss Harriet H. Hanson, Wentworth, N.H., manuscript in Harriet H. Robinson Papers, Radcliffe Library

What Has Become of the Girls?

Freeport, Armstrong Co. Pa.
March 30, 1848

DEAR VOICE:—I take this opportunity to write a few lines to you. I hope you will succeed in the noble cause in which you are engaged, for your object appears to be the elevation and amelioration of the laboring classes. Although I differ with you on the subject of Association, still I believe you are actuated by noble motives. When we cast our eyes abroad both on the old and new world, there appears to be a general commotion; the laboring classes seem to be waking as from the sleep of ages, and are beginning to enquire after their long lost rights. There is one object in which all reformers ought to unite, and that is, the restoration of the soil, which is an element, and is necessary to man's existence, and ought therefore to be free. If every man had his plot and his cot, we should not hear of so much misery and destitution from abroad, nor see so much slavery and dependence at home; the sons and daughters of New England, who are now doomed to incessant toil, would be independent and happy; the black slavery of the South would cease to exist, for all men might then sit each under his own vine and fig tree with none to molest or make afraid. I would like to know what has become of the girls that used to write for the *Voice* when it was published at Lowell. I do not feel so much at liberty in writing as when the girls wrote for the *Voice*. I remain with the greatest respect,

Yours, for the right,

MARTHA HALLINGWORTH

Voice of Industry, April 14, 1848

Married

"Married, in Gill, Mass., Oct. 21st by Rev. Mr. Miller, Geo. H. Wells, Esq., of Marietta, Ohio, to Miss Urania S. Richards of Gill."

Miss Richards left the "City of Spindles" about seven years since for the West, and has been an efficient teacher in that section. Sisters of New England, "Go ye and do likewise." The cake is received, and is of a superior quality; according to request have "passed it round."

M.E.[3]

Voice of Industry, November 5, 1847

The *New England Offering*

INTRODUCTORY REMARKS

In presenting to our readers the first number of this magazine, we have but few words to offer. Its pretensions are but slight, and its principal claim upon the public is the fact that it emanates from the female manufacturing operatives of New England. Yet, if we believed it destitute of intrinsic merit, we would not obtrude this offering upon the shrine of literature. We feel that we can make our little periodical as pleasant and as useful as any of its size, and more interesting to that class for whose improvement and amusement we write and publish. We trust that all contributors will unite with us in preserving a calm, candid, charitable spirit in their compositions, and feel free to speak in this manner of what they please. We wish to make it eminently New England in its tone,—that its fiction shall not be based upon the English novel of the eighteenth century, nor its argument upon the French theories of the nineteenth. If we had more room, we would do more ourself to make it what we would like; but we can give no variety, if we give long articles. A series of *Dialogues on Labor,* another of *Tales Illustrative of Factory Life,* besides other sketches, fantasies, &c., we have had in preparation for our anticipated readers; but we must give them up for the present. One of our contributors will furnish an instructive series of articles, the results of her own observation and experience, which we trust will be appreciated by those for whom she writes.

There can be no greater mistake among the operatives, that those who have left the factories cease to remember and to care for those who are left to labor there. They do think of them, sympathize with them and are willing still to labor for their good. They would be doing something in the community for their benefit, and something with them for still greater progress and excellence. They would smooth the way for a ready recognition of their claims to places among the good and intellectual, whether they shall leave the mill for other and more responsible situations, or choose to remain at their mill labors, there to be and to do good. We trust that all who can aid us with the purse or the pen, will not be backward in their efforts to assist; and we will cheerfully respond, with every effort in our power, to make our magazine and their cause respectable and respected.

HARRIET FARLEY

New England Offering, April, 1848

On the *New England Offering*

The first number of a monthly of 48 pages, with the above name, is on our table. It is beautifully printed, and is altogether prepossessing in its external appearance. It is made up of articles written by females who are or have been employed in the mills, and, as a literary work, does credit to our "Factory Girls." We are particularly pleased with the "Uncommitted Sin," by the *Editor,* and "Prose Poems" by *Lucy Larcom.*

The work has one prominent defect, or what seems such to us, though in the eyes of many it may be a merit. Its pages show no proofs that the swift and animating life-currents of the Present Age flow through the veins of those who have given their contributions to its columns. It breathes none of the Hopes, the Aspirations, the high Purposes, which should actuate the young women of our country at the present time. We do not ask or expect that every publication that is issued shall be devoted to some special Reform, or even to Reform in general, but we do ask and expect that every thing that claims to be *living* Literature, shall breathe the spirit of the age which gives it birth. The Literature of our time should bear the same relation to the Industrial and Social Revolution now in progress in the world, that the Literature of seventy-six bore to the Revolution that gave *political* Liberty to our Fatherland.

With a kind greeting to the Editor and her fair Contributors, and a hope that future numbers of the *New England Offering* will breathe a truer life-tone and higher aspirations, we will close our somewhat extended notice.

M.E.[3]

Voice of Industry, April 17, 1848

The Factory Girl's Come-All-Ye[4]

Come all ye Lewiston fact'ry girls,
I want you to understand,
I'm a going to leave this factory,
And return to my native land.
    Sing dum de wickety, dum de way.

No more will I take my Shaker and shawl
And hurry to the mill;
No more will I work so pesky hard
To earn a dollar bill.

No more will I take the towel and soap
To go to the sink and wash;
No more will the overseer say
"You're making a terrible splosh!"

No more will I take the comb and go
To the glass to comb my hair;
No more the overseer will say
"Oh! what are you doing there?"

No more I'll take my bobbins out,
No more I'll put them in,
No more the overseer will say
"You're weaving your cloth too thin!"

No more will I eat cold pudding,
No more will I eat hard bread,
No more will I eat those half-baked beans,
For I vow! They're killing me dead!

I'm going back to Boston town
And live on Tremont street;
And I want all you fact'ry girls
To come to my house and eat!

Phillips Barry, "The Factory Girl's Come-All-Ye," *Bulletin of the Folk-Song Society of the Northeast*, No. 2 (Cambridge, Mass., 1931), p. 12

Farewell to New England

Farewell to thee, New England!
   Thou mother, whose kind arm
Hath ever been my shelter;—
   The stern, and yet the warm!
Amidst the grief of parting,
   Each pulse is beating high
With pride that I'm thy daughter,—
   Best land beneath the sky!

And thou, old Massachusetts,
   At bidding thee farewell,
My caged heart shrinks and flutters
   As in some wizard's spell.
In brighter hues may blossom
   The valleys of the West,
But, should they rival Eden,
   I'd always love thee best.

O, spirits of the Pilgrims!
   Suns, beaming from the Past!
Upon your wandering daughter
   A warm reflection cast!
Like wind-borne flowery odors,
   Air of the Pilgrims' home,—
Still breathe around my spirit,
   Wherever I may roam.

Farewell! thou little village,
   My birthplace and my home,
Along whose rocky border
   The moaning surges come;
The name shall memory echo,
   As the exiled shell its wave.
Art thou *my home* no longer?
   Yet, keep for me a grave.

Farewell! thou busy city,
    Amid whose changing throng
I've passed a pleasant sojourn,
    Though wearisome and long.
My soul is sad at leaving
    The dear ones, not a few,
I've met within thy mazes,
    So noble and so true.

O, friends! upon love's altar,
    Still doth a taper burn?
Then keep it, bright and golden,
    To gladden my return.
And if the distant prairie
    Must hide the wanderer's tomb,
Unto that shrine of radiance
    Will my freed spirit come!

LUCY LARCOM

New England Offering, September, 1849

Letter from a Factory Girl

To the Editor of the Daily Evening Voice:[5]

Lowell, July 2, 1866

A victory on the side of Labor has occurred here, which I fear has not come under the notice of "Observer."

I will try and give you the account, hoping you will publish it for the encouragement of others who labor under the supervision of soulless men. It happened in the "dressing-room" of the Merrimack Corporation.

All who are acquainted with the mills know that the dressing room is at the best an uncomfortable place to work. In the room mentioned there are fans communicating with the air outside, and when running they add much to the comfort of the dressers. But it required a little more water to run the fans, so the agent determined they should be stopped. Not satisfied with this, he also ordered that the girls should put up their own size. This would enable him to discharge from two to four men.

But the girls, determined not to submit, called a meeting and voted unanimously not to start their frames till the size was put up for them and the fans set in motion.

The next morning they prepared their work as usual; then sat down to wait for the size and the cool breath of the fans.

The overseer informed Col. Palfrey (for this the agent delights to style himself) that the girls were firm in their resolve. I do not know the exact conversation which passed between them, but the overseer soon returned with the order that the men should attend to the size, as before.

The girls then inquired if the fans were to run. The overseer said no. They then told the overseer that he could go directly back and tell the Colonel (undoubtedly thinking to themselves *long-eared Palfrey*) that they would not compromise.

The result was, the agent succumbed, and the girls went to work on their own terms.

FACTORY GIRL

Boston Daily Evening Voice, July 15, 1866

My Experience as a Factory Operative

To the Editor of the Daily Evening Voice:

Thirty years ago I was a factory girl in the city of Lowell. I was ambitious to do something for myself in the way of earning money to pay my expenses at an Academy; and being too young to teach school in the country, not strong enough to do housework or learn a trade, I went into the card-room on the Fremont Corporation. My work was easy; I could sit down part of the time, and received ($1.75) one dollar and seventy-five cents per week beside my board. Being fond of reverie, and in the habit of constructing scenes and building castles in the air, I enjoyed factory life very well.

After a few months my parents removed from a country town to Lowell, and I went to board with them on the street, and then I began seriously to reflect on the realities of life.

For a delicate girl of fourteen years of age to be called out of bed and be obliged to eat her breakfast without any light, and then frequently wallow through the snow to the factory, stay there until half-past twelve, then run home and swallow her dinner without mastication, run back and stay there until half-past seven, is, to say the least, very unpleasant and unnatural, and exceedingly hurtful to the constitution.

I attended school three months during the following summer; then worked about eighteen months longer in the factory; afterwards worked in the weave-room, in all three years, but only about six months at a time, as my health would not allow me to work longer. The labor of attending three or four looms thirteen hours per day, with no time for recreation or mental improvement is very severe.

The habit of standing on the feet frequently produces varicose veins; and though the girls seldom complain, for they know it is useless, yet it is a fact that factory girls are great sufferers in this respect.

In those days the morals of the girls were well guarded, and they were generally treated respectfully by the overseers, and I think lived well on the corporations.

They were generally daughters of our New England farmers and mechanics, some of them were well educated. Many of them had learned trades. Some of them were of a literary turn and get up improvement circles. And I will say in truth that if the hours of labor had been only eight instead of thirteen, I should prefer working in the mill to house work, enjoyed the society of the girls, and the noise of the machinery was not displeasing to me; but after one has worked from daylight until dark, the prospect of working two or three hours more by lamp light is very discouraging.

In 1849 I was thrown into the society of several young women who were daughters of mill owners; and the contrast between their condition and that of the operatives was so great that it led me to serious reflection on the injustice of society. These girls had an abundance of leisure, could attend school when and where they pleased, were fashionably dressed, were not obliged to work any except when they pleased; indeed, they suffered for want of exercise; and while they were so tenderly cared for, lest the "winds of heaven should visit their faces too roughly," the operatives toiled on through summer's heat and winter's cold; many passing into an early grave in consequence of protracted labor, and many others making themselves invalids for life.

For one, I could never see the justice of one set of girls working all the time in order that another set should live in ease and idleless. Cowper says, "I would not have a slave to till my ground, to fan me while I sleep, and tremble when I wake, for all the wealth that sinews bought and sold have ever earned." But many of our people in Massachusetts are quite willing to make fat dividends on the labor of anybody they can hire, widows and orphans, boys and girls of tender age; and when they cannot obtain American girls, they send across the ocean for operatives, and then allow them just enough to keep them from starvation.

I am satisfied from my own experience, as well as from observation of the working classes for many years, that nothing can be done for their education or elevation, until the hours of labor are reduced. After one has worked from ten to fourteen hours at manual labor, it is impossible to study History, Philosophy, or Science.

I well remember the chagrin I often felt when attending lectures, to find myself unable to keep awake; or perhaps so far from the speaker on account of being late, that the ringing in my ears caused by the noise of the looms during the day, prevented my hearing scarcely a sentence he uttered. I am sure few possessed a more ardent desire for knowledge than I did, but such was the effect of the long hour system, that my chief delight was, after the evening meal, to place my aching feet in any easy position, and read a novel. I was never too tired, however, to listen to the lectures given by the friends of Labor Reform, such as John Allen, John C. Cluer or Mike Walsh. I assisted in getting signers to a Ten Hour petitions to the Legislature, and since I have resided in Boston and vicinity have seen and enjoyed the good results of that improvement in the condition of the working classes.

A WORKING WOMAN

Boston Daily Evening Voice, February 23, 1867

Jennie Collins and the Dover Strike

WHETHER it is wise for women to strike as do men, for higher wages, may be a question, but they have at least the same right. The strike at Dover, N.H., still holds out, and Miss Jennie Collins of Boston has espoused its cause in right good earnest. Last week she went up to Lowell, Mass., and rallied the factory women and girls there to the rescue in their behalf. They gathered by the thousands in Huntington Hall, one of the largest in New England, to listen to Jennie's appeal for their sisters in Dover. Her address is reported at considerable length in Massachusetts papers, but the following passages must suffice for these short columns:

She rejoiced that the Dover girls held out, and she had no doubt but they would eventually be restored to their old places at the former rates of compensation. The women all over the country, she believed, when they understood the facts, would allow the Cocheco goods to rot on the shelves before they would purchase them, and she was bound to do all in her power to advertise the facts. George Peabody,[6] she thought was not the philanthropist he might have been with his vast wealth, for, in all his munificence, he has failed to alleviate the poverty of those to whom he was specially indebted for his remarkable success in life; but yet he was everywhere extolled as the prince of benefactors, and the great nations of the world have united in paying honor and tribute to his memory. If, she added, he had searched out suffering and injustice and afforded relief, his memory and good deeds would live longer than the acts of his life, which are perpetuated by monuments and Institutes. In further describing the oppression of the working women in the eastern states, she said it seemed to her that their condition was worse than that of the black women of the south; but she was reluctant to believe that the partiality was on account of color. To secure substantial relief from the present and prospective wrongs she counselled them to organize thoroughly among themselves, and then stand firmly by each other in resisting the oppression of cotton aristocracy and heartless stockholders and overseers. Referring briefly to the Women's Rights movement, she alluded to the execution of Mrs. Surratt,[7] when there was not a voice, except that of her own daughter, raised to save her; but when Jefferson Davis, with his hands dripping with the blood of thousands, was brought to the bar of justice, who but the tender-hearted Horace Greeley came to the rescue![8] but for a poor woman, who was not positively guilty of murder, he had not a word of sympathy, or of mercy. Such a circumstance as this, she thought was a strong argument for Woman Suffrage, and for legislation to allow women to hold office. What she wanted most was an organization to secure the protection of the working women of the country against the cruel encroachments of capital and every true woman of the country would unite and rejoice in the movement.

After Miss Collins's address the following preamble and resolution were adopted:

WHEREAS, The Cocheco Manufacturing Company at Dover, N.H., have reduced the wages of their operatives by twelve percent, and have thereby unnecessarily created great suffering and distress, while the affairs of the company are in a highly prosperous condition, they having for years a dividend of sixteen per cent, per annum and increased the value of their stock to $172 beyond its par value share; therefore,

RESOLVED, That the conduct of the Cocheco Manufacturing Company in thus reducing the wages of their operatives is unjust and oppressive, and deserves the execration of the community; that we tender to the victims of their meanness and tyranny the assurance of our warmest sympathies, and that we call upon the press to assist in holding up to public reprobation the harsh and cruel conduct of the Cocheco Manufacturing Company.

The New Hampshire *Patriot* says the stock of the Dover factories has fallen in the market since the strike from $750 on the shares of $5 a par value, to $665, and that the general belief is that there was no necessity for the reduction of twelve per cent in the wages of employees. The best operatives have left for Lowell, Lawrence and Lewiston, and it is believed to be impossible for the company to start up all their works during the winter.

The Revolution,[9] April 22, 1869

New England Factories

DEAR REVOLUTION: I thank you for the timely words uttered through your columns, in behalf of the eight hundred noble, but oppressed women who took part in what is termed the Dover strike.

In this, capital struck at the women. In order to prove this, I must give you an idea of factory life thirty years ago. Then the work of a weaver was to attend to two looms. Although they toiled thirteen hours, they could look out of the window, comb their hair, read a book, converse together, and frequently contribute articles to the press. Then there were two powerful opposing parties, and everything connected with factory life was a party issue.

You are aware that when a number of individuals, desiring to be incorporated in a manufacturing company, petition the legislature for that privilege, the legislature regulates the conditions if it gives them a charter, but the corporations have the privilege of issuing their own by-laws.

Before the operative puts on her apron, she is obliged to go to the counting-room and sign a contract, one of the most despotic codes that was ever issued in a free country, called a regulation paper.

In the favored days of factory life, the fairest women in the New England States were employed in the mills, but every one of them had a home to go to in the hot summer months of July and August.

Although the stockholders made a dividend of seventy-five per cent they were determined to have a set of operatives who would be wholly dependent. Hence they gathered women from every place that was possible, the main consideration being to have those who were without homes and friends. In consequence of the best men and women being engaged in the slavery question, the groans from the factories were not heard. Probably they would not be heard to-day were it not for this fact, that before the war, working women in the City of Boston could get board for $2.25 per week. Now they are compelled to pay $6, and oftentimes more.

As the corporations have boarding-houses for their operatives, poverty has driven large numbers of them back to those living tombs. Now for the Cocheco Company. They receive on their Prints two cents a yard more than any other company. I have said in the begining of this article that two looms were a girl's work. Then they reduced their wages and added another loom. Again they cut down and added still another loom. Again and again this was repeated until now a girl's work is six and seven looms.

That was not the only outrage imposed upon them, but formerly a piece of cloth measured thirty yards, now there are twelve more added to it, making it in all forty-two yards at the same price. A short time ago this company purchased a machine to press warps for the looms at an enormous price, by which two hands can perform the labor of fifteen. In consequence of stock being low in the market, the stockholders issued a *regular prerogative* to reduce wages twelve cents on a dollar. The poor victims remonstrated, but they were told that if they run *eight* looms they would make the same as before the reduction.

Allowing that stock was low in the market, no reduction was made in the salary of the agent and the supernumeraries (the dry pumps). The *men* in the factories produce nothing. If the stock is low in the market why not let the men and women share the consequences equally. Another point I want thoroughly understood. There are forty-eight thousand factory girls in Massachusetts. They consume on the average six calico dresses a year, ten yards in the dress. From this you can see that the factory girls are the largest patrons of their employers. The strike is virtually ended, and many are compelled to yield, but the company have nothing to triumph over. Hostilities have not ceased. It is only an armistice, for I found among the strikers who gathered from day to day in Exchange Hall in Dover, during the strike several graduates of the Boston grammar schools, who stood first in their class. They demand just laws, and they will have them. Mr. Fulton asks if the working class of women can vote themselves more wages and more leisure? To-day, while ten hours are a legal day's work for a mechanic, women and children work eleven. Then he says women on the platform are out of their proper places. Fifteen years ago a similar strike took place in Manchester, N.H. They appointed a committee to wait on the agent. He refused to meet them, but instead, he sent the mayor out to read the riot act, but the women were afraid of the bullets from the cotton chivalry, so they went back. Fifteen years have elapsed, the working women have the platform and tongues to use, and no man now dares to come into an orderly meeting and read the riot act. We working women will wear fig-leaf dresses before we will patronize the Cocheco Company.

Heaven bless THE REVOLUTION *and its two noble women.* I thank you in behalf of the hundred thousand working women of Massachusetts.

JENNIE COLLINS

The Revolution, April 29, 1869

The Factory Girl

She wasn't the least bit pretty,
    And only the least bit gay,
And she walked with a firm, elastic tread,
    In a business kind of way;

Her dress was of coarse, brown woolen,
    Plainly but neatly made,
Trimmed with some common ribbon,
    And a hat with a broken feather,
And a shawl of modest plaid.

Her face was worn and weary,
    And traced with lines of care,
As her nut brown tresses blew aside
    In the keen December air;
Yet she was not old, scarcely twenty,
    And her form was full and sleek,
But her heavy eye and tired step
    Seemed of wearisome toil to speak.
She worked as a common factory girl
    For two dollars and a half a week.

Ten hours a day of labor,
    In a close, ill-lighted room,
Machinery's buzz for music,
    Waste gas for sweet perfume;
Hot, stifling vapors in summer,
    Chill drafts on a winter's day,
No pause for rest or pleasure
    On pain of being sent away;
So ran her civilized serfdom—
        FOUR CENTS an hour the pay!

"A fair day's work," say the masters,
    And "a fair day's pay" say the men;
There's a strike—a raise in wages,
    What effect on the poor girl then?
A harder struggle than ever
    The honest path to keep,
And to sink a little lower—
    Some humbler home to seek,
For rates are higher—her wages
    Two dollars and a half per week.

A man gets thrice the money—
    But then a "man's a man,
And a woman surely can't expect
    To earn as much as he can."
Of his hire the laborer's worthy,
    Be the laborer who it may;
If a woman do a man's full work,
    She should have a man's full pay,
Not to be left to starve—or sin
    On forty cents a day.

Two dollars and a half to live on,
    Or starve on, if you will,
Two dollars and a half to dress on,
    And a hungry mouth to fill;
Two dollars and a half to lodge on
    In some wretched hole or den,
Where crowds are huddled together—
    Girls and women and men;
If she sins to escape her bondage
    Is there room for wonder then?

                                        J. A. PHILLIPS

Machinists' Monthly Journal, September, 1895, p. 3

NOTES

1. The *New York Times* of May 15, 1977, carried the following dispatch from Columbia, S.C.: " 'I just started to smother after I had been working in the spinning room for a few years,' Flossie Strickland said. She paused to catch her breath, then continued: 'My work began to slow down. The boss man came around and told me I wasn't moving fast enough. I stopped taking a lunch break. But I still couldn't make my quota.' She paused again. 'It was all that cotton dust flying around. I couldn't breathe. I finally had to quit work five years early—no pension, no medical compensation, not even one of those sheets we were making.' If her doctor's diagnosis is correct, Mrs. Strickland is a victim of 'brown lung,' a mysterious illness that poses a serious health threat to many textile workers. . . .

Brown lung, known medically as byssinosis (from 'byssus,' the Greek word for cotton), is a respiratory ailment that impairs lung capacity and leads to coughing and shortness of breath. . . ."

2. Mary Emerson had been secretary *pro tem* of the Lowell Female Labor Reform Association.

3. Mary Emerson.

4. The song, expressing the determination of the factory girls to leave the mills rather than continue under existing conditions, was learned by Mrs. Mary E. Hindle in 1875, but it was probably current before 1850.

5. The *Boston Daily Evening Voice* was launched in 1864 by printers who were locked out for belonging to a union. Lasting until late 1867, it was the first daily labor paper published in the United States, and it devoted much attention to the problems and struggles of the factory workers in the New England textile mills.

6. George Peabody (1795–1869), merchant and banker who founded and endowed Peabody Institute, Baltimore, and Peabody Museums at Yale and at Harvard.

7. Mrs. Surratt was executed for being implicated in the assassination of Abraham Lincoln.

8. The reference is to the fact that Horace Greeley (1811–72), editor of the New York *Tribune,* urged in editorials that Jefferson Davis (1808–89), President of the Confederate States of America, not be brought to trial for treason. Davis was released by the government and never prosecuted.

9. *The Revolution* was launched as a weekly after the Civil War by Susan B. Anthony (1820–1906) and Elizabeth Cady Stanton (1815–1902) as a reform journal advocating woman suffrage, the rights of labor and other causes. Its first issue appeared on January 8, 1868.

Index

351

DATE DUE